THE LIFE OF GEORGE LANSBURY

George Lansbury, leader of the Labour Party, about 1935

THE LIFE OF
GEORGE LANSBURY

by

RAYMOND POSTGATE

LONGMANS, GREEN AND CO
LONDON · NEW YORK · TORONTO

LONGMANS, GREEN AND CO LTD
6 & 7 CLIFFORD STREET LONDON W I
ALSO AT MELBOURNE AND CAPE TOWN

LONGMANS, GREEN AND CO INC
55 FIFTH AVENUE NEW YORK 3

LONGMANS, GREEN AND CO
215 VICTORIA STREET TORONTO I

ORIENT LONGMANS LTD
BOMBAY CALCUTTA MADRAS

First published 1951

*Printed in Great Britain by Richard Clay and Company, Ltd.,
Bungay, Suffolk*

FOREWORD AND LIST OF SOURCES

I HAVE not concluded this *Life* with a formal estimate of George Lansbury's place in history, though it would be expected and I had intended to do so.   For this I have two reasons.   The first is that I think 1951 is too early in time.   He belonged to a generation of remarkable men, mainly of working-class origin: Keir Hardie, John Burns, Will Crooks, William Morris, Will Thorne—even Arthur Henderson and H. M. Hyndman—all these were men of similarly great energy and decisive personality.   We can begin to recognise certain common features among them; but it is too early, yet, to evaluate how much they have done and how long their work will last.   The second reason is personal.   I worked with him for many years, and I loved and respected him as I never expect to love and respect a man again.   This deep admiration has not, I do believe, prevented me from painting a faithful portrait.   But it impedes me from making an abstract and professional appraisal; I think and hope that when the reader has finished my story he will find arise from it automatically all the general reflections that are necessary.

I pass from this to a list of the sources which I have used:

Oral.   My thanks are due to four people who read through the whole text of the book and helped me greatly by their criticism and information: My wife Daisy, G.L.'s daughter; my sister, Margaret Cole; William Lansbury, G.L.'s eldest son; Sir Francis Meynell.   They are none of them responsible, of course, for anything which appears in the book.   I also made great use, naturally, of my own recollections of G.L.   I was made foreign sub-editor of the *Daily Herald* in 1919, and thereafter worked with him, sometimes very closely, until near the end of his life.   Many anecdotes and statements in this *Life*, not otherwise ascribed, were told to me by him.   I was assistant editor of *Lansbury's Weekly*, and prepared most of his books for publication.

Printed. The primary printed source is Lansbury's auto-biography, *My Life* (1928). Wherever a statement is given as by him in the text, it is drawn from this book, unless otherwise identified. Subsidiary sources are the following books by him:

My Quest for Peace (1938). An account of his journeys in 1936 and 1937.

Looking Backwards—and Forwards (1935). A volume of disconnected reminiscences.

The Miracle of Fleet Street (1925). The story of the *Daily Herald*.

What I Saw in Russia (1920).

These, of course, must be supplemented by the files of the *Daily Herald* and *Lansbury's Labour Weekly*. There are innumerable articles by him in other papers, which I have not attempted to index, and there are also election addresses, pamphlets, leaflets and so on. Propaganda books by him which should be consulted are: *Your Part In Poverty* (1915), *These Things Shall Be* (1919), *My England* (1934), *Labour's Way with the Commonwealth* (1935). There are occasional copies to be found of two election newspapers directed by him: the *Bow and Bromley Worker* and the *Middlesbrough Election News*. I have also found of great assistance Mr. Hellicar's collection of cartoons and cuttings dealing with the later period of his life, which is in the Poplar Central Library.

Edgar Lansbury's *My Father* (c. 1933) is an admirable portrait of G.L. as he was at that date. Life in the Lansbury home in the early 1900's has been described by Daisy Postgate in two articles in the *Fortnightly* (Nov.–Dec. 1948) entitled ' A Child in George Lansbury's Home '. Margaret Cole in *Makers of the Labour Movement* has given a brief sketch of his life and an appraisal of his importance.

To some extent G.L. was a lone wolf, and, though he appears frequently in such general Labour histories as Cole and Postgate's *The Common People, 1746–1946*, he is not often mentioned in the biographies of other Labour leaders. But incidental information is to be found in Fenner Brockway's life of F. W. Jowett, Mrs. M. A. Hamilton's life of Arthur Henderson, Margaret Cole's life of Mrs. Webb, and Snowden's autobiography. Valuable references are also to be found in Mrs. Webb's *Our Partnership* and G. D. H. Cole's *History of the Labour Party from 1914.*

Manuscript. A pile of thousands of letters to G.L., of a few by him, and of a large number of memoranda, drafts, speeches and other papers were examined for this book. They have been handed over to the British Library of Political Science (London School of Economics), where they are being indexed, and will in due course be available to students. To these have been added copies of the letters (a mere handful, alas!) from G.L. which were lent to me as a result of a public appeal.

This does not complete the list of the records left behind him for his biographer, and although the story of the disappearance of the rest does not reflect very flatteringly upon my alertness, for completeness' sake it must be told.

Some time before his death George Lansbury sent me, as his biographer, most of the papers mentioned above and with them several boxes apparently containing mostly official papers about the second Labour Government. These he wished particularly to be studied, for his reputation to be cleared from the attacks made by Snowden and others. I did not go through them at the time; I looked at some of them casually, and saw they were marked ' Property of His Britannic Majesty's Government ' (not, for what the distinction is worth, of the Crown); some may have been labelled ' Secret '. When he died, a further jumbled mass of papers arrived; these I looked at, but not thoroughly, as I had agreed with the publishers not to commence writing this book at least until the war was over.

In 1943 I received some letters from Mr. Norman Brook on the notepaper of the War Cabinet demanding the return of certain secret Cabinet papers—not specifying them—which had been in George Lansbury's possession. I replied, as was true, that I was far too busy with official and Home Guard duties to sort G.L.'s papers then, but that when I came to do so after the war I would keep an eye lifting for any documents to which he was not entitled.

The next year William Lansbury, as G.L.'s executor, received a letter on the same notepaper from Sir E. E. Bridges, which seemed to threaten penalties if these unspecified papers were not returned. I thereupon wrote to Bridges, asking him what was up, and repeating that I could not myself yet sort through the papers that G.L. had given me before his death.

There followed correspondence which I may not print, as it was marked ' Confidential ', and my later request for permission to quote from it was parried by a demand to see first what I was going to say. But the upshot was that I agreed to see the Treasury Solicitor, in February 1944. He assured me, with the persuasive suavity which one would expect, (1) that legally the papers for which they were searching ought unquestionably to be returned immediately to the Cabinet offices, and penalties would fall upon the executor otherwise, (2) that they knew what they were seeking, and that was ' a dozen or at most a score ' of very secret papers of a special kind, of which he showed me a specimen (printed, on blue paper, and with a red warning at the head, it was of a kind well known to most civil servants). As it was impossible for me to sort Mr. Lansbury's papers, he would send an official to collect them; they would extract these few documents, and return everything else.

After considerable thought I agreed, and handed to an official well over thirty boxes which seemed to me likely to contain the wanted papers.

There then happened several things which made me regret my action.

In the first place, *all* the papers that I had sent were seized. So far from a dozen being kept, nothing whatever was returned. I was sent, it is true, a set of signed applications to subscribe to the *Labour Gazette* in 1893; but if this was an official's jest or what I have never fathomed.

In the second, I found a transcript of the final resolution of the Labour Cabinet in 1931, stating without qualification that the Ministers were entitled to retain what they pleased.

In the third, I found portions of a correspondence between G.L. and the secretary of Mr. Churchill (at this time Premier) from which it could be deduced that the demand for Cabinet papers had been made by the Government of 1934, and it had been objected that that Government might do as it pleased with its own records, but had no right over those of previous governments. Both for themselves and their heirs the two statesmen seem to have repudiated the claim as illegal, and that repudiation had been acquiesced in.

In the fourth, I belatedly remembered that G.L. had told me something to this effect ten years before, adding that as the papers were the property not of the Crown but of the Government of the day, no legal question could arise.

With this extra information I made repeated applications for the return of the papers which I now felt had been improperly taken from me. I may only say here that these applications were refused.

After Mr. C. R. Attlee took office I again applied, but he replied that the papers were ' Crown property ' and I would not ' be given access ' to them.

I do not think, for reasons given at length in the chapters affected, that the damage done has been as serious as it might have been. In fact, there are only two points where I suspect that darkness still remains which might have been lifted; and I may well be wrong even there. But the story raises the question of how far Ministers, as public servants, are entitled to withhold the records of what has been done in the service of the public. Though this is not the place to decide this, I felt that the facts should be published for future reference.

R. W. P.

CONTENTS

PLATES

Frontispiece

George Lansbury, leader of the Labour Party, about 1935
(*Photograph by Runham, Barnet*)

Facing page 14

Mrs. Ferris, George Lansbury's grandmother

The Rev. J. Fenwick Kitto

Facing page 15

The Lansbury family in 1899

Facing page 96

Propaganda post-card, 1911

After a meeting in Victoria Park, on South African outrages, with Poplar comrades, about 1905

Facing page 97

George Lansbury, signed portrait, 1911
(*Photograph by Lena Connell*)

Facing page 288

George and Bessie Lansbury, about 1925
(*Photograph by Lafayette, Ltd.*)

Facing page 289

George Lansbury, after resigning the leadership
(*Photograph by Whitney, Huntingdon*)

Chapter One

GEORGE LANSBURY was born in 1859, and died in 1940. Among the first events which he remembered was a mid-Victorian election, with hustings at which the candidates stood, with electors pushing through a shouting, fighting, half-drunk crowd to record their votes openly, with jockeys on horseback in gay colours rushing off to fetch new electors when their candidate seemed to be losing. Among the last was being hurried down to a steel-and-concrete underground shelter, lit by fluorescent lights, under a monster bank, when the air-raid siren had gone in the Second World War.

He had seen a country in which no working man had the vote, where the word Socialist was forgotten, where the last Chartist Society had only just dissolved and the trade unions organised hardly one worker in twenty, alter into one where all men and women voted equally, where two Socialist Governments had held office, and every other working man was a unionist. The main railway lines were still being built when he was born; when he died they were partly out-dated by motor-coaches and air travel. He had seen compulsory schooling for all take the place of dame-schools for a small minority; he had seen accepted epidemics and high child mortality vanish before new health regulations and better local administration. He had seen his beloved London double itself in size and cover the marshes and green fields that he had known as a boy; he had seen its inhabitants change in habits, clothes, height, food, appearance, games, language, and even smell. For the larger part of his life he had known his country as the most powerful State that there was in the world, or had ever been in the world. For from, say, 1815 onwards only the most ignorant and fool-hardy ruler directly defied the British, and for those that did, from Canton to Omdurman, there was exemplary punishment. This power, as great as any of past empires, if not so brutally enforced, was far more widespread: the indication of disapproval

I

shown by the arrival of a couple of British cruisers could occur anywhere in the world where salt water reached. Only the partly nominal possessions of the seventeenth-century Spaniards equalled the British Empire in size: nothing equalled it in authority. To the end of his life, Lansbury instinctively felt that what London could be persuaded to see was right mattered more in the world than almost anything else. Yet when he died Britain was engaged in a struggle with a barbarian antagonist double its size, whose very nature would have been incomprehensible in 1859, and whose victory was far from improbable.

No other eighty years had seen such great and such important changes. They were watched, and taken part in, by a man whom his contemporaries realised to be a lay saint. In the later years of his life, a daily picture paper referred to him, unaffectedly and with no suggestion of mockery, in a leading article simply as ' Good George Lansbury '. This was what he was to most; his love, and incessant work for his fellows could not be overlooked by anyone. Some who saw this added silently the comment that his heart was better than his head; they saw, or wished to see, in him only a sort of Father Christmas, whose advice they could not reject as wrong, but might successfully dismiss as unworldly and coming from someone with no knowledge of human wickedness and political necessities. Those who had worked with him, or even merely those whose memories reached back beyond 1935, knew how wrong this was. Lansbury was a man of very keen observation and political shrewdness. Like Robert Owen, he had been a successful business man, though on a smaller scale. He could deal with opponents with cunning and with friends with tact; he was a brilliant administrator locally, and (so far as he was allowed) nationally. Few people saw more clearly, or were more qualified to interpret, the changes that went on around him.

He was not even a saint in the conventional meaning of the phrase. He was not meek, nor simple-minded, nor passionless. He was, indeed, by nature a man of very strong, almost violent passions, held in check and directed by a very firm will and by ardent Socialist and Christian principles. He used to say—half jesting, but half not jesting—that the reason for his teetotalism was that if he once took to drink he would not know when to stop. His anger and pain at injustice or cruelty could affect him so violently as to make him momentarily ill: even after no more than one of his usual speeches to a large audience he would often be drenched in sweat and shaking from the energy he had put into it. To the end of his life those who knew him well and could read his face would sometimes see flash in it the signs of impatience or anger, struck down at once by his ever-watching conscience. Kind he was, overwhelmingly kind; but it was never the kindness which rose from thinness of blood or simpleness of mind.

The day of his birth was February 21st, 1859, and the place was a tollhouse between Lowestoft and Halesworth in Suffolk. This strange birthplace was his because his father was a migrant. He was a timekeeper for Thomas Brassey and Co., the railway contractors who were covering the East of England with the new railroads. Where the ' navigators ' went (' navvies ' was still a frowned-upon abbreviation) George Lansbury senior had to go. The child's earliest memories were of repeated moves, from one set of long rows of wooden huts to another. The huts were put up only to be abandoned as soon as that part of the line was finished: no water was laid on to them, and there was only communal sanitation at a short distance. Frequently all or part of the row was burnt down: little George remembered two such fires, both being caused by warming-pans. These were things that looked like vast frying-pans with lids: they were filled with red-hot cinders, closed up and then rubbed up and down within the sheets before bedtime. If the pan was too hot, or left for long in one place on the bed, the straw mattress would blaze up.

He also remembered the frenzied energy with which the navvies dug and shovelled, and the immense meals they ate of bread-and-cheese and beefsteaks. Nearly all of them, too, drank equally immense amounts of beer and spirits: drunkenness was an everyday, or an every-night occurrence. From other sources we know that among the drunks was often enough his own father.

There is little else that is known of the elder Lansbury, but George spoke frequently of his mother, Anne, obviously a stronger and more lovable character. She, too, drank to excess (and the memory of his parents' life was one possible explanation of his own rigid teetotalism); but that common failing did not prevent her having an incisive mind and a spiritedness which she passed on to her son. She was Welsh, from Brecknock: she ran away from home (or at any rate from domestic service) to be married at sixteen. When he was seven, his mother took young George to help her make her peace with his grandmother, old Mrs. Ferris. She lived then at Clyro in Radnorshire; and the boy never forgot their welcome. Though she did not expect her, and had not seen her for ten years, the tall, straight-standing old Welshwoman hugged her daughter without a word of reproach, 'and then smothered my baby brother and myself with kisses'. He remembered, too, seeing a meeting of the local Hunt, with an uncounted number of hounds, with ladies on side-saddles and gentlemen in pink coats, and deciding that a fox must be a destructive monster of great size and ferocity, requiring the services of so many public-spirited people to kill it. His mother and grandmother were both Radicals—very possibly the older woman was more clearheadedly so than the younger. At any rate, it was she who first talked politics to the boy on her annual visits to London that followed the reconciliation. She was a Nonconformist and a strict Sabbatarian, whose principles admitted of one exception only—the purchase every Sunday of *Reynolds'*, which she taught her grandson to read; and so supplied him with his first political literature.

His earliest continuous recollections were of a home near to Sydenham; the years were probably 1866 and 1867; he was seven or eight years old. Many of his memories were, naturally, isolated pictures. The first recollection of a policeman, in a long blue frockcoat and a top-hat, with a big staff at his side, glaring down at a small group of small boys who had been illegally playing on the unfinished railway line, and were now running away like young rabbits. The recollection of another day when the young family of four (the full number was ultimately nine) were playing or crawling round the door of their home, and suddenly a small crowd appeared, in the centre of which was something being carried. It was a couch, borne by four men, and on it lay their mother with a broken leg. Months passed, during which the housework, care of the children and care of the invalid fell upon the next-door neighbour and her

4

big daughter, with what help the oldest Lansbury child (a girl of nine or ten, at the most) could give. It was at that time, Lansbury used to say, that he learnt the truth of the saying he most frequently quoted at his rich friends—'It's the poor that help the poor'.

At Sydenham, too, he had his first schooling, in the front room of one of the small cottages in that still rural area. His recollection of his education was dim: he remembered much more clearly the 'big Granny's cap' that the old dame who ran it wore, and the fact that, as a specially good pupil, he was allowed to thread her needle for her. He learnt his letters, and probably some simple arithmetic; he sat on the floor and sang nursery rhymes with the rest of the children. His most vivid memory was one of that now-vanished monster, the Crystal Palace: he saw General Tom Thumb there, and believed that he saw the original Siamese twins. He most certainly saw Blondin walk from one tower to the other along a rope, wheeling a barrow with a man in it; and watched his elder brother Jim being sick on the ground with the terror of it, and a grown-up woman being carried out in a dead-faint.

The family's next move was to Greenwich. Here his schooling was even worse than in Sydenham: he learnt much more by sitting on the pier and listening to the men telling stories of the great sailing-ships which daily passed up and down the river. Once he listened to an argument which he afterwards knew to be historic: it was one of the last disputes over which of the famous fast China clippers would arrive with the 'new season's tea' for which the City merchants were waiting. Before steamers replaced them, these ships used to race each other from the Far East; and in the yards across the Thames shipwrights were still sawing and adzing planks, and placing them on the ribs, to make new sailing-ships to challenge the champions.

At Greenwich, too, he was first introduced to class distinctions. It was a gentle introduction: it consisted of being taken with other children, dressed in his best, thoroughly washed, hair combed and oiled, to the home of the manager of the company. Not one of the children had ever before seen such furniture, such glass, such fruits, cakes and pastries, or, above all, such a remarkable thing as a piano. It was huge to their eyes; it had an

B

enormous tilted back and, apparently, heavy green drapery over it. Very daring, the small boy squeezed up close to the grand lady and touched one of the white ivory keys. He was sharply reprimanded by his mother; but the hostess was kind, and allowed him to strike a whole chord with his small hand. Kinder still, she read to him that day and afterwards, *Cinderella*, *Jack the Giant-Killer*, *Little Red Riding Hood* and *Dick Whittington*, pointing out that the moral of the last was that hard work, truthfulness and honesty led to riches. As yet, he did not question that moral; but he was already old enough to be puzzled by the contrast between the manager's wealth and his family's poverty.

Listening to his mother, he heard in these years the names of Derby, Gladstone, Cobden and Bright, of Cavour, Mazzini and Abraham Lincoln. But the most dramatic piece of his political education was a tempestuous election in 1868 which resulted in the return of David Salomans for Greenwich, and the confirming of the right of Jews to sit in Parliament—a thing that then seemed a final blow to the dying cause of anti-Semitism.

'The hustings were set up on Blackheath [he wrote]. The franchise was very restricted: all voters had to declare publicly on whose side they intended to vote. All parties openly practised bribery. On this occasion [polling could then last several days] a huge crowd gathered round the polling places on the Heath. My mother and another enthusiastic woman took me and my brother to see the election. How we came back alive I cannot tell. We were pushed and squeezed, spat at and hooted because we wore Salomans' colours and cheered every time his jockey rode past with figures telling how the poll was going [the colours were red and white, striped]. I have been in many an election campaign since that day, but I have never been nearer death. People talk of rowdiness and uproar at public meetings nowadays: the worst scenes with the Irish and suffrage agitators were mere parlour games to what used to take place in the good old days when voting was free and open, and bribery was carried on as an honourable occupation.'

About the end of 1868 the family moved again, first to Bethnal Green and then to Whitechapel. He was now in East London, his home; and for seventy years, with one short break, he lived there. East Enders were his people: he loved them and defended them—even to the extent, sometimes, of excusing their drunkenness and violence—he was convinced that they were the best people on earth, the most affectionate, loyal, kind and capable. But the East End when he settled there was a very different community from to-day's East End. For one thing, there were hardly any Jews. The Jews came later, as refugees from Russian terror. The steady stream of poor Russian and Polish Jews in the last quarter of the nineteenth century is commonly regarded as an inrush of poverty and misery, debasing the East End by spreading conditions such as were exposed in the tailoring trade at the turn of the century. Lansbury remembered it as something quite different. A high proportion of the refugees, from Stepniak onwards, were anarchists, nihilists and social revolutionaries—men with high principles and a defined working-class philosophy. They were each one a nucleus of education and resistance, and largely responsible for the slow improvement in London conditions. All of the Jews, in any case, by the care they took of their children, put to shame (and soon outnumbered) the existing foreign colony. For already in the sixties and seventies there was a foreign colony, an enormous undigested population of Irish. The Irish fought among themselves, frequently and furiously, men and women stripped to the waist and reeking of whisky and porter; but they never interfered with the English, and civilly interrupted their battles to let them pass. The East End was also much smaller: Romford was in the country, and the marshes of the Lea were open spaces. Lansbury watched the great eastward suburbs being built:

'I have seen these marshlands turned into towns [he wrote]. Do you know how it's done? First, millions of tons of house and road refuse are shot down. After it has sunk, a small layer of concrete is put down, and up go the " desirable working-class residences ". There are miles of streets in East London which have been built up in this way during the past fifty years. The houses in many instances are no more than slums held together by each other. United they stand, divided they would all topple over.' (*My England*, p. 62.)

Smallpox, cholera and typhoid fever swept the East End at regular intervals: ' free diarrhœa mixture ' was provided every summer as the only preventive. The sole hospital was the

7

London Hospital in the Whitechapel Road, a quarter of its present size at that. Drinking-water was stored in foul tanks, with green and grimy slime on bottom and sides. He remembered being regularly marched, with his fellow schoolchildren, to church to pray for the ending of smallpox or typhoid; or being told that ' God had been pleased to take home His loved one ' when one of his playmates disappeared. He listened sometimes to an early group of free-thinkers who met on Bonner's Fields; but whenever his mother suspected that he or his brother had been there she rushed them over to a Primitive Methodist Chapel in Bonner Lane, where the pastor specialised in terrible descriptions of the torments of hell. For once and twice he was shaken by these, but soon after he was unaffected (' hardened ' was the phrase used), and ever afterwards was contemptuous of that sort of terrorist religion.

He was more influenced by Lord Shaftesbury's Evangelical Mission in George Yard in Whitechapel—not by whatever doctrine was taught there, but by the charity enforced by its founder. The Mission gave free meals, and shelter to tramps and ' down and outs ', and Lansbury remembered the attacks on its policy by the Whitechapel Poor Law Guardians. The Guardians fiercely resented the implied criticism, and issued statements denouncing Shaftesbury for pampering idlers and won't-works. Though he was only twelve, ' I somehow knew what it was all about,' Lansbury writes; and he took the side which he took all his life.

But these were no more his usual interests than they would be those of any other small boy. He was not a specially good, nor even a quiet child. He was probably, if anything, rather more boisterous than his fellows in a very boisterous crowd. Careering round the streets banging at housewives' doors, playing football—which largely consisted in fighting and kicking other players—leaping from barge to barge on the Thames, and once at least nearly meeting death in the water: he showed in these years a boyish exuberance which he never quite lost. (Unlike very many earnest reformers, he really loved the noise that children make; the yelling in a school playground was music to him; and nothing excited him so much as a romp in Epping Forest where no one but himself was over fourteen.) In the sixties the Lansbury children's favourite playground was the newly opened Victoria Park in Bow, with its impressive park-keepers in top-hats, frock-coats and red waistcoats, and its mysterious and inaccessible island in the centre of the pond. On this island is a pagoda, which they believed was inhabited by Chinese who came out at night to take care of the swans, ducks and other water-fowl.

His schooling was intermittent. He went to the school of St. James the Less in Bethnal Green till he was eleven, when he left for a year to go into an office. (He also ran away about this time into Herefordshire, where he took a job as potboy in a pub, and left after two days because of the filthiness of the spittoons he had to clean; but he did not often talk of this escapade.) Then he went back again for a couple of years to St. Mary's School in Whitechapel, where at last he came under a really able master, Michael Apted. But even here all the children (who were the aristocrats of the neighbourhood, paying fourpence a week, unlike the ' charity sprats ' down the road) were taught in one great room. He learnt reading perfectly, a good deal of mis-cellaneous history (mostly English), geography, and arithmetic well enough to run a business in later years. He was not properly taught grammar; his handwriting remained poor and his spelling was always imperfect. He acquired a taste for literature; but this he learnt mostly from Mr. Tarling, the Superintendent of the Band of Hope which he joined, who encouraged him to learn by heart pieces from Shakespeare, Thomas Hood, Aytoun, and some forgotten Victorian favourites like Bell and Massey.

He was often asked in later years whether children of his day had a happier and healthier life than in the nineteen-twenties and thirties. He never hesitated in the answer. He had seen so immense a change, such a diminution of disease, starvation, drunkenness, fighting, desertion, thieving, cruelty, raggedness, filth, bad housing and administrative callousness, that any praiser of the ' good old days ' was rapidly and finally confuted by a stream of facts drawn from his personal knowledge. Yet sometimes he would admit a longing for the highly coloured gaiety of festivals which have now disappeared and left no successors. He has left (in *Looking Backwards*) a description

9

of one, ' Fairlop Friday ' in July.   It was an annual outing for
the shipwrights in Dockland.   They went out to Fairlop near
Barkingside, then a country place: they travelled in boats, of
course, as shipwrights should.   But the boats were not sailing
on the river: they were mounted on carts and drawn each by
four horses gaily caparisoned and ridden by jockeys in brilliant
colours.

' Sometimes four very large boats, fully rigged, would take part.
The boats were filled with men all dressed up and some place to go.
They all looked most important to us, and to judge by the jollity which
prevailed were all well supplied with the sort of drink which is said to
make glad the heart of man, and later on makes his head and stomach
very much the reverse of glad.'

The boats went in slow procession all round the streets of
Whitechapel, with many stops for more drinks, ending up at
Fairlop, where there was a big dinner, and a fair with sideshows
and various amusements of which he knew only by hearsay.   But
the great moment for which the children waited was the return
of the procession to Whitechapel shortly before midnight.   The
laughter and singing—for drunkenness had not usually yet turned
to quarrelling—and general gaiety were enhanced for them by
' the glory and grandeur of . . . the fireworks and lanterns,
which together with masses of coloured lights made us youngsters scream with delight '.

The Franco-Prussian War of 1870 was the first event that
interested him seriously in politics; though he was only eleven,
he read and listened avidly.   There is a story which shows how
carefully he studied his facts even at that time: it is his recollection of a group of adults wondering what was the meaning of the
Tsar's action in tearing up the Black Sea Treaty, and of a small
boy in the centre explaining to them, in a dead silence, what the
treaty was.   It was, George Lansbury said, a pact signed at the
end of the Crimean War which forbade Russia to build or maintain warships in the Black Sea; it had now been cancelled by the
Tsar because the other chief signatories were distracted by the
Franco-Prussian War; and this, concluded the child, was a bad
thing, as, if one side could at any time cancel a treaty, then no
international agreements would ever be binding.

His source of information and his chief tutor was John Hales, the Irishman who was secretary of the First International founded by Karl Marx and others in 1864. Hales did not relay Marxism to him; indeed, Hales was not a Marxist at all, but an Irish nationalist, a Radical, and a working man very conscious of his class interests. It is unlikely that he did more than impress the boy with a sense of solidarity with the working people of all the world, a hatred of oppression and an as yet indiscriminate love of freedom of thought, speech and action. He revealed to him, that is, his own innate beliefs and principles: later experience was only to strengthen, not to change, the views he had begun to hold at the age of eleven.

For the moment, naturally, he was only a spectator. Politics for him consisted in attending, open-eyed but not entirely uncomprehending, the meetings in Tower Hamlets and round about addressed by Captain Maxse, George Odger, W. R. Cremer, George Howell and other forgotten Radical politicians. Only once did he pass from passive to active: some time towards the end of this period he helped to rescue the great atheist, Charles Bradlaugh, from a violent mob in Hyde Park. He had come to listen to him—as a Republican and Radical orator, not as a secularist—but was prevented by the yells and scuffling of a crowd of opponents. It was clear that a number of them, headed by medical students, had determined to break up the meeting, wreck the platform and beat up the speakers, 'smashing over the head all who got in their way'. Bradlaugh's top hat was trampled on and his frock-coat torn from top to bottom; and, in order to save him, Lansbury and others linked arms and formed a protective ring, getting him slowly through the mob to Marble Arch, which was then the actual gateway to the Park. Here the medical students made a fierce rush, banging and slashing at the boys' wrists and arms, but without success. Bradlaugh was put into a hansom cab and driven off—he seemed, Lansbury noticed, not altogether grateful to his saviours. He was a tall man, lion-headed, with enormous physical strength and no sense of fear whatever. He kept looking back at his assailants, going unwillingly, as if he thought he could by his own strength of body and dominant personality quell some thousands of screeching young men.

Chapter Two

THE year 1875, when George Lansbury was sixteen, saw at least three events which changed the course of his life.

First, his father died (his mother re-married not long after). With his eldest brother, Jim, he took over his father's business unloading trucks (mostly of coal) for the Eastern Counties Railway, in the arches at Whitechapel, and into barges at Thames Wharf, Blackwall. Described as a ' contractor's job ', it was chiefly plain coal-heaving; it probably developed his physique and made him into the powerful and tall man that he later was, but it also may have strained him and been responsible for various illnesses which followed. Often he worked at night—from one to seven in the morning—going home for bath and breakfast, allowing himself (even at that date) the minimum of rest, and spending the afternoon if possible at a cricket match, or at a political meeting, and in the evening, not infrequently, going to the House of Commons gallery. He became close friends with many of the guards, platelayers, greasers, shunters and signalmen employed by the railway at the Spitalfields, Brick Lane and Bishopsgate depots. He saw, and never forgot, ' two shunters, a guard and an inspector crushed to death because they were not quick enough in stepping out from the trucks, or in between them '—deaths which could have been prevented if the Company had been willing to go to the small expense of providing poles for uncoupling wagons.

This year, also, he began to ' walk out ' with a pretty school-girl of fourteen, named Elizabeth Jane Brine, whom he had met at St. Mary's School. For both of them this was the beginning of a love-story which had no change and no looking backward; it was a Victorian romance of complete constancy and unaltering affection on both sides; in his own belief hers was the most powerful and important influence on his life and character. Yet at the moment, if, so far as the young lovers were concerned, the course of love ran smooth, outside interference was shortly to disturb it violently.

The third important event was that he came under the direct personal influence of the Vicar of Whitechapel, the Reverend J. Fenwick Kitto. Mr. Kitto has long been dead, and there are none now who remember him; but it is clear he was a man of exceptional personality and probably of radiant goodness. He was among the first East End clergymen to attract crowds to his church by the beauty of his services. The Low Church parsons who surrounded him followed the Evangelical tradition, which had declined from austerity into mere ugliness. Their ritual, and even their buildings, differed little from those of the bare, and almost deliberately hideous, dissenting chapels which speckled the East End. They spoke of love, but they seemed more concerned with hate. They rejoiced in descriptions of hell's torments: they hated so many things—tolerance, beauty, colour, ceremony and Roman Catholics. To-day Mr. Kitto's services would not be attacked as inordinately ' High '; but he restored chanting and singing to their proper place, the Elizabethan prayer-book was read as it deserved to be, his church was lovingly adorned, and the ceremonial of the services was followed out enthusiastically. He had no outstanding intellectual qualities; his thinking never went beyond the simpler dogmas of orthodox Anglicanism; he was not infrequently stumped by some of the fairly easy posers his young charges put to him. But his character, and the example of his life, brought about a profound change in Lansbury's thinking and way of living. For him, and for many other young men, Mr. Kitto was to the end of his life a man whose example should be followed, and whose approval it was immensely important to retain. The first supper to which Lansbury and several other youngsters were invited at the vicarage was an alarming experience:

' I had never seen an evening dinner or a meal served by servants, so I sat looking at my plate, wondering what next was coming on. A superior person asked me if I would have some " blancmange "; she might as well have said " poison ", because the word had never come my way before. Seeing my discomfort Mr. Kitto called down the table, " Have some cornflour, George? " and of course I said yes.'

Under Mr. Kitto, Lansbury experienced what was then the common phenomenon of a ' conversion '. There was no wickedness, no life of sin, for him to be converted from; nor had he ever doubted the truths of Christianity; but, as with most schoolboys, they had had no reality for him. Now they became suddenly real; they shaped his mind, and shaped it finally. Many years later, it is true, he was invaded by doubt, and even sent his children to an Ethical Sunday School; but he recovered himself after a few years, and never afterwards regarded the period as anything but one of darkness—a wavering from the faith, deeply regrettable and to be spoken of as little as possible. The outward signs of the change that came over him between sixteen and eighteen were a renewed energy in the Band of Hope, the joining of a 'Stephenson Total Abstinence Society', and an immense activity in Mr. Kitto's own society, the Whitechapel Church Young Men's Association. Its twelfth rule said bluntly, under the heading FOUNDATION: 'That nothing be done in connection with the Association that is not in strict accordance with the Word of God'. It ran devotional meetings, Bible-readings, lectures, debates and educational classes. Its members read essays to each other, and used a small library and a 'reading-room supplied with periodicals of a pure tone'; they organised entertainments, cricket matches and other sports. In all these Lansbury, and his old school friend Wait Chester Sewell, were so energetic that they were soon committee members.

A place for reading, a hall where debates could be held and entertainments organised, an association that ran cricket matches —these were things badly needed in Whitechapel in 1875, and there were, no doubt, many very enthusiastic young members who were merely working off their energies in the only place that they harmlessly could. Not so Lansbury and his intimates: they were not the later type of 'muscular Christian' to whom the cricket bat was as important as the Cross. They worked so ardently only because they were certain that they were doing the Lord's will. They had been caught up in the great Protestant tradition that had been running strongly for two and a half centuries in England and has only failed in the last generation. There still exists a small bundle of letters from Lansbury to Sewell, some of which, from their tone and phrasing, might almost have been written two hundred or more years before. Sometimes there is a distinct echo of the

*Mrs. Ferris, George
Lansbury's grandmother*

The Rev. J. Fenwick Kitto

The Lansbury family in 1899

Annie,   George Lansbury,   Bessie Lansbury

Constance,   Doreen

Dorothy,   Edgar,   Nellie,   William, Daisy

(*Absent: Bessie   Dead: George   Unborn: Violet, Eric*)

correspondence of a man for whom he had no great affection, Oliver Cromwell.

His first preserved letter to Sewell, in August 1877, is concerned chiefly with his troubles over taking Sewell's class while Sewell was ill and the problem presented by another tutor boxing a boy's ears. But in October of next year he is deep in religious discussion.

'You say you do not feel that you have repented of your sin. I will tell you as near as I can what I think true repentance is. I think that when you have accepted Christ you repent of your sins by that act. You show that you mean by His grace to lead a better, purer and holier life. I do not think that we have any right after we are converted to be sorry; we should rather be rejoicing at having such an unspeakable gift in our possession. . . . Dear Wait, do try to make yourself happy by God's grace. You cannot do it yourself: you must trust Him and Him alone. He only can shield you from sin. . . . I am sure that I cannot express half I feel in regard to Bess and Alice; it does seem a glorious thing that we should all four be Christians under one God and one banner; doesn't it make your heart warm?'

'Bess' was, of course, his own betrothed; 'Alice' the future Mrs. Sewell. Like all his letters, this one was imperfectly spelt. 'As' was usual for 'has'; verbs ending in '-e', like 'have', kept the 'e' in the participle ('haveing'); capital initials were used for emphasis as well as to mark the beginning of a sentence; words beginning with 'ex' received the 'x' only ('xcept'); punctuation consisted of one mark which could be regarded at will as a full stop, a comma or a dash. These idiosyncrasies have not been reproduced: they were common to many self-taught Victorians. They have no significance, except in the sentimental recollections of those who received his highly individual letters.

In March or April of the next year, 1879, his health broke down, and he was sent away to 'Poplar House', near Redhill in Surrey, apparently a convalescent home or hospital. The letters do not make the position wholly clear, but they refer to the beautiful scenery, to a kind 'Matron', and to a visit from Mr. and Mrs. Kitto which raised him greatly in the esteem of his fellow-patients. He had time to write to Sewell at length (April 16th):

'I do sincerely hope that your religion is getting firmer and stronger every day. You know, dear Wait, I think there is too much theology in your religion. . . . I think too that you look for the answers of your prayers too soon. You know that in praying there must be no doubt and mistrustfulness: it must be simply trusting Jesus and Him alone, and waiting His own time and pleasure for the answer to our prayer; so, dear Wait, do try to trust Him, do try to see Him as he really is, your true and only Saviour.'

Ten days later he wrote that he had a relapse into whatever was his illness.

'I was really very bad . . . but you know it has cost rather a good bit of money for me to come here . . . so don't tell anyone about this letter. Give my love to my boys [his class at Whitechapel] and tell them that please God I shall be at School on Sunday fortnight. Tell them if they want me back and love me they must pray that God will be pleased to restore me to health and strength. I should be glad if they would pray for me in school. You might speak to Budd because I do really feel the need of their prayers just now. Of course don't make any fuss about it: if you think he would rather not don't say anything about it; but you can remember me yourself at any rate at the teacher's meeting Sunday week. Dear Wait, I long to be home and once more working for God.'

It is almost a relief, among all this seriousness, to find a more human distress (April 28th):

'I must thank you most of all for your kind letter; it quite cheered me up. I was feeling so miserable when I saw the postman coming. I have not had a letter since Wednesday from Bessie. I have written her two and have written another one just now which she will get tonight. So you may guess I did not feel very grand when the postman gave me the letters and I saw there was none from her.'

Many people who met Bessie Lansbury late in life saw only a retiring, soft-voiced and shy woman, mother of twelve children, and obviously wholly occupied by care of them, of the house, and of one of the most energetic and restless husbands in the country —a woman with little knowledge of politics, and no interest in economic and philosophical questions, whose range of thought was bounded by the home. No picture could have been more untrue, at least of the young Bessie Brine. Her mind was as inquiring and active as her young admirer's, if not as profound; we have his word for it that her character was as strongly formed. She had been more carefully educated—her handwriting and spelling were better than his. She shared all his activities in the St. Mary's Band of Hope, playing the harmonium there. She was invaluable to him and Sewell in the propaganda warfare they carried on in the Whitechapel Young Men's Association, copying out and improving their essays and resolutions. Even after her marriage she tried to carry this on: there is a later letter from George Lansbury to Sewell saying that he must allow Bessie ' at least a fortnight ' for dealing with his essays, ' as she has generally got so much work cut out to do each day '.

The earliest remaining literary work of George Lansbury is an essay for the Whitechapel Association on the need for Irish freedom: it is very well-informed for a boy of seventeen (as he probably was), but the comments of his colleagues, written on the facing pages, will not allow him the sole credit. ' Judging by the signature I do not think Mr. G. L. wrote this paper himself,' observed one; another, who seems to have been a Tory put out of temper by Radical opinions, said, ' I sh'd advise Mr. L. to ask the Lady who wrote his paper to make a reformation in her " o's " as in some cases they are so deformed as to have the appearance of " a's ", producing very peculiar results.' The hand was Bessie Brine's: the thought, however, was of course, as it always was, George Lansbury's. But her interest in politics was genuine and to some extent independent. One of her few remaining letters is an early one sent from Wincanton in Somerset, where she was staying for a short holiday: it contains an unexpected phrase for a love-lorn girl of sixteen in July 1877.

' It is such a beautiful place but very lonely. Oh, I do miss you all so, you would never believe. I do wish George was down here. I should feel so happy then. Now I have left George behind I feel I have left everything. I should like you all to be down here. There are such lovely lanes shaded with trees, just wide enough for two to walk along comfortably and talk politics a treat.'

Her better education, indeed, was a barrier to their courtship. Through her suitor's prejudiced eyes, her mother appears a bad-

tempered snob, and her father, afterwards ' Grandfather Brine ',
a domineering brute with a Lancashire accent.   He was probably
descended from James Brine, the Tolpuddle Martyr: if so, he
inherited little of his ancestor's broadmindedness.   Both the
Brines considered that their Bessie was endeavouring to marry
beneath her, and tried to stop her by the peremptory means
natural to Victorian parents.   But it is not always remembered
that the overbearing Victorian parent implied and produced the
rebellious Victorian child: Bessie had more spirit than they
allowed for.   The month after her Wincanton holiday the
explosion came.   A letter of George Lansbury's tells half the
story:

' Dear Wait . . .

' Mrs. Brine has gone wrong again.   I had such a row with
her last night.   As briefly as possible I will try and tell you what it
was all about.   Last week Bessie had her hair cut a little; well,
yesterday she found it was too short to do it up as she generally does,
so she wore it down her back.   Well, her mother as soon as she saw it
told her to put it up but Bessie said she could not.   Mrs. Brine
appealed to the Bully.   He told Bess he would murder her if she did
not put it up—well, at last she went and put it up in some style or
another and it was forgotten till teatime when it came up again and
there was another row.   The upshot of it was she, Bessie, would not
go to Church, but as soon as her mother and Bully had gone she came
round to me at Chicksand Street and wanted me to take her to Putney.
But I took her home forcibly and thought I might arrange it somehow
with her mother.   But Mrs. B. no sooner saw me than she told me
that Bessie and I would have to part.   I treated it as a capital joke and
told her I knew I should have to—till Wednesday.   She then got
indignant and called Bessie, Lizzie and Alice over to rights.   Lizzie
was a bad girl, Alice a gossip and you and Alf—well, I don't know how
to qualify her language at all, but it was simply outrageous how she
went on.   I was worse than all.   When I told her that Bessie was not
proud and that she and the Bully were the only ones that said she was,
she said I had no right to say so as I did not know anything about
Bessie.   I told her that I must disagree with her in that I had known
Bessie for two years and that I thought I was a little justified in saying
that in my opinion and in the opinions of an army of friends who all
say that she is not.   Well, after that she went on abusing Bessie.
She did not call her a fallen woman, but everything besides—a low

girl, a fast girl, and, there, I don't know what she did say hardly; only that I was mad, nearly stamped my foot, and banged my umbrella about and told her it was to her eternal infamy to say so and that till she and the Bully altered I would not cross her doorstep again; and with that I went into the other room and found that Bessie had gone out leaving the door open behind her. I went back and told Mrs. B.; she said she could not help it, but she would hand her over to her father. I said " oh " and goodnight.

' I went out to find her. I did after running about for an hour. I went to Mrs. Farquhar and she wanted to know how it would all end, and I told her I supposed it would end either in us all drowning ourselves or taking arsenic. She was righteously indignant: I should like her to have Mrs. B. for an hour or so. Well, at last I found Bessie waiting at our gate for me. She would not go home, and it was then past 10, so I found Lizzie and Alf and Alice and had a committee; and at last Bessie was to go home—last night or this morning if not last night. She was going to sleep with Alice. But they were going to see Mrs. B. first. The reason she would not go home was she was afraid of that great hulking Lancashire bully of a Father. He told her mother when he found she had gone out he would break her neck when she came home, and you know his hands and feet are not very light. I don't know what to do. I cannot write and must not go out with her. But I shall when I get the chance. I do wish you were here.'

How exactly the crisis was solved is not known; but Miss Brine was returned to her home without disaster or scandal, and her parents gradually accepted Mr. Lansbury as a tolerable suitor. But the two were by no means able to marry at once. George's illness had saddled him with a debt, and he and his brother were now responsible for the two younger children in the family. He worked with renewedly ferocious energy at the contractor's business: he was proud of his strength and his ability to do two men's work. Once he recklessly attempted to wind the winch of a coal-shoot alone. The shoots were on hinges, and at one moment the winch-winders—there were always two of them—had to take the whole weight of the shoot. Despite his strength, the shoot was too heavy for him alone; the winch-handle shot round and struck him on the head, putting him out of action for the rest of the day. At that he was lucky: if he had held on to the winch-handle he would have been flung into the air and fallen twenty feet into a coal-barge, probably with a broken neck. Such accidents taught him a little caution—not much, for to the end of his life he worked himself to the last ounce of energy. He had a particular spur now to earn money: he even economised, which was all his life unnatural to him.

'Dear Chester,' he wrote in August 1878 to Sewell, 'I am getting quite economical now. I go a whole day and spend only a half-penny, and that is for the *Echo*. I hope it will last: I mean to try. I have much pleasure in telling you that Bessie is about to buy a large lamp like my mother's. So you see we mean business. My duty is to pay off my debt: she knows all about it. It will not take long now.'

It took longer than he thought: they were not married till 1880, five years after their engagement. In the intervening two years Lansbury completed the first stage of his political education. He was a Christian Radical, and for him, as for many others, the great political struggle was the fight between Gladstone and Disraeli. He records that he managed between 1875 and 1880 to hear ' most, if not all, of Gladstone's great speeches on the Eastern Question, in the House of Commons, or Blackheath, or at Newman Street Hall' (off Oxford Street). So profoundly impressed was he by that tremendous voice and that great earnestness of passion, that fifty years later he could repeat verbatim a long passage from the great man's speech on Montenegro and Bulgaria; ' I can hear his voice and see him now ', he wrote. Already he had begun to wonder a little over his leader's incomprehension of all social questions—his utter lack of understanding, for example, of such things as the demand for an eight-hour day—but he was too much moved by the campaign for peace and for the freedom of small nations, including Ireland, to criticise openly. Peace was his greatest love, and next to that the freeing of oppressed nations from their bonds. Only afterwards did he become a Socialist; and it was perhaps of some psychological importance in his last years that his love of peace was the earliest of his political convictions. At the moment, however, there was no contradiction. Gladstone's party was preventing Disraeli from going to war with Russia to help the Turks. The prevention of this war would mean the freeing of the small Christian nations of the Balkans. And Gladstone's party was also the only one from which any social reforms could be expected.

At last, on May 29th, 1880, George Lansbury and Elizabeth Brine were married at Whitechapel Church, by Mr. Kitto. They went away for a short honeymoon near Coleston in East Anglia, having been slightly embarrassed by good friends soon after the train left the old Bishopsgate Station of the Eastern Counties Railway.

'You may thank,' he wrote to his brother Jim, ' all those very kind and affectionate gentlemen who so kindly cheered as we passed. The reason I did not look out was the carriage was full and everyone stared at us as though they knew we were just married. Who told Ward? I could see his broad face grinning, and old Stockley—I thought he was coming over the parapet. Bessie was quite pleased. She thought herself very grand to have a lot of people waiting to cheer her. Well, we shall be home about half past: get Arthur to let Chester Sewell know, and Mrs. Brine.'

Of their married life he himself in 1935 wrote all that needs to be said:

' I don't feel I can write about my wife who, from the time I first met her, exercised an influence over my life which no words of mine will ever adequately express; and also, I feel she stands in a relation to me on a quite different footing from anyone else, man or woman. A sweetheart with whom one lived, talked and walked during a period of more than fifty years cannot be described, or her influence weighed in any worthwhile balance. So I leave out of this account the one who through all our long years of courtship and married life shared all my joys and sorrows, my failures and successes, and who knew me for what I am, as only a lover and wife could. Neither of us were sexless persons, but both of us believed marriage was for eternity; and this, when the tide of tempers rose, or when adversity swept down, kept us young enough in heart to be able to say: " No matter, we have still got each other; let's forget everything else ".'

Chapter Three

A YEAR after his marriage, in 1881, George Lansbury's mother died, leaving two young boys for him and the other children to look after. At the same time his first child was born. It was not long after that he became restless in his partnership with his brother Jim in the contracting business; and dissolved it. He had, indeed, been uncomfortable since his marriage, and had sounded Mr. Kitto on his chances of becoming manager of one of the new Board Schools; but the unease, whatever it may have been, did not become unbearable till some time in 1882. Then he tried his hand at several enterprises: one, running a coffee-bar as part of the social services attached to Whitechapel Church, lasted as long as eighteen months. Then he left because the sedentary indoor life made him ill. Other jobs he left because he detested the competition in which they involved him. 'I fled from one good job,' he wrote afterwards, 'because I found myself fighting a near relation for good conditions, only to find myself landed into a shop which ruined an old-established shop a little way down the road.'

With such scruples, he and his young wife were, as he said afterwards, 'willing dupes' of a propaganda that was plastered all round London. The Colonies were anxious for British immigrants, and no one was more eager and less responsible in his statements than the Queensland Agent-General. Australia was represented as a land where there was work for all, where any man could carve out for himself a good living in a virgin country, without harming anyone else. Hard work it would be, and out-door work; but who would be daunted by that? You could be your own master and no man's enemy.

As a matter of fact, Australian towns were already full of drifting unemployed; and why the representatives of the Colonial governments should have gone on with their recruiting, like clockwork toys which, wound up, cannot stop, is not clear even to-day. It was not the need for cheap labour: the

22

wharfsides were already packed with cheap and unwanted labour which was no use and might become a public charge. But continue with it they did; and among their recruits were the two young Lansburys, now with three small children (Bessie junior, Annie, and George junior) and George's young brother aged twelve. The children were three, two and under one respectively; only one could walk, and the voyage would not be easy. But the earthly paradise on the other side of the world would be compensation enough.

If they had realised it, a warning of what was ahead for them came as soon as the party left Waterloo. They were now ' only emigrants ', part of that immense outward wash of human beings that spread from the British Isles in the last half of the nineteenth century: like others, they received no more consideration than cattle or freight. The train was allowed to take a whole day to reach Plymouth, dawdling round the longest way; in the town itself they were accommodated for the night in a lodging-house which was verminous. Next morning they went on board the ' Duke of Devonshire ', a very long, narrow, grey ship, with both steam and sail—a four-master. It was a cargo-boat in fact, transformed into an emigrant ship by dividing up the hold into ' a set of boxes partitioned off '. There was no cabin accommodation, as they had been promised: nothing but bunks consisting of deal planks with a mattress laid upon them. When they set sail, in May 1884, further disadvantages showed themselves. The ill-balanced old ship rolled, pitched and tossed: all but the most experienced sailors among the five hundred emigrants were seasick and stayed sick; Mrs. Lansbury was only well during the small periods when they were in port. The food provided by the company was insufficient to maintain life. The family had a capital of something over £100, and had prudently laid in a stock of food, ' or we should literally have starved '. The second engineer and the boiler-maker, ashamed for the company, shared their food with the sick women, including Mrs. Lansbury. ' I think my wife was kept alive by these means.'

The children, however, suffered very little, if at all; dirt was never a hardship to a child, cramped quarters are less cramped for the very small, and they were adequately fed. Passage through the tropics was a joy. Every day, in the perpetual sun, their father plunged them in a great tub of salt water filled fresh from the sea, and excused them the customary scrubbing on the ground that they were now clean enough. He even shook the strict conservatism of the English housewife: ' Most mothers followed my example and gave up washing their children in basins '. Malta, Port Said, Suez, Aden; heat, Roman Catholics, crucifixes, Muslims and ' traders ' who climbed aboard and were really thieves who had to be thrown into the sea head first by the officers. Lansbury had an impulse to intervene until it was explained to him just what ' the natives ' were after. At Colombo he went ashore and into the heathen temples: it was the first time he had seen with his eyes a religion which was not the Christian, and the elaborateness of the carvings and the size of the buildings made him thoughtful. At Batavia he did intervene: Javanese women loaded the boat with coal, and the manners of the Dutch overseer seemed to him insulting: he went up to him and abused him roundly in good loud Cockney English, for treating women ' as if they were cattle '.

In the Indian Ocean he had an experience which he thought was a narrow escape from death. The ship ran into a monsoon.

' As a boy I had read of the sea running mountains high, but one must see this kind of thing to appreciate it. Our big ship would sink right down as into a great valley of water and waves, and coming towards us were huge mountains of water which seemed as though they must overwhelm us. But somehow, like a cork, our vessel rose up. It seemed sometimes as though the boat must smash in two. Everyone was sick; even I was ill for about two hours. In addition we starved nearly all these three days, in fact, very few people wanted anything except to lie still. I think that had we been told we were going to the bottom it would not have made much difference. I am certain it would have made very little difference to my wife and myself. We had our children with us, and had the feeling that we should all go together. But of course there is an end to everything, and there was an end to this monsoon. It came when the heavens opened and the rain commenced to fall. The great torrents of water from the sky beat down the sea. I heard that rain could beat down an angry sea, but should never have realised it had I not seen the water

24

from above literally beat the waves down and thus produce a great calm.'

At last, on a clear, sunny day in July—the Australian winter—the 'Duke of Devonshire' sailed slowly and smoothly into Brisbane river. The banks were beautiful, and at that time quite unspoiled, with clean white houses peacefully nestling in the green. The emigrants sang together a song: 'Safe Home at Last', and some of them literally danced for joy.

'As we went round the bend of the river, however, and came in sight of the town itself, the houses became more closely packed together, the streets, which we could see quite easily from the ship, looked ugly and squalid, and the first glimpse of a friend's face on shore sent our hearts into our boots.'

Big groups of unemployed were waiting for them on the quay—some of them men whom they knew, who had left England but a few months before with equally high hopes. The emigrants landed among sullen or compassionate faces, and were marched off to the 'Immigrants' Home', a filthy building with no amenities, crawling with vermin, and with big rats running across the room. There they were left to fend for themselves: Authority had finished with them.

Lansbury had never before been unemployed: it was a new experience for him to go from address to address in a city, vainly offering his strength and intelligence. The hundred pounds steadily melted away. The family found a small house, almost a hovel, in the well-named Fortitude Valley, and each day he went out to try to get work. For some while he worked at the last resort of Victorian labourers—stonebreaking. This even his physique could not stand: finding he earned no more than a shilling a day, he quit, suffering acutely from neuralgia. From this he moved to a better job, in a slaughter-house, driving the van. He was fairly well paid, but his fellows in the slaughter-house were on piece-rates, and he noticed how senselessly they drove themselves as a result. They seemed to lose all human feeling, he recorded: they were brutalised, and would have cut their fellows' throats as easily as those of the bullocks and sheep. He left this job because he would not work on the Sunday: his employer, a Roman Catholic, tried to argue him out of it, but he was obstinate, although his family was near to being very hungry. Forty years later he still thought he was right. ' I think Moses was really inspired when he laid down this principle ' (of the Sabbath rest) he wrote.

There was no one, and no institution, to help the Lansburys but themselves. They were meeting Victorian free competition at its purest. There were no social services, and no trade unions. Protest meetings by the unemployed were met by offering jobs to a handful of the more energetic or violent. There was no person who would offer even sympathy, except the Bishop, a mild old gentleman named Hale, who seemed to have almost the only kind heart in Brisbane : even he was convinced of the virtues of free competition, and surveyed the un-Christian society round him with a melancholy helplessness.

When everything seemed hopeless, Lansbury was offered a job by a farmer who had driven in from a village named Harrisville, some eighty miles away. The salary was to be £40 a year, plus an ample allowance of flour, meat and sugar, and a charming little furnished cottage, away from the farm, and in lovely surroundings.

Not until later did he find out that his employer was one of those whom Australia does not boast about, who ' left his country for his country's good '; and that he himself was the victim of the oldest and most successful fraud practised on employees. He had been brought out to a place from which he could not escape without money, under conditions which made it sure that he would always be in his employer's debt. It was a fairly common swindle in Australia at the time : the Harrisville employer was only a little more ruthless than his fellows, and more expert a slave-driver on the farm. Lansbury wrote to Sewell in September of 1884 :

' I am about 40 miles up the bush under the worst old tyrant it has ever been my lot to meet with. He has got his match in me for I take none of his cheek : and to-day I would not work in the pouring rain (and it does rain here) so he grumbled and I came home and had a day's holiday. I work very hard, from sunrise to sunset. I have acquired several accomplishments since I came here. I can milk very well, also load hay and other various forms of farm work.

' We live in a hut of one room cut in two. We can see the stars over our head at night and the sun by day. The nights are very cold but the days are very hot: I don't know what it will be like in summer. I earn the enormous sum of 13/4 per week. They give me 20 lbs. of flour, 20 lbs. of meat, 1 lb. of tea, 4 lbs. sugar also, weekly. The meat runs alive as soon as we get it so that my 13/4 is spent in buying milk, eggs etc. for us to live on.

' It is a dead sell to send poor people out here: they are not wanted . . . If I come back to London as I hope to in a couple of years I shall join the Christian Socialists and get them to start me lecturing on emigration. Mr. Kitto and these good people know nothing of the numbers of new chums that die out here miserably, especially the poor children. No one thinks we shall bring up our three, though we are trusting that our good Father will bring us *all* through safely.'

The ' pretty cottage ' was a ' humpie '—that is, a wooden building stuck up on four stumps, with the ridgeway worn away so that the sky could be seen through it. Rains, when they came, nearly flooded them out. The ' furniture ' consisted of planks laid on tree-stumps as beds, two cupboards, a table and a bench— to which the Lansburys added, startling their employer, their sole impressive piece of furniture, an American organ. The ' lovely scenery ' was indeed fine, as the Australian bush can be, but it was wild, and snakes infested the long, rank grass around. Until they were used to them, the family were also discomposed by the fat and woolly little Koala bears, and the hideous night-long yells of the laughing jackass.

Lansbury consulted frequently with his fellow-worker on the farm, an Irish Land Leaguer, on ways of escape. The Irishman offered various suggestions drawn from his experience, such as burning the farmhouse down, wrecking the machinery, or knocking the farmer on the head: but Lansbury was not the man to accept any of them. He had relaxed his principles on one point only: he did the milking on the Sabbath, for, as he said himself, the cows had never heard of the Sunday rest.

His employer made the mistake of bringing the local M.P. to explain to him that prison would be the result of ' breaking a contract freely entered into '. This was the sort of threat which he was already fully able to cope with: he lectured the M.P. upon the cheating promises made by his Government in

London, and read him extracts from the letters he was going to send back home describing conditions in Queensland. 'The poor man was rather taken aback', he records; and whether because of that or because, despite his peaceful principles, he was a very powerful, very angry and possibly dangerous man, his employer soon afterwards let him go—though without any wages.

Back in Brisbane, he took various jobs one after the other—first mowing oats on an outlying farm, then laying the Brisbane cricket-ground in the city. He had hoped to see the English cricket team, due over in a fortnight's time, play on it; but he learnt that cricket watching was not a pleasure for workmen. Another job, parcels delivery, came along, and although he was a keen follower of cricket, he never saw any play upon the ground he laid out.

His thoughts were mostly concentrated on saving other East Enders from walking into the trap in which he had been caught. He wrote regularly home to counter the effect of the Queensland Government's pamphlets and leaflets.

'Every one of their statements I emphatically deny,' he wrote to Sewell in March 1885. 'Mechanics are *not* wanted. Farm labourers are *not* wanted and do not get paid well at all, and are worse fed. Pick-and-shovel men are *not* in demand. Hundreds of men and women are not able to get work. Another statement that I heard over and over again thrust down the throats of the people was that those who had sisters or grown-up-daughters could not do better than send them out here—that those poor white-faced girls who were working in factories or at sewing machines should come out here where they would get good wages as domestic servants. Now, I distinctly say that the girls are not wanted here. The streets are foul day and night, and if I had a sister I would rather *shoot her dead* than see her brought out to this little hell upon earth. Hundreds of girls work 12 hours a day in farms, factories at sewing machines and other work for 12/- a week and domestic servants get 6/- and 7/- a week for slaving from daylight to dusk for a family of 6 or 7. I don't wonder the girls go on the streets for besides sending out hundreds of girls unprotected the Emigration people send out hundreds of single men who, thrown upon their own resources, go into all kinds of vice and crime.'

He was offered a partnership in the delivery business: but he was sick of Australia, and would not stay. By May 1885 he had received from his father-in-law enough money for the homeward journey—this time in the S.S. ' Mercaro ', as passengers and not emigrants. Conditions were pretty bad, all the same: the ship was rat-infested, and Mrs. Lansbury was ill the whole way home. There was little exciting about the journey except a visit at Suez from some tall and very handsome Sudanese who, in the excited passengers' view, might have been personally concerned in the dreadful murder of General Gordon which had just been reported.

The family arrived penniless in the London they had left two years before. Lansbury now found that his father-in-law was not, after all, a ' Lancashire bully ', but a kind-hearted if rather testy old man from Somerset. The day after he landed, Mr. Brine found him a job in his Whitechapel saw-mill and veneer works. Though he expected, and received, full and hard work for the wages he paid, he was at the beginning an understanding taskmaster, and allowed his son-in-law ample time off for the furious campaign that he started at once against the emigration recruiters.

Chapter Four

LANSBURY's thoughts were still concentrated upon the swindle that had been practised on him and thousands of other emigrants. He was not a Socialist—his reference to joining ' the Christian Socialists ' had been a vehement phrase to express the extremity of his anger—and he was satisfied that separate agitations against individual abuses would lead to all the necessary reforms. On him the immediate task had been laid of exposing the Queensland fraud. He supplied Wait Sewell, and anyone else who would listen, with elaborate lists of facts and figures, some of which still exist. The winter of 1885–86 was exceptionally cold: recurrent snowstorms swept the East End, but that did not prevent Lansbury holding repeated meetings on Mile End Waste, a barren open space that has now vanished. Often he set up his platform on a crust of frozen snow, so hard that there was no danger of either it or the audience falling through.

His speeches, and his letters to the *Echo*, at last had some effect. A conference was called for the beginning of February 1886; the Bishop of Bedford took the chair, the Member of Parliament for Whitechapel, Samuel Montagu, was present, and so were all the Agents-General for the Colonies. Young Mr. Lansbury was the chief speaker at the morning session: he gave a direct account of conditions in Queensland. The Agent-General for that Colony, the first but not the last to be so unwise, felt that he could deal easily with this common working man, earning only thirty shillings a week, and abused him roundly and confidently as ' a work-shy man '. Lansbury's rejoinder, in his second speech, was so effective that the conference was swung completely over to his side. A deputation was sent to Osborne Morgan, the Under-Secretary for the Colonies, who as a result set up an ' Emigration Information Department ', which for the next fifty years, by posters and pamphlets, in post offices, labour exchanges, and so on, gave free and honest advice to emigrants; and put an end to a peculiarly cruel deception.

As he left the hall, Lansbury was stopped by Montagu, who said to him: ' You must let me get you into the House of Commons. You are just the sort of man we want there.' Lansbury was flattered, and blushed with pleasure; but he regarded it as no more than a politician's extravagant compliment.

He had other things enough to occupy his mind. His wage of thirty shillings for a hard week's work was good pay, as East London rates went, and he had all the hardwood he needed for the home fires free. Nor did he pay rent for the little four-roomed cottage in St. Stephen's Road, Bow—' two up and two down ', with a small wash-house attached. But the family now ran up to six, and his wife and he lived in poverty, and did so for years. What energy he had over from his work and his meetings he put into acting as unpaid ward secretary for the local Liberal Association. He did hear again from Montagu; when there was a sudden general election in 1886 the M.P. asked him to act as his agent. He agreed; was given three weeks off by Mr. Brine; took the magnificent salary of three pounds a week; and put Montagu in with a larger majority for less money than he had ever spent before. He was asked to stay; but refused, and went back to work at the saw-mill. However, he was promoted from ward secretary to general secretary to the Bow and Bromley Liberal Association—still at no salary. It selected as candidate a fairly advanced Radical, J. A. Murray MacDonald, and as motto ' A happier, more moral, and more equal life for all '.

This should, he felt, have satisfied him and his colleagues; but it did not. They were disquieted: ' somehow none of our minds would stop working '. Freedom, peace, equality before the law—there was no question but that these were good; but they were not enough. ' Peace, Retrenchment and Reform ': it was a slogan that was getting dull. In a short sojourn at Tottenham, Lansbury had come into contact with a branch of the new Social Democratic Federation; and since then its propaganda had been beating upon him. He either listened to or read the debate between Charles Bradlaugh and H. M. Hyndman on Socialism. This conflict, like the meeting between Feargus O'Connor and Richard Cobden a generation before, had an effect far beyond the usual influence of such meetings; the victory of the Socialist was clear to all but the prejudiced; the antagonists were most eminent champions of their sides. Bradlaugh was more than a free-thinker: he was a Republican, a Radical, a proved defender of free speech, a man of unexampled courage and determination, and among the best speakers of his day. Hyndman had the hardness of Stalin, the vanity of Trotsky and the logic of Lenin. It was his misfortune, not his fault, that economic circumstances did not allow him to play the part of any of those three: the revolution for which they were all prepared and waiting should, by Marxist rules, have occurred in the most advanced capitalist country, Britain, not the least advanced, Russia. Directly in touch with Marx, though he quarrelled with him by his own fault, he was the sole effective transmitter of his philosophy in England for a quarter of a century. He never spared others, but he also never spared himself. His squat, formidable figure, with bushy eyebrows and a huge beard, perfectly dressed in top hat, frock-coat and striped trousers, was regularly to be seen in Hyde Park and Trafalgar Square, handing out leaflets or denouncing the British governing class. To a down-and-out workman who asked him how he dared dress like that, he answered mercilessly: ' Because your class are idiots enough to enable people like me to do so.'

It may be that Hyndman was the greatest political influence upon George Lansbury. Lansbury now met a group of men of great energy, courage and intelligence, and of intense individuality, who founded the modern British Socialist and trade union movement. He was to be for a later generation to some extent the incarnation of their remarkable qualities. He knew and worked with them all; and there were several who had a greater claim on his affections than Hyndman. William Morris he esteemed more as a man. He had a greater respect for the brains and character of Sidney and Beatrice Webb (' You are two of the most selfless persons I have ever met,' he wrote to them later). John Burns he felt he understood, and he never lost a certain wry liking for him, despite his fantastic vanity and his early desertion of the Labour movement. With the dockers, Will Crooks from Woolwich, Harry Orbell from Tilbury, Ben Tillett from Poplar, or with the burly gas-worker Will Thorne, he felt a complete understanding, an almost physical sense of

unity that he had with any man or woman of working-class
origin who was treading the same political path that he was.
(It was this feeling which in later years was a part of the wide
and genuine affection—a two-way emotion—that linked him
with hundreds of thousands, if not millions of his fellow-
citizens.)   But none of them had the direct effect on his mind
that Hyndman had: no one else thoroughly and of deliberate
intention changed his opinions and his method of thinking.   It
was Hyndman, by his own admission, who showed him that in
attacking the royal family and the monarchy he was attacking
a false—indeed a non-existent—enemy; the enemy was the
capitalist class.   Hyndman's influence, and that of Hyndman's
disciples, such as the ex-officer H. H. Champion and the printer
Alf Watts, persuaded Lansbury and his wife to read and study
Marx and Engels.   The two of them attended patiently groups
which went through and discussed Engels' *Socialism, Utopian and
Scientific*, and Marx's *Capital* (whether in fact he ever completely
finished the latter work is not quite sure—he was a little evasive
when pressed upon that point—but certainly in the next ten years
he absorbed the whole Marxist doctrine).   It was Hyndman's
advice which set him to work in which he was more unquestionably successful afterwards than any other—that of local administration.   Hyndman pointed out to him that before long, there
was no doubt, the working class would take over the control of
the country, and it was the duty of himself and other workers to
learn how to administer it.   It was a revolutionary task to become a guardian, a councillor, and even in due course an M.P.;
and in each case to become a complete master of the job.

The Socialists to whom he listened did not all speak with one
voice.   Hyndman and the Social Democratic Federation said
clearly that any continued association with the Liberal Party was
idiocy, if not treachery.   No alleviation of poverty was possible
except by integral Socialism—that is to say, by the public
ownership of the means of production and exchange, which could
only be secured by the expropriation of the existing owners.   It
was obvious day-dreaming to imagine that either of the two
parties, Conservative and Liberal, who were controlled by the
employing classes, and were in principle opposed to Socialism,
would assist in this—in fact, of the two, Hyndman had less

contempt for the Tories. Already, however, there was a dissident policy, provided by the Fabian Society, and voiced with especial persuasiveness by Sidney Webb. (For Bernard Shaw's advocacy of Fabianism, Lansbury had little liking: the two men neither greatly liked nor greatly respected each other: indeed, they scarcely understood each other's language. The same was true, later, of another Fabian, H. G. Wells: if they had spoken their more uncharitable thoughts, the two writers would have described Lansbury as sentimental, and he would have described them as self-centred.) The Fabians considered, and for some years seemed to be justified, that the Liberal Party was democratic and its leaders were responsive to new ideas. By infiltration and pressure, from above and below, it might well be hurried into Socialist measures. It was pedantry to refuse to try out this policy because of a philosophical dilemma based upon, ultimately, a sort of revolutionary romanticism.

Lansbury's final break with Liberalism was the result, characteristically enough, not of argument, so much as of two personal experiences. (He did apparently attend the foundation of the Second International in Paris in 1889; but the debates seem to have made no impression on him. Only the bare fact is recorded.) On nothing did the East End Radicals feel more strongly than on the oppression of Ireland, and in 1889 he persuaded, in perfect orthodoxy, a number of the then very powerful working-men's Radical clubs to send a delegation of twelve to ' see what crimes are being committed in our name '. They were led by a clergyman, the Reverend Fleming Williams, and received a boisterous welcome from the Dublin Nationalist leaders. John Dillon and Edward Dwyer Gray took the lead in fêting them, though Lansbury already noticed that Dublin seemed ' a city of the past ', with no life to it but what was provided by passing political excitements such as their visit. The party broke into three; one section went west, one south, one north. Lansbury went north, to Dundalk, Newry, Belfast, Carrickfergus, Draperstown and Londonderry. They saw what they expected to see. Spies and informers sat with them at their meals in hotels; police, in and out of uniform, shepherded them around, and took obvious notes at all their meetings. The Irish peasants welcomed them, and showed them their smallholdings and their cabins; and these last were as bare and miserable as they expected. Some questions that Lansbury asked stayed unanswered. The housing conditions in the towns were vile enough to shock even an East-ender, and the poverty was worse than the worst of London's; but when he asked the Nationalist leaders for their policy upon these matters they had no answer to give. They appeared not to have considered them: they were content to say that such problems would be dealt with after the end of British rule. He noticed, also, that all parties, Irish and English, agreed in asking for State aid for the Irish peasants, and upon the rightness of legislation fixing rents for Irish peasants. On his return to London he asked his colleagues in the Liberal Association how such demands could be right and the demand for the legal fixing of wages and hours for British workers be completely wrong. At first he asked in simple inquiry: before long his demand became louder and more suspicious, and had behind it the mass of the Bow and Bromley Association.

The second event which swung him over to the Socialists was his own experience at the Manchester conference of the National Liberal Federation in 1889. Soon after his return from Ireland he attended a delegate meeting of London Liberal and Radical organisations at the National Liberal Club; here he carried a motion calling for the legal enactment of an eight-hour day for all Government and municipal employees. It was upon such questions that the struggle between Liberalism and Socialism was fought at this date. The Socialists' enemy was merely free competition, whose horrible results they could see in every industrial area. Cartels, combines, international financial empires were not yet any problem: monopolies scarcely existed, and the Marxist Social Democratic Federation was the only one which even in theory contemplated the possibility of the monopoly capitalism of to-day.

Nor was nationalisation of one single industry or trade as yet a practical policy: a first battle had to be fought out over whether it was permissible at all for Parliament to intervene by law to lay down conditions controlling free enterprise. If Lansbury, like others, thought that the slow and bitterly-resisted passage of the Factory Acts meant that opposition to this on principle had ceased, he was soon shown he was wrong. His success at the London Liberal Conference had seemed to be overwhelming, and he had been named as delegate to the national conference at Manchester, to present the eight-hour resolution. This was a more serious threat than 'London ranting'. Strong voices were called for to put Lansbury down. John Morley, whose authority as a theorist and guide was unique in Liberal circles, issued a statement denouncing the resolution in such terms that it was clear no compromise was possible. When Lansbury asked him to explain the difference between fixing rents in Ireland and fixing hours and wages in England, he replied coldly that he had no time to enter on the question. Even the 'Left', as it would now be called, was intimidated. Both H. W. Massingham the Radical and Sidney Webb the Socialist wrote to Lansbury asking him to withdraw his motion. The time, they said in a phrase he was to learn to detest, was not ripe. It would be better to wait until the Liberal iron-masters and coal-masters in the North had been converted.

Lansbury was not going to wait for that event, or for any other blue moon. He remained equally obstinate at Manchester when the conference met next month. J. Murray MacDonald, the candidate for his own constituency and associated with him in the resolution, took him to Shaw Lefevre, who used all his considerable powers of persuasion to charm the difficult delegate. Lansbury insisted that he was a duly accredited delegate, with a resolution which he was instructed to present, and that he had the right to be heard.

The caucus thought otherwise. When he clambered on to the platform at the great Free Trade Hall, the chairman, Sir James Kitson, rang his bell with the persistence of a muffin-man. Lansbury nevertheless tried to speak: half the great audience howled at him, the other half, equally noisy, howled on his behalf. After a few minutes, on a signal from the chairman, stewards closed in upon him and removed him, gently, indeed, but unquestionably by force. From that moment, he said afterwards, his connection with Liberalism in fact ended.

Emotion as well as reason was working upon Lansbury, and emotion pulled him two ways. He joined wholeheartedly in the London struggles of the S.D.F., both for the unemployed and for the right to speak in Trafalgar Square. The longer these lasted, the deeper became his conviction that his true place was with the Socialists. On the other hand, his personal ties with Murray MacDonald and his other Liberal friends were very strong, and tightened continually by their own generous behaviour and their obvious anxiety to help the masses of the people in the only way they thought possible. Their purses were always open for the strikers or unemployed for whom he appealed. They made the most earnest efforts to retain him within the party; and though their proposals were such as meant a very considerable advancement to him, financially as well as politically, they were never offered to him in such ways that even the most suspicious could think them a bribe. Murray Mac-Donald and Bolton King sent him down to Warwickshire to be interviewed as a successor to P. H. Cobb, the retiring Liberal member: he could have had the seat, it was made clear, but he came back and told MacDonald he felt he could only run as a Socialist. Jane Cobden was elected Councillor at the first London County Council elections, in 1889; she was then unseated by the Courts on the ground that women were not eligible. A group of West End Liberals appealed to Lansbury to run for her seat, as he had been so effective a speaker for her on women's rights. They would put up all the money. Once again he had a struggle in his mind; once again he eventually answered that he could only run as a Socialist. Then his one-time would-be patron, Samuel Montagu, was brought in to persuade him. Montagu, afterwards Lord Swaythling, was not only a very rich man and a very powerful Liberal M.P., but also commanded Lansbury's respect for his sincerity and kindness. He had an interview with him in the House of Commons, interrupted rather absurdly by John Burns' recurrent inquisitive attempts to find out what the two men were talking about. Lansbury recorded the gist of Montagu's appeal:

' Sir Samuel asked me what I was going to do with my life, pointing out that if I really desired to help the masses he would help me, that his influence would get me a safe seat, and once in the House of Commons with his backing my future and my work for the people was secure. I told him I had become a Socialist and wanted to preach

D

Socialism. He replied: " Don't be silly, I am a Socialist, a better Socialist than you. I give a tenth of my riches every year to the poor." I said: " Yes, I know how good you are and respect you more than it is possible to say, but, my dear friend, we Socialists want to prevent you getting the nine-tenths. We do not believe in rich and poor and charity. We want to create wealth and all the means of life and share them equally among the people." He said: " But think of your wife and children; how much nicer it would be for them. I will give you a start now in Whitechapel at five pounds a week as my agent, and we will get you a seat in this place at the first opportunity. You can preach all the Socialism you like: all I ask is support for the Liberal Party, which is the best instrument even for your Socialism." I did not like to hurt his feelings by blankly saying no, so after a two and a half hours' talk with him I promised to talk it over with my wife and write him my decision. I did this and wrote him next day that both of us had decided that my place was with the Socialists, that we were very grateful to him for all his goodwill and kindness, but could do no other.'

In the end, by a typical compromise, Lansbury agreed to see his local Liberal candidate, Murray MacDonald, through the 1892 election; and to leave the Liberal Party the day after the poll was declared. Each believed that upon Lansbury's decision the election would turn; and so it was. The election was fought on a minimum of money (Lansbury's fee was opulent—twenty guineas for four weeks, on MacDonald's insistence). Keir Hardie came across from his victory at West Ham to help. MacDonald was returned: the same evening Lansbury and his colleagues packed up, left the Liberal committee-rooms, and declared themselves the Bow and Bromley Branch of the Social Democratic Federation. The parting was friendly: Lansbury sincerely liked and admired Murray MacDonald, and to the end of his life kept hanging on his study wall the gold-and-red testimonial presented to him by the Liberal Association when he left.

Events had brought too much pressure on him for him to stay. The year 1884 had begun another of the terrible depressions that (as Hyndman argued in his *Commercial Crises of the Nineteenth Century*) were bound to recur every ten years or so in the capitalist system, and would end in a universal crash.

The East End, like every other British city, was packed with unemployed, who were often enough literally on the verge of starvation. Nothing was done for them: the workhouses to which they were coldly referred had changed very little since Dickens' days, and nearly all the other relief available was supplied under conditions like those laid down by the Charity Organisation Society, which habitually gave its charity in a patronising manner and after intimate personal examination which, he thought, would destroy all self-respect. (It is from this period that there dates Lansbury's especial dislike of this organisation: he consistently described it as hypocritical, heartless and brutal, and urged kind-hearted people, whatever they did with their money, at least never to give it to the C.O.S.) Meetings held to call attention to the sufferings of the unemployed—even meetings advocating the respectable Liberal remedy of land reform—were dispersed by the police. Lansbury was part of one which received a ' Land Charter ' from an eccentric named John de Morgan and attempted to march down Whitehall to present it to the House of Commons. It was attacked by the police and driven into Old Scotland Yard, which was then a dead end. No sooner was the shouting and singing crowd packed into the Yard than it was, to all appearances, deliberately charged by a force of mounted police. Lansbury was seriously bruised: he afterwards decided that it was the most dangerous scuffle with the police he was ever in. This although he was also present in Trafalgar Square in November 1887 when Alfred Linnell was actually killed in a scuffle with the police, and walked in the procession, led by John Burns, which wrecked the Pall Mall Club windows in January 1886 and caused the Lord Mayor's Relief Fund to leap up from £30,000 to £79,000. He spoke in Hyde Park, too: he was flattered to occupy the same platform as Cunninghame-Graham, Michael Davitt and John Burns, though less flattered when the last named, who already felt that he alone should occupy most of the speaking time at any meeting, pulled his coat-tails five minutes after he had started and repeatedly said in his deep voice: ' Time! time! time! '

Not improbably what made his decision inevitable (as with so many others) was the famous Dock Strike of 1889. As the years pass by that date seems to grow more and more important, and some suspicion of its immortality seems to have touched those who lived through the year. Until that time it had been assumed, tacitly and sometimes openly, that a large part of the British people was unable to help itself. Trade unionists, after repeated failures, had decided that unskilled workers—'labourers' in the Victorian phrase—could never be taught permanent solidarity. 'Unskilled' unions would always be ephemeral. 'They cannot be organised: I have tried it myself,' said Edwin Coulson, who had pulled the bricklayers out of misery. Social workers had for years been among them, and knew their wretchedness, but in their reports of their ghastly conditions they always stressed the complete degradation of the unskilled workers—especially around the London docks—and their imperative need for guidance and control by those in happier circumstances.

The full story of the London dockers' strike cannot be told here. It burst with the suddenness of a bomb, in the hot August of 1889. There was only one man among the dockers themselves who could be classed as an 'agitator', Ben Tillett, a thin, pale-faced teetotal worker at a tea warehouse (the vestigial union which existed at the outset was called the Tea-workers' and General Labourers'); the other two leaders, John Burns and Tom Mann, were engineers who belonged to the S.D.F. and came down to help for no other reason but that of class solidarity. The strikers asked no more than a guaranteed sixpence an hour (the famous 'dockers' tanner'), regular hiring which would prevent the savage rush to be taken on at the dock gates whenever a ship came in, and the abolition of 'contract work' which meant that 1,000 petty gang-leaders were used as instruments to grind down their fellows. The dockers had no resources, they were regarded by the companies (and even by themselves) as the most degraded of men, incapable of loyalty or any common action, and the outcome of the struggle seemed certain. Only the brilliance of the leadership, their own unexpected doggedness, and the widespread support that they received from fellow-workers from as far away as Australia brought them eventual victory. Lansbury was among those who worked ceaselessly to help them: on thirty shillings a week he felt himself a rich man, and was 'proud to go round every Saturday collecting pennies to help those half-starved ones'. He learnt something from them himself, too: he had not till then held a union card, and Will Thorne, the gas-worker, convinced him that he must hold one. There was no union, it was true, particularly designed for a worker in a saw-mill, but that was not a sufficient excuse. He took out a ticket in Thorne's Gas-workers and General Labourers' Union, and continued to hold it, through various changes by which it became the National Union of General and Municipal Workers, until the day of his death. At nearly all the Labour Party Conferences, although he seemed the typical representative of a local Labour Party, he was in fact a union delegate; and when he ceased to attend as a member of the union delegation because of a difference on policy at the end of his career, the breach gave him genuine distress. His union card had become for him a symbol of his unity with his fellow-workers: when he decided to become the delegate of the Bow and Bromley Labour Party, much as he loved that party, it was as though an estrangement had been recorded and made definite.

Chapter Five

WHEN Lansbury walked out of the Liberal Party rooms in 1892 he walked into the profession in which he spent the rest of his life—that of Socialist propagandist. More 'Socialist' than 'trade unionist': it is true that he organised immediately after the great 1889 strike a very wretched group of East End workers called 'bass-dressers', and at all times he flung himself—a volunteer even before he was called—into every industrial struggle; but his propaganda was in general based not upon any individual strike or demand, but upon the misery around him and the need for Socialism. He believed in liberty, equality and fraternity, giving full value to each of the three words ; and almost invariably his speeches came back to those three final principles. For nearly fifty years from his conversion this propaganda was his preoccupation, over-riding everything else. Often several times a week, almost every week-end, he would be addressing meetings anywhere in Britain. For his family, as his son Edgar wrote, this life of his became a regular routine; they learnt to watch out from their bedroom window for the fast train from Liverpool Street, which passed within fifty yards of the house ; and their father, disregarding the astonishment of his fellow-passengers, would come to the carriage window, push out the red flag which he carried rolled up with him, and wave it to his children till he was out of sight.

Nearly half a century—1892 to 1940—of unceasing devotion to a cause brought its rewards. ' G.L.' built up a personal connection with more of his fellow-citizens than probably any other man of his generation except Keir Hardie had done—certainly a closer connection than any propagandist will ever do again, now that the great age of meetings is over. A historian has to go back to the famous figures of an earlier generation—Gladstone, Spurgeon or Bradlaugh—to find anyone else who was personally known to, and loved by, so many people. Established trade union leaders might, in appearance, have more supporters: they would hold up in Trades Union Congresses and Labour Party Conferences cards marked ' 150,000 ' or ' 300,000 ' voters, and no one could deny their right to do so.   But many, many more people—many more, often, of their own members—knew George Lansbury, and trusted and loved him in a way which they did not their own worthy general secretaries and presidents. They had seen him and heard him ; they had known that he would come down in all weathers and at great personal inconvenience to speak to audiences that, at first, might consist of no more than a couple of dozen of idlers.   They knew that it was largely due to the patience of himself, and many others like him, but unremembered, that these couple of dozen had slowly grown to a couple of thousand, and then to many more.   (Lansbury was one of the very few who could, when he was at the height of his powers, be sure of filling the Albert Hall in London with its ten or twelve thousand auditors—indeed, there was a time, in the high day of the *Daily Herald*, when his colleagues as automatically took the Albert Hall as a local secretary would book the parish hall.)   They knew that no personal vanities or political ambitions moved him, but only a steady enthusiasm for the cause, which they in a degree shared; for they had met him and talked to him, over the tea or cocoa and home-made or Co-op-made buns and sandwiches which were all he could be offered or wanted: they had seen that he never wrapped himself in the solemnity or aloofness of his more pompous colleagues, but enjoyed nothing more intensely than conversation and argument with the rank and file of the movement.   He believed—and his every word showed it—that all men were equal in their rights ; one of his most unvarying anxieties was that the humble, ordinary workers should receive all the credit that they deserved— which he, mistakenly, often held to be greater than his own. His books, his reports of his journeys, the despatches printed in later days in the *Herald*, are incessantly slowed up and made more difficult to read because they are loaded with lists of the names of obscure comrades who had helped him in his work, and who, he feared, might be forgotten.   He reaped the reward in the form of a vast network of admirers; he could not, it is true, organise them to vote for him or to carry so much as one resolution in the Party conference, or even in one union; but he had what he valued more, an affection whose quality and extent cannot even be explained to those who did not see it and remember it.

This lifetime mission was unpaid. For a brief moment, some months in 1896, he became a staff speaker for the S.D.F. ('on the whole, the best organiser the Federation ever had,' said Hyndman); but he soon abandoned it. He greatly disliked taking money for preaching Socialism: it seemed to him something that, of its nature, must be done for love. It is probable, too, that he did not care for being under orders in such a matter. The more intelligent of his adversaries told him that, despite his Socialism, he was a great individualist. It was true: but he did not merely value his own individual independence, he wanted independence and dignity for every working man and woman. (This, for him, meant every man and woman; he did not think that any person of ordinarily decent character could really *not* want to work for his living—people might be misled by propaganda, or have had a bad education—say at a public school—or be spoiled by early luxury; but as soon as they realised that they were parasites, even the dullest and richest would be ashamed, and try to change.) Socialism was for him above all a means of ensuring security, and therefore independence, for the ordinary man: of all the attacks which Conservatives made upon it, only one ever disquieted him, and that was the charge that State Socialism, as the Webbs and the older Fabians advocated it, might make men slaves of the State as soon as they had escaped from being slaves of the employer.

It was strange that the period in which he threw all his energy into this unpaid missionary activity was also one in which his financial condition began to improve. At the beginning of the nineties his circumstances had been as difficult as ever. In an undated letter of about 1893 to Sewell he said:

'Just a line to say that it is quite impossible for us to accept your more than kind invitation. We would gladly have done so had it been at all possible. Bessie and I both dislike having to say no and to as usual say we can't afford it but this is the plain truth. One of the difficulties of our life is to make 20/- stretch to 22/- or more. I wish for Bessie's sake very often it were otherwise but at present I don't see any chance of it being other than it is. I often think she had me for better or worse and that so far as money is concerned it has been

all worse and no better.   What the end of it all will be I don't know:
one can only hope and after all if one does one's duty that is everything.   It seems to me that one ought not to have principles at all in
this age; they always come in the way in a most inconvenient manner.
Now I won't write any more in this strain or you will think I am
miserable *which I ain't*.   How are you?   I hope well; are you having
good weather and have you read all the literature? '

But at the end of the nineties, twenty or thirty shillings became
something like three pounds a week, and though his family
increased steadily throughout the period, still, at the prices of the
nineties, that income raised him above the poverty line, and his
elder children can remember the change.   He had been out of
work in 1895, writing round for jobs; there seems to have been
a dispute with his father-in-law.   But after he had been less than
a year with the S.D.F. old Mr. Brine died in an accident, and
Lansbury took over the firm.   It needed great energy and
shrewdness to run a competitive enterprise like an East London
saw-mill and timber business and also to be a travelling Socialist
propagandist; but Lansbury had both.   The business prospered,
and a photograph taken round about the turn of the century shows
him, ginger-whiskered and benevolent, in the centre of over
twenty employees, soon to rise to sixty.   Too many of
these, for a strict economist, were lame ducks—half-useless
employees taken on because they had had a misfortune or
because a comrade had intervened on their behalf; but there
were never more of these than the business could carry; and it
was noticeable how many of them in time fulfilled the
hopes which Lansbury had had when he took on these
' unemployables '.

The heaviest load in these years, he always declared, fell upon
his wife.   Not only had she to run the household on a very
narrow budget, to cope with a young and ever-growing family,
to bear the children, and to run and keep mercilessly clean a
house in the dirty East End with little or no assistance; but
always, at any hour of the night, she would be waiting up to
receive him with a hot drink and warm food, and an interested
inquiry on how the meeting had gone.   The family brought its
sorrows and anxieties.   Two of the children died—little George
at the age of five; Doreen, one of twins, in 1902.   Willy, the

eldest boy, ran away to sea, but his parents in due course accepted this philosophically.

His propaganda was nearly still all by the spoken word, and throughout his life he remained a better speaker than writer. His writing could be vivid, as the quotations in his book show, but it was always untutored, and often verbose. What seems to be his first written and published work dates from this period; it is, oddly enough, rather more carefully and effectively written than much that he wrote later, when he felt more at ease with a pen. It is dated 1897, and is a paper on 'The Principles of the English Poor Law' which he read to the Central Poor Law Conference at the Guildhall that year. (As will be explained later, he was by then a member of the Poplar Board of Guardians.) It describes briefly but well the principles of the Elizabethan Poor Law, and that of 1834, and goes on to combat the attempt which was once again being made by the Whitechapel Guardians to enforce the latter in all its vigour. It was being argued that the very penal workhouse regime in Whitechapel had reduced pauperism. He tested this claim by facts:

'Standing here as one who lived some of his best days in Whitechapel, I contend that the comparisons made between it and other Unions are entirely wrong. The great stream of Jews and foreigners which has pressed out the Gentile population from Whitechapel, and is now rapidly filling up St. George's, Stepney, and Mile End, is more accountable for the decrease of pauperism in that Union than any methods of administration possibly can be. . . . In 1871 the number of foreigners in the Whitechapel Union was 8,130. In 1891 there were 17,961, and although many of these are very poor it is but a small percentage that go to the Guardians. . . . To talk of the Whitechapel Guardians as having abolished pauperism is to talk pure rubbish; that they have shifted it none will deny.'

Close economic argument he did not particularly care for: even in this pamphlet he prefers to stress the effect of the Poor Law on human lives; but he nevertheless produces a carefully reasoned plan for amelioration of the Poor Law which in some parts anticipates the famous 'Minority Report' he signed in 1909. He does not formally propose to abolish the Poor Law, but to break off great segments of it, so that very little is left.

46

The old (since the average Victorian worker could not save) were guiltless if they were destitute; they should therefore have old age pensions. Children were even more obviously guiltless: they should, ideally, be removed from the Guardians' control altogether, but in the meantime boarding-schools ('barrack schools' was the grim phrase of the day) should be established, where a proper education should be provided, ending with technical schools. No child should leave before it had been properly educated and made 'fit to start in a trade'—at the age of sixteen. Foster-parents, boarding out and baby-farming should be abolished. For the able-bodied destitute, who alone remained, he claimed 'the organisation of labour'. He was more vague about this, but seems to have envisaged a nationally financed system of agricultural colonies with workshops attached. He ended, with but little success, by asking his audience to 'go back to your several Unions and administer the Poor Law along the lines I have sketched out and to remember—

> That all before us lies the way,
> Give the past unto the wind;
> All before us is the day,
> Night and darkness are behind.'

The S.D.F. had not been deterred by the disastrous results of its first election efforts—a candidate in Hampstead polled exactly 27 votes—and Lansbury was put up for Walworth in North London at a by-election in 1894. Immediately he had his first brush with Hyndman. The Federation was still attracted by the idea of violence. 'Bullet, Bomb, or Ballot Box' was a favourite slogan. Champion, an ex-army officer, had actually drilled unemployed in a vague hope of leading them in a battle for a 'Commune of London' which Hyndman had once provisionally dated for 1889. Lansbury's election address contained a quotation from the American poet Lowell which the great man considered sentimental, and in addition the explicit sentence:

'The object of the work of Social Democrats, whether such work be done in Parliament, or County Councils, or any local authority, is to bring about, *by peaceful means*, the transformation of society from

47

a competitive system which is sapping the life blood of our people, to a cooperative system.'

Hyndman criticised the address pitilessly at the meeting of the S.D.F. executive, probably in the brutally sarcastic manner which Marx and Engels favoured, and Lansbury was embarrassed and shaken. But a colleague whispered to him, ' Stand up to him: it's your address—not his ', and he stuck to his text.

Nor did Hyndman hold his defiance against him. Lansbury fought Walworth twice within a few months. There is no account remaining of it but his own: it shall be quoted as he wrote it:

' The first thing that our election committee had to consider was that there was no money—no money at all. I do not remember how the rest of us proposed to deal with this difficulty, but I remember declaring that it was a matter no one need bother about. I must have had a private faith that money would come along. Anyway, however unjustified my attitude was, I was lucky in the event. Money did come along. William Saunders, the retiring M.P. gave some, I think Charles Dilke sent a subscription, and William Morris and others helped.

' The strain of the election campaign that followed would have been too great for many men, but I was just thirty-six years of age and in the prime of condition. I was proud of my strength and energy and used them fully. My working hours earning my living were from 7 a.m. to 7 p.m.—one o'clock on Saturdays. Every night and all day Sunday I walked or rode, often with my wife and our friends, Tom Glossop and his wife, from Bow to Walworth and back. I was speaking almost incessantly at street corners, in public halls, and in schools. Naturally and rightly the chief work fell on me, but I was supported by Morris and Hyndman, Frank Smith and Keir Hardie, Harry Quelch and Herbert Burrows, Dr. and Mrs. Pankhurst, and hosts of others. Each night we held enormous meetings at every street corner in Walworth. From all appearances it was clear that neither the Liberal nor the Tory candidate was in it. Our doubts gradually vanished into a certainty of success. We found our strength growing daily, and the affection and support of the electors for our programme became more and more obvious. The costers became my heartiest supporters. Soon the only matter in question for us was the size of my majority. Some of us expected it to be very high indeed.

' Then, on polling day, came the counter-blow which for years was to send Socialist candidates down like ninepins. The Liberal workers ran around the division with the cry, " You are splitting the progressive vote! You are letting in the Tory! " Our vast audiences melted away at once. They returned swiftly to their old homes, and when the poll closed I was safely at the bottom. My vote in my first election was exactly three hundred and forty. '

At the general election a few months later he tried again, but now his vote was only 204.

' All of a sudden an old Irish woman with tears in her eyes and voice, flung her arms round me, smothered me with kisses and said, when we had both somewhat recovered, " Never mind: you are bound to win. Don't you ever despair." She may have said lots more that I did not hear. I know I was choked and crying like a child, because in a flash I realised that people like this poor woman were beginning to trust me, and I wondered if I could prove worthy of the love and confidence given me.'

Two hundred and four votes was not so ignoble a score as it would have been later. Youths and women had no votes, and many M.P.'s were returned by no more than 5,000 votes, instead of 25,000, as to-day. But the result was poor enough, compared with the hopes of the Socialists for revolution by Parliamentary methods. For revolution it was to be; Lansbury was only one of many to anticipate, eagerly or with terror, a profound social convulsion: even the Fabians expected a fundamental change, and only questioned its convulsive character. They had, indeed, originally inserted in their programme a demand for the nationalisation of the means of production and distribution ' without compensation ': the line was only thin which separated them, as the extreme Right, from the extreme Left of William Morris's anarchists, who hoped to see the Houses of Parliament turned into a large dung-shed. All these sections could, without a feeling of inconsistency, come down to Walworth to speak for an S.D.F. candidate like Lansbury. Fierce verbal disputes on tactics already divided them on the surface; but all sections in fact realised that the most immediately important duty was the exposure of what the Liberal policy of free competition was every day doing to the life and wealth of the nation. Indeed, at Bradford in 1893 nearly all the Socialist bodies of importance (except the Anarchists, who were already fading away) made a serious attempt to come together on what was effectively a programme to do just that.

The Fabian Society, with its several provincial societies, attended, Bernard Shaw among the delegates; so too did the S.D.F.; there came also a recently founded Scottish Labour Party, a large number of unattached societies and even some union branches. Among the more noticeable figures were an Ayrshire miner named James Keir Hardie, and a brilliant journalist named Robert Blatchford, who was editing a new paper called the *Clarion*. The conference agreed on the need to run independent Labour candidates for parliamentary and local elections, and so took the name of the Independent Labour Party (I.L.P.). Immediately it became the largest Socialist body in the country: though the central Fabian Society lost all interest and concentrated on permeating the Liberals, and the S.D.F. withdrew *en bloc*, it remained so; and it was fairly sure that Lansbury would in due course be drawn into it.

In the twenty years which had passed since he first took notice of politics there had been changes so encouraging that the figure of 204 votes could not be of real significance. In 1875 there had been no Socialist society at all. Now there were two national Socialist parties, one (the I.L.P.) with 280 branches; there was an extremely active and intelligent centre in London, the Fabian Society, which was a sort of co-operative socialist brain, pouring out facts and arguments and disturbing every periodical and every politician. The great Liberal Party was distracted and torn by Socialist arguments and steadily being robbed of its best propagandists; there was a good number of Socialist papers up and down the country, including this particularly convincing weekly, the *Clarion*, whose readers were already forming themselves into clubs using the new safety bicycles, and appearing in droves in the most backward centres and startling the yokels by holding Socialist meetings. Twenty years before, trade unions had been weak bodies, their members had been nearly all only skilled craftsmen, with good wages, who treated their unions mainly as insurance societies whose chief duties, beyond paying friendly benefits, were to hold the common labourer off the skilled man's job and to keep the peace with the employer. Now the union membership was double or treble what it had been; the union members included masses of unskilled workers; the unions no longer bowed to 'the boss', but had learnt it would be for their strength they would be respected, and in certain cases had forced some of the most powerful employers to grant higher wages and better conditions.

In the seventies it would have been difficult to find any ordinary politician or writer who did not accept as a proved fact the belief that conditions were rapidly improving and free competition was an admirable device for increasing prosperity. Now, despite the obvious dislike of the political leaders of both parties, the disastrous results of uncontrolled capitalism were being discussed on either side. Books like Charles Booth's *Life and Labour of London* were widely read. Parliamentary inquiries and Royal Commissions, such as those on the Housing of the Poor, the Depression of Trade, the Poor Law and the Social System, continually produced new and more revolting disclosures. Light is the first step to cleansing. Light was being repeatedly blazed upon every dark and dirty place: it was clear to even the pessimists that, despite ill will, some cleaning up was going to follow.

The governors of this society which was so unwillingly being shown its diseased places had also changed their character, though this change was less universally noticed. Competition was still the rule: business men fought each other ruthlessly, and the cheaper product drove out the dearer. Trade agreements were rare; price-fixing was rarer and usually ineffective. The proprietor of a business was still usually an individual or a family: the anonymous company was not yet the standard unit. But behind this jungle-strife, red enough in tooth and claw to please the most orthodox economist, the beginnings could be seen of the stiff and regulated monopoly capitalism of the nineteen-thirties. The bigger units, as Marx had prophesied, were beginning to eat up the smaller. It needed only a moderate prophetic gift to see that a time would soon come when these bigger units would abandon their internecine struggles, and the first 'rings' would come into existence. At the same time, a different type of employer was beginning to dominate both the great parties. From the eighteen-twenties to the eighteen-sixties the opinions and needs of the textile magnates fill the debates in Parliament and the discussions in the Press. Even the examples given in books of simple economics are drawn from mills, and expressed in terms of spindles or bales. There might almost have been no other industry of importance in the island but the making and selling of cotton- and wool-stuffs. But the mill-owners by now were being elbowed out by iron-masters, steel-masters, coal-owners and engineers. Lansbury, when he had tried to push the National Liberal Federation into approving the eight-hour day, had been urged to wait for the consent, not of the Manchester magnates, but of the North-East coast. The town most commonly associated with the new power was, however, neither in Durham nor South Wales: it was Chamberlain's Birmingham, where an enormous number of various metal trades were centred, and whose chief citizen was years in advance of his time in advocating a mingled programme of social reform and Imperialism.

For Lansbury and his fellow-Socialists were to have to realise that their propaganda could not for long confine itself to the ruin caused by capitalism at home. Textile capitalism—Manchester Liberalism in its political form—had been on the whole a pacific force. All that it asked for was a big navy to keep the water-ways of commerce clear: it would even have minded very little if the British Empire (except the priceless market of India) had dropped away. But iron and steel capitalism was not prepared to speculate philosophically about Canada joining the States and Australia declaring itself independent: on the contrary, it had added during the eighties millions of square miles in Africa to the Empire. Cotton goods can safely be sold to native potentates; but if you are selling railways, it is safer to control the country yourself; it is almost essential to do so if you are proposing to mine coal or gold. Four years after the Walworth election the new needs of British business men were to involve the country in the Boer War, and to force the Socialists to make up their minds on an entirely strange set of problems.

Chapter Six

LANSBURY fought the first and most famous 'Khaki election'—the 1900 election, which came near the end of the Boer War—as a Social Democrat in the Bow and Bromley division. A cutting, undated, has been preserved, reporting his adoption meeting. Nobody mentioned the Boer War—not the chairman, Harry Quelch, nor the distinguished attendance, 'including Messrs. J. Vandy, S. Oliver, Brook, Glossop, Purdy and Metivier, Miss Annie Johnson, Mrs. L. Wilson and Mrs. Lansbury', nor even the candidate. They dealt exclusively with the right of a Socialist to stand, in face of the charge of splitting the progressive vote, and the total failure of the Liberals to do anything to help the workers.

'Mr. Lansbury said . . . [the M.P.'s] knew that if the unemployed problem was dealt with the capitalist system would have to be dealt with, and commercialism, as it exists at present, practically destroyed, if any remedy was to be found. Any individual member of the Liberal or Tory Party could say what he liked so long as when he got into the House of Commons he voted in the lobby with his Party. Mr. Lionel Holland could air all sorts of advanced theories but when he got to the House of Commons he had to obey the Whip.'

But even if the S.D.F. intention had been to fight the election on economic and social issues, the electors would not allow it. Nor did the candidate himself whole-heartedly want to. He was attacked as a 'pro-Boer', and he accepted the description delightedly. The election was uproarious, and he never stood a chance of victory: even the 'jingoes'' children chased his children about the streets and pulled their hair, and the whole campaign was conducted on that level. At Mile End Vestry Hall, Shoreditch Town Hall, Trafalgar Square and elsewhere his meetings were turned into free fights by drunken patriots. ' I again got soundly beaten', he wrote; as a matter of fact, he polled

E

2,558 votes against the Conservative's 4,403, which was not at all discreditable in that intoxicated year.

The S.D.F. opposed the Boer War on logical grounds, because it was opposed to the British governing class. There were Socialists found (among the Fabians) to support the war, on the equally logical ground that the war was favouring a large unit against the sort of small one which was outmoded by all Socialist economic theory. But Lansbury's opposition was much more than logical. He disapproved of the war as a wicked thing; his opposition was moral. It was part of a deep change in his mind which was gradually taking him out of the Marxist S.D.F. and back into the Church of England. He did not, it is true, see any further into the South African future than his contemporaries; no man foresaw that the Boers who were now being defeated would take effective control of the whole country in a generation's time, would infect the English with their own racial arrogance, and from a pious group of defeated farmers become the narrowest oligarchy based on a colour bar in the world. At the time all that was obvious was that Alfred Milner and Joseph Chamberlain had organised the quarrel with the Transvaal and the Orange Free State, that they had rejected sincere if belated attempts by Kruger and Steyn to compromise, and that the ' Uitlanders ', on whose behalf they were supposedly acting, were a group of Rand financial adventurers, mostly of very bad character, and many not even British. A great imperial Power had picked a quarrel deliberately with two small and rustic communities.

> ' And sword in hand upon Afric's passes
> Her last Republic cried to God '—

wrote G. K. Chesterton, and it would have seemed a just summary to Lansbury and most other pro-Boers.

But it would not have commended itself to a Party which objected even to a quotation from Lowell in an election address. That Party did indeed have a morality—a very austere and selfless morality—but it was one that it believed to be based exclusively upon reason. It required all its members to subordinate all their personal feelings and ambitions to the cause. It even compelled all candidates for public office to write out, sign and deposit with itself forms resigning their offices, to be used if they faltered or failed to support the class line. Not even small deviations could be overlooked: Lansbury's branch was among those which censured Harry Quelch for putting on a morning-coat to meet the Prince of Wales. Socialist songs, and those only, opened and closed all branch meetings, which were often enlivened by the reading of ' extracts from historical and economic writings '. In after-years Lansbury believed this rationalist period of his life to be ' only a year or two '; but it is probable he was under-estimating it. His son Edgar put it at ten years. Certainly, those of his twelve children who were born in the nineties were not baptised; and during that period they were sent by him to an Ethical Sunday School, run ' by that prince of teachers, F. J. Gould '. Prince of teachers he was indeed; but anyone who consults, say, his book *The New Testament*, will see he was also a militant atheist. The time was in any case long enough to make a strong impression upon the family: when Lansbury rejoined the Church, and there was what might almost be called a mass-baptism of young Lansburys, one of the children at least was so established in her freethinking views as to spend the rest of the day under the bed nursing her resentment.

When exactly he was re-admitted to the Church he has not recorded. It was about 1900, and family tradition is that he began to go to a church in Barkingside—at first slightly shame-facedly, and then resolutely. He preserved notes for a speech in which, among other things, he defended his change; but they are not dated. They begin in the ordinary way of notes for a Socialist speech—not wholly comprehensible to anyone but the speaker:

WORK

' Subject we all know something of.
' Some of us perhaps in need of work.
' Others *over*-worked.
' The problem to-day is: how to reconcile these differences.
' We must first of all recognise that they can't be reconciled.
' Our industrial life depends on these inequalities.
' Then, useless work.
' *Adulteration*. Crockery, etc.
' *Advertising*. Lying. Early to bed and early to rise, etc.'

But when he got down to the subject most at his heart (though it was not the official subject of his speech) he wrote out what he meant to say more fully.

' I am a Socialist pure and simple, in that I am where I was. The difference is that I have come to believe that the motive power which should, and which *will* if men allow it, work our social salvation, is the power which comes from a belief in Christ and His message to man. [He went back in his writing to give a capital H to " His " : you can almost see his mind changing.] I know as well as anyone that economic changes are necessary, that in fact they are fundamental, but I also see that these changes are not brought about by merely declaring they are economic. . . . I think that the moral law which I believe in should have freer play to mould and alter our lives. And therefore I come to this—

' That none of us are too poor or too helpless to do some work for others.

' Hypocrisy in the Church? Yes, and so there is in other places.

' But what is that to us?

' Is the ideal true and real in our hearts? Are we helping to bear the burdens of others?

' Are we doing anything in our day to try and assist people to realise they should be something more than machines? . . .'

The pencil notes on the back (presumably his answer to critics) invite speculation. ' J. Bright. First thing is *fundamental*. What shall we do? Ireland. *Religion* a tool.' But it is not from such speculation that we shall discover what Lansbury's religion was.

His religion was a very personal thing to him: he rarely spoke of it in any detail, and theological discussion he almost actively disliked. It is difficult, for one who does not share it, to describe his faith; but the most immediately noticeable facet of it was that he was a churchman. It was the Church of England of which he was a member; it was, in part at least, his strong sense of history which held him there. No one who watched him at one of his favourite tasks—that of taking parties of children round the Houses of Parliament—could have failed to see how vivid was his feeling of the continuity of English history and how anxious he was to make the children aware of their own place in the story. Even when he was facetious (' that old josser who looks as if he could do with a square meal ') about the august dead, it was to cover his earnestness. So, too, there is no doubt that the actual words of the Anglican Service held an especial attraction for him because of their history: the ceremony too, though with more reserve, for he shared to the full the Victorian distrust of Rome and Rome's practices. Later in life, when he was First Commissioner of Works, he visited Kirkwall Cathedral in the Orkneys. He walked silently through the magnificent red-stone building, noticing the windows from which the stained glass had been smashed out and replaced by uncoloured panes, the niches from which the statues had been battered down, and the yellow cane-bottomed chairs replacing the destroyed pews. As he left he sought for some words to express his shock, and finally said to his companion: ' Ray, I would prefer that the Romans had it.' It was the severest condemnation he could express.

He distrusted Rome because it interposed a priest between a man and his conscience, because it presented to the layman a body of doctrine and rules of conduct (including political doctrine, such as Leo XIII's condemnation of Socialism) that he must accept and should not test, item by item, by his own conscience, because it provided one man—the Pope—with a position and authority for which no man was fit. Politically, he also found the Roman priests too regularly the enemies of Socialism for him to trust them; but anti-clericalism of the Continental type was all the same completely alien to him.

He did not, for all that, sympathise doctrinally with the Low Churchman and Nonconformist. He was instantly distinguishable from the ' lay preacher ' type of Socialist, like Arthur Henderson. He never preached: if he ever at all delivered a sermon (which is doubtful), it would have been from the pulpit of an eccentric Socialist church, such as Conrad Noel's at Thaxted. He would read the lessons; he would take a class or a women's meeting on a weekday (which tended to become a Socialist meeting); he would even attend sometimes at Convocation— that is, he would do all that a layman should; but the boundary between those in orders and those not in orders was not one he wished to overstep. Indeed, he did not till quite late in life particularly care even for the company of clergymen, except for that of militant Socialists like Noel or P. E. T. Widdrington. He judged them more by their performance as Socialists than as clergymen: Cosmo Lang, when Bishop of Stepney, had been among his most frequent correspondents; after he became Archbishop, he said, 'I fear I am one of Mr. Lansbury's great disappointments', and the silence that followed was most informative.

Lansbury was separated from many of the Low Churchmen and Nonconformists by their narrowness, their intolerance and their dislike of innocent pleasure—one of the things which he was most delighted to promote. Because he was a teetotaller, and a man of unexampled purity in his own life, they continually expected him to put down by force drinking and ' sexual licence ', and were as continually disappointed. When he was First Commissioner of Works he was pressed by them to forbid the sale of beer in Park restaurants, and to harry homeless lovers in dark corners; they were baffled by his steady refusal. Nor could they understand his wish to brighten Sunday—to encourage Sunday games, and even to open cinemas on that day.

These were his dislikes; it is less easy to say what were his positive beliefs. He did not believe in Hell. He was not in the least interested in such posers as ' Who was Cain's wife?' and, if questioned upon miracles, was apt to answer frivolously that he had not been present on the occasion. He believed in a future life: when his wife died he was quite plainly confident that he would shortly meet her again. He believed that the teaching of Christ was a universally valid rule of life, and that Christ himself was exceptional to such a degree that the word ' divine ' could properly be used of him. He was not a steady church attender, though he never willingly missed the Easter services. Opposed as he was to all superstition, he astonished many of his friends in later years by joining the Theosophists. He explained it by saying that he found himself ' able to accept the only condition of membership imposed by the Theosophical Society, which is that all who join shall work together to establish a universal society based on Brotherhood '. His membership remained formal; he took no part in its mystical hocus-pocus; and it may well be that his joining was no more than an acknowledgment of the immense help he and the *Daily Herald* had received from individual Theosophists.

Prayer perhaps provides the most searching test of Christian belief, and on this we have fuller information. In 1932, when he was Leader of the Labour Party, he wrote a letter to *The Times* calling all Christians to unite in ' effort and prayer ' to solve destitution. There were more agnostics than Christians in the Party he was leading, and it says much for his influence that his letter was not repudiated. But his son Edgar, who was closest to him politically, felt some explanation was needed, and wrote as follows, without being disavowed:

' There was more wisdom in father's call " for effort and prayer " than his critics could grasp. He is not such a fool as to expect God to step down from some incredible throne and sweep away unemployment and destitution just because a few thousand Christians beseech Him to do so. What he expected was that " those who call themselves Christians " would put the efficiency of prayer to a real test. In his own case he had found that prayer resulted in a clarifying and purifying of his mind so that his course seemed straighter and clearer and his efforts more fruitful. Prayer for him was not a matter of asking favours. I am sure he has never prayed for anything or anybody. I have known him to be questioned at meetings by agnostics and socialists as to what good prayer or Christianity could do for the working classes. And always his answer had been, " I don't know what good it can do them; I know that for me prayer is an inspiration and that it leads to work and renewed effort". Clearly if one doesn't like work and effort one had better not pray. I think the terms " meditation " and " self-examination " might fitly describe what father calls " prayer ".

' His call to Christians was inspired, not by the belief that their voices would reach the ear of God, but by the knowledge that if " those who called themselves Christians " prayed sincerely, they might themselves discover the will and the power to move mountains of ignorance and misunderstanding concerning the causes of " unemployment and preventable destitution ".'

He believed in God: through the Church of England he found a communion with the Spirit to which he gave that name. That church was for him the chosen and clearest channel of communication. Others, he recognised, might find other channels in other churches, or no church at all. ' A religious person, in my view, is one who shows his love of God through love of his neighbours.' There is a little more that can be said, in words comprehensible to a non-Christian. His own systematic attempt to explain his belief is to be found in *These Things Shall Be*, a book consisting of six small sermons on the six verses of his favourite poem by Lowell.

One criticism, however, must be mentioned. Those who disagreed with him, unchristian Socialists and unsocialist Christians alike, frequently charged him with using his God as a political instrument. What was Socialist, they said, was always found to be God's will: God's will was also opposed to proposals that he disliked even within the Party. This was a crude mockery, though it was the same mockery as was made of his first leader, Gladstone. But it had this truth: for Lansbury, Christianity was Socialism:

' Kneeling with others at the altar of the sacraments will and can bring no real peace unless those who so kneel spend their lives as brothers and sisters; and this is quite impossible within a system of life which depends upon the ability of the children of God to dispute, quarrel and fight for their daily bread.'

He would also say that Socialism was Christianity, but of this he was less certain. Around him were too many selfless comrades, working themselves to death for the cause at the same time as they proclaimed their conscientious atheism. But he not improbably comforted himself by reflecting that they were doing Christ's work without being aware of it. Indeed, he would defiantly apply the name ' Christian ' to the most unlikely persons: criticised for calling a life-long friend ' a good Christian gentleman ', he insisted on letting the words stand, saying, ' Although he lived and died a Jew, it makes no difference; Joseph Fels loved his fellow men. That was enough.' But though he excused Socialists who were not doctrinal Christians, no conscious and avowed Christian should, he felt, have failed to be a Socialist. ' Christ was the first Socialist ': this was not to him an epigram, but the most banal statement of obvious fact. It was not only written out patiently again and again in the Gospels, it was the only practical meaning at all that could be

attached to Christ's mission on this earth. Too many clergymen, of all establishments, evaded this truth: their reasons were
but too obvious, and though, as a Christian, he had the duty not
to condemn them, it was too much to ask him not to be aware of
their failure. This it was which made this earnest churchman
avoid, as far as he courteously could, the company of the average
clergyman. 'All who approve and accept', he wrote, 'competition and struggle against each other as the means whereby
we gain our daily bread do indeed betray and make of no effect
the will of God.'

It was certain that a Socialist holding these views would not
be a permanent member of the S.D.F. and follower of Hyndman.
The date of the transfer of his interest from the S.D.F. to the new
'Labour Representation Committees' is not recorded; it was a
gradual process, probably round about the year 1903. These
Committees had been set up in 1899 and 1900, as a result of an
agreement the chief parties to which were the Independent
Labour Party (I.L.P.) and the Trades Union Congress, for the
promotion of independent Labour candidates backed by the Party
and by such trade unions as chose to assist. The first Annual
Report of what was then called 'The Borough of Poplar Trades
and Labour Representation Committee' survives: it shows a
year's working ending December 20th, 1904, and George
Lansbury, as Treasurer, holding the sum of £3 19s. 3d. It
had had a rapid success for so young an organisation—seven
councillors and two aldermen on the Borough Council, and five
on the Board of Guardians. There were branches of six unions
represented on the Committee, but the bulk of support came
from Lansbury's own union, the Gasworkers and General
Labourers.

The Socialist group had a great deal more influence on both
Council and Guardians than its numbers would explain: indeed,
a very few years later an official Inspector from the Local Govern-
nent Board was to record that Mr. George Lansbury and Mr.
Will Crooks were largely responsible, by their personal influence,
for causing a party which had only reached ten members to
dominate a party of twenty-two. Of these, the most persistent
in attendance and most dominating in character was Mr. Lansbury. He had been elected a Guardian as long ago as 1892,

and ever since then had been working to alter completely the whole system of poor relief—a thing of immediate interest to almost every other family in Poplar, as things were in the nineties and nineteen-hundreds. He did not work alone: besides the cheerful and beloved Will Crooks, he had Mrs. Wilson the Social Democrat, Harry Kay of the Dockers' Union and one or two others to help him. His success was due not to numbers, but to his pertinacity in showing to his colleagues on the Guardians things that they did not wish to see. Some of the other Guardians were ' delegates of interests '—house agents representing slum landlords or representatives of the dock companies, whose duty it was to keep expenditure down at all costs, and whose eyes and ears were closed. But most of them were small tradesmen—milkmen, chemists, builders and so on— whose worst object was merely a trivial corruption over minor contracts. ' You scratch my back and I'll scratch yours,' was their policy as he described it, ' where jobs and contracts were concerned.' They were not prepared for major villainy: when Lansbury showed them conditions like those described in *Oliver Twist* they were discomposed and ashamed. They were following his lead, and voting money for his plans, years before his Party secured a majority either on the Board of Guardians or the Council.

He began his work dramatically enough. Everyone assumed that the abuses attacked half a century ago by Dickens had ceased to exist. Only the incurably shiftless, it was believed, would go into the workhouse: honest workmen could always live by labour. Once there, these worthless wretches were treated with Christian kindness, by self-sacrificing officials, at the expense of oppressed ratepayers. There was no urge for a politician to question that agreeable theory—for anyone who accepted relief became ' a pauper ' and could not vote. It was not until this smug restriction was lifted that local government ceased to be the preserve of small shopkeepers and other minor Tories.

' My first visit to a workhouse,' Lansbury wrote, unfortunately giving no date, ' was a memorable one. Going down the narrow lane, ringing the bell, waiting while an official with a not too pleasant face

looked through a grating to see who was there, and hearing his unpleasant voice—of course, he did not know me—made it easy for me
to understand why the poor dreaded and hated these places, and made
me in a flash realise how all these prison or bastille sort of surroundings
were organised for the purpose of making self-respecting, decent
people endure any suffering rather than enter. It was not necessary
to write up the words " Abandon hope all ye who enter here ".
Officials, receiving-ward, hard forms, whitewashed walls, keys
dangling at the waist of those who spoke to you, huge books for name,
history, etc., searching, and then being stripped and bathed in a
communal tub, and the final crowning indignity of being dressed in
clothes which had been worn by lots of other people, hideous to look
at, ill-fitting and coarse—everything possible was done to inflict
mental and moral degradation.

' The place was clean: brass knobs and floors were polished, but of
goodwill, kindliness, there was none. There is a little improvement
in the ordinary workhouses of to-day (1928) but not much. Most of
them are still quite inhuman, though infirmaries, hospitals, and
schools are all vastly improved. But thirty years ago the mixed
workhouse at Poplar was for me Dante's *Inferno*. Sick and aged,
mentally deficient, lunatics, babies and children, able-bodied and
tramps all herded together in one huge range of buildings. Officers,
both men and women, looked upon these people as a nuisance, and
treated them accordingly. Food was mainly skilly, bread, margarine,
cheese, and hard, tough meat and vegetables, and occasionally doses of
salted, dried fish. Clothing was of the usual workhouse type, plenty
of corduroy and blue cloth. No undergarments for either men or
women, no sanitary clothes of any sort or kind for women of any age,
boots were worn till they fell off. The paupers, as they were officially
styled, were allowed out once a month and could be visited once a
month. Able-bodied men were put to stone-breaking or oakum-
picking. No effort was made to find work for men or women. Girls
came in to be delivered of their babies, went out, and in course of time
came back again. On one visit I inspected the supper of oatmeal
porridge. On this occasion the food was served up with pieces of
black stuff floating around. On examination we discovered it to be
rat and mice manure. I called for the chief officer, who immediately
argued against me, saying the porridge was good and wholesome.
" Very good, madam," said I, taking up a basinful and spoon, " here
you are, eat one mouthful and I will acknowledge I am wrong."
" Oh, dear no," said the fine lady, " the food is not for me, and is

good and wholesome enough for those who want it." I stamped and shouted around till both doctor and master arrived, both of whom pleaded it was all a mistake, and promptly served cocoa and bread and margarine.

' This little incident set my colleagues and me storehunting. We visited the workhouse early morning and late at night, discovering many gross irregularities such as calico in stock in place of linen the Board had paid for. Then we tried to discover where all the stores went to, and finally found our stores were short by thousands of yards. After weeks of toil we impeached the officers and proved gross negligence, if not worse, and applied to the President of the Local Government Board for an Inquiry. I do not know how many months passed before the Inquiry was held; when it did take place we received not the slightest help from the Local Government Board or its officials. Our own officials, whose conduct was under investigation, employed a Queen's Counsel, Mr. McMorran, and the task of prosecutor fell on me. We won our case, and the officials responsible were sacked. The manner in which Whitehall did its utmost to burke an inquiry into these irregularities, and the alacrity with which they rush inspectors down to investigate cases where they consider too much relief is given is worthy of the attention of those who are willing at all times to think the central Ministry must be right and local Guardians wrong.'

There were only five of them at that time on the Board of Guardians, but the impression caused by their work was such that only two years after their election Lansbury was called to give evidence to the Royal Commission on the Aged Poor, on which sat the Prince of Wales (afterwards Edward VII) and Henry Broadhurst, the stonemason who had become a Privy Councillor.

Unlike the trade unionists of the preceding generation, Lansbury was not intimidated by such a summons, nor anxious to conform in dress and manners to his new surroundings. Rather, like all his colleagues of the early Socialist movement, he was ' spiky ', and anxious to emphasise his independence of, and difference from, the rich men and women who were now taking an interest in the poor. Charles Booth, the famous author of the study of the London poor, invited him to dinner before the meeting of the Commission. ' I had never been out to dinner before,' he wrote stoutly thirty-five years later, ' and of course possessed no dinner uniform, and never have done.' He noticed that nobody seemed shocked by his failure to put on a boiled shirt, except the butler and the footmen. His only embarrassment came from the presence of a footman behind his chair all through dinner, breathing down his neck and trying to anticipate his desires.

The next morning, before the Commission in the House of Lords, he found that Henry Broadhurst was the least sympathetic to his views, and—to his surprise, as he candidly admitted—the Prince among those most willing to learn.

' The Prince of Wales was the first to start cross-examination after the chairman. I did not know what I was expected to do, but I know that I tried to treat him just as respectfully as I had done the chairman, so I called him Sir. He was evidently interested because he picked out from the points I had made the questions which were at least the most interesting to me. He referred to the need for underclothes and no uniform, and in reply I said : " Certainly they need those, just like you and I do." Then we got on to the question of the sort of institution, and I remembered I had just before visited the Royal Hospital and Home for Incurables, and so I said that that seemed to me to be the kind of place which aged people who had no homes of their own deserved. Then came the question of food, which finished us, because he asked what I meant by variety, and himself said : " Well, a biscuit occasionally ", and I could not help but just finish it all by saying: " Well, if you give them biscuits you will also have to supply them with teeth ".'

The biscuits, it should be explained, which were provided for paupers were thick, round, hard objects like dog biscuits. He reproached himself later for one piece of discourtesy: when the Prince of Wales afterwards handed round cigars he looked over his head and pretended not to see, instead of civilly saying that he did not smoke. This ' rather nonsensical ' behaviour, he wrote afterwards, was a result of his S.D.F. training and his censuring of Harry Quelch. But he did not fail to make use instantly of his contact with royalty: on his return to the Board of Guardians he told his colleagues that the Prince had clearly shown his opinion that the paupers should have better food, of a kind that would not break their teeth. He had also thought they should have underclothes and no uniforms. The Board, with wide-eyed loyalty, immediately voted both the reforms which had such august approval. Tailors and dressmakers were engaged; the dietary was wholly reconsidered; the workhouse master was, in addition, told to draw up a scheme for 'leave' for inmates.

He organised, or rather revived, another method by which a minority could successfully press its views on authority. This was the method of mass-deputation, which in after years some of his colleagues were to wish had remained forgotten. When he was young, Robert Lowe, the Chancellor of the Exchequer, had been frightened out of a tax on match-boxes by a descent on the West End of the miserable women who made them, and would have been thrown out of work. Haggard, filthy and dishevelled, the ragged harridans who appeared had so shocked respectable Westminster that the Chancellor had abandoned the tax rather than look into the abyss which had opened before him. Remembering this success, Lansbury collected the unemployed to call first upon the Guardians, and then upon the 'Board of Works' (a body which shortly afterwards was absorbed in the Borough Council). They filled the galleries, and even stood behind the Councillors' seats. 'How can we discuss this matter with men standing six or seven deep behind us?' complained the chairman. 'The room ought to be cleared.' But before it could be cleared, the Councillors felt it wise to listen to four or five quite orderly speeches; and afterwards to vote arrangements which provided work, of one kind or another, instead of 'relief', for nearly a thousand men.

Then, with Mrs. John Scurr, Mrs. Cobden Sanderson, Mrs. Sumner, Will Crooks and others, he organised a deputation of a thousand women to interview the Conservative Premier, Arthur Balfour. (Mrs. Pankhurst heard of it, and tried to turn it into a Suffrage demonstration; but he evaded her.) The women were not allowed to approach the House of Commons *en masse*, but went to the Caxton Hall, and sent small groups across to the House. Balfour listened to Lansbury and Crooks on the main deputation, exhausted but patient; in reply, after some words of sympathy and a description of his difficulties, he raised his hands

and exclaimed, ' What can I do ? ' This confession of helplessness in the face of unemployment was enough for the East-
enders; it was placarded thereafter throughout the country.

The Poplar Guardians shared with the Whitechapel Guardians
the ownership and administration of a school called the Forest
Gate District School: they appointed the restless Mr. Lansbury
as one of the managers. The Poplar Guardians had no suspicion
that it was anything but satisfactory, nor had their Whitechapel
colleagues, who anyhow were firm believers in the theory of
' deterrence '. This was a principle laid down by the Poor Law
of 1834—that the relief supplied by the Guardians should be
more unpleasant than the most unpleasant method of earning a
living outside, in order to ' deter ' the people from applying for it.

' My first view of the school [wrote Lansbury] was a most dis-
heartening one. The buildings are in Forest Lane, Stratford, and are
built on the barrack system—that is, long dormitories for scores of
children to sleep in, very little accommodation for recreation, and at
the time I first saw it the children were dressed in the old, hideous,
Poor Law garb, corduroy and hard blue serge, and the girls with
their hair almost shaved off, with nothing at all to make them look
attractive in any sort of way. The food was quite coarse and I should
think at times insufficient. It was apparent that the place was
organised and controlled as a barracks. I daresay the superintendent,
who had been a military man, was, according to his light, quite a
decent person, but then his light was deficient. . . .

' After our first committee meeting we were taken downstairs,
where a seven course dinner was to be served. It was this which
made me very disgusted with the middleclass men and women who
controlled the institution; they could let little girls who they knew
must be starved, stand and wait on them while they ate chicken, nice
soups, sweets, etc., all at the expense of the rates. I am glad to say
that when, later on, we bought out Whitechapel and took over the
school all this sort of thing was abolished. We were very badly let
down by the Ministry of Health in our dealings with Whitechapel over
the purchase of these buildings, but it was no use our attempting to
work in double harness with Whitechapel.

' I was elected chairman and remained chairman for over twenty
years, until my other work made it impossible for me to continue,
although I remained a very irregular member of the committee. No

sooner did we get control of the school than we appointed a new superintendent and matron, and although neither of them were Socialists they both have proved themselves most splendid officials.'

The Forest Gate School became the Poplar Training School: it is, and has been for years, famous in its own right. It was moved to Shenfield in Essex in 1907, where it has been ever since; after over forty years the Borough is proud both of its buildings and of its staff and children. Nor was there any doubt in the inmates' minds over who was responsible for their happiness. Years later, when Queen Mary inspected the school, Superintendent Dean carefully coached the children in their behaviour and in the loyal song they were to sing when Her Majesty finished her visit and appeared at the head of the steps with Mr. Lansbury. But, alas for his plans, no sooner did they see the two of them appear than the children forgot all their lessons, broke rank and surged forward, shrilly crying, ' Good old George! Good old George! '

The most spectacularly successful of his activities was due to a discovery of some neglected powers. Sir Henry Fowler, President of the Local Government Board in 1892, had ruled that it was within Poor Law Guardians' authority to lease and work land, if they deemed fit; this permission had remained unused and almost unnoticed. Lansbury persuaded his colleagues to look around for suitable land on which they could offer farm work to the unemployed, instead of keeping them in idle misery, either on out-relief or in the workhouse.

Laindon Farm Colony from the Poplar Guardians, Hollesley Bay from the Government's Central Unemployment Committee were the immediate results of Lansbury's agitation; in after-years they were copied by many other authorities in England and Scotland. But he would have denied strongly that the credit was all, or mainly, due to him. Both these experiments were made possible by a new friend whom he made in 1904, one of two friends who had an especial place in his life and affections, and on whose financial generosity so many of his projects depended. This was Joseph Fels (the other friend, whose influence came rather later, was Lady de la Warr). Fels was a small, active, confident, very Jewish-looking American capitalist.

He had made a fortune in soap (' Fels-Naphtha ' was literally a household word in his day), and he added to it steadily. Challenged by his indignant rivals to divide up his money, he used to reply: ' I shall go on making as much money as I can; and I will use it to prevent people like you and me being allowed to do so any longer.'

Fels had already founded a Vacant Land Cultivation Society, as part of his propaganda, and hearing of Lansbury's activity in the East End, got an introduction to him from Keir Hardie. Lansbury was evasive to the point of rudeness: he was already thoroughly tired of rich men who wasted his time by lecturing him on his wildness and their own purity of motives. But once he had ' petulantly said Yes ' he was captivated. Fels' generosity and devotion were combined with a financial shrewdness that placed his gifts and loans in the most useful places and on conditions which made it very difficult for them to be wasted. The combination was irresistible: Lansbury never respected a man who was a fool with his money.

Fels' most famous donation was one which enabled the Russian Social-Democratic conference of 1907 in London to finish its agenda and go home. This was the conference at which Lenin carried the day against Martov, the Bolsheviks against the Mensheviks; and Fels' money may have changed history. H. N. Brailsford (*Plebs*, May 1948) says he was approached desperately by Theodore Rothstein for £500, without which the conference would collapse.

' I could not myself produce £500, but after a little reflection I thought of a man who might. Joseph Fels was born in Russia, and had fled in his early days from the land of pogroms to New York. So I guessed that he might have a fellow-feeling for these rebels stranded on our shores. Not that Fels was a socialist. He was a convinced Henry Georgeite, who believed that all would go well with mankind if only we would adopt the single tax on land values. But for all that, Fels was no bigot and he had not forgotten his hatred of the Tsar's tyranny. So off we went, Rothstein and I, to Fels' office in the City. He received us in the friendliest way, listened patiently, and was on the point of saying " Yes ", when he pulled himself up and said that he must first consult his almoner. My heart sank—until I saw in the doorway the familiar, kindly features of

George Lansbury. Of course George agreed that this would be a splendid way of using superfluous wealth! '

Walter Coates, Fels' business associate and friend, was almost equally generous. There is a typical letter from him dated January 1906, which seems to refer to the attack made upon the Guardians and the Farm Colony:

' I can't but feel that you are very much worried over the money your fight will cost. It will cost the same win or lose. Let me pray of you to drop that out of your mind altogether. *Go ahead* and if it is necessary for you to spend £1000 more to get the right number of workers, spend it. I want to assure you that both Joe and I feel that any money help we can give you towards helping *your work*, is the best spent money we spend. I want to say right here you have brought more sunshine and hope into our lives than any other man has—so let's drop the question from now on. For my own part you may spend my money as if it were your own, and I'll tell you when I am hard up.

' Good luck, old man, and don't budge for anyone.

' I'll also tell you frankly when I stop feeling for you as I now do.'

It was Fels' money which made possible both Laindon Farm Colony and Hollesley Bay, partly by loan, partly by outright gift. Laindon Farm Colony was first in time: it consisted of a farm called Sumpners, of about 100 acres, outside Laindon in Essex. It was in wretchedly bad condition, as was so much Essex land. The Tariff Reformers said the multiplication of these derelicts was due to Free Trade; the Socialists said it was due to Capitalism; whichever was right, Laindon was a particularly distressing sight. The soil was both sandy and sour; the existing crops were mainly brambles and weeds. Fels bought it for £2,125 and leased it to the Guardians for a ' pepper-corn ' rent. They, when they took it over on March 5th, 1904, were allowed to supply clothes, and to maintain the wives and families of the men who went there; but they were not allowed to give them any money. Fels provided them with sixpence a week pocket money, and this pitiful sum was among the charges of coddling and waste which were brought against the Poplar Guardians later. But meanwhile two hundred men were getting a living, they were recovering their health and their self-respect, and 100 acres of waste land were turned into orchards and gardens. They even built a reservoir, damming a small river. In later years Laindon was used mostly for older men, but at this time its inhabitants were nearly all young men. Gerald Balfour, the Conservative Cabinet Minister, came to inspect it, and was startled and distressed to find how many of them had served in the Boer War and had since been discarded by society as useless. It was apparently the first time that he had himself seen what happened to ex-soldiers.

Hollesley Bay, under the Central Unemployment Committee, was a bigger project; but it, too, could not have been started but for Fels, who lent nearly £40,000 for three or four years free of interest. Lansbury, C. H. Grinling of Woolwich, or another member of the committee spent every week-end at the colony, arranging classes, lectures and recreation. Some men were able to bring out their families and live in cottages on the estate: these benefited the most, but all the men, by their enthusiasm and their rapid rise in skill, showed ' that unemployed townsmen can easily become expert gardeners and agricultural workers '.

Both at Laindon and Hollesley Bay fruit-growing and market-gardening were the main occupations; it was reasonably doubted if ordinary mixed farming or stockbreeding would have been so successful. Fels had not discovered a panacea. But the attack (for there was one to come) upon Hollesley Bay was not to be based on any such dry reasoning; nor was it to come from the natural enemies of such experiments. Laindon was safe, because Laindon was owned by Poplar. But Hollesley Bay was vulnerable; it was to have very few years of life as it had been planned originally.

The enemy was not the existing Conservative Government. If anything, that Government was friendly to men like Lansbury. It was acutely conscious of its unpopularity, and of the election due at latest in 1906. Even its successes had turned to its disadvantage. The results of its victory in South Africa had not been a mining boom to pay the cost of the war—on the contrary, large payments had to be made to the Boers. Chinese slaves were being imported into the Rand mines—no doubt to put

white miners out of work, and under disgusting conditions—
and ex-soldiers were begging in the London streets. Moreover,
the nation had by now a bad conscience over the war, and was
taking it out of those who were responsible for it. The Government had passed an Education Act which was a great advance
in itself, but the advantages given to the Anglican schools had
turned every Nonconformist into an anti-Conservative agent.
Its liveliest member, Joseph Chamberlain, had taken up the
cause which was varyingly called Tariff Reform, Protection,
Fair Trade or Imperial Preference. But he had secured only
languid interest from the Colonies; and at home he had convinced the working and middle classes that he would raise the
price of food, and the City of London that he would wreck its
position as the world's financial capital. He also deeply divided
his own party: in order to prevent a split he left office to carry
on his propaganda, while Balfour, as Prime Minister, promised
to take no action on his programme. This subtle manœuvre
saddled the Conservative Party with all the opprobrium of
desiring to tax food without allowing it to come out with whole-
hearted propaganda in favour of Tariff Reform.

In such circumstances almost the only hopeful line of policy
was to show an anxious interest in the unemployed—to revive
hastily, and on a political deathbed, a Disraelian spirit, and hope
that the Liberals would be inconvenienced. One item in this
policy was an Act which set up the unemployment committee
already mentioned. Another was the appointment in 1905 of a
large and influential Royal Commission to report on the Reform
of the Poor Law. It was a time when audacity might pay, and
could anyway do no harm. The Government named as Commissioners a group of clergymen, Poor Law officials, Charity
Organisation Society officials, and politicians, and added to them
a woman who was already prominent as a Socialist theorist, Mrs.
Sidney Webb. To the theorist it added the practitioner, the
rash man who had used the Guardians' powers to their extreme
legal limit, Mr. George Lansbury.

Chapter Seven

BALFOUR resigned at the end of 1905: Sir Henry Campbell-Bannerman, the Liberal leader, took office and at the beginning of 1906 ' went to the country '. The Conservatives had expected to lose a few seats: they met a disaster. From 310 they fell to 130 in numbers; the Liberals had 399 seats, an absolute majority over all others. Unluckier than Mr. Churchill, forty years later, Balfour was never forgiven by his party for his electoral miscalculation: the catch-cry ' B.M.G.' began to be whispered about within a very few months, and he was ultimately replaced by the narrow Bonar Law, a man whose later action in encouraging the Ulster threat of civil war had bloody consequences which have not yet fulfilled themselves.

But for the minute a possible change in Conservative leadership was the least of the results which attracted political conversation. More interesting among subsidiary subjects was the emergence of an entirely new Party, more extreme, in the general belief, than any other—the Labour Party. There had, of course, been working-men M.P.s before, a dozen or half-dozen respectful and respected members of the Liberal Party: there had even once, for one Parliament, been a single Conservative working-man member. There had been two stray ' wild men ' before: Keir Hardie, who had momentarily captured West Ham in 1892, and John Burns in Battersea. Burns had now become respectable enough to be offered the Cabinet post of President of the Local Government Board. (He accepted in a phrase which confirmed middle-class observers in their opinion of working-men who rose above their station: ' I congratulate you, Sir Henry; this will be the most popular thing you have done '.) But now there were no fewer than thirty independent Labour M.P.s, with Hardie as their leader; and soon, by decision of the Miners' Federation, thirteen miner M.P.s were, nominally at least, added to their number, and taken away from the Liberal Party. Nor was the influence of the sinister new force confined to the new

Party. In 1901 the once famous ' Taff-Vale ' judgment had decided that a trade union could be made to pay for all the financial damage caused by a strike—even though the strikers who caused it might have acted without the union's authorisation and the strike have been called against its wish. Sir Henry's Government was prepared to modify this ruling, which might have bankrupted every union in the country; but when it proposed a compromise Bill, Liberal member after member rose in his place in the House to say in effect that he owed his seat to a promise to secure the outright repeal of this decision; and an outright repeal was forthwith provided.

Interesting—and to several Liberals alarming—though this incident was, the chief importance of the election seemed to be quite clear. It seemed to have violently reversed what had been the trend of nearly a quarter of a century. From 1832, for fifty years, political history had been the story of continual advance by Liberals. To begin with they had altered the constitution, wiping out the long roll of rotten boroughs which their opponents mainly owned or purchased. Then they had remodelled local government and turned out a great pack of Tory and Anglican office-holders. They had cut at the economic roots of the great Conservative landlords by repealing the Corn Laws. By a policy of free trade, of financial and administrative reform, and of peace, they had altered the England of the Prince Regent into the England of Mr. Gladstone, an England where Liberal ideas reigned always, and the reign of Liberal governments was interrupted by little more than the necessary intervals for repose.

But by the eighties this unexampled succession of sunny years seemed to be breaking. The Tory interludes did not appear to be any longer momentary successes secured by stealing the Whigs' clothing and adopting their programmes. The reasons offered by the despondent varied and were often contradictory: the cause was alleged to be Mr. Gladstone's preoccupation with Home Rule for Ireland, or his unwillingness to consider reforms, or more simply his old age and obstinacy; or the attractions of a flashy and bloodthirsty imperialism; or the failure of the Liberal Party to adopt that imperialism; or the mysterious absence, from 1894 onwards, of large subscribers to Liberal funds; or the treachery and skill of Joseph Chamberlain; or even the dramatic adulteries of Sir Charles Dilke. But for whatever reasons, the Liberals in 1906 had had to look back on no less than twenty years of Conservative rule, interrupted by a mere three years (of the Gladstone–Rosebery administrations) which not the most loyal could look back to with pride. Now it was proved, 399 times, that the long interlude was only an interlude; the Conservative Cabinets were only the results of a series of unlucky accidents; the heart of the country was Liberal.

No man foresaw the alternations of violence in the women's question and of feebleness in the Irish question, and the vacillations on all questions, by which Asquith was to lead his Party to disaster and ultimate disruption. Enthusiasm was, if anything, enhanced by the first actions of the Government. Apart from the passing of the Trades Disputes Act, already mentioned, in its first year, it produced a reasonably good Education Bill— which the House of Lords, quiescent while Tories had ruled, tore to pieces. It passed a Workmen's Compensation Act which brought relief and protection to some six million workers. At the beginning of 1907 it infuriated the Conservatives, but satisfied the conscience of the nation, by restoring self-government to the two conquered Boer Republics. Its Budget introduced a graduated income tax and heavier death duties on large estates; it passed a Small Holdings Act of which great things were expected, and a number of minor measures which received more moderate applause. If it was charged with slow or insufficient performance of its promises, it could always point to the malicious delays and mutilations of its Bills by the House of Lords. Morley's scheme for India (introduced in 1907, and approved in 1909), if condemned by Hardie as inadequate, was at least an attempt at reform. The Old Age Pensions Act and the Coal Mines Eight Hours Act were benefits indisputable by anyone.

But by then the stock of goodwill was running out. The growth of unemployment, and the Government's shuffling over women's suffrage, were the chief reasons named at the time for the fall in Liberal popularity: they were undoubtedly the most effective causes. But many had lost their faith in the Government well before 1909. Lansbury had been among the earliest to be disillusioned. He had not, it is true, been a propagandist for the Liberal Party at the General Election; but he had spoken very vigorously against their opponents, especially upon such subjects as Chinese indentured labour in South Africa, and it was not long before he looked back on his speeches with embarrassment. The whole period, indeed, started badly for him. Instead of staying to fight the general election in Bow, where he was well known and might well have carried the seat, he persuaded himself it was his duty to leave that seat to an apparently well-intentioned and progressive Liberal, and to go up to Middlesbrough to turn out Havelock Wilson, the seamen's leader. Wilson had been elected as an independent Labour M.P., with Hardie and Burns, and had without a trace of embarrassment passed to the Liberals. His union policy, too, was one of alliance with (or subservience to, as you pleased) the shipowners. It was clear to the local I.L.P. that an example must be made of him; Joseph Fels subscribed the necessary money; meetings bigger than anyone else's were held. But Lansbury did not turn Wilson out; instead he was at the bottom of the poll, with only 1,200 votes. Moreover, he ran into a personal disaster. The day before the poll he ' did the usual tour through all the wards, finishing up in the big market-place . . . more dead than alive '.

' How I got home I had no idea [he wrote]: my mind is a blank; I have no memory of it. . . . In the middle of the night I was seized with terrible pains. I screamed out prayers and entreaties for release. I must have been a most alarming and difficult patient: for I was really ill and in the most acute pain. Polling day passed with me still ill, and I heard the result lying in bed wondering if I should ever see my wife and home again.'

He had, in fact, been in great danger; Mrs. Lansbury had been telegraphed for, which at that time and in those circles was the equivalent of a warning of approaching death. What exactly was his illness he covered with a Victorian reticence; but it seemed that his violent exertions had caused the rupture which he suffered from ever after—possibly some other complications as well.

While he was slowly recovering from this, it was made clear

to him that the accession of John Burns, the ' Man with the Red Flag ', to the presidency of the Local Government Board meant no assistance to him in his Socialist policy locally—indeed, it meant an attack on him personally as well as upon his most loved projects. What moved Burns must remain uncertain until his papers are published or made available for students: he may have been a more complex character than he seems, and his motives may have been more mixed than they appear. On the surface, however, he seems merely a man of enormous vanity and limited abilities, jealous of his late colleagues and anxious to ingratiate himself with his new colleagues. Very vain he certainly was: Mrs. Webb, in her acid diary, called him a little later ' a monstrosity . . . a non-responsible being, a creature too crazily vain to be appealed to as one self-respecting man appeals to another '. He had already shown in small ways his jealousy of Lansbury: soon after he was, in a larger matter (the Insurance Acts), to announce his delight at ' dishing the Webbs '. But, with all this truculence to his one-time fellow-Socialists, he was meek to his permanent officials. Certainly, he made no changes for the better (or, so far as is known, any change at all): he accepted and defended the policies they had approved.

The affairs which mostly concerned Lansbury were the province of one of his officials named James Davy, whose object, improbable though it seems to-day, was to enforce a return to the ' principles of 1834 '. The central principle of the Poor Law of 1834 (as has been said) was ' deterrence ': relief was to be given in such a way and to such an extent that the life of a pauper would be more disagreeable than the most disagreeable way of earning a living outside. This was ensured in various ways, of which the favourites were humiliation, underfeeding and overwork. In its pristine days, the law was so administered that everyone needing aid whom it was not provably illegal or physically impossible to force into the workhouse was compelled to go there. Here he (or she) was separated from his family, both as a punishment and to prevent ' breeding '; he was compelled to wear a hideous uniform; he was contemptuously treated by the officials; his work was such as would cause ' a strong man effort '; his food was inadequate and distasteful. Even his death was as unpleasant as might be—medical attendance

77

was at the best summary, church bells might not (at one time) be tolled for him, and the funeral was ignoble.

> *Rattle his bones*
> *Over the stones*
> *He's only a pauper whom nobody owns.*

In many places, however, this system had been modified by the passage of time. Of course there were still Guardians, like Lansbury's neighbours of Whitechapel, who observed the old rule, in letter and spirit. Displeased with him, and complaining as their predecessors had complained of Shaftesbury, the White-chapel Guardians had even improved upon it. Years before it was thought of, or even lawful, they had invented and applied a Means Test. They had made their workhouse accommodation so repulsive that no person would willingly use it; they then, without much regard to their constitutional duties, decided that relief outside the workhouse should be refused to everybody, whatever their condition, unless the incomes of all their relatives had been disclosed to the Guardians, and their contributions approved as adequate. It would be unfair to say that Burns, or his department, actively approved of this elaboration; but it took no steps to prevent it, and it did take steps to put down the rival policy of the Poplar Guardians, which was having too many imitators. They considered it their duty to treat paupers well— to restore their self-respect, not to break it down further by humiliations; to feed them well, so as to make them capable of earning their living ; and to give them work chosen for its usefulness, and not for its deterrent character. To Davy and his officials this was not only making Poor Law relief more attractive than certain occupations outside the workhouse (there are people still who can remember just how degrading and miserable some of the East End trades were in 1906), but it was also condemned by sound economic law. It was subsidising the paupers out of the rates, which in a final analysis meant out of the wages of those who were employed. They contended, so seriously that Lansbury himself was disquieted by the argument, that eventually the Poplar policy would lead to a fall in wages, as the faintly similar Speenhamland policy had done a hundred years before.

To end this dangerous policy—to give Whitechapel the victory over Poplar—Davy had two weapons, one for distant warfare, and one for in-fighting. His long-term attack was through the new Poor Law Commission. As the official in charge, he could supply evidence that would secure a reaffirmation of the principles of deterrence; and a reform of the administration by the elimination of the Guardians and the handing of their duties to bodies such as the County Councils, which would not be so irresponsibly lenient. The short-term attack was direct. It was to undo the reformers' work at Laindon and Hollesley Bay, and if possible convict the Poplar administration as a whole of maladministration, waste and corruption.

Hollesley Bay was vulnerable: it was under central authority. By simple administrative action, it was converted back into a deterrent workhouse. No more lectures, no more visits by Grinling and Lansbury, no pocket-money from Joe Fels, no independence and ' pampering' at work—just a penal colony which happened to be more out of doors than between four walls. Lansbury watched in helpless fury: he never forgave the officials of the Local Government Board or its successor, the Ministry of Health. Thenceforward he ascribed to them a perpetual malicious intent: he saw them as persons who wished to inflict suffering and humiliation on those who lacked money, and who would go a very long way in trickery and obstruction to punish local authorities who tried to be humane. Davy and his colleagues came next, he felt, in infamy to Loch and his colleagues of the Charity Organisation Society, and for the same reason— not so much that they failed to relieve poverty, but that they broke the spirit of the men and women whom they controlled.

The attack on Laindon and the general policy of the Poplar Guardians had to be less summary: the Guardians were a constituted authority. To deal with them, a formal inquiry was set up by the Local Government Board; Davy was the inspector in charge; the first session was held on June 7th, 1906. An inquiry under the Local Government Board was not subject to the rules of procedure which govern the Courts, and the first days of Davy's investigations provide an exuberant crop of evidence for the traditionalist lawyers who condemn lay tribunals. The inspector himself had already announced his verdict on the question he was to investigate. His exact words are not recorded; we know of the fact because Lansbury told him that 'you knew why' the Guardians were sorry to see it was he who had appeared as inspector, and Crooks expressed his regret 'that you have already expressed an opinion'. There were present the inspector, the Guardians, headed by Crooks and Lansbury, and a lawyer named E. Robb, instructed by the 'Municipal Alliance', the name of the local Conservative Party.

Robb opened proceedings by a polemical speech; some of the Guardians at once tried to question him; Davy forbade it. Any questions, he said, must only be put through him.

'MR. LANSBURY: I take it other people will do the same?
'MR. DAVY: Never mind about other people.'

Robb continued. The orders given for food, drink and clothing for the workhouse were recited. All bulk orders for institutions, read out in a series, sound enormous; these were no exception. They sounded the worse because in several cases the lowest tender had not been accepted; in others, by splitting the tenders and accepting the lowest items out of each, the Guardians apparently might have made a saving; in all cases the 'best' quality was stipulated. Crooks or Lansbury, now and later, tried to point out that the omission of the word 'best' in contracts was the equivalent of inviting the contractor to send rubbish to the workhouse; that contracts could not be split at will, as low prices on one or two items were deliberately quoted to secure the whole order; and that 'lowest tenders' often came from known sweaters, or suppliers of bad milk and meat. Davy stopped them: Robb's speech was a speech, and not evidence; therefore it must not be interrupted or controverted. Days later the answers were permitted: but meanwhile the Press had had its headlines. Robb went on to further accusations. Laindon Colony was packed with criminals who terrorised Essex; 142 persons were on a piece of land which needed only twelve. Guardians every day thronged to Poplar workhouse, where they drank beer at the ratepayers' expense in the cellar, and were frequently rolling drunk. The master, Madeley, was a reprobate. 'We shall have all this in the *Daily Mail* in the morning,' cried Crooks, in baffled despair.

The master was then called, and the examination permitted by Davy would hardly have been tolerated in a regular court. Firstly, he was questioned upon a matter which was *sub judice* and should never have been gone into. A contractor named Jacobs had served a writ on him, and Robb examined him on this, trying to make him say that he had accepted a bribe from Jacobs. The Guardians tried to intervene to prevent this attempt to make a man incriminate himself; they were met by a sneer:—

'MR. DAVY: Of course, if Mr. Madeley wants legal advice he can be recalled after an adjournment.

'MR. LANSBURY: But you are making him give evidence against himself.

'MR. DAVY: He is my witness.'

In the afternoon something of a different picture appeared when Lansbury examined the workhouse master. The questions and answers that followed (pages 62 onwards of the verbatim report) are a good example of a technique which Lansbury developed greatly in later years—the bringing out, by what Davy described (in irritable quotation of Lansbury himself) as his 'sweet reasonableness', of facts which the authorities did not wish to have stressed. There was no luxuriousness in the paupers' diet, it was shown. When the dietary was changed, it was changed to that laid down by the Local Government Board itself—worse diets, such as Whitechapel's, were presumably a defiance of the Board. Inquirers from social and religious organisations had continually visited the reformed workhouse, and so had inspectors from the Board: they had all approved, and had sent along others to learn from it.

The interlude was short. Robb, allowed if not encouraged by Davy, resumed in a second examination what would now be called his smear campaign. Madeley was questioned on whether he ever went to the West End. What did it cost him? Had he had dinner at Frascati's? (There was no one to inquire by what right he was asked how he spent his spare time, or what it all had to do with the procedure at Guardians' meetings.) A fresh attempt was made to make him say he had accepted a bribe— four pounds was the sum named—and Jacobs, the carriage contractor who had issued a writ against him, was called to confirm this. After forty years, even the verbatim record is no longer immediately comprehensible; but it is clear that Lansbury and Crooks were enraged by the baiting of Madeley, and their cross-examination put Mr. Jacobs into a state of great discomfort. ' Give me cold water! ' he cried at the end, adding with a resurgence of hope: ' I would like brandy after that.'

There was, in fact, something here that Crooks and Lansbury were trying to hide. Madeley had for years managed the Poplar workhouse exemplarily: his wife had been an exemplary matron. But she had fallen ill, and the master had become infatuated with a nurse who had once been employed in the infirmary. He had broken off the connection, and the Guardians had relievedly decided that they need not be aware of the incident. But shortly before the inquiry he had gone back to his new love, and Lansbury had written him a long personal letter (not preserved) in which he told him that he should quietly resign to start life again elsewhere. This he had done; but for the sake of Mrs. Madeley—an unhappy and needlessly shamed middle-aged lady —the Guardians wanted the story concealed. Robb and Davy, however, ultimately dragged it out from her and from others: it was part of the picture they wished to draw of the Poplar work-house as a cross between a brothel and a public-house. To destroy this, the Guardians had to call evidence on the most trivial points. Anderson, a Guardian who had been charged with being drunk, testified that he was secretary of the Steve-dores' Union, and, like many seafaring workers, walked with a rolling gait, which was demonstrated in court. McCarthy, a Post Office worker who had visited the workhouse daily, proved that he was chairman of the Visiting Committee, which had been censured under the old regime for not visiting often enough, and so letting the workhouse get into a disgraceful condition. Detailed evidence was called to show that when Madeley offered visiting Guardians a glass of beer, it was from a barrel of his own at the far end of a trestle table, and not ' the ratepayers' beer '.

It was no good: a section of the Press had found a good story, and would not let it go. The *Daily Mail*, the *Daily Mirror* and *Punch* enjoyed themselves most: the high point was perhaps a cartoon portraying Crooks and Lansbury (both teetotallers and non-smokers, in fact) with cigars in their mouths ordering a fresh barrel of ratepayers' beer to be rolled out from the workhouse cellar for their use.

On June 21st, at last, Corrie Grant, K.C., appeared for the Guardians; in the presence of that distinguished lawyer, an old friend of Lansbury's, the proceedings became more decent. Nothing further grotesque occurred, except perhaps a wrangle over whether Guardian McCarthy was in fact offered jellied eels by the workhouse master on one of his visits. Grant dominated his clients as well as the inspector. When a contractor charged the Guardians with corruption over dustbins, Lansbury shouted, ' He is an infamous liar! ' Grant turned on him, and in a voice which drowned his (and Lansbury's voice was enormous when he chose) said, ' Quiet, Lansbury! You are spoiling your own case.' In the afternoon, Lansbury subduedly apologised to the Court. ' Do you apologise to me? ' cried Palmer, the dustbin man. ' No, I do not,' roared Lansbury: for once, Grant and Davy were united in silencing him.

In the procession of strange witnesses appeared one who, even more than the rest, seemed a stray from a Victorian novel. He was a specimen of a creature whom Lansbury and his colleagues hoped to extirpate, a creature who is not even a memory to the present generation—the perpetual pauper. Yes, he said, he had been many years in the workhouse. All the Guardians, all the officials, were gentlemen. He was often in the hall, and would see anyone who came in. Had he seen any drinking in the cellar? He did not wish to answer any queer questions. Had the master his own keg of beer? ' I am a pauper.' Did the Guardians come often to see the master? ' I do not know; I am a pauper, understand that.' He had no eyes, no ears, no opinions; the Court stared at this wraith, and let him go.

The chaplain, who had been rebuked by them for neglect of duty, testified that the Guardians were biased and uncouth men. The doctor stated that he could not trust them: they had failed to support him. On what? On his refusal to sign a chit authorising the master to allot beer to paupers given foul work, such as cleaning sewers. Alcohol should be given only to the sick: paupers could perfectly well clean sewers without being given beer, he considered.

The Essex Chief Constable appeared to testify about Laindon.

He was prepared and eager; he hated the Londoners with the twisted malice of an Essex rustic. But it was Corrie Grant he had to face now, and his evidence was severely tested. The Laindon men were undesirable characters, he said. They terrified the countryside. They had criminal records. Precisely how many had such records? Well, seven or perhaps eight. Out of how many? Out of two hundred. And what were they convicted of? Drunkenness. They were fined, no doubt; what were the fines? Between half a crown and four shillings. Apart from this drunkenness, had the Chief Constable had complaints? Certainly he had. How many? Two —one definite. By now he was angry, and threw up at the Guardians Joe Fels' gift of pocket money. 'A great deal of mischief has arisen from the sixpence a week,' he snapped. 'They do not spend it on mineral waters.'

The local constable followed, trying to support his superior. The Laindon men had worried him. 'They have changed postal orders for a shilling and even one-and-six; and said they came from their wives.' They had been 'rowdy'. But he was an honest policeman: examined by Grant, he said outright that that was true only at the beginning. 'Lately they have been a very decent class.'

Lansbury hardly needed to point out that nearly two hundred men had been employed on 'land that only needed a dozen', for the reason that the intention was to rehabilitate the men by teaching them spade husbandry and other agricultural arts—not to cultivate a farm with the smallest possible labour force. The case against Laindon had fallen down by its own weight.

By now Davy had to hear the Guardians' evidence, the most noticeable part of which was Crooks' own. But the Press was no longer greatly interested, nor was the inspector himself. However, Crooks made it clear that the heavy rise in the poor rate was due to economic causes; the slump of 1904 had struck Poplar's dockland very heavily, and from the early nineties onward the better-class inhabitants had been moving steadily out of Bow. The rateable value of the borough had fallen as steadily and at the same time as its needs rose. Moreover, there had been a previous inquiry into the Poplar Guardians, in 1894, forced on the Local Government Board by the very group which was now being accused. It had been conducted by Mr. Lockwood, Q.C.; and Crooks took the Court right through the record of his discoveries and the laborious and drastic reforms that the Guardians had enforced as a result. Then there had indeed been peculation—not a glass of beer given to a visiting Guardian, but van-loads of stores sold by officials, whole bales of cloth missing. There had been real corruption—not a disputed four pounds from a coach proprietor, but a systematic percentage on contracts. Dirt was thick in the workhouse and infirmary; rat manure floated in the skilly and cocoa. The officials were drunken and idle; the workhouse was the scene of violence and fighting. The older men were beaten by the younger and their food seized from them. Yet the Local Government Board had been curiously unwilling then to support the Guardians: even after they had dismissed the thieving officials, it had been anxious that they should have a pension.

Some more weighty inhabitants of Poplar were called to confirm the picture of the Poplar Poor Law. Miss Grant, headmistress of the chief girls' school, testified that the Guardians' policy was the only practical way of lifting up the people of Poplar at all; she saw its results in her own pupils. Her decisiveness silenced even Robb. To Lansbury's surprise, the local officer of the Charity Organisation Society followed her with an equally wholehearted eulogy. He had had, he admitted, to reproach the Guardians occasionally with being gulled by plausible rogues; but their policy was the best thing that had happened in the East End for years. Any attempt to reverse it would be a disaster. He had reported in detail more than once to his headquarters, with full facts and figures, upon its effect in rehabilitating men whom the Society had thought past redemption: despite Davy's fidgeting, he conscientiously read into the record the full texts of his conclusions.

The inspector had had enough. Before long he indicated that he felt the whole subject had been sufficiently ventilated. No, he needed no more accounts from Laindon. No, he would not visit the Colony, nor see the men and the work they did. All he would do was to thank those present warmly for their aid, and retire to draft his report.

The report, when it came, was naturally hostile. The most

was made of the stories of glasses of beer, of too-high contracts accepted, and of gossip about the master; the least was made of the answers provided by the Guardians. Lansbury, in his autobiography twenty-odd years later, spoke of it with a still-indignant contempt. Wrong-headed it certainly was, but he failed to make allowances for a strain of peculiar honesty in it. Davy had a conscience; it was a particularly Civil Service conscience. It had not prevented him letting the inquiry be rigged, as far as it might be; it had allowed him to record charges which were unproved and to permit questionings which were scandalous, if not actually illegal. Yet, if he was unscrupulous in assembling the papers for his file, what was on the file, however it got there, must be given its due place in the final summary. Anyone who has worked closely with Civil Servants will recognise the scruple. And among what had found its way into the file was evidence which made it impossible to strike down the group which had been the real target of the Board. What suspicions remained unallayed lay upon the old-style Guardians: the Labour group was unblemished. Particularly, the great twin antagonists of the Board must be exonerated.

' Mr. Crooks and Mr. Lansbury [wrote Davy] are busy men, holding a number of offices which entail continuous work, and naturally would not have time, even if they had the inclination, for doing the routine work of managing an institution like the Poplar Workhouse. . . . They neither ate nor drank with the workhouse officials, and they suggested more than once to the Local Government Board that the contracts should be altogether taken out of the hands of the Guardians. . . . There is most conclusive evidence that they at all events derived no personal profit from the existing system.'

Lansbury paid no attention to—does not even seem to have noticed—his own financial exoneration. This was typical of him. His probity was so absolute, his knowledge of his own complete disinterestedness so clear, that he never willingly would notice or reply to charges of such a kind. He felt that truth would prevail, that his whole life was an answer to such an accusation, if an answer was needed, and that the subject itself was distasteful. It was a purity—a prudishness, if you will—

which was to do him a disservice years later, when he came into conflict with Lloyd George.

No action followed the report: the attack on the Guardians had failed. Madeley went to New Zealand; the Guardians resumed their old policy (though it may well be that contracts were more closely scrutinised and the Master's barrel vanished from the cellar); Lansbury was re-elected Guardian with a thumping majority. The first of three conflicts with Poplar had ended, as the next two were to do, in the discomfiture of the central authority.

But the results of Davy's use of his long-term weapon—the Royal Commission on the Poor Law—were less clear-cut. Davy's plan, and the first steps to its frustration, are briefly laid out by Lansbury's fellow-Commissioner, Mrs. Webb, in her diary (quoted in *Our Partnership*, page 322):

' *December 2nd* (1905): I had extracted from Davy, the assistant secretary of the L.G.B., in a little interview I had had with him, the intention of the L.G.B. officials as to the purpose and procedure they intended to be followed by the Commission. They were going to use us to get certain radical reforms of structure; the boards of guardians were to be swept away, judicial officers appointed and possibly the institutions transferred to the county authorities. With all of which I am inclined to agree. But we were also to recommend reversion to the principles of 1834 as regards policy; to stem the tide of phil-anthropic impulse that was sweeping away the old embankment of deterrent tests to the receipt of relief. Though I think the exact form in which this impulse has clothed itself is radically wrong and mis-chievous, yet I believe in the impulse, if it takes the right forms. It is just this vital question of what and which forms are right that I want to discover and this Commission to investigate. Having settled the conclusions to which we are to be led, the L.G.B. officials (on and off the Commission) have pre-determined the procedure. We were to be spoon-fed by evidence carefully selected and prepared; they were to draft the circular to the board of guardians; they were to select the inspectors who were to give evidence; they were virtually to select the guardians to be called in support of this evidence. Assistant commissioners were to be appointed who were to collect evidence illustrative of these theories. And above all we were to be given opinions and not facts. Charles Booth and I consulted what line we should take.   To-day at lunch I put Lansbury (the working-man on the Commission) on his guard against this policy.'

The unconscious patronage in that last sentence illuminates the doubt which a biographer must have over this famous Poor Law Commission.   Through the absence of other records, and the brilliance of her own, Mrs. Webb's account of it has become authoritative, and probably will remain so.   We see the proceedings through her eyes.   The Commission is harried and dominated by her; the necessary evidence is organised and prepared by her.   At the end she fails indeed to carry the Commission with her, but Sidney Webb writes out, using the work she has done, a Minority Report which becomes one of the most important social documents of that generation.   She secures for it the signatures of three other Commissioners beside herself: a clergyman named Russell Wakefield, ' the working-man ' whom she had kindly warned against Davy, and Francis Chandler, a Carpenters' Union secretary with a straggling beard, so meek that she almost forgot him.   (' But he will have to agree to whatever we decide on.')

All her life she was convinced of her perfect success in such manipulation.   A little earlier she had written in her diary about a similar operation: ' Of course, they unconsciously resent having situations " prepared " out of which there is only one way—i.e. ours! '   Late in life, when she prepared her diaries for publication, she could still say: ' Skill in social intercourse was my special gift. . . . I could insinuate myself into smoking rooms, business offices, private and public conferences, without arousing suspicion.'

Rarely can a clever woman have been so profoundly self-deceived.   The publication of her diaries has shown that she had a more attractive, indeed more lovable nature than the world knew: but the picture they draw is misleading for the years 1906–09.   At this time her manner and manœuvres were arousing not suspicion, but plain hostility.   The softness of youth which had made her face beautiful had gone.   Those who met her saw a strong-featured, middle-aged woman, with a beak nose and bird-like eyes.   Her favourite gesture was to fling out a rather claw-like hand at an interlocutor; her favourite opening a long-drawn and highly individual ' A-a-ah, Mr. Blank! ' on an alarming and almost predatory note. The world was by now well aware it was being ' managed ', and increasingly resentful of it. Her colleagues, outside a narrow circle, found themselves considered not as collaborators but instruments: movers of amendments, packers of committees, exhibits in her social museum, and sources of factual information; but not framers of policy. Lansbury himself never believed that the famous Minority Report was an all-Webb production to which he had painfully put his proletarian pen. He regarded himself as having at least modified it. He did not, indeed, consider himself as having offered anything like an equal part to that of Mrs. Webb, nor is it questioned that Sidney Webb wrote the actual text of the report. But neither of the Webbs had had any practical experience of the administration of the Poor Law. Lansbury had had a great deal; resisting one of Mrs. Webb's arguments, he wrote to her: ' *Experience*, which I admit may not be so valuable as a complete and thorough grasp of economic theory, has taught me this cannot be.'

He was not the man to press any claims to authorship, and the amount of his collaboration, if any, can probably never now be decided. It is certain, anyway, that from the first day Mrs. Webb worked him very hard. Short notes in that famous illegible scrawl began to pour into the house in Bow. Often they were passed from hand to hand, or from eye to eye, for deciphering: frequently Edgar, the second son, was the only one who could ascertain their meaning. They were always requests for information, or suggestions for new work—sometimes very fruitful, as was the one which resulted in Lansbury (in the strange company of Loch of the C.O.S. and two others) crossing to Hamburg in 1908 and making a close study of the German system of poor relief. This was the first time Lansbury had investigated seriously and systematically the institutions of a foreign country; from Australia and Ireland, for all his quick wit, he had brought back emotions rather than facts.

Davy's plan for the Commission, though he did not know it, was defeated by its second or third meeting, and this defeat, unquestionably, was Mrs. Webb's doing. So far from hearing a few routine witnesses and issuing a report which would be suggested to it by the permanent officials of the Board, the Commissioners found themselves plunged into a detailed investigation of all the existing methods of relieving poverty, of their effects, their administration, and their costs in terms of life and efficiency, as well as money. Indeed, they were compelled to investigate not the Poor Law, but poverty; and whenever they faltered their hands were forced by Mrs. Webb's willingness herself to undertake or arrange for the particular investigation in question. At first they were willing enough to let her work: but before long they realised that her gifts were Greek gifts, which, so far from saving them trouble, only led them on to make their inquiries more profound. She notes in her diary with glee the time when the chairman, Lord George Hamilton, showed open alarm at her offer to provide yet another memorandum.

' " You might elaborate the one you have already presented," said Lord George in a frightened way ', she wrote.

Three great sub-committees were appointed: the Statistical Committee, the Evidence Committee and the Documents Committee; and while their proceedings and the separate inquiries were producing reports which became classics against their will, Davy was digging his grave with his mouth. He and his colleagues recited to the Committee the 1834 doctrine in its crudest form. ' The pauper ', he told it, must be reduced to a condition below that of ' the poorest independent labourer '. His degradation should be forced home to him ' first, by the loss of personal reputation (what is understood by the stigma of pauperism); secondly, the loss of personal freedom, which is secured by detention in a workhouse; and thirdly, the loss of political freedom by suffering disfranchisement '. Margaret Cole, in her *Beatrice Webb*, quotes some further remarks:

' The work in the workhouse should be both monotonous and unskilled. You have got to find work which anybody can do and nearly everybody dislikes doing. You have got to give him something like corn-grinding or flint crushing, cross-cut sawing or some work of that sort, which is laborious and which is wholly unskilled.'

When Lansbury objected that this was, surely, unjust to men thrown out of work by a trade depression, and not by their own fault, Davy, angry at the reappearance of an antagonist who should have been crushed, replied brutally: " The unemployed man must stand by his accidents. He must suffer for the general good of the body politic.'

Revolted by this harshness, distracted by Mrs. Webb's creeping barrage of facts and figures, the Commission came to one unanimous decision: that the Poor Law should be abolished. This grand announcement was the limit of their agreement: from that point the Majority and Minority diverged.

The Majority Report was an ill-considered jumble of suggestions which in no way could have carried out the principle that it had laid down. It was mainly to the effect that voluntary relief for the destitute should be organised and co-ordinated, with the State stepping in to supplement charity when it was inadequate. It was so preposterously inadequate that no attempts were ever made to implement it: indeed, it is difficult to find any record of it ever having been mentioned again. It was the Minority Report alone, then and later, which attracted public attention. It became a guiding programme for Socialists (and even for some Liberals); it was subjected to closer study and bitterer controversy than any other State Paper of its time. It was never fated to be carried out as a whole at one time: it was implemented piecemeal—by Old Age Pension Acts, Minimum Wage Acts, Trade Board Acts and so forth—until forty years later the third Labour Government could claim to have completed it almost in its entirety.

The best short summary is that of Margaret Cole, in her book just quoted:

' Briefly, the Report stated that people became destitute from a variety of causes, from old age, from ill-health or accident, from mental disease, from the loss of the bread winner, from wages that were too low to support the family, or from inability to find work. All these causes, it said, should be tackled at source, by responsible people with expert knowledge, and the various forms of prevention and relief co-ordinated into a nation-wide plan. E.g., old age should be provided for by a State pension system. The local authorities, through their medical and educational services, should arrange for the help needed by children, by sick and crippled people, or by lunatics; the problem of those whose wages were too low should be tackled by national fixing of minimum rates of pay; and that of the unemployed by a policy of public works administered nationally and locally. The Poor Law as such, should disappear altogether, and the local authorities should appoint Registrars of Public Assistance whose function would be, in the first place, to keep a register of all who were receiving public funds from any source whatsoever, and secondly, to assist with relief grants persons who had fallen into destitution and were not adequately catered for through any of the sources mentioned above.'

The Asquith Government had no intention of putting such a programme into effect: at this distance of time it is easy to see that it was impossible that it should have had. The Webbs did not think that it was impossible: to force its hand they organised, with their usual efficiency, a ' National Committee for the Prevention of Destitution ', whose campaign was highly educational, but politically quite ineffective. It agitated the Radicals, it is true; and Lloyd George's reforms of 1910–13 were in part designed specifically to deflect it: but that was all that could be said.

Lansbury, expecting less than the Webbs, was less disappointed. His final summing up, politically, was in an article for the *Commonwealth* (of March 1909, immediately after the completion of the Report). In it he picked out as the important demands of the Minority Report such things as that child-bearing should henceforward be treated as a physical change in health, like a fever, and should be allowed to cause no more suffering, that the care of children should be taken entirely away from the Guardians (who at this date allowed between 1s. and 1s. 6d. a week per child) and passed over to the educational authorities, and that all diseased persons should be removed from the Guardians and their workhouse infirmaries and put under a health authority. But, he decided, the most important result of the Commission was none of these minority recommendations; it was its unanimity on the need to destroy the Poor Law. Unlike the Webbs, he had already decided that the policy of cajoling and tricking Liberal or Conservative ministers into carrying out Socialist policies had reached the end of its usefulness (if it ever had any): inquiries such as this must have mainly an educational effect, and admissions of principle (or confessions of failure), such as the unanimous declaration on ending the Poor Law, were all that could be turned to immediate political use. His energies and thoughts were turned wholly to independent Labour politics: while working with the Webbs on the Commission he had also been coming into closer touch with the only political party which was following the policy which he felt to be his own. For many years he had been a rogue elephant in propaganda. He had, already, a solid group of supporters and admirers in East London; from this lair, as it were, he would go out and trumpet up and down the country, addressing meetings and making converts, but identifying himself closely with no other body but the Bow and Bromley local party. This was the life he liked and understood: it gave him full independence, limited responsibility and, within a certain area, great authority. But he could see that it would not do for long: he must become part of the larger movement, and in these years he became a prominent member of the Independent Labour Party. Still, he was never ' an I.L.P.-er ' in the usual sense of the word. He never belonged to the close group which included Keir Hardie, Philip Snowden, Bruce Glasier, Ramsay MacDonald and Fred Jowett. He could leave the Party when the time came without a pang: the party members, when they counted their most typical and devoted leaders, by no means always included George Lansbury.

Chapter Eight

THERE was no alternative, in the 1900s, for any Socialist like Lansbury but the Independent Labour Party. If there had existed then the local Labour Parties which were set up under the constitution pushed through in 1918 by Arthur Henderson and Sidney Webb, he would have joined one of these; and his after-history would have been different, and perhaps politically more successful. But until 1918 the Labour Party had a peculiar, a strictly half-and-half character. It was a marriage, and not always a very happy and cordial marriage, between the trade unions and the Socialist Societies. If you were a delegate to Conference you came from one side or the other: such a person as 'a member of the Labour Party' did not exist. As a union delegate, you would have to observe the decisions of your union and vote accordingly. These, in general, were far from being Socialist: your union Executive (which was usually the effective controlling body) was likely to consist of orthodox Liberal working-men, spattered with an occasional Socialist, a few Radicals and even possibly some Conservatives. If you were not a union nominee, but merely wished to be a delegate (or a candidate) on the basis of the Party programmes—which already contained strongly Socialist sentiments—you must come as a representative of one of the Socialist societies. Here you had but little choice. Apart from a few tiny local bodies, there were but three Socialist societies affiliated. The first, the Fabian Society, was a self-conscious group of middle-class intellectuals. Its delegates attended because, as Fabians, they were interested in all activities of the working-class. Their most eminent leaders treated the Party with extreme contempt (the extremity of contempt consists in not even troubling to condemn): one of them has recorded that the sending of delegates at all was regarded as a fad of E. R. Pease, the General Secretary. The second was the old S.D.F., which Lansbury had but recently quitted: picking up a few new members and changing its name to the British

Socialist Party (B.S.P.) towards the end of this period, it nevertheless changed its nature not at all, and remained the small and uncompromising *élite* which he had left; in any case, it was momentarily (in 1906) not affiliated to the Labour Party. The organisation which immeasurably overtopped all others was the Independent Labour Party—the I.L.P.—founded in 1893. Any Socialist who wanted to give practical effect to his ideas and was not a Trade Union worthy had, willy-nilly, to belong to it.

The ' I.L.P.-er ', with his circular red-enamel button in his lapel—a gold S, for Socialism, twined round the party initials—was an easily recognisable figure before the 1914 war. If a man, he was often rather white-faced, voluntary asceticism adding to the effects of the underfeeding and over-work common among the British working-class; if a woman, straggly-haired and given to ' sensible ' clothes at a time when these involved ugliness as well as sense. But a profound earnestness and independence of thought was the I.L.P.-ers' most distinguishing characteristic: the world is the poorer for their disappearance. Unlike the S.D.F., the I.L.P. was indulgent to oddities and to indiscipline, thinking that the truth would come out through the least-expected mouthpieces. Unlike the S.D.F., too, it had no hostility to Christianity—great numbers of its members were professing Christians (more usually Nonconformist than Anglican), and its favourite speakers dwelt frequently upon the contradiction between Christ's gospel and the miseries of capitalist society.

Youth and enthusiasm have been spotlighted too often since 1900 for them to secure our admiration for their own sakes: equally earnest, devoted, bright-eyed and clean-limbed have been the young men and women who shouted, ' Heil Hitler! ' ' Duce! Duce! Duce! ' and ' Stalin! Stalin! ' It is only fair to underline how different was the I.L.P. enthusiasm from the organised zeal of any National Socialisms. The I.L.P.-er might have illusions about the selflessness of Ramsay MacDonald, he might weep too easily at the perorations of Mrs. Bruce Glasier; but he was an independent man or woman; he thought his own thoughts, and was never an item in a claque. He had joined the I.L.P. because he defied and resisted the world around him: he could be charged, often enough, with being unreasonable, sentimental, quarrelsome and even ignorant. But one thing he never was, and that was what a later generation called a dope.

A quite small group of men, all of marked character, gave inspiration and (within limits) direction to this Party (and through it, intermittently, to the Labour Party as a whole). They were far from being alike; some, indeed, actively disliked each other. But they all had common characteristics; a blindfold man, hearing them speak, could have said: ' That is an I.L.P.-er '. The steadiest of them all—the most placid, who did most to hold the group together—was the perpetual treasurer, T. D. Benson. The most important, of course, was their grand old man, Keir Hardie. How hard it is, after forty years, to explain to those who never saw him the importance of a man like Keir Hardie! Each year another one of those who knew him dies, and another witness to his value is removed. The later world sees him only as a man with a big and rather woolly growth of beard and whiskers, with a kind expression and no doubt a heart of gold, with a touch of theatricality about his appearance. (It may be, too, there was a certain self-consciousness about his cape and the large scarf knotted about his neck: Hardie was a platform speaker, and knew the value of accessories.) What did he write? Nothing worth preserving. What did he do? ' He inspired a generation '—but that is a phrase so vague that it carries no meaning.

Lansbury and Hardie, whom he greatly resembled, suffer from a disability that may well deny them their right place in history—the weakness of the spoken as compared with the written word. There have been other cases in which a later generation of historians has completely falsified the facts, because histories are written in libraries, where men read only the printed word. The most illuminating parallel that occurs to one is that of Cobbett and Hunt, a hundred years earlier. In the history of the Reform struggles under the Regency they were almost surely of equal importance—indeed, Hunt may well have been of greater, for he stood his ground when Cobbett ran to America. But Hunt spoke, Cobbett wrote. As a result, nothing is remembered of Hunt. A specialist here and there may know that he wore a white hat, and made that headgear a sign of Radicalism: if he is very meticulous he may add that Hunt had a lisp, calling his

Propaganda Postcard, 1911

D. Bowman (Queensland M.P.), George Lansbury, M.P., J. Keir Hardie, M.P.
Tom Richardson, M.P.

*After a meeting in Victoria Park, on South African outrages, with Poplar
comrades, about 1905*

Tom Williams, Dick Palmer (with sons), Tom Payne, George Lansbury,
Alf Watts (with daughter), Charlie Sumner, — Bronick

Workers of all
Countries Unite
You have nothing to lose
But your chains
You have a World to gain"
March 18. 1911

Yours always
Geo. Lansbury

favourite place for mass meetings in London 'The Sulley Theatre'. A few more people will know that he spoke at the Manchester meeting which turned into the massacre of Peterloo; and that is all. But biography after biography is written of Cobbett; his works reappear in *Everyman's Library*; cardinals and *Times* reviewers discuss his importance. And there is no evidence that he converted one more person by his pen than Hunt did by his tongue.

So, too, the time is near when historians will ascribe the conversion of half a generation of Englishmen to Socialism to the writings of Bernard Shaw, H. G. Wells, the Webbs and a few others. It will probably seem absurd, in the 1980s to affirm that the influence of Hardie and Lansbury was greater than all of the others put together: but one does not need to be very old to remember a time when that would have seemed to be a truism. Shaw's plays were laughed at consumedly by West End audiences (though their runs were short and not always profitable); the Webbs' books were read by an *élite* and slowly relayed to town and county councillors, who might carry out their suggestions; Wells' books amused a great many by their stories of the moon and of aerial invaders, inspired a less number to dream of a better-organised society, and encouraged several young women to sleep with males to whom they were not married. Later, their influence was to be much greater. The written word remains; their works were like the repeated blows of hammers. But in the early years of this century their influence, outside London at least, was less than that of Hardie, Lansbury and other speakers who week after week personally argued the case for Socialism in bare and crowded halls all over the island. These men met the doubts of the half-converted; they discussed with infinite patience the immediate problems of Socialists in each town; they provided, in the unassuming but undeniable honesty of their characters, evidence that a Socialist could easily be a better man than the 'get-rich-quick' business man whom Liberal politics held up as a model. You could not, after about nineteen-ten, cross-question Shaw upon his Prefaces: even Wells' *Anticipations* (if, on twenty-three shillings a week, you could afford to buy the book) would not provide an answer to every question that tormented a young worker in Cleckheaton or Galashiels.

But he knew that if he went to a meeting which Hardie or Lansbury or another such speaker addressed, his question would be
answered, and answered patiently and understandingly. He
knew that if no meeting was announced, it would nevertheless
not be long (if his I.L.P branch went to the trouble of organising
it) before one was held. He knew that after the meeting the
speaker would be glad to meet workers like himself, would talk
to them as one friend to another, and would reassure him that he
belonged to a class which was the equal of any other in the world,
and in whose hands (if it chose) lay the future of humanity.

Hardie had been selected as first chairman of the Parliamentary
Labour Party, in 1906, because no other choice was conceivable:
but after a year he was as relieved to vacate the office as the
M.P.s were to see him go. He could represent and understand
the workers: as a lone ' Member for the Unemployed ' he had
had a place and work to do in Parliament. But for the detailed
and finicky work of a Party leader he had no heart; for the
compromises involved in co-operation with the Liberal Party he
had an active distaste. Yet those compromises were necessary:
over half his fellow-M.P.s owed their seats to Liberal votes, and
many more than half the trade unionists who supported the Party
were still Liberals. After trying out two or three trade unionists,
the Party, to his relief and its own, settled on the second most
important ' I.L.P.-er ' as its leader, the highly presentable James
Ramsay MacDonald, one of the two M.P.s for Leicester (the
other being a Liberal).

If it is difficult to explain to a later generation the importance of
Keir Hardie, it is doubly difficult to explain that of Ramsay
MacDonald. It is difficult, indeed, to portray the man at all.
He was to attain the highest office in the State, to head the first
two Socialist Governments, to inspire extreme devotion and
extreme contempt, to turn on his own party and drive it to the
worst disaster it had known. A man (one would say) obviously
of strongly defined and possibly violent character, whether he
be hated or admired. Yet this, most of all, he was not. His
most contemptuous opponent, Winston Churchill, called him
' the boneless wonder ': he was not so much a boneless as a
hollow man. The outside can easily be described: reasonably
tall, slim, well-proportioned, with a noble head and handsome

profile, a big and flowing moustache; early-greying dark hair, with a big quiff at the front. The voice exceptionally fine and deep, resonant with a great variety of tone and sufficient of a Scots accent to give it charm. The manner all that could be required of courtesy and dignity. But the contents of the splendidly delivered speeches were very small—they amounted in earlier years to no more than generalities about the Socialist future and to involved warnings against rash actions; in later years they amounted to nothing at all, and some of his speeches then were incomprehensible in the literal sense of the word. His opponents could not say roundly, as they did of Lloyd George, that the man lied; for they rarely were certain of what he meant. Nor could they say that his mind was vacant and that he had no political guidance to give. He had a political theory—or at least a political metaphor—at this time. Society to him was an organism: it could be described in biological terms, and its future could be predicted as assuredly as Darwin could trace the evolution of species. In his *Socialism and Society*, published in 1905, and running at once into two editions, he elaborated this thesis. Society was moving at its own pace towards Socialism. It should be assisted on its way, of course: but the prodding which MacDonald was prepared to give it was of the gentlest kind. What was immediately clear to him was that the Liberal Party must be supported against the Conservatives: 'independent Labour' politics in the sense which Hardie and the I.L.P. founders had envisaged them could do nothing but harm.

He was supported in this by the private convictions of a majority of his followers, but what served him in his authority was much more his knowledge of Parliamentary technique and his admirable Parliamentary manner. It is not easy, if you are leader of no more than forty or fifty M.P.s, many half-inarticulate, to arrange for speakers on every subject of importance, to brief them, to prevent them losing their tempers, to draft motions, to supervise questions, to secure the proper share of Parliamentary time, and of seats upon committees, and so forth. All this his predecessors had failed to do, and MacDonald did excellently: he received the trust that is the fair reward of good work. But as he gained increasing trust within the Parliamentary Labour Party he was, in this period, beginning to lose it within his own

I.L.P. The distrust was most marked in the man whose name for thirty years was most closely linked with his own, to their common discomfort, Philip Snowden. Snowden's origin was somewhat similar to MacDonald's. Both knew real poverty when young (MacDonald as the illegitimate son of a Scotch girl of straitened resources; Snowden as one of the children of a Yorkshire weaver); both early came into the ranks of the lower middle class. Snowden was a Civil Servant until a bicycle accident crippled him for life; those who watched him hobbling about the House of Commons on his sticks could not but wonder whether the accident which had twisted his body had not also twisted his mind. For he was a bitter man: his thin nose and close lips, his bright and often burning blue eyes, his head sunk into his shoulders, reminded observers of what they had read of Robespierre. The anger of the disinherited spoke through him, their resentment of the injustice which they suffered, their hatred of oppression and their contempt for their oppressors. The scorn which he felt for his opponents was too often also sprayed over colleagues who failed to rise to his exacting standard. But it is also true that this hard man could, among his own people, speak so movingly and gently of the future and of the community of all who were working to the same end, that years afterwards they would say he was the only really great speaker whom they had ever heard.

Other 'I.L.P.-ers' were less striking characters. Most, like Snowden, had little knowledge of, or interest in, the trade unions. Little J. R. Clynes, of the General and Municipal Workers, bristling like a terrier, was the only one whose feet were equally in both camps. Bruce Glasier and his wife Katherine were favourite speakers of the Party, whose warm-heartedness compensated for Snowden's acerbity. Glasier in appearance was something of a weaker Keir Hardie—his beard fuzzier, his face kinder but weaker. There was a streak of obstinacy in his character, however, as contributors to the *Labour Leader*, which he edited, found out. Snowden once announced that he had for three years refused to contribute to this, the official party weekly, because of a disagreement with Glasier. It is typical of both men that Snowden did not consider the disclosure could reflect upon him, and that Glasier was completely unaffected by it. Ethel Snowden, Philip's wife, was a speaker more of the emotional quality of the Glasiers, but she was already giving most of her energies to the cause of women's suffrage. The man among the eminent ' I.L.P.-ers ' to whom Lansbury took the greatest and most immediate liking was Fred Jowett of Bradford, a strong, stocky working-man with a firm, full, round, reddish face and a short moustache—a steady man, an immovable Socialist and a hard worker. The procedure of Parliament seemed to him wasteful and antiquated, and to compare unfavourably with the rules of the Bradford town council : he made himself an expert upon House of Commons reform. On this subject Lansbury took his views all his life from Jowett : he returns to it more than once in his writings, but does little more than re-phrase his colleague's proposals.

Lansbury realised he had to be a member of the I.L.P., but he still hoped that he might at least be excused from the discipline of the Labour Party, so infected with the Liberal trade unionists from whom he had just escaped. A general election must come before long : he had been adopted by the Bow and Bromley Party as their Parliamentary candidate. Could he not run just as ' a Socialist ', and so retain his independence? The career of Victor Grayson seemed to give him an opportunity to plead his case, and he prepared a careful article for the *Labour Leader*.

Grayson is hardly a name to the present generation; his story can be briefly told, and does not appear important; there must, it seems, have been some vivid quality about the man, some dynamic force in his speaking, to explain the impression that he made. In 1907 Colne Valley in Yorkshire, the seat for which Snowden later sat, fell vacant. A young Unitarian preacher, black-haired and fanatical, named Victor Grayson, was put up by the local I.L.P. He was not a member of the Labour Party; he spoke, he said, only for the unemployed and disinherited, and would have nothing to do with that time-serving clique. He beat both the Liberal and Conservative candidates (Snowden alone speaking for him); insulted the Speaker and the House in a carefully stage-managed scene; and toured the country, rousing his audiences to a bitter rage. (His after-history was mysterious. In 1910 he lost his seat and disappeared; he re-

H

appeared momentarily in 1914, being billed at the Liverpool Olympia as ' Private Victor Grayson, of New Zealand, the Anti-German Cyclone '; he got in touch with a friend in 1919 from whom he expected some financial assistance; fixed an appointment which he did not keep; and was never heard of again). In 1909 he stirred up a revolt inside the I.L.P. against the leadership, making no distinction between MacDonald and Hardie: all were equally contaminated. He was sufficiently successful to prevent several of the more eminent ' I.L.P.-ers ' from accepting the seats on the National Administrative Council to which they had been elected.

Lansbury felt that Grayson's successes might open a way to a general relaxation. Grayson, he wrote, despite the unreasonable way in which he had behaved in minor matters, was in principle right. This the Party Conference had recognised. The widest tolerance was now the only possible rule: look at the way Snowden, for a personal reason, had declined to write for the *Labour Leader*. Look at the speeches which Steadman and Shackleton, two Liberal trade unionist M.P.s, delivered, without anyone asking for them to be expelled. Would it not be wise if candidates like himself were allowed to continue to call themselves ' Labour and Socialist ' candidates, and not have to promise to accept the Labour Party whips?

The plea was not accepted. Nationally it was not even considered; locally it had some success. In the year 1907, with his insatiable appetite for work, Lansbury had contested Woolwich for the London County Council, polling the then startling figure of 7,600, but not being elected; in March 1910 he was successful, with Frank Smith and R. C. K. Ensor making a group of three ' independent Labour ' councillors, who defied Webb's and Crooks' policy of working with and through the Progressives (as the Liberals were called on the Council). But that it was easier to permit. The Progressives had lost control of the Council, and both groups were in opposition; Webb himself was no longer a member after 1910; alliance with the Progressives had anyhow never been laid down as an official Labour Party policy. But Parliament was a different matter: every M.P. was under a spotlight, and the Party policy had been discussed freely every year at Conference. Lansbury, reluctantly enough, realised that he must at least outwardly, and in some obvious essentials, conform.

The election came in January 1910: there were three candidates in Bow and Bromley; Alfred du Cros (Conservative), Stopford Brooke (Liberal) and George Lansbury (Labour). Lansbury believed he would have won had it not been for a last-minute denunciation of him by Dr. Clifford, a once-famous Nonconformist leader. However, at least the Liberal was a lamentable last (2,167 votes against 2,955 for Lansbury and 3,695 for du Cros): henceforward the conflict in Poplar was to be Socialist against Conservative only.

In December of the same year the collision between the Liberal Government and the House of Lords forced a fresh general election. This time there was no Liberal candidate in Bow; moreover, the immensely popular Chancellor of the Exchequer, Lloyd George, made a pointed and unsolicited reference to the need to vote for ' my friend, Mr. George Lansbury ' in an East End speech. His new-found friend was rung up by three separate Liberal journalists next morning, asking: ' What response do you make to Mr. George's generous gesture? ' ' None,' he answered. But the Chancellor's speech had turned some waverers, and though his opponent was a clever, Fabian-trained, restless little Tory named L. S. Amery, he beat him by 4,315 votes to 3,452. Lansbury was now one of the very few working-men who could write M.P. after their names. There were only forty-two Labour members out of over 600; and not all of them were working-men. Each was on an eminence: what each one did was subjected to a curious attention from which the rank-and-file Liberal or Conservative was largely free.

It is surprising that he had the time to take up the new task at all. A brief list of the work he was already doing illuminates his unparalleled energy better than any description could. He was, as before, a Borough Councillor and a Guardian. What these two posts might involve is shown by the disclosures of the 1906 investigation. He had no regular secretary to help him in this or in any other work; he depended on his memory, on his own handwritten notes, and on unskilled assistance in the family. He had just taken on additionally a post as a London County Councillor: the L.C.C. organisation by Committees was skilfully devised to extract the maximum work from its members—so skilfully that Lansbury always cited the Council as a far more competent body than Parliament.

He was continuing, with no relaxation, his steady campaign of propaganda up and down the country—often organising meetings as well as addressing them. He was, in Bow itself, a sort of universal consultant—doing by himself the work which ' Citizens' Advice Bureaux ' try to do to-day. Almost daily the house in Bow was called at by men and women who were in legal, personal or financial difficulties and wanted ' G. L.' (the initials were by now commonly used) to advise and help. The advice was almost invariably good and well-informed, and quite invariably kind. The assistance was limited by his own straitened circumstances: the Lansbury family was no longer a poverty-stricken family, it is true, but it was never well-to-do. Its standard of living remained throughout his life working-class.

He had also to run successfully the small timber business without which none of this activity would have been possible. The elder children, out at work, were costing less, and, it may be, bringing something in; but any such economies were consumed forthwith by the needs of a family which was always growing up and demanding more food, more clothes, more education, more room. Lansbury in all had twelve children (a genealogical table of whom is at the end of this book), and though at no time were all twelve in the one house together, the absentees' places tended to be taken by grandchildren. (His eldest daughter, Bessie, died in 1909, leaving three children.) By far the greater responsibility for this tribe fell on Mrs. Lansbury. Still, there was never a time when Lansbury became the sort of distant father, rarely seen, whose business kept him separated from his children's lives. With all of them he had, as far as he possibly could, the closest and most intimate relationship. From the days when he could bath them until they were grown and married men and women, everything that they did was of the most intense and sometimes embarrassing interest to him. He was a Victorian patriarch all his life: he did not, it is true, ever try to force on them any course of action against their will, but he would have been deeply hurt not to know at all times what they were doing and why. He was most at ease when he drove the family, for an outing or the annual holiday, in a horse-drawn brake which it filled by itself, himself holding the reins, and supported and comforted by the immense clatter and chatter of his family behind him. Every year this happened; sometimes more than once a year. His children remembered it; they remembered, too, how all his attention was concentrated upon the outing. The public cares seemed to have been blanked out from his mind.

Nor was this ceaseless activity accompanied, as it is so often with men of business, by an abstention from study and reflection. Lansbury was all this time a voluminous reader. The papers which came to him from his various authorities were numerous, and were carefully studied. A flood of journals, mostly but not all propagandist, already was reaching the house, and they were read with alacrity. Time was found even to read novels and plays—generally, it is true, old and approved ones. Moreover, at this time he added a new and difficult subject to his interests—India.

An increasing number of dark-skinned comrades was among the callers at the house in Bow. Annie Besant, once a Socialist and now in India, sent many of her Theosophist followers. For Lansbury, the chief question was answered as soon as asked: if India wanted self-government, she must have it. The Indians —from Lajpat Rai, the pioneer of trade unionism, to Pundit Motilal Nehru, the Congressman—who called on him found that they had no need to argue their case. In what way could Mr. Lansbury help their cause? Was there any specific injustice which he could get righted? These were the only questions that they were asked. Not all of them, at this date, even demanded Home Rule within the Empire; none at all, so far as is known, asked for anything more. It was not till seven years later that the Indian Congress took the rather daring step of electing a Home Ruler, Mrs. Besant, as its President.

Chapter Nine

THE year 1910, when Lansbury entered Parliament, seems in retrospect to be Britain's apogee. In this year the British Empire was at its height: it was not only one of a long series of years of prosperity, it was one in which there were fewest shadows perceptible for the future. British power was at its apparent maximum—no Power was Britain's superior, and none was thought to be her equal. (It was not until 1921 that, exhausted by a great war, Great Britain contemplated allowing another Power—the United States—to have a navy equal to her own.) The Boer War had, it is true, shown weaknesses: but these had been remedied, and had in any case been due to years of peaceful policy—a thing of which no humane man could be ashamed. The widespread wealth, still Victorianly abundant in the better quarters of all the cities of the island, was gradually being diverted, in some degree, to more deserving objects than wealthy backs and bellies: social reforms—education, pensions, medical aid— were being introduced sedately and without disturbance. No one who has lived through the period can visualise the immense and largely unconscious feeling of security which penetrated all classes except the very lowest. The world was firmly set: its habits might be modified by earnest agitation, but its pattern could not pass away. This certainty, which is the heritage of almost everyone who had reached the age of, say, fifteen by the year 1914, marks them out from their juniors, whose mental background has been fear and uncertainty. Psychologists may know which state of mind is more desirable: it is undoubted which is more serene.

It was this very sense of security which was to make wilder than they need have been the political extravagances of the following four years. When the ice is many inches thick, skaters may caper as wildly as they will—they can brawl, they can drop heavy weights, they can light fires on the Thames. If they had not been so sure that, somehow, Britain would remain the same, that food and protection would always be provided, would the Suffragettes have started their campaign of burning, rioting and destruction? The syndicalists have organised strike after strike, up to the brink of a general refusal to work? The Carsonites have progressed from violent oratory to gun-running? Irresponsibility is often a sign of profound inner confidence.

The year 1910 was full of indications of power, of technical advance and of social progress. At the funeral of King Edward VII, on May 22, there was a procession of potentates such as had never been seen before, or would be seen again, in any country. The ruling monarchs of the German Empire, Denmark, Greece, Norway, Spain, Portugal and Bulgaria walked in the cortège, the heirs to the thrones of Austria-Hungary, Turkey, Rumania and other less-known countries, and close relatives of the reigning monarchs of Russia, China and Japan. A 'Japan–British Exhibition' opened at the White City 'demonstrating the resources of the allied empires', and a conference was arranged for next year of what were still happy and proud to be known as 'the Colonial Premiers'. May 31 was 'Union of South Africa' day, which not only welcomed a new member of the family, but recorded also (for most Englishmen) the voluntary righting of wrong by the conqueror. The world was at peace: there were no reasons for war, and the Chancellor publicly declared the nations' continued expenditure on armaments 'insane'. There was even published a book called *Europe's Optical Illusion* (soon changed to *The Great Illusion*) by a Mr. Norman Angell, which had an enormous sale and was taken to prove that war was financially impossible nowadays.

Two sensational technical advances were made during the summer. A French firm called Pathé used a new machine called the Kinematograph to record events of historical importance, and then to show them on a screen to audiences. The moving pictures were very clear, in black and white, with (of course) occasional flashes and blobs and tears, and they did not jiggle about very much; they were, indeed, marvellous, though what precise use they would serve was not clear. The same objection could not be raised against the second great innovation: the Eiffel Tower in Paris began to send out wireless signals to ships. This was an immense aid to navigation: moreover, on the last day of July a murderer named Crippen was arrested on an Atlantic liner by the use of a wireless message. Technical advances in other spheres did not receive so much publicity: these two themselves were not British in origin, and in the basic industries the quality of German competition was becoming definitely annoying. There was, however, as yet no general alarm.

The year was not, it is true, one of new social legislation. Recent years had been full of new Acts, and they were only now beginning to operate. In this year there was only one advance, and that was a proposal to remove obstructions rather than an advance in itself—the passing on March 29th in the House of Commons of the ' Veto ' resolution declaring that the power of the Lords should be clipped.

In truth, the immediate political condition of the country, looked at closely, was the least satisfactory part of a generally satisfactory society.

The Parliament which Lansbury joined in 1910, and the Government which he, nominally and indirectly, supported, were very different from those which he had seen take power four years before. Both were poorer in quality. The 1906 landslide had uncovered some oddities, but also some real talent and genuine enthusiasms. But 127 seats had been lost since 1906: the Liberals now numbered only 272; and, as is always the case in Parliament, the ' marginal seats ' had been held by the young, daring and intelligent, the safe seats by the party hacks. The change in the Government was even more marked: in particular the substitution of H. H. Asquith as Premier for Sir Henry Campbell-Bannerman was a disaster whose character was only slowly becoming evident. Campbell-Bannerman had been a strongly-built Radical, a man of courageous principle and firm character. When the news of the dissolution of the Duma and the crushing of the Russian revolution by the Tsar was received, his pronouncement was deliberate: ' The Duma is dead: long live the Duma.' His successor would have had neither the honest emotion which impelled that cry, nor the wit to see that it was true statesmanship.

The verdict of many historians on Asquith is that he was a Whig: by that is meant that for him, as for his Whig predecessors, politics was a game of In and Out: reforms might be necessary, but chiefly as a means of ensuring that you and your colleagues were the Ins. A skilled politician was one who evaded or side-tracked every difficulty as it arose, and stayed in office the longest possible time.

The new leaders had considered Sir Henry artless: they were themselves above all artful. The local and immediate skill by which Asquith, Lloyd George, Colonel Seely, Mr. Churchill, John Burns and the rest ducked or deferred all the problems set them by the women's movement, the Irish question or the Labour unrest was unprecedented. Each device was cleverer than the last; each led the Party deeper into a tangle from which there was no escape. For behind all this manœuvring there was neither honest conviction nor (except in the case of Mr. Churchill and probably Lloyd George) political courage. The Liberal Party was given its death-wound by its own leaders between 1910 and 1914: the split during the war only hastened an extinction which was already inevitable.

An example of their short-sighted but undeniable cunning was their treatment of the Labour Party. The election figures (Lib. 272; Lab. 42; Nationalists 84; Cons. 272) gave that Party, with the Irish Nationalists, the power of balance; in theory it could turn the Government out, and could therefore have expected greater authority and some deference. It received less than ever. The Liberal leaders were smart enough to see that though the Labour men could have permitted themselves some exuberances in 1906, when the Government was firmly established, MacDonald could not allow them in 1910 to speak or act in a way which might turn the Cabinet out. He would put up with almost any treatment rather than that—he and his group, that is, could safely be ignored and insulted; and they were. Nothing was more important to them personally and politically, for example, than the repeal of the Osborne Judgment. This was a decision handed down by the Law Lords in 1909 to the effect that it was illegal for Trade Unions to spend their money upon electing and maintaining members of Parliament. This threatened to extinguish the Party, as well as depriving its M.P.s of their salaries. It fought the elections of 1910 in the greatest financial embarrassment. The Liberal Party was pledged to amend this, but it deliberately made its humiliated ally wait until 1913 for a reversal of the Judgment, which even then it made partial and inadequate. (A union could henceforward only subscribe on behalf of those of its members who did not claim exemption.) True, it saved the M.P.s from ruin by passing the Payment of Members Act in 1911—but that was to its own interest, for it wanted no inconvenient by-elections.

But tormenting the unhappy Labour Party was the least of the problems on which the Government had to exercise its wits. The four great problems which it had to meet, in the order of their occupying the centre of the stage, were what were called the Problem of Social Unrest, the Question of Women's Rights, the Irish Question, and the German Menace. The first was deflected, momentarily, by the attack on the Lords. The other three the Government failed to meet at all: the story of its decline is a dull farce that ends in murder.

The fight with the Lords was already well under way when Lansbury entered the House—indeed, the December election was mainly due to the reluctance of King George V to create Peers to break down an opposition with which he not improbably agreed. It was a fortunate diversion. Real wages were going down; working class discontent was rising almost monthly; alleviation of some kind was expected from a Government whose claim to be progressive had been so loudly proclaimed at the recent election. The discontent was rapidly developing into a class struggle of working-man against employer —the most inconvenient of all struggles for the Liberal Party, which depended upon the employing class for its funds and policy, but on the workers for its votes. The ideal solution would be to turn the wheel of history back and set both classes once again against the landed interest, as had been done eighty years before. Out of this struggle the Liberal Party had been born: if it could be revived, would not the Party revive too? ' The People *versus* the Dukes ': the cry was ready, the dog-fight started.

The majority of the Conservative Lords were rich, greedy, stupid and old: they were no match for a Welsh attorney. They had walked straight into Lloyd George's trap. He presented a Budget which proposed some small taxes upon land—too small to be in any way oppressive or in fact of any fiscal value. He accompanied this proposal with some of his most skilled and unrestrained invective against the great landlords. Losing their tempers, as they had almost surely been meant to do, the Peers broke through precedent by striking the duties out of the Budget. It was only the climax of a series of malevolent interferences: but it was indefensible outside the House (as Lloyd George knew it would be), because it was so obviously due to greed of money and because it was an invasion of what had for generations been regarded as a purely House of Commons sphere.

It is a great advantage to have fools for your enemies. Lloyd George needed to do nothing more than insult the Peers in public speeches—one of the more famous of these was the Limehouse speech in which he announced his unexpected friendship for Lansbury. The enraged noblemen did the rest for him. The terms of the Budget were swiftly forgotten: what was now in dispute was the right of the Lords to hold up or alter legislation at all. No sense of reality stopped these foolish men: they accepted the battle on this ground, and even showed their stupid and spoiled faces on platforms up and down the country, arguing to voters that they were their natural rulers by culture and birth. The fight went on for two years, involving satisfactorily widespread enthusiasm and raising no inconvenient economic questions. Would the Lords, twice defeated at the polls, give way? Would the King have to create just under 500 Liberal peers to break their resistance? All the country, and not only the 499 Liberal worthies waiting in the party corridors, watched breathless through 1911. A sigh of mingled delight and disappointment rose when the ' Die-hards ' were turned out of their last ditch and the Parliament Act was passed. The Act was no solution of the problem of the Lords: it merely removed Money Bills from their purview, and permitted the Commons to pass other Bills over their veto after roughly a two-year interval.

There had to be more thought behind the other devices used to meet working-class discontent. The Poor Law Report, with its unfortunate proposals, so widely publicised and so regrettably practical, saw to that. The Insurance Acts, covering health and unemployment, and passed in 1911 and 1912, were the Liberals' reply. Their object was scarcely disguised: John

Burns went about saying: 'This has dished the Webbs!' and in May 1911, just after the Chancellor's speech, C. F. G. Masterman, the clever young Liberal M.P. who was Lloyd George's chief assistant, came up to Lansbury and said, grinning with glee: 'We have spiked your guns, eh?'

The provisions of the Acts were briefly these.

One part of the Act—the second and smaller scheme—was for unemployment insurance. It applied to only a few trades—building, shipbuilding, mechanical engineering and iron-founding, vehicle-making and saw-milling. Slightly over two million workers were affected by it: each worker paid twopence halfpenny a week, his employer the same amount and the State would contribute one-third of what those two paid. The contributions would be collected by the employer, who would stick fivepence in stamps upon his workers' cards and take twopence halfpenny off their wages. For this the worker was entitled, male or female, to seven shillings a week when out of work—up to a total of one week for every five stamps and never for more than thirteen weeks in the year. The scheme was operated through the newly-set-up Labour Exchanges—places whose professed object had merely been to cramp the exploitation of workers by various ravenous private labour agencies, but which were to become in the next quarter of the century the most important buildings in many workers' economic life. Limited though it was, this part of the Act served (partially at least) to put out of practical politics the Labour Party's Right to Work Bill, which it had presented to Parliament at regular intervals, only to have it denounced by the Liberals as nonsensical economically and morally wicked.

Part I, however, was far wider-reaching and excited much greater attention. It dealt with Health Insurance, and it covered some fifteen million people. It was in no way equal to the 1948 scheme, but it did provide, so far as benefits were concerned, something which the average working-man (or woman) had hardly dreamt of before. He was to have his own family doctor (almost at once known as 'the panel doctor'); medicines were to be supplied; sickness benefit while he was ill would be payable; for women a 'maternity benefit' was to be paid. Stamps were used, as for unemployment insurance. Threepence a week was paid by every employer for each worker; male workers paid fourpence and female threepence; the State put twopence in the kitty. The scheme was to be self-supporting: nevertheless, for threepence or fourpence the worker would get ninepenn'orth of medical assistance. The existing health insurance societies—the Oddfellows, the Hearts of Oak, and the more sedate trade unions—were not to be put out of action. Far from it; though perverse contributors could draw their benefits from the Post Office, they were encouraged to join the existing societies, who would administer the scheme as soon as they were recognised as Approved Societies. The implication of this arrangement was not immediately realised. But there were several trade union secretaries who considered that if their society's financial arrangements were made sufficiently sound to be ' approved ', there might be a very large increase of membership indeed from these fifteen millions.

The presentation of the scheme in 1911 (it came into effect in 1912) started an uproar which amply replaced the din caused by the Lords' resistance. Doctors, Conservative ladies, and Left-wing Socialists all clamoured against it. But there was an irresistible slogan embedded in the proposals: it was ' Ninepence for Fourpence '. Lloyd George (as he always did till 1922) had calculated correctly: it had an almost universal appeal. If it had not had, his Conservative opponents, accommodating as ever, would have made it irresistible. They packed the London and provincial halls with vulgar meetings. Shrill women from the suburbs and solid women from the shires swore ' never to lick stamps ' for ' a Slimehouse lawyer ', so that their housemaids could have some resources or some attention when they were ill. There was no real strength behind this defiance, and the large ladies who uttered it had too little imagination to know what was its effect on ' the lower orders '.

It was this campaign which foredoomed any attack on Lloyd George from the Left. MacDonald and most of his party were in favour of the Bill, but at first there was a powerful opposition, whose leader was Lansbury. After a little hesitation, Snowden joined him, and to them were added Keir Hardie, Will Thorne, Jim O'Grady and Fred Jowett. At one party meeting the Members were split exactly half and half (Lansbury reported secretly to the Webbs). More than half—twenty-seven—M.P.s voted with him after that. Lloyd George infuriated Austen Chamberlain by saying that ' Lansbury had taken the position of leader of the Opposition '. MacDonald wrote to Jowett's Bradford supporters saying that their Member took instructions on how to vote in the lobbies from Lansbury instead of from the Whips, and that unless this ceased he, MacDonald, would have to resign. The rebels' case had a sound basis in logic. Until this moment it had been assumed that if social reforms were needed, the State should pay for them, and take the money from those taxpayers who could best afford to contribute. This it was that caused such resistance to free education, to school meals, to sanitary regulations, to the provision of water supplies, or to the relief of the unemployed. The class struggle came into each such proposal; and the governing class was not going to pay a penny more than it had to. Now, it seemed, Lloyd George's ingenious advisers had by-passed the whole financial problem. The working-class would pay for its own relief. Part of the money would come directly out of the workers' pockets. Part would nominally be paid by the employers, but everyone knew that, as it was a statutory charge, it would merely be added to the price of the goods, and once again be paid very largely by the working-class. The State's contribution might still (through the Income Tax or taxes on luxuries) be taken from the rich, or in the future be taken from them so; but it was going to be a third or less. A new and very smart way of financing ' reforms ' had been invented. It would be extended and invoked whenever a fresh campaign to raise the workers' standard of life was started. The trick would work until the working-class realised that it was being fooled into putting money out of one pocket into another; and that might not be for decades.

The argument might be logical, but it was ineffectual; the chant of ' Ninepence for Fourpence ' prevented it ever being heard. MacDonald never had any occasion to implement his threat of resignation: indeed, it probably would not have been made otherwise. Still, it is impossible not to feel some sympathy with him in his dealings with his new recruit. Hardie defied rules from time to time, but his was an exceptional position, and he could in the last resort always be relied on to support Mac-

Donald's authority. Thorne and O'Grady only broke loose under great provocation. Snowden was persistently vitriolic and openly contemptuous; but he generally managed to see that his protests were within the Party constitution, and he worked very hard at the duties and subjects assigned to him in the House. Lansbury alone behaved as if Party discipline did not exist, and Party policy was what each Member considered right in his Socialist conscience. Within the House he generally, but not always, voted as the Whips would wish, and spoke more or less in agreement with what might be considered, by a latitudinarian observer, to be Labour policy. Outside, in his voyaging up and down the country, he accepted no restraint at all. He denounced the Executive, the Insurance Bill, the evasions over women's suffrage, and the whole policy of co-operation with the Liberals as roundly and as candidly as if no Party decisions on these points had ever been made. Nor did he denounce them in any measured way. Lansbury in the early nineteen hundreds was not the white-haired and kindly ' G. L.' who was so loved in the thirties. The white whiskers were ginger, framing a face which was not then one of Roman dignity so much as of rounded enthusiasm—the mouth tending to drop open in moments of excitement, the expressive eyes restless and emotional. Slightly out of fashion already, with his whiskers and the ' boater ' he wore as frequently as his bowler, he was a genial and beloved figure, respected for his hard work and his selfless enthusiasm, but not, as yet, for his wisdom. He was carried away, by his own admission, once he was on a platform: there were many to respect and work with him, but not many to accept his guidance.

One time when he was reproached for acting independently, it was his colleagues who were proved wrong. Sir Rufus Isaacs made a warm defence of himself and Lloyd George against a charge of buying Marconi shares at a time when they had private knowledge that the Post Office was about to enter into a very profitable contract for wireless transmitters. His denials appeared at the time to be all-embracing; Lansbury alone continued to be unconvinced. He said in the Commons that the behaviour of the Ministers throughout the debate had been most uneasy, and he asked for further inquiry. The *Daily News* next morning said that he was the only man in the House evil-minded

enough to doubt the Ministers' word. Lansbury, in fact, had in
his pocket anonymous letters which gave a pretty accurate
account of what had occurred, but (he wrote twenty years later)
' I hadn't the courage, and I haven't even now, to use anonymous
letters '. Very few weeks had passed when it was shown that
the Ministers had been far from frank: they *had* bought, and
profitably bought, shares in Marconi's. However, the Company
concerned was the American, not the British, Marconi, which
would gain no direct benefit from the Government contracts.
The Ministers escaped anything worse than a damage to their
reputations.

Lansbury introduced a Bill for holidays with pay, which got
no farther than the first reading. He tried, but failed, to adjourn
the House on the prosecution of Tom Mann and the Bowman
brothers for publishing and selling a ' Don't Shoot! ' leaflet
addressed to soldiers. He very nearly succeeded in getting onto
the Statute Book a Bill giving Church of England clergymen the
right to sit in the House of Commons, as Nonconformist parsons
did. It was ' talked out ' by Sir Frederick Banbury, an elderly
Conservative M.P. who had achieved some fame by a device
commoner in the American Senate than in England—that of
talking rubbish at inordinate length in order to prevent the con-
clusion of business.

This was only one of the forms of obstruction which the Conservative Party had started. It is an historical oddity, at the
least, that the Party which considered itself the support of law
and order should have taken the first steps to making Parliamentary government impossible. Banbury's resurrection of the
' filibuster ', once employed by the Irish, was the least dramatic
device. His colleagues sensed the weakness of the Liberal
Government, felt that they would defeat it at the next election,
and believed that they should have done so at the last. They
behaved like loutish fifth-formers to a headmaster who was
scared of them and was due to lose his job next term. They
shouted and yelled insults—one even threw a book at the
Treasury Bench. They organised the chanting of schoolboy
insults: ' Go out and get a drink! Go out and get a drink! '
they roared at Asquith, whose alcoholic habits were certainly
no worse than those of some of their leaders. Sometimes actual

fighting seemed very near: Lansbury noted the two Cecils as among the most 'vulgar and rowdy'.

But Lansbury's attention was more occupied by another subject: his anger was greater against the Government than the Opposition. It was not unexpected to him for noblemen to behave like louts, nor even for them to cover up and defend preparations for armed rebellion in Ulster (though he did not, any more than the others, yet realise how serious that might be); but the violence and evasion of the Government towards the women who were demanding the vote both surprised and enraged him. Pretty soon he felt this subject become more important than any other for him. It even eclipsed for a while his devotion to Socialism: it soon filled his whole horizon.

Chapter Ten

THERE were two causes fighting for primacy in George Lansbury's mind in the years 1911 and 1912, and it might have been expected that the women's cause would have come second. For the other claimant, the workers' struggle—'*the* cause' by definition for every Socialist—was especially acute in these two years, and he was affected more closely by it than before. The two years were filled with great strikes, upon a scale never seen before, in which, of course, his sympathies and energies were wholly on the workers' side. The first to come out were the sailors and firemen, in 1911: starting with Southampton, Goole and Hull, they closed almost every port of size in the island. They defeated a traditionally autocratic and very angry set of employers, securing long-overdue increases in wages. The dockers followed in August: they had not secured a rise since 1889, and their victory was equally complete this time. Next a general strike, an almost complete hold-up, a thing never seen before, silenced the whole city of Liverpool the same month. Then there followed another new thing, a railway strike—not a complete one, but successful enough to force the Government to intervene and give the workers several concessions. The miners came out in March 1912—'about a million of them' estimated the frightened Board of Trade—and were only got back to work by a Minimum Wage Act. In August of that year the Transport Workers' Federation unwisely called a second national strike: it failed because of inadequate response in the provinces. Lansbury worked hard to save the strike in London. There was no relief in those days, except from the Guardians, and these would generally refuse to assist men 'wantonly refusing work'. It was the sight of their own starving children which in the end defeated the dockers. Lansbury did his best, and he was already an expert in raising money: among the few records of this period which remain is an exchange of telegrams with the Archbishop of Canterbury, in which he tried to induce the pontiff to start a Red Cross fund or to intervene with the employers. ' You know how keen and deep is our sympathy with the starving sufferers ', was all the assistance he got.

He was already on the committee of a new paper called the *Daily Herald*, having been bustled into it almost forcibly by Ben Tillett; this paper, which will be described later, was syndicalist in tone and closely connected with the new strike movement. There was every emotional reason for him to throw his energies into the class struggle. Yet he turned aside almost entirely during these two years: in his devotion to the women's suffrage struggle he nearly severed his connection with the Labour movement. He acted with extreme impetuousness, and in one instance (as he would admit in later years) with considerable unwisdom. Rashness was not so surprising in 1912 as it would have been a few years later: but that he should have neglected so completely the cause to which he had given his life is even now astonishing.

The reasons for his complete obsession for a short while in the women's movement were, of course, many. Something must be allowed for the dramatic nature of the injustice to the suffragists. Four hundred M.P.s were pledged to support ' votes for women ', and yet by repeated Parliamentary tricks the vote was withheld. Suffragettes were sharply punished for trivial violences like stone-throwing, while open organisation for armed civil war and mutiny by the Carsonites was completely unpunished. Again, the demand for the vote was not only one that was obviously just, but it was one which could have been granted with the greatest of ease. But it is probable that the final reason for Lansbury's extreme anger and whole-hearted self-sacrifice was one which would not really have commended itself to the Pankhurst family and their followers if they had realised it. Lansbury was a Victorian father of a family: he believed, with all his mind, in sex equality; with all his emotions he believed that women were weaker vessels who needed protection. He saw women being manhandled by policemen and by roughs; he saw them tormented and brought to the verge of death by forcible feeding and the Cat and Mouse Act—a quite deliberate cruelty due to individual and named politicians, cold Asquith, sly Lloyd George, priggish McKenna. The sight, for him, was like the sight of a lout kicking a child: the anger it provoked was similarly noble but unrestrained.

It drew him from support of the Suffragists to support of the Suffragettes. To an audience which has probably forgotten both words it must be explained that the first—the Suffragists— were law-abiding women and men, mostly organised in Mrs. Fawcett's National Union of Women's Suffrage Societies. Their weapon was reason: they used public meetings, processions, petitions and propaganda. There was no trace in their publications of any ' anti-man ' mentality; their principles and methods would normally have been Lansbury's. Their organisation was democratic: decisions were taken by properly elected national conferences after careful discussion in local branches. None of these things were true of the Suffragettes, the members of the Women's Social and Political Union. Constitutional procedure in their opinion was a failure. Any form of agitation which attracted attention should be used: breaking up meetings, throwing stones, smashing windows, rioting in the House of Commons, cutting up golf greens, slashing pictures in the National Gallery, burning up the contents of pillar-boxes, firing houses, and whatever else a woman could think of. There was a marked contempt for men as men within the W.S.P.U.; though it has been exaggerated, there may have been a certain amount of sexual abnormality. The Union was not at all democratic; it was from the beginning directed authoritatively by six persons: the Pankhurst family (Mrs. Pankhurst and her daughters, Christabel, Sylvia and Adela) and Mr. and Mrs. Pethick Lawrence. Adela went abroad. Sylvia fell from grace by organising working-women in the East End—there was an odd strain of snobbishness in the directing circles of the Union. Then there were four left: the Pethick Lawrences, in the middle of 1912, could no longer put up with the autocratic methods of the remaining Pankhursts, and parted from them amicably. Then there were two: Christabel went to Paris to direct the movements from safety, since not all the leaders could be in prison at once. Her mother went to prison, hunger-struck, was reduced to extreme weakness, was released, was rearrested, hunger-struck again—and so forth, twelve times in all. She was no longer a general; she was a front-line soldier and almost a casualty. Then there was one: the autocrat Christabel, who was by now flinging her devoted and hysterical followers into the conflict with as much sense as one can find in the nursery rhyme.

The Union arrived at this condition by a series of steps which were forced on it by circumstances, or by the folly and cowardice of the Liberal Government, as it would have said. ' Militancy' itself had been almost an accidental discovery. At the end of 1905 Sir Edward Grey was addressing a Manchester meeting upon the programme of the Liberal Government which would shortly take office. Annie Kenney, in the audience, tried to ask a question on women's suffrage; Grey (who supported it) would not answer. Christabel Pankhurst also tried to ask it. They sent up the question in writing: still Grey refused to answer. Then the two girls made what was called ' a scene '. Large-hatted, with long skirts to their ankles, and broad leather belts round their waists, they stood up and cried—no doubt a little shrilly and embarrassedly—' Votes for Women! ' and that it was shameful for a politician to refuse to answer an important and reasonable question such as theirs. They were ejected, with a great deal of noise but no roughness: they found that large numbers of the audience waited to hear what they had to say when they spoke outside, that the Liberal dignitary found it necessary to make a special explanation of his views on suffrage to the Press afterwards, and that the papers gave their protest more space than a year's peaceful propaganda had secured.

The lesson was learnt: meetings were regularly interrupted henceforward by women who cried ' Votes for Women ' and waved small green, white and purple flags. They even called out ' Divide! divide! ' from the Ladies' Gallery of the House of Commons in May 1906 to Members who were prosing along over a resolution on the suffrage, but they were a little abashed by the universal disapproval this aroused. (Later they were able to get to the point of throwing bags of flour at hostile Members from the gallery, and until 1940 there existed a grill in front of the gallery to prevent this recurring.)

Their next tactic was to organise mass deputations—' mass ' at this date means fifty to a hundred persons—from suffrage meetings to march to the House of Commons. These deputations would be stopped by the police, whose duty it had been since the Gordon riots to prevent any large assemblies near the House; the women would refuse to go back; there would be a decorous scuffle and several would be arrested. Next morning there would be court cases, charges of obstruction, speeches from the dock, fines and excellent propaganda. The Liberal Government, however was artful enough to deal with that; the police were instructed to arrest the women, but not to charge them. They were released after the deputations had been dissolved: there was no chance for propaganda. Something else had to be done: the W.S.P.U. decided upon 'technical assaults' which could not be ignored. Mrs. Pankhurst, taking the initiative, slapped Inspector Jervis in the face on the steps of the House of Commons. At this date there was still courtesy between the antagonists: Mrs. Pankhurst's slap was the gentlest and most formal touch, and the Inspector made a point of stating that no offence was taken. But even though arrests followed, the Government stayed indifferent: nominal or at least little-noticed sentences followed. The next step was stone-throwing and the breaking of windows. This at least could not be ignored: the Press was filled with gratifying denunciation. More severe sentences were imposed. Then, in prison, the suffragettes thought of two new devices. They first refused to obey prison rules: this had a double advantage, for it called attention not only to their cause but to the maladministration of Edwardian prisons and the petty spitefulness of their regulations. Next they refused to eat any food. The Home Office kept them until they were very weak and sick, but it was not prepared to let them die. The 'hunger-strike', as it was called, was at first successful.

The first Parliament of 1910 passed a Conciliation Bill as far as the second reading: it met most of the women's claims, and the Suffragettes, on the appeal of the Suffragists, held up their campaign. The squabble with the Lords followed; there had to be a new election, and in the new Parliament the Government abandoned the Conciliation Bill, promising an Adult Suffrage Bill, which might be amended (if the House chose) so as to enfranchise women. The Prime Minister, Asquith, announced that on such an amendment he would oppose giving the vote to women, and the Suffragettes, with the equivalent of ' I told you so ', re-started militancy.

Over the winter of 1911–12 the Suffragette campaign was intensified. It had not yet reached the stage of arson: it consisted chiefly of stone-throwing and interruption of meetings. But the Government, unable or unwilling to repress the far more dangerous activities of the Ulstermen, seemed to be relieving its feelings by increased viciousness towards the women. An age which has seen the horrors of Nazism finds it difficult to realise how shocked humane Englishmen were at what was now a systematic routine. The women who made their protest were sent to prison, where, as was expected, they went on hunger-strike. They were then ' forcibly fed ': this, which sounds a mild process, was a very painful and ineffective one. The instruments used were brutal, the shock was violent, the intake of food was negligible, and within a short while the victim was reduced to prostration. She would be discharged, not exhausted, but seriously ill. (The *Lancet* published a medical report emphasising the dangerous nature of the treatment.) But the preoccupation of the Home Office was to see that no woman actually died while in prison: in this it succeeded, but the correspondence of M.P.s was full of desperately anxious letters from the friends of women whose survival was uncertain.

There were stated to be 186 women suffering from this particular persecution when the Government, in March 1912, decided upon a stroke intended to break down the W.S.P.U. Mrs. Pankhurst and Mr. and Mrs. Pethick Lawrence, as the Union's directors, were arrested and charged with ' conspiracy '. The charge was unexpected: if political conspiracy was to be revived as a crime there were several guiltier defendants insulting the Government daily from the Ulster benches in the House of Commons. But women had no votes, no arms, no Orange Lodges: the three leaders were sentenced to nine months in the second division. Public protest secured their transfer, as political prisoners, to the first division, but when they discovered that this privilege was not to be extended to the ordinary suffragette, they went on hunger-strike. In June they were released— Mrs. Pankhurst in a dangerous condition and unable to stand.

The next day (June 25th, 1912), Tim Healy, kind-hearted

and witty Irish M.P., with unusual solemnity asked the Prime Minister if he would not at least discharge some other ill women who, as everyone knew, would have to be let free in a few days. ' Why keep up this endless torture? ' Several Liberal M.P.s tittered, and Mr. Lloyd, a young and smart Tory, rose to ask if ' any more concessions to law-breaking ' would be made. Asquith was more than usually contemptuously official: ' Any one of these prisoners could leave prison to-morrow,' he said, ' if she would give the proper undertaking.' The arrogant tone, and the recollection of the desperately ill women that he had seen, was more than one of the Members could bear. A roar of indignation came from a corner below the gangway. ' You know they cannot,' shouted Lansbury. ' You know it is dishonourable to ask them. You disgrace yourself.' Laughter turned to clamour, though Asquith maintained his usual still silence. But Lansbury meant to be listened to: he pushed his way to the Treasury bench and shook his fist in the Premier's face. ' You are beneath contempt,' he told him. ' You drive women mad and then tell them to walk out! You, to talk of principle! And you too,' he said, turning to the Conservatives, who were yelling at him by now, ' you ought to be driven out of public life. These women are showing you what principle is. You should honour them, instead of laughing at them.'

By this time the whole House was in an uproar: Asquith scarlet with embarrassment, Lansbury white with anger, the Speaker repeatedly ordering him to be silent, the Members leaping up and crying out. At last Lansbury went back to his seat; his passion exhausted, he argued for a little with the Speaker, who insisted that he should leave the House. Will Crooks came across to him to persuade him to obey: he hesitated and looked, unexpectedly enough, to Ramsay MacDonald. After all, he probably thought, MacDonald was his party's leader. MacDonald urgently signalled him to go; he left the House heavy-hearted. A colleague on the National Administrative Council of the I.L.P., Harry Dubery, met him in the lobby and was scared by his haggard pallor. He walked slowly with him to Westminster Bridge and on to the underground station, intentionally chattering to him about trivial Council matters, in the hope of distracting his mind. The M.P. looked so ill that Dubery wanted to see him home to Bow, but dared not offer to; he went home fearing his friend was on the edge of a breakdown. Lansbury went to bed sick and despairing.

The next morning he was astonished to find himself a hero. In all his life he never received, for one action, such a flood of gratitude and praise. His explosion of anger had come at the right moment; thousands of women and men seemed just then to have reached the point of exasperation. The many hundreds of letters and telegrams which poured in during the next two days would have shaken a far more cold-blooded man. A large box full of them still exists: one only, and that anonymous, is hostile (saying, ' If you do not exercise more self-control you will in time lose your reason '). The rest are of every tone, but all enraptured. They are exuberant: ' I wish you *had* hit Asquith!!! ' (Marianne Dale); ' I only wish you had pulled old Asquith's nose ' (L. B. Warden); naive, ' I think you should have a knighthood ' (Ada Blundell), ' I thank you on behalf of the Virtuous Sex ' (anonymous); upper class, ' Mrs. Henderson and Family desire to expre∫s their thanks ', ' the Rev. R. B. L. and Mrs. Exon wish to express their gratitude '; working-class, ' As an East-End working-woman I thank you from my heart ' (Ellen Spencer), ' Allow a working-woman to thank you . . . women like myself who have familys to keep and can do so little to help do indeed feel grateful ' (Mrs. B. Palmer); critical of his silent colleagues ' perjured hirelings ' (Robert Horsfeld), ' blighters ' (H. D. Harben); and plain laudatory: ' You were roused by a brutal laugh at the sufferings of women who were neither near nor dear to you ' (Mrs. Rebecca Scott-Hamilton): the *Daily Herald* in its leader said three times ' Thank God for Lansbury! '

One letter, more sympathetic than might have been expected, tried to call him back to moderation.

' I wanted a word with you, for one thing to tell you how deeply obliged I was to you for taking my advice ' (to leave the House), wrote MacDonald. '. . . As you know, I am not made as you are and—probably it is a great weakness—I always regret scenes. I would run to the wilderness to avoid them. But you stood manfully up, and if I thought you were right, I would offer you the most unqualified praise. But, my dear man, are you sure you are right?

Is all this going to enfranchise women? I wish I saw clearly on that point. I am sure you feel you are doing the best thing, however, and so long as that is so do not let me or anyone else take your enthusiasm out of you. It is valuable for the righteousness which you in your way and, I hope, I in mine are trying to help along.'

The appeal might have been more successful if it had not coincided with a long article by MacDonald in the *Daily Chronicle* denouncing the Suffragettes, and all who behaved in a disorderly manner, as enemies of women's freedom. Lansbury did not indeed make any more scenes in the House, but he started, for the first time, a systematic attempt to reverse Parliamentary policy and undermine Parliamentary leadership. He circularised a large number of local I.L.P.s, Labour Parties and similar bodies with a proposal for a new Parliamentary policy. It was not a policy supported by either H. N. Brailsford or Keir Hardie—the women's best friends and most trusted advisers in the Labour movement. Brailsford considered that the Party should only vote against the new Reform Bill on the third Reading, if by then women's suffrage had not been included in it. The other provisions of the Bill were, after all, all improvements on the existing system. Hardie considered the Party should vote continuously against the Bill until women's suffrage were included in it. But this would not do for Lansbury. Advised now only by Mrs. Pankhurst and Christabel, and by his own emotion, he proposed that the Party should be instructed to vote against *every* Government measure until the introduction of an official measure for women's suffrage. This would have involved some very serious decisions—for example, voting with Carson and Bonar Law against Irish Home Rule—but so indignant were many local Labour Parties that Lansbury got a very considerable favourable response.

Not only MacDonald felt that now he had gone unforgivably far. To object to Party policy at M.P.s' meetings in the House was fair enough, to make unauthorised scenes under provocation was excusable, to speak in violent terms in the provinces could be overlooked: but to attempt to mobilise their own constituents against his fellow-M.P.s was something that it was not safe to tolerate. Lansbury himself later admitted that the Parliamentary Party's reaction was ' justifiable ', though he always added that he, too, could not honestly have acted otherwise than he did. Anyhow, its reaction was sharp enough. It condemned the terms of the circular, it condemned the action of issuing it at all, and it required that in future Mr. Lansbury should conform to the policy of the Party of which he was a member and in whose name and with whose aid he had carried his seat.

In reply he could have done one of three things. He could have obeyed and promised good behaviour in the future; but nobody who knew him expected that. He could have ignored the demand and hoped that it would be forgotten; in view of the universal respect for his integrity, that was not impossible. Or he could have accepted the implications, resigned from the Party and become a solitary Independent in the House; he would probably have been fairly happy in that position. Instead, he crossed to Boulogne and consulted with Miss Christabel and Mrs. Pankhurst, who persuaded him there was a brilliant fourth device. This was, to resign his seat and contest it again as a suffrage candidate. The advice was as bad as it could be; but it could not have seemed bad to them. Women's suffrage was the only cause in which they were interested : none of Lansbury's other interests appealed to them at all. Like their own Union members, like themselves, he was merely a piece on the board in the game of chess that they were playing. To have an M.P. resign over the treatment of the Suffragettes, to have a by-election fought on the question of votes for women and no other subject at all—this was superb propaganda. If the M.P. concerned broke his political neck, what of it? If the word had been invented, they would have said that Mr. Lansbury was 'expendable'.

That he was over-worked and over-tired is shown by the manner of his resignation. He did not inform his colleagues on the I.L.P. Council—that may have been deliberate. But he also forgot to inform, let alone consult, his supporters in the Poplar Labour Representation Committee (as it was still called). They felt slighted, and, because they knew certain things about an electorate that neither he nor the Pankhursts realised, they thought his action a foolish one. Moreover, Joe Banks, their railwayman secretary, did not care twopence for women's suffrage, and that side of the election organisation was run sullenly by a man in a very bad temper. The Pankhursts sent down a young woman organiser who refused to work with the Labour people at all: ' the Union would never allow us to work under the men ', she said. Arthur Henderson, in charge of national Labour Party affairs while MacDonald was in India, prevented national speakers coming to aid Lansbury, thus starting an antagonism not healed for many years. Lloyd George, who had supported him in 1910, now told his friends ' Blair, the Conservative, is my man '.

The candidate had to rely upon his own energies and the enthusiasm of his personal friends. That might well have been enough. He was untiring, and his supporters were moved with something of his own flaring enthusiasm. Even Mrs. Lansbury, who rarely intervened, sent out a short letter to the electors. And the suffragette speakers, however difficult they might be to work with, at least never spared themselves. But there was a hostility which only the old stagers in the local Party had foreseen. The electors were angry. They had put George Lansbury in a post plenty of people would have been mighty glad to have, and he had walked out of it. He was annoyed at the way the women were treated, was he? All right; he could have stayed at Westminster and said so. If he didn't want the job, he needn't have it. ' There are still people in the division,' he wrote in 1928, ' who never vote at an election because they will not vote against me, but will not vote for me because of the action I took in 1912.'

He went to the poll in October 1912 and was defeated: his majority of 863 was turned to a minority of 731. The shock was severe to him; momentarily it was even worse to the suffragettes. Their young organiser, wrote Sylvia Pankhurst, ' exclaimed, " What will Christabel say? " and then opened her mouth and cried noisily like a child '. By the W.S.P.U., however, the disaster was soon forgotten; but Lansbury was more severely shaken.

There were correspondents enough to assure him that everything was well. Christabel, in a great splashing handwriting, wrote, ' The real victory is what you have done, and not what the electors have done '. Even Mrs. Fawcett, her constitutionalist rival, wrote to say, ' No great effort for what is right is ever wasted '; Joe Banks, perhaps remorseful, congratulated him ' on the splendid fight you put up for the women '. The letters from working-men were on the whole rather different in tone from the Suffragists': ' How ungrateful the rank and file are,' said Will Thorne, but added, ' no constituency could be won on *Votes for Women* ', not even his, with 4,000 majority. Ben Tillett was furious, but ' the selfish thought creeps into my heart ' that Lansbury could now be used for ' the greater work of the movement '. Lansbury brooded over his defeat, and in the end he deduced from it a general principle, which might be briefly stated in the two words: ' Never resign '. A Socialist might leave a job which he had taken up because of overwork, ill-health or a genuine knowledge of his own unfitness, but not for any other reason. If he had undertaken some work or occupied a certain post, then he must stay there doing all that he could to carry out his instructions, until he was expelled or his con-stituents dismissed him. Nothing else would be understood. Resignations ' on principle ' or ' to call attention ' to this or that would be regarded as self-indulgent (or, as he more mercilessly put it, ' childish '); quite probably they were so.

Probably it was lucky for him that he lost his seat: he was over-working seriously, and Harry Dubery was not the only one who was anxious. But though the pressure on him was relaxed, he was unwilling to rest. He now had two preoccupations: one was the *Daily Herald*, in which he began to take a much more consistent interest, and the other remained the Vote. Since he had been turned out of Parliament, he was a common soldier in the struggle, and he deliberately set out to share the sufferings of the Suffragettes. His speeches contained set incitements to violence (always with the distinct exception of ' anything that might endanger life '). His home was a centre for the organisa-tion of illegal or banned meetings. Once one of his daughters, Daisy, dressed up as Sylvia Pankhurst, who had been tracked down there by the police when she was on the run: the girl ostentatiously left the house, and was at once set upon by the police and carried off to the station, while Miss Pankhurst left sedately by another exit and appeared on the platform at the meeting in the Roman Road Baths which the police had deter-mined she should not address. (Here Lansbury's instinct to secure the maximum publicity out of everything did not desert him. There still remains a Counsel's Opinion secured upon a suggestion that his daughter should proceed against the police for false arrest; Bradlaugh was the only other politician who would have thought of that.) When the Poplar Borough Council cancelled its lettings of halls to militants and would not hear him speak, he 'swept to the floor all the Town Clerk's books and papers and all the documents he could lay hands on'; his family assisted the cause by breaking windows and throwing stones.

Two skilled blows (as it seemed) had been struck at the women. The one, the least expected, was that when at last the motion was moved in the House of Commons to amend the Adult Suffrage Bill to include women, the Speaker ruled the amendment out of order. That, and no more; the whole Parliamentary campaign had to start from the beginning again. The second was that the Government had discovered, as it thought, an ingenious means of countering the hunger-strike, which was christened the 'Cat and Mouse Act'. It provided, in effect if not in set terms, that when a suffragette went on hunger-strike she could be detained until the doctor certified her life to be in danger; she could then be released and allowed to recover; then rearrested and held until she was again at the gates of death; then released, and so forth indefinitely. Inhumanity was rare and disgusting in 1913; the device was not universally applauded. It provoked Lansbury, among others, to court arrest. On April 10th, 1913, at the Albert Hall (already his favourite rostrum), he said: 'When you are tricked and deceived, when Parliament betrays its sacred trust, you have a right to rebel. Let all of us here stand shoulder to shoulder with the militant women! Let them burn and destroy! For every leader that is taken, let a dozen more stand forth!'

A few days later he was arrested, and prosecuted (of all things) under a law of Edward III (I Edw. III, c.16). Not only did this classify him as 'a wanderer, a beggar, or a piller from across the seas', but somewhere about 1515 a copying clerk had left out a 'not' in the statute which made it even more grotesque. Everything possible was made of this, and Archibald Bodkin, the prosecutor, was extremely vexed; but the end was inevitable. Lansbury was sentenced to be bound over or to serve six months;

he refused to be bound over, and was taken to Pentonville, and went on a hunger-and-thirst strike.

As a preparation, he had taken nothing but water for some days before. In a few days he was very weak, and the East End became very restless. A special issue of *The Worker* (a paper issued by the Poplar Labour Representation Committee when it thought fit), dated August 1913, was sold over half London. The whole of its second page was filled with an address ' To my Bow and Bromley Friends ', telling them how ' The Liberal Government . . . have cast me into jail without trial by jury ', while they allowed ' without prosecution Sir E. Carson, Bonar Law, the Duke of Abercorn and F. E. Smith to arm with cannon, bayonet and guns an army in Ulster ', and ended naturally as he would have ended any other letter :

' With love and best wishes,
' Always,
' George Lansbury '.

In prison, he records,

' A young chaplain came to me and rebuked me because I was hunger-striking, saying I was defiling the temple of the Holy Ghost— my body. I asked this bright young spark if he was a Protestant. He said " yes " so I replied : " You are able to come here and insult me because two men named Latimer and Ridley allowed their temple of the Holy Ghost to be destroyed by fire because they would not submit to the laws of the land, just as I will not submit to the laws of the land as to what I shall say about political agitation." The young man cleared out without saying another word.'

Dainties were placed before him (' poached eggs and a pot of freshly made tea ' he remembered fifteen years later, with genuine longing), but he resisted. Thirst strikes are more dangerous than hunger strikes; he was a middle-aged man who had till recently been an M.P. and was widely loved in the East End; the Government wanted no trouble; in a short while he was released under the Cat and Mouse Act, and was never troubled again.

During these years, when Lansbury and others like him were devoting their energies wholeheartedly to ' the vote ' it was not, as Mr. Dangerfield and other historians have thought, an un-requited gift secured by the art of the Suffragettes. In the short run Lansbury may have been the victim of the Pankhursts' strategy, though he himself never thought so. But in the long run the Socialist movement benefited at least as much as the women. Each side was educated by the other. The Labour movement, trade unionist or Socialist, had until about 1910 been predominantly a male movement. It was forced, slowly and sometimes unwillingly, to admit the principle of sex equality—to accept women comrades as equals and to elect them to committees and to offices. The lessons learned during the suffrage cam-paigns were gradually assimilated—the women might be un-reasonable, but no party could do without their courage and devotion. The Labour parties and I.L.P.s found more and more women among their members and relied on them more and more. The German, French and Italian parties, which had no similar experience, were the worse for it; and are suffering from it to this day.

The Suffragists themselves benefited no less. When the agitation for the Vote started, it was a lineal descendant of the Victorian ladies' agitation started by the *Englishwoman's Journal*. Dr. Pankhurst himself had been a Socialist, but, except for Sylvia, his family and their followers soon forgot this. Women should have men's rights: that was all that was needed. Privileged women should be the equals of privileged men: there was, on the face of it, no reason to go beyond this, and in fact both Christabel and Mrs. Pankhurst ended up as Con-servatives. But many other suffragists, less dogmatic than they, saw that their only unwavering friends were extreme Socialists like Lansbury, Hardie and Brailsford. They read the books which their new friends read, listened to their speeches, and took in their papers. They found that injustice to women was not the only, nor perhaps even the most profound injustice that existed. They began to divert some of their energy, and some of their money too, to ending social injustice. There began, in 1910, a conflation, a blending together of two hard metals, which many years later was to make the British Labour movement able to survive disasters which wrecked its Continental fellows.

Momentarily, however, all that seemed clear was that the Suffrage movement was checked. The Government had hardened its heart, and one by one the suffragettes were being exhausted. Miss Davison's suicide on the Derby course shocked a few and silenced for a while the more vulgar sneers, but it did not shake the Government's resolution. Lansbury, like many others, continued to give all the support he could to the women, but all they could do seemed to be ineffective. Insensibly he found himself returning to Socialist activities. Even in his letter of resignation from the National Council of the I.L.P., in which he had spoken chiefly of their desertion of the women's cause, he had reminded them that the Labour Party had also failed in its Socialist duty. When Hardie and his colleagues had founded it, he said, their object had been to create a workers' party independent of Liberalism. The policy of MacDonald and the executive had resulted in creating a group which was as tightly tied to the Liberal Party as ever Broadhurst had been. There had been, after twenty years of work, no change at all.

The argument was unanswerable, not only by those who had criticised his devotion to the W.S.P.U., but also by himself. Gradually he found himself losing his fixed concentration on Votes for Women and returning to his old interests. Particularly, he attended to the new daily paper, the *Daily Herald*, of which he was a director.

Chapter Eleven

WHEN Lansbury became editor of the *Daily Herald* in 1913 he was fifty-four—in fact, when he took over detailed daily control in February 1914 he was fifty-five. He had lived the greater part of his active life, one might have imagined. If he had died then he would have left an honourable name behind him. But it would have been a local fame—he would have been, like Peter Lee, a man greatly loved and long remembered in a certain area, and in after years recognised by historians who made a special study of his time or his region. It was only in his fifties, his sixties and his seventies that he became, in the words of a future premier, ' one of the best loved men in the world '. He became this, most of all, as editor of the *Daily Herald*. Even when this is written, more than a quarter of a century after he left the editorial chair, the paper which has for so long been in the majority-ownership of a commercial firm has a hold on the loyalty and affection of its readers which dates from his reign: traces of his manner and teaching are still observable in its columns. But nobody in 1913 would have expected him to become a great editor. He had had no experience in journalism. Afterwards, raking round in his memory to produce some qualifications, all he could remember was that some time in the eighties he assisted to edit ' a Radical-Labour weekly called *The Coming Times* ' which has completely vanished, and that earlier still he wrote for a manuscript magazine of the Whitechapel Young Men's Association. (The Vicar, Mr. Kitto, considered that it had agnostic tendencies, and set the contributors to reading Butler's *Analogy*, which killed both the magazine and their interest in theology.) It may have been partly his lack of technical equipment which made him so excellent an editor. There are three men, belonging to the three great parties, who were outstanding editors in the early part of this century—C. P. Scott of the Liberal *Manchester Guardian*, J. L. Garvin of the Conservative *Observer*, and Lansbury of the Socialist *Daily Herald*. None of them, it is surprising to note, was a particularly good writer: Scott has left nothing memorable, Garvin was wordy, Lansbury, though he could write admirably on occasion, was on the whole a clumsy stylist. But they all possessed the five essential qualities of a great journalist. They had wide knowledge and practically limitless interests; they had unusually quick apprehension (which is the foundation of a 'news-sense'); they had an absolute and immovable conviction that what they believed and wrote was true and just; they were swift to find and generous to reward talent in their colleagues; and finally they had what is loosely called 'personality'. They filled a room when they came into it: very soon after any one of them had spoken, it was a very stupid person who did not realise that here was a most exceptional man.

The *Daily Herald* was founded in 1911, in a very different Fleet Street from to-day's. Fifty thousand could be an influential circulation for a daily, 250,000 was a large one. There were over half a dozen independent London evening papers, including the *St. James's Gazette*, the *Pall Mall*, the green *Westminster* and the pink *Globe*. There was a large and prosperous provincial Press, greatly outnumbering the London Press and possibly in certain circumstances of more weight. There were no 'Press barons'; the man of importance in a newspaper office was still the editor. The days were far away when six members of the House of Lords would control the daily reading of a majority of the population (Lords Kemsley, Rothermere, Beaverbrook, Southwood, Camrose and Layton) and a sale of less than a million copies be insignificant. Only one paper, Alfred Harmsworth's *Daily Mail*, foreshadowed that period; its influence in no way corresponded to its circulation and it was despised by its own party, whose leader had described it as written by office-boys for office-boys.

The first *Daily Herald* was a strike-sheet; London journeymen printers were locked out by their masters for demanding a forty-eight-hour week, and instead of hanging idly round publichouses, brought out their own daily paper in support of their claim. The first number came out on Wednesday, January 25th, 1911, and sold 13,000 copies. There had never been a Labour daily before, and the 1911 issues are a collector's curiosity.

The compositor-journalists stuck very closely to their trade interest; when a correspondent suggested that Trade Unionists should take only papers like the *Daily Herald*, they were shocked, saying, ' Our contemporaries serve the very useful purpose of keeping large numbers of printers in employment '. But its three months' life—it closed on April 28th, ' having fulfilled its immediate purpose '—suggested to others than its proprietors the possibility of a permanent daily for trade unionists, and a committee was left behind to deal with the project. £10,000, it was optimistically felt, would be enough to start on; T. E. Naylor of the London Compositors and Ben Tillett of the Dockers were the active members of the Committee, and C. W. Bowerman, secretary of the Parliamentary Committee of the Trades Union Congress, lent them his lethargic support. The £10,000 was cut to £5,000 and then to ' less than that '; in fact, when they brought out their first number on April 15th, 1912, the reckless sponsors had barely £300 left over from immediate expenses. They had no editor—a leader was provided by ' a professional writer ', which the Committee unanimously declared intolerable, and the secretary, W. H. Seed, wrote another as best he could, and carried on until a regular editor was appointed (whose politics turned out to be such that the staff mutinied; Rowland Kenney was the first permanent editor). On the first night all the provincial trains were missed and the London agents were kept waiting for hours; work was carried on all in one huge room (at first with only one sub-editor) in which journalists, compositors, committee-men, members of the public and strike deputations all milled round together. Throughout its life the pre-1914 *Daily Herald* maintained something of the same amateurish, inconsequent and enthusiastic character. Its chances were made the worse because Clifford Allen, a young ' I.L.P.-er ', was soliciting, with MacDonald's authority, subscriptions to ' Labour Newspapers Ltd.', a body which was to (and later did) start a rival Labour Party daily, to be called the *Daily Citizen*, and to follow official policy. The directors had not realised that the ' 230,000 sale ' of the *Herald's* first few numbers was a curiosity circulation which would rapidly fall and figures would fluctuate wildly between 50,000 and 100,000. Nor had they allowed for the time that must elapse between the immediate payment of the wages bill, the printers' bill and the paper merchant's bill, and the collection of accounts from newsagents. By May 6th, 1912, Ben Tillett was writing a frantic appeal for money, 'AT ONCE! AT ONCE!! AT ONCE!!!' In October the paper was in danger of closing down—the issue of the 23rd said simply: ' We may come out again or we may not '. They did— they always did until the outbreak of war, because their readers would not let them die. On that particular night they survived because a clergyman reader and his wife came in with £150 of their savings and laid them on Lansbury's desk; on another because the staff shared out equally as its weekly wage what was in the cash-box, and received eighteenpence each; on a third because the machine-minders, when paper was refused, searched the basement of the Victoria House Printing Company and used up all the odd ends of reels, of varying size and colour, which accumulate in a printing-house. Once, when the bailiffs were actually in, Lansbury, Tillett and Robert Williams, the Transport Workers' secretary (a big, pale-faced Welsh coal-trimmer with a Neronic nose), stood in the doorway orating about the workers' struggle and preventing them moving the furniture until help came. Ben Tillett in later years said that he used to drink with Mr. Farrow of Farrow's Bank in his office in Ludgate Hill until the banker, dignified and bearded, if slightly tiddly, would go to a locker and extract from it bearer bonds of high value and press them on him ' for the sake of the workers '; but this may have been only a fantasy.

Lansbury had written for the second number an article promising that there should be no censorship, and from that day on Tillett saw that he did more and more work for the paper. So well-loved a man and so skilled a raiser of funds could not be allowed to escape; and, as was often the case on committees that he attended, Lansbury's influence became more and more dominant—especially when Tillett was worked to exhaustion by the great dock strike of 1912. But his power was not over-whelming—the replacement of Kenney as editor by Charles Lapworth, for example, was against his vote. When he took over the editorship later, the change was a small step from the influence which he had already acquired as chairman of the Board of Directors; but the growth of his power was gradual, and the minutes from which it might have been traced have been destroyed.

From its first week the *Daily Herald* justified his promise of ' no censorship '. It printed anything that the libel laws would permit (and at least five times what they would not). To get into its columns a writer had only to be a rebel; he had to be an enemy of the existing capitalist system, and what he was in favour of mattered less. It had contributors of almost every colour. Bernard Shaw, it is true, sent a postcard to Lansbury refusing to help (' Neither you nor anybody else can keep a daily Labour paper going '), and H. G. Wells, who wrote for it only once, sent a more malicious refusal. But Belloc and Chesterton wrote regularly for the paper, for little and sometimes no payment; so did younger writers: Gerald Gould, the poet; Langdon Everard, the humorist; Rebecca West, for a fortnight, at nineteen, ' Woman's Editor '; G. D. H. Cole and William Mellor, two Socialists just down from Oxford. Most brilliant of all was the Australian cartoonist, Will Dyson, whose drawings are still collected by amateurs.

Lansbury delighted in freedom more than anything else: the discordant clamour which arose from the *Herald* columns delighted him, for the reason that it showed the universality of the determination to put down oppression and poverty. But he did not fail to see that it was discordant. Chesterton and Belloc were writing to express their fury at the dishonesty and decay of the Liberal Party (particularly at the Marconi case): they delighted in the great strikes of the years 1911–14 because they regarded them as a protest against petty tyranny and great corruption. They were not really Socialists at all; they were fumbling round for a way of restoring small proprietorship, and they were to end as Roman Catholic propagandists. They had practically no sympathy with the next most vocal section of *Herald* writers, the Suffragists, who almost every day had a whole page at their disposal in which the wrongs of women were denounced and their reactions (even those of rather witless destruction of doubtful Velazquez paintings and the burning of the contents of pillar-boxes) were sympathetically celebrated. They were almost equally isolated from the pacifists (the word did not exist then; ' pro-Boers ', over a decade old, was the

nearest equivalent), who persuaded the editor to print denunciations of war as violent as the ' Don't Shoot' leaflet for which
Mann and the Bowman brothers had been prosecuted. (The
denunciations passed unnoticed and the principle of free speech
seemed to have been vindicated.) The reports of Parliamentary
debates were headed ' The House of Pretence', and anyone
who imagined any good could come out of Westminster was
kindlily or brutally mocked; but any M.P., especially Lansbury,
who tried to use the Commons machinery to right a wrong was
warmly and illogically thanked and encouraged. The loudest
voice among the ' rebels', at least after Lapworth took charge,
was the Syndicalists'. The word is now almost forgotten, and
the theory was killed by the General Strike of 1926; perhaps it
must be explained. Syndicalism was a philosophy of the class-
war: ' industrial unionism' was its less pedantic name. It held
that Parliaments were merely a deception, and no fundamental
social change could come through them. But all production,
and therefore the whole structure of society, depended upon the
industrial workers. They were robbed ' at the point of production'. They had merely to refuse to produce for profit, and
society would collapse; once the workers ' folded their arms',
the struggle would be over. Not only industrial exploitation
but the State itself would disappear. As practical men (and the
Syndicalists felt they were essentially practical men among
visionaries), they realised that the existing unions could not
carry out such a programme as ' the social general strike'. There
were nearly 1,800 separate unions, where there ought to be at the
most fourteen. Numbers of them were little units in which
plumbers, pattern-makers, carpenters and other craftsmen met
together to pretend that their craft was still of importance and
the labourer who tried to invade their trade could be kept out.
All these must be swallowed up in roughly a dozen great unions,
each covering a whole industry and able to call out every man in
that industry in support of his fellows. The State could not
touch them; the members need simply refuse to work. Every
strike was a Heaven-sent means of enforcing the idea of solidarity
upon the average worker: so far from avoiding strikes, the class-
conscious worker should welcome them. When the union
members had been sufficiently educated to hate and despise their

bosses, and when their unions had been reformed in their organisation and been completely federated together, then, with or without a general strike, the fourteen great Industrial Unions would coldly take over the fourteen great divisions of industrial production, and capitalist society would cease to exist.

The idea, had they known it, was eighty years old; the journals of Robert Owen's Grand Consolidated Union in 1833 expressed almost identical hopes. But their forces were more formidable. The dockers, through Robert Williams' Transport Workers' Federation, had something near to an ' industrial union '. The railwaymen, in the new National Union of Railwaymen—whose secretary, oddly enough, was a man named J. H. Thomas, who detested all this talk—had an almost perfect model of an industrial union, with internal craft representation. The area miners' associations were federated in the ' Miners' Federation of Great Britain ' which produced (mostly from Wales) more Syndicalist speakers than any other union. All these three were linked in a ' Triple Alliance ', which in itself seemed powerful enough to call the social general strike. There were quite a number of people, indeed, who hoped, or feared, it might be tried in the winter of 1914.

Under Lapworth's editorship, Syndicalist propaganda began to take precedence of any others. Wherever a strike occurred, it was supported. The paper never ' deplored ' strikes; it never even denied that it encouraged them. Challenged, it answered: ' We have considered the matter. We have considered every phase of it and we say: " Prepare your organisation and then strike ". STRIKE AND STRIKE HARD.' Industrial news was presented under the running head ' The War that really matters ', and even to this day the pages are exciting. Very few other journals have managed to make industrial reports interesting; they are almost always relegated to an inner page, and resolutions of even the largest branches are ' spiked ' with a sigh. Lapworth and his colleagues were able to make the *Herald* readable because they believed, and showed in their editing, that all these minor disputes and wordy resolutions were part of an unending war which was going to turn the rich out of their castles.

Lapworth's editorship made great improvements in the paper.

The new Syndicalism might be sour and shrill, but it gave a general direction to a paper when it had seemed to be a chance collection of disapprovals and of casual news paragraphs. The size of the page was reduced to that of the present *Daily Mirror*, from the old ' bedsheet' size of *The Times*. New type-faces (perhaps due to Francis Meynell, typographer son of the poet Alice Meynell) were used; Dyson's cartoons were given a whole page. But the greater skill of the editorial work was accompanied by a greater venom: Lapworth and his colleagues were not content to attack the system, but denounced everyone who compromised with it. ' The *Daily Herald* contains the noblest aspirations and the basest adjectives in the English language ', was a verdict which Lansbury treasured as the fairest summary. He was once forced to public rebuke by the savagery of one article, compelling the paper to print on October 2nd, 1912, ' my strongest protest against your attack on Philip Snowden ', whom it had called a traitor to be watched. ' It is unworthy of any journal devoted to Labour. If we cannot disagree without charging each other with all manner of social meanness, then there is no hope for the Labour movement.' The *Herald*, answering with the greatest deference, nevertheless repeated its views, and from then on there was distrust between Lansbury and Lapworth.

The older man held the editor in check, and deleted his more ferocious epithets. He defended him publicly, admired his make-up and his journalistic skill, brought in money, and even organised the ' *Herald* League' of supporters up and down the country, which began to give the paper a steadier basic circulation. But when, at the end of 1913, he accepted a pressing invitation from Fels for another visit to the States, he began to doubt whether he dared leave the paper to Lapworth uncontrolled. It would probably receive writs for libel, of which it had too many already, but more serious was that its ' good old gospel of hatred ', as he called it, would become even bitterer. Nor was it at all certain that it would survive. Ceaseless appeals for money had kept it going from month to month, but it was being slowly strangled by the rope which is round all Left-wing journals. When they most needed it was just the time when its readers could support it least. While the dock strike was on, for example, the *Herald* had produced several evening editions, costing some hundreds of pounds, and infinitely valuable to the dockers. But just at that time thousands of its would-be readers could not even spare the halfpenny to buy it, and the union could not subscribe a farthing. If the paper was to go on, individual helpers had to be solicited, and they were almost all insistent that Lansbury's policy should be followed. Henry Harben, a rich shareholder in the Prudential, who had helped him in reorganising the business side, was giving or lending money of his own: so were several earnest-minded theosophists. Lady de la Warr and other suffragists were subscribing heavily; so, through her, was an American lady whose name was held secret (it need be no longer—Mary Dodge). Many others, with resources from two figures to four, were prepared to help, and a public subscription had reached £11,000. They all subscribed in confidence in George Lansbury—not in Lapworth.

The ' *Herald* League ', indeed, considered it could take over the editing, and there had even been a time when the ' comps ' had wished to do so. But these proposals were not financially practicable; after a severe internal struggle, which still troubled him twenty years after, Lansbury took the apparently preposterous decision of using his casting vote to terminate Lapworth's editorship (on generous terms) and appointed himself editor just before sailing for the States. Other solutions had been proposed: one of the more absurd was the appointment of the rake Frank Harris, who had been seen by Tillett on the Riviera, and had promised that the paper should be conducted in accordance with Christ's teaching, which he would insist should be rigidly followed. But it became in the end clear that it was Lapworth or Lansbury; and that question had but one answer. His editorship (he came back from America in February 1914) caused but two important changes: one was the elimination of an undertone of personal spite, which helped the circulation, the other was the deletion of ' racing tips ' which damaged it severely. Lansbury did not only think gambling wrong (he also disapproved of drinking, but did not refuse brewers' advertisements), he thought it grotesquely silly; he could not believe that the workers could really wish to waste their money so stupidly or that the absence of ' tips ' could injure the circulation. When, in 1919, the *Herald* was revived as a daily, he was overborne by his colleagues and agreed to include them; but he was never easy in his mind. One sub-editor remembers a repeated scene of those days: Taylor, the long, thin, dark journalist who was 'Templegate' the tipster, rising from his seat as the editor came in and saying, 'Well, G. L., we had five winners yesterday', and being answered, 'That's fine, brother; I'm very glad', in a tone of great dejection; and these two excellent men looking at each other in distress, each respecting the other, anxious to avoid hurting the other's feelings, desiring nothing so much as the success of the paper, and yet aware of a high fence of misunderstanding between them that nothing could overleap.

Under his editorship it remained what it had been, for him and all its readers, more than anything else: a weapon in the workers' struggle. The Trades Union Congress and the better-established unions were in general opposed to *Daily Herald* policy, though some of their officials, in a sort of bemused acquiescence in anything that called itself trade unionist, had sat on its committee long after it had been openly hostile to them. The majority of the well-to-do unions were 'craft' unions—that is to say, they were unions of plumbers, pattern-makers and so on, who regarded the general labourer who shifted from trade to trade as a threat to their privileged position, and sometimes also as a lower type of human being. Their officials, reasonably, also considered the propaganda for a dozen industrial unions as a direct threat to their jobs and salaries. Their resistance to syndicalist proposals was reinforced by the great number of 'insurance members' who had joined the unions as a result of Lloyd George's Act. These were men who had enough sense of their class interests to choose as their 'approved society' a union rather than a company, but cared and knew too little of trade union theory even to attend branch meetings, let alone support agitations to reconstruct the whole union organisation.

But the resulting petrifaction was on the surface: the years from 1911 to 1914 were years of unceasing industrial upheavals, strikes, lock-outs and boycotts. The angry men involved in them needed some means of communication and some way of co-ordinating their actions; what their unions could not or would not give them they found in the *Daily Herald*. Its columns are full of reports, resolutions and articles which are effectively the ' rebels' ' communications with each other. The records of those years show many instances in which union executives adjure their members not to come out on strike, to go back to work if they are out, or to refrain from helping their fellows by refusing to handle ' black ' goods, and in which the *Daily Herald* urges them to do the opposite; and they often follow the paper's advice, and not that of their leaders.

The history of the journal under Lansbury's influence is thus to some degree the industrial history of Britain in these years. Its concentration upon the class struggle was the condition of its survival—the divisions between the suffragists, the Socialists, the Syndicalists and Chesterton's followers were blurred by the realisation that almost daily the paper was fighting actual injustices, and, whatever might be its political errors, was always intervening on the side of the poor against the rich. The very first news-story that it had to handle gave its keynote; it was the sinking of the ' Titanic '. Other papers recorded well enough the shock of the loss of the fastest, most richly equipped and safest ship in the world and the hundreds who went down with it. The *Herald* analysed the figures: 121 steerage women and children passengers were saved, 134 drowned; 246 first- and second-class women and children were saved and only twenty drowned; fifty-eight of the 173 first-class men were saved. ' They have paid ', it said of the White Star line, ' 30 per cent to their shareholders and they have sacrificed 51 per cent of the steerage children. They have gone to sea criminally under-equipped with the means of life saving, they have neglected boat drill, they have filled their boat with cooks and valets, with pleasure gardens and luxurious lounges; they have done all this to get big profits and please the first-class passengers. And when the catastrophe came they hastened to get their first-class passengers and their chairman safely away. Fifty-three children remained to die. They were steerage passengers ! One hundred and thirty-four women and children slain. They were steerage passengers ! '

There is much invective hidden away in the old *Daily Herald* files which deserves resurrection for its style alone; those who can find a file should turn to the issue of June 28th, 1913, for a

rather less bitter but cruelly amusing attack on the Labour Party
by Chesterton. Most of its writing, however, was harsher than
his, for it was connected with immediate conflicts, and its
material supplied by men actually suffering from the poverty and
hunger it denounced. As one turns over its pages, one sees it
in the summer of 1912 supporting first a strike at the Earl's Court
Exhibition, then the Great Northern railwaymen for coming out
despite their officials, then the crew for walking off the White
Star boat ' Olympic ' until its safety arrangements were made
better than those of the ' Titanic ', then the London tailors in a
sudden strike, and finally the two months' struggle of the
London dockers, already mentioned, in which the men and their
families were reduced to extreme distress, and Ben Tillett, on
Tower Hill, prayed for their most insolent enemy : ' God strike
Lord Devonport dead ! '

A full account of the *Herald's* industrial action (which was
also its political action) would be unreadable; it would consist
of an unceasing stream of small and large strikes supported and
encouraged without regard to the wishes of the union leaders,
and covering almost every trade in the country. Even in those
years of furious energy they were far from being all even partially
successful; but no economist has yet been able to work out a
truthful balance-sheet of strikes. How many reductions were
prevented, how many improvements graciously granted because
of the employers' knowledge that the workers would fight if
they were not ? Industrial truculence paid in many cases where no
strike occurred at all.

Two of the disputes in which the *Herald* intervened have to
have a separate mention—the Dublin lock-out of 1913 and the
building dispute of 1914. The Irish workers' conditions were
worse than the English; their organisations were feebler, their
slums more horrible, their masters more oppressive. But in
recent years there had been some relief, due largely to two devoted
men : James Connolly, a great Socialist theorist and organiser,
and James Larkin, a great Socialist speaker and organiser. They
had been mainly responsible for founding and running a hard-
fighting industrial union—the Irish Transport and General
Workers' Union, which took up the defence of almost any group
of workers who wished to join it. In many cases—notably

a big Wexford strike—it had compelled employers to grant better conditions and to agree to negotiate with their men. It was this latter compulsion which Irish employers most resented: under an especially ruthless autocrat named W. M. Murphy over 400 of the most powerful Dublin employers in September 1913 united in a society whose object was quite simply to destroy the union. All their employees were required to sign a ' document ' (a device first tried out eighty years before in England) either resigning from the union or promising never to join it. Hideously poor though they were, the Dublin workers refused, and roughly 100,000 of them were locked out. Arithmetically it is certain most of them could not have been members of the union at all. The employers could not understand an apparently insane defiance. The *Herald* readers could; it was an assertion of manhood. But they found that the British trade union leaders, who resented Larkin's industrial unionist propaganda and bellicose tactics, considered that the dispute was none of their affair. The journal set out to force them to join in.

It had plenty of material, for there can have been few cases where so little was to be said for the masters and so much for the men. The Dublin workers' conditions were disgusting, the aggression of the masters flagrant, and their character brutalised— ' Cry aloud to Heaven for new souls! ' wrote ' A. E.' to them in an Open Letter which became famous. The death rate in Dublin was the highest in Europe bar Russia; 21,000 families lived in one-room ' homes ', men worked seventy hours a week for from twelve to seventeen shillings—such were the facts the *Herald* columns printed and *Herald* meetings advertised all over the country. The organisers called it ' carrying the Fiery Cross ', and the indignation roused justified the phrase. Wide support was secured by it for the Irish workers: subscriptions poured in, and the Co-operative Movement sent shiploads of food. The British union officials, reluctantly enough, were forced to intervene and offer mediation; their efforts, like those of more eminent persons, were frustrated by the barely civil refusal of the employers. Still, the *Herald* failed in its dearest hope—to secure strikes by any workers asked to handle Dublin goods. Some few workers came out, but instances were rare. A boycott of that kind might perhaps have broken the Dublin employers' obstinacy, but it might also (the union leaders argued) have broken the British trade unions. The campaign succeeded in arranging for English friends to house and feed the children of locked-out men: but this the Dublin priests forbade. The children (they feared) might come into contact with Protestant beliefs. Dyson's cartoons on the Dublin lock-out reached a new brilliance; so, too, did the printed words. But man cannot live by words, and neither the food-ships nor the subscriptions of English workers could feed what was something like a third of Dublin. The children, though their souls might be saved, were dying from hunger; slowly, as the winter went on, the Dublin workers went back on what terms they could get.

The London building dispute of 1914 was less dramatic, but it was on the *Herald's* doorstep, and it arose directly out of the Dublin dispute. It shows with peculiar clarity both the *Herald's* aspirations and the typical difficulties with which the ' rebels ' had to deal. The building trades were a network of craft unions—two masons' unions, two bricklayers', two if not three builders' labourers', the painters', the plasterers', two carpenters', two plumbers', the slaters', and the sawyers'. These societies never co-operated, and they often quarrelled—one of the plumbers' unions recorded, with a sort of collectors' pride, that it was ' in dispute ' at one time with five other trade unions. The trade was, as a natural result, infested with non-unionists; a particularly uncompromising group of Syndicalists (or industrial unionists—there was no real difference, in Britain) was occupied in the triple task of trying to fuse all these unions into one industrial union, of rounding up all the non-unionists, and of directing a campaign for better wages and conditions. Murphy's partial success suggested to the London master-builders that they might dispose of their local Larkins; they, too, presented a ' document '. It was less arrogant than the Dublin paper, for the climate was less propitious in Britain. It merely required all their employees not to refuse to work with non-unionists, under pain of a one-pound fine. But their workers refused, and on January 24th, 1914, practically the whole of the London builders were locked out. Even the non-unionists would not sign; they were thus out of work, and living on the grim charity of the Poor Law Guardians, because they would not sign a promise not to strike against themselves. The London master-builders, like Murphy's colleagues, could not understand.

The lock-out went on through January, February and March to April 16th, when the master-builders decided to withdraw their 'document'. The union officials, and the *Daily Citizen*, announced that this must end the dispute; the *Daily Herald* declared that the builders should insist on their freedom to deal with non-unionists. A ballot was held—the first which might show the relative strength of the 'rebels' and the moderates. The master-builders' terms were refused by 23,481 votes to 2,021. The lock-out continued through the summer; in May the union officials agreed with the master-builders on a new set of terms, with many minor concessions and the threat that unless they were accepted a national lock-out would be enforced. Once again the 'rebels' and the officials—the *Daily Herald* and the *Daily Citizen*—were opposed; Lansbury and his colleagues were naturally elated by the figures of 21,017 against acceptance and 5,824 for. No national lock-out was called, but one union (the masons') went back to work.

During all these upheavals the writers in the *Daily Herald* had been trying to harmonise the opinions of their variegated supporters. A theory brought in from the *New Age* by G. D. H. Cole, William Mellor, G. R. S. Taylor, and W. P. Ryan, was what was called Guild Socialism or 'National Guilds'. It was that society should be so reorganised that industries should be controlled and regulated by the workers within them, as the medieval guilds had been, seeing that standards of craftsmanship were observed and nobody was exploited. (This secured the approval of Chesterton and his followers.) To make this possible, the thousand-odd unions should be remodelled into a few revolutionary industrial units, so that they could take the factories, mines and workshops away from the capitalists who ran them. (The support of the industrial unionists could be assumed for this.) But it was contrary to public policy and to national justice for the interests of the workers in each industry to be supreme; miners or railwaymen (for example) could hold up the community to ransom, and teachers who could not do so might be made to suffer. Therefore, the State should *own* industry, and the workers in each industry should *control* it. (This might reconcile those Members of Parliament and ' State Socialists ' who were not, like Philip Snowden, opposed to trade union action or principle.) The formula was neat; it was to be criticised in the future as no more than neat, because it did not compose the difference between those who were working for a peaceful change, by agreement and by the ballot, and those who wanted a revolutionary change carried out by recurrent blows, as violent as possible, against the employing class. There was a clash of temperament as well as theory. ' AGREEMENTS MADE UNDER COERCION ARE NEVER MORALLY BINDING,' said a double-page *Herald* ' streamer ' headline on May 15th, 1914, urging the London busmen and builders to repudiate their obligations as soon as convenient; the criticisms this roused could not be silenced by the Guild Socialist formula.

But the formula had its value. If it had been remembered in the late nineteen-forties it might have lessened some of the troubles of nationalisation; from 1913 onwards it held together rebels who might otherwise have fought each other. In 1914, indeed, Lansbury and his colleagues had some reason for optimism. They had a programme which, if it did not prevent discussion (and the paper thrived on arguments), at least enabled all its supporters to co-operate without sacrificing any of their principles. They had a band of supporters throughout the island, organised by George Belt in the ' *Herald* League ' and linked by the paper, whose power and enthusiasm were shown by the record of the Larkin meetings and the builders' polls. Finally, the subscriptions of admirers, and the financial re-organisation under Lansbury's administration, had put the paper on so sound a basis that it could within a few months pay its way.

Their reasonable hopes were destroyed, with many others, by an event which the journal foresaw no more than its con-temporaries. Not until the last day of July 1914 did it realise the immediacy of the danger: ' WAR IS HELL ' it told its readers then. Like nearly all the British nation, it had neglected foreign policy. Its eyes, like those of its fellow-citizens, had been fixed upon the other three of the four chief problems which troubled the Liberal Government. These four, as they have been listed

L

in an earlier chapter, were the Suffrage question, the Irish question, the Social question and the ' German menace '. The Suffrage question had been not so much answered as slurred over. Sporadic protests by women still occurred; the *Daily Herald*, the *Daily News* and a few other papers still protested; Mr. McKenna, the Home Secretary, treated his prisoners less harshly; the anxiety was less tense. The Liberal Government had been ' firm ', as its supporters said; its M.P.s had not fulfilled their promises to those who had no votes and seemed likely not to suffer from it. The Irish question had turned itself into a carefully organised armed revolt of Ulster: the Orangemen, directed by Sir Edward Carson, F. E. Smith and Sir James Craig, had provided themselves with a provisional government and a partly equipped army to frustrate the Home Rule Act which had passed the Commons. A mutiny at Curragh in Ireland among the officers who might have had to put down this insurrection had been condoned—no punishment had followed, which is usually the sign of a collapse of governmental authority—and an attempt to bring in arms for the supporters of the Government policy was met with shooting (at Batchelor's Walk in Dublin). The social question, which the *Herald* had done so much to make louder and more acrid, had been answered partly by the Liberal social reforms, partly by the dragon-fly journeys of Lloyd George and Sir George Askwith, flitting from place to place, and by special negotiations settling conflict after conflict as each arose. But the fourth and worst question—the international danger—had not been faced at all. The Liberal Government, apart from occasional emotional speeches by the Chancellor (Lloyd George) or the First Lord of the Admiralty (Mr. Churchill), had been as willing as its fellow-citizens to leave foreign policy to the experts. But Sir Edward Grey, the Foreign Secretary, was no expert. Nothing whatever was done by the Liberal Government to remove the danger of war: the sole advance towards international peace—the foundation of the Hague Court of International Justice—was the result of the initiative of the Tsar of Russia. Great Britain slid into the war of 1914 not as a result of imperialist intrigues or ambitions by the Government, but because of its incompetence, of its ignorance of what was developing around it and its unawareness of its duty to

take some action to prevent disaster; in short, as Humbert Wolfe
wrote later, because of

> ' the ineptitude
> which, like a slattern bringing food,
> just slipped, and let the whole world smash '.

Chapter Twelve

THE *Daily Herald* was a war casualty. From August 4th, 1914, onwards readers wanted war news and only war news, and this it could not provide as efficiently as its capitalist rivals. A fortnight later it was losing money so rapidly that it raised its price from a halfpenny to a penny; the change wrecked its circulation, and on September 6th the directors decided to turn it into a weekly and make the best composition they could with their creditors. By this means a weekly *Herald* was able to survive and a daily to revive after the war; less prudent, its rival, the *Daily Citizen*, tried too long to continue as a daily, and vanished into complete extinction. About the same time Lansbury (unwisely, as he realised very soon) sold up his private timber business.

At first the *Herald's* pages showed no very clear understanding of what war meant. For a short while its editor and contributors seemed to have thought, like the traders who put up notices ' BUSINESS AS USUAL DURING ALTERATIONS TO THE MAP OF EUROPE ', that life would go on essentially unchanged—that, with the addition of the great anxiety of the war, their preoccupations might still be the old questions of the class war, the reform of trade unions, the oppression of women, and the freedom of Ireland. There were very few people who guessed that such problems would disappear from politics, either, like the Suffragettes, never to return, or, like the Irish, to return in a different and far more dangerous shape. The war was thought of as larger, bloodier and more destructive than the Boer War or the Afghan wars, but nevertheless as still something that the nation watched, encouraging its soldiers, supplying them and succouring their dependants. Only slowly was it discovered that the scientist, the farmer, the engineer, the miner, the railwayman, the writer—everybody, in short, was a part of the war. The apparent origin of the war, as well, was accepted as uncritically at first in the *Herald* as elsewhere. To fight or not to fight had been in

August a moral question to be decided by an estimate of the various wrongs committed. Serbian agents had murdered the heir to the Austrian throne—that was wrong, and many people had agreed with *John Bull's* poster ' TO HELL WITH SERVIA ! ' and sympathised with the Austrian ultimatum. The Russian Tsar had come to the aid of a smaller Slav nation; this, if precipitate, was excusable. Instead of helping to keep the peace, Austria's ally Germany was believed to have egged her on—a graver wrong. But a far worse wrong was the Kaiser's deliberate invasion of Belgium, a small and peaceful country, in defiance of treaties. It wiped out any memory of the crime of Serajevo: the *Herald*, like nearly all the rest of Britain, assumed at first that nothing else could have been done but to declare war and fight it to the end. Far in the future were the disclosures of Aehrenthal's deliberate use of the Serajevo murder to secure war on Serbia, and of General Sukhomlinov's revelation of how he and Yanushkevitch forced general mobilisation (and there-by war) upon the Tsar; nor did even the *Herald* appreciate the economic pressures behind the whole crisis.

With this temporary uncertainty of mind, and with the smaller preoccupations which a weekly brought, Lansbury's attention was more and more turned to his personal and almost paternal work in Bow. Dislocation of industry in the first few months of the war caused unemployment; in addition, the unexampled and unexpected rush of volunteers into the forces meant that millions of women and children suddenly became ' soldiers' and sailors' dependants '. The War Office, which knew no more about the modern soldier than it did of modern war, treated them fre-quently with the parsimony and patronage suited to Mrs. Tommy Atkins of the Boer War. Their allowances were inadequate, they were deprived of reliefs to which they were entitled, the forms they were given and the questions they were asked seemed to them (at that date) inquisitory, they were not infrequently insultingly treated. A general distress was added to the many particular troubles: the Government, having no idea of the economic results of a great war, made no effective attempts to control prices, which began to rise at once. The trade unions, by patriotically pledging themselves not to strike in war-time, deprived the workers of their only means of countering this loss in real wages; but no comparable restraint was shown, or (probably) was possible, by industrialists and traders. Advantage was taken from the first month of the shortage of materials: a new word, ' profiteer ', shortly appeared to describe a new person. The rise in the price of food was, of course, the most serious to Lansbury's neighbours: no adequate steps were taken to check it. Between 1914 and 1916 the freight rates for grain from the Argentine, for example, rose from eleven shillings to nine pounds a ton, yet it was not until October of the latter year that the Government took control of corn and wheat imports, and even then home production was left uncontrolled.

In such circumstances a much larger amount of Lansbury's time was spent in direct help to his fellow-citizens in Bow. His house was a centre for every sort of aid—advice on domestic problems, instruction on how to secure pension rights, prevention of evictions, assistance in reversing all sorts of personal injustices, administration of private and public relief, and very often direct financial aid. During these years he became for much of Poplar the ' father figure ' which he was later for a wider area of England. A not-too-friendly glimpse of him at work is recorded in the memoirs of Sylvia Pankhurst, *The Home Front*, which shows both his own methods and the opposition from an ' extreme Left ' which now, for the first time, began to criticise him. Miss Pankhurst, who ran a sort of small *Herald* called *The Women's Dreadnought*, came to ' the Bow West Ward Committee ' (a relief committee, apparently) one day to find ' a little woman, flushed and tearful ' facing it. ' George Lansbury's big sing-song voice with its Bow accent admonished her in a fatherly style: " Now you go home and have a good try! " ' Miss Parkhurst says that the woman was ' not disposed to be meek and contrite ' and complained that ' *someone* ' was speaking against her; eventually Lansbury told her that if she didn't ' try ' they would have to stop the food tickets. After she had left there was a dispute: the origin of the trouble turned out to be that the woman had been found drunk and dancing a hornpipe in the Roman Road. She had six children, and her husband was in jail. Lansbury said she should not get drunk on public money; Miss Pankhurst replied that she only got from them food-tickets on which she couldn't get drunk (but she might have sold them), and that once a woman had been accepted as 'unemployed through the war', no further questions should be allowed. The local parson was insistent on severity; but every London borough is a village, and Lansbury knew all the villagers. 'She used to be a decent little girl,' he said, appealing to his colleagues ('lachrymose,' snorted Miss Pankhurst), and got her another chance on condition Miss Pankhurst saw that she behaved herself. This Miss Pankhurst on principle failed to do, and apparently no more was heard of the case.

Within a few months, when munition production got under way, unemployment almost disappeared. By the same time the anomalies and injustices in the treatment of servicemen's dependants were largely removed, and Lansbury and his colleagues had to clear their minds and decide on their policy about the war, which was now clearly not going to be a three-months' march to Berlin. In so doing they made the *Herald* probably the most powerful and incomparably the widest-circulated 'anti-war' journal in the country; they also gave Lansbury a national eminence which he had not had before, and a particular type of influence which was at one time exceeded in its sphere only by Ramsay MacDonald's. The first direct and uncompromising demand that the war should stop seems to have been an explosive article by Francis Meynell in the Christmas number for 1914; it was provoked by a literary critic named Edmund Gosse, an arbiter of taste who had compared the rivers of blood in Flanders to a purifying 'Condy's fluid'; it was followed by others.

With the change in the paper went a change in friends and collaborators. The two most famous *Daily Herald* contributors were the first to go. Will Dyson, after an uneasy period of drawing pictures deriding the harriers of soldiers' wives, left after a pacifist caption had been written underneath one of his cartoons without his permission. G. K. Chesterton fell ill in December 1914, and when he recovered came down to Fleet Street to tell Lansbury he felt he should contribute no more. 'I can see him now,' Lansbury said, 'looking apologetic, with his hand on the door-handle. I told him we would let him write exactly what he pleased. "Yes, I know you would, George," he answered gently, "but, you see, we don't any longer *mean* the same thing."' Of the old staff there soon remained only

W. P. Ryan, who took Lansbury's place as editor when he was away; Jimmy Butler, the sports writer, whose term of service with the *Herald* was to exceed all others ; and Langdon Everard, the humorist. New names, or names known only a short while before the war, began to predominate among the contributors and advisers: John Scurr, W. N. Ewer, Gerald Gould, H. N. Brailsford, Evelyn Sharp; Cole and Mellor almost alone gave among the columns of pacifism industrial news and comments which recalled the older paper; Robert Williams of the Transport Workers' Federation was almost the only trade union leader who still co-operated.

Lansbury never had an organisation behind him (the ' *Herald* League ' was a small body, the Bow Labour Party a local affair), but what he now gained, and was to have for twenty years, was a group. He was the head and the centre of it, but never its dictator. In Bow he was something of a local monarch; but not in the *Herald* office or in *Lansbury's Weekly*, which followed it. The members of the group continually changed, but some considered themselves his intellectual superiors, and none deferred to him as a master. He both gave and took; the inspiration, the solidity, the confidence and courage in difficulties came largely from him; it was others who provided the programmes, the ideas and the practical research. What ' the *Herald* people ' (more rarely, ' the Lansbury group ') thought and would do became henceforward a thing of great if intangible importance to the organised working class, and so in due course to the nation. This magnified his influence, but it also clarified it; in the next twenty years he was not only a more important but a wiser man than he had been; nor did he fall back into a mental isolation until the very last years of his life, when his old friends and advisers were either dead or in disagreement with him. This continual intercourse kept his mind young beyond its years, and an essential strain of humility made him invariably willing to learn; one typical memory which has a faintly absurd charm is of his frowning forehead as he tried to assimilate an exposition, by Gould and Meynell, of why Walter Crane's designs for May Day posters were inadequate by modern theories of art.

At first this group had very small success in its immediate task. In May 1915 the journal risked asking leaders of ' advanced thought' and of trade unionism to declare themselves upon the peace terms which should be required from Germany. Seldom can a journal have provoked a more discomposing answer. H. G. Wells furiously denounced ' Krupp-Kaiserism ' and cried, ' Let us see it through! ' Shaw thought the question erroneously phrased. Arnold Bennett demanded enormous indemnities, annexations and ' a ceremonial passage of Belgian troops down Unter den Linden '. Robert Young, of the Engineers, wanted large indemnities; the other union leaders—James O'Grady, Harry Gosling, Will Thorne, G. N. Barnes, J. H. Thomas and so on—in phrases of varying indignation demanded to fight to the end and wanted no discussion at all. Robert Williams and Philip Snowden thought a statement on war aims desirable; but their support was to be expected. Readers of the old *Daily Herald* may have stretched their eyes on seeing that the most sensible and reasoned replies came from their old enemies, Ramsay MacDonald, with a thought-out list of frontier changes, and Sidney Webb, with a detailed scheme for a League of Nations.

The *Herald* was not, of course, alone in opposing the continuance of the war, though its voice was the most powerful. There were the I.L.P. with its *Labour Leader* and half a dozen M.P.s, the British Socialist Party (successor to the S.D.F.), which expelled H. M. Hyndman and ran *The Call* as a successor to *Justice*, and groups of unofficial ' shop stewards ' in war industries who undertook the duty of protecting the workers' standard of life (which the engineering unions had resigned) and so found themselves in growing hostility to the Government. After conscription was introduced in March 1916 there were also some 16,000 ' conscientious objectors ', about half of whom were refused the exemption which they desired, and underwent sufferings which were rather extensively commiserated in the paper (though they were more serious than in the Second World War—three dozen were sentenced to death, and it was not known that they would be reprieved).

The First World War, indeed, differed in many essential respects from the Second. First, it was arranged by no one. Positive intention, deliberate planning of a world war can only be alleged plausibly of a few officials in the Austrian Foreign

Office and the Russian War Office—perhaps, too, of the Serajevo murderers. The heads of governments were guilty in various degrees of failing to prevent war and playing with matches in a powder-room; they pursued selfish or imperialist objects, were too witless to see where their actions would end, and lacked courage and speed enough to stop the disaster they had started. There was nothing like the calculated invasions and destructions of international law that preceded the invasion of Poland in 1939. Secondly, the antagonists were of a similar political character and belonged to a like civilisation. A large part of the British public was in time convinced by writers like Horatio Bottomley and Harold Begbie, and the speeches of more responsible politicians, that the Germans were innately a different race, trained by a state-philosophy of ' Prussianism ' for war and nothing but war; and that they must be crushed in utter defeat, beaten to their knees and squeezed until the pips squeaked—there was a remarkable choice of violent metaphors. (A hundred years earlier, with more excuse, the same description was applied to the French.) By contrast, the Allies were held to be freedom-loving and democratic: their troops were universally gentle-manly, while abominable atrocities were committed by Germans, who boiled corpses to make soap, cut the breasts off nuns and the hands off babies, and hanged priests upside down in their own church-bells as living clappers. They were unscrupulous imperialists whose intention was to conquer the whole world, whereas the Allies did not ' covet an inch of territory ' for them-selves. The atrocity stories were to be mostly disproved, and the secret treaties to show the Allies as greedy as their adversaries. But the most important difference between the First and Second World Wars was that the German State under the Kaiser was essentially of the same character as the British, and certainly more democratic than the Russian. Though its powers were less, the war could not continue without the consent of the Reichstag any more than of the Commons. The German Reich franchise was nearly as wide as the British. Within the Reichstag walls, Karl Liebknecht could denounce the war as freely and as bitterly as Philip Snowden; Hugo Haase could secure more votes than Ramsay MacDonald for a moderate motion on peace. Ever since the days of the French Revolution and Napoleon, political democracy had been spread over Europe, roughly in the steps of the French armies. A map of Napoleon's conquests and satellites in 1812 is oddly like a map of Parliamentary institutions in 1912; even the varying degrees of French domination correspond uncannily to the extent of democratic advance within each country. As one travelled east, political democracy weakened; it was secure in France, Belgium and Holland, somewhat weaker in Italy and Germany, still feebler in Austria-Hungary, and a mere shadow in Russia. But in all countries, up till 1914, it was growing stronger year by year, and growing in the same pattern. More and more power was being transferred to the elected assembly from the Crown, more and more citizens were gaining the right to select the assembly. Inter-parliamentary communications, and particularly the 'International' which linked all Socialists, strengthened and hastened this process: the prolongation of the war and its monstrous bloodshed and misery ended it and wrecked the civilisation that depended on it. Twenty-five years later there was, in fact, to appear what the Bottomleys and Lloyd Georges pretended existed already—a State organised for war, based upon the tormenting and massacre of its fellow-citizens, knowing no freedom of speech or thought, and deliberately educating its children to be thugs. For its appearance, those who prevented an early peace had a great responsibility.

After the first great German sweep through Belgium to Northern France had been stopped at the Marne, the war had become a grinding of the two armies against each other along a long line from Switzerland to the sea. Two great bloodstained ditches ran from the ocean to the mountains; within them, as Henri Barbusse said, were 'not two armies fighting each other, but one great army committing suicide'. Barbed wire protected each side, and to attack the opponent was certain death; but the generals on neither side had intelligence to see what is clear to us to-day. The military writing of the day is full of a mystical exaltation of 'will', of the value of the 'offensive spirit', and of the power of artillery. Throughout 1915, 1916 and 1917 the same technique was used: a heavy bombardment cut the wire and warned the defenders—it also churned the soil into impassable mud if it was low-lying, as at Passchendaele—and when it was over the soldiers would advance, often shoulder to shoulder, as though they had been on the parade-ground at Wellington Barracks. The defenders, waiting in their dug-outs, would receive them with machine-gun fire which could not miss; they would die in hundreds, and their successors would march over them to meet the same fate; and at the end of it all a few hundred yards' advance would have been made. Falken-hayn, the German commander who planned the attack on Verdun which lasted through so many months of 1916, had realised the only possible use of this form of warfare; he defined his objective as to kill as many Frenchmen as possible. Haig and Nivelle, the British and French commanders who directed a similar policy on the Allied side, had not even the excuse of his clarity of objective. They still believed that somehow they would ' break through ' by these means, and for months cavalry units were kept prepared in reserve to ride through the gaps which were to be torn. When new weapons, such as the tank, were presented to them which might have ended the deadlock, they either refused them or used them so diffidently that the enemy had ample time to counter them.

While this massacre, which there are no words to describe, was prolonged by idiocy, what it is no more than fair to call perfidy accompanied it in diplomacy. Of one thing the hundreds of thousands of men who filled ' Kitchener's Army ' and were sent to the Somme and Passchendaele were certain—that they had enlisted and were fighting in a wholly honourable cause: the defence of a violated small nation and the restoration of the rule of justice and law internationally. They did not know, until the middle of 1918, when the *Herald* and the *Manchester Guardian* published the secret treaties found by the Bolsheviks in the Tsar's archives, that the Allied Governments had pledged themselves to precisely the sort of territorial aggrandisements that they charged the Kaiser with desiring, and themselves had solemnly dis-owned. When Outhwaite, a Liberal M.P. disquieted by rumours, asked the Foreign Secretary in May 1916 to deny that Britain was bound to go on fighting until the Tsar annexed Con-stantinople, Sir Edward Grey answered smoothly: ' The honourable member is asking for a statement which I do not think it is desirable to make.' Yet a year and two months earlier the Russian Foreign Office had recorded in writing the arrangements made: Russia was to annex Constantinople, the Dardanelles, with the hinterland to both, and two islands in the Ægean; Ispahan and Yezd in nominally independent Persia were to come under Russian 'influence', while the 'neutral zone' in that country should be abandoned to Britain. Other treaties in 1915 and 1916 gave Italy the South Tyrol and Trieste in Austria (the rest of whose seaboard was to be annexed by Serbia), Valona in Albania, twelve Greek islands called the Dodecanese, and a great slab of Asia Minor. Russia was to take 'the provinces of Erzerum, Trebizond, Van and Bitlis' with part of Kurdistan from Asiatic Turkey; France Syria and some more of Asia Minor; Britain Southern Irak, Haifa and Acre. Rumania was to have Transylvania and the Banat from Hungary.

Until these arrangements were revealed, the opponents of the Government had little to go upon but their suspicions, and their success was small. The Government was twice changed, but by palace revolutions, and not by popular discontent. In May 1915 Asquith dissolved his Government and brought the Conservatives into a coalition; he felt it necessary, despite the alarm caused, to offer a minor post—as President of the Board of Education—to Arthur Henderson, who had taken MacDonald's place as leader of the Labour Party. (It was a gamble, but a risk which must be faced, said the *Daily Mail* bravely.) He also gave posts to Ulstermen—although he had no Irish Nationalists in his Government—a piece of folly which had its share in provoking the Dublin rebellion of Easter Week, 1916. In December 1916 he was turned out of office by his most eminent supporter, Lloyd George, who split the Liberal Party in half to do so: but the new Government, though a reaction against Asquithian incompetence, was in no way a reaction against 'jingoism'. Official speeches repudiating anything but a fight to the bitter end and a 'knock-out blow' became more common, and their tune was more rather than less violent: suppression of pamphlets, prosecution of speakers, prohibitions of meetings became more and more frequent. The seizure and suppression of the *Herald* was discussed once at least, but dismissed as imprudent. Lloyd George instead sent for Lansbury, offered him breakfast and (according to Lansbury) assured him that his thoughts were perpetually upon the means of securing an early peace, that he knew Haig to be a butcher who massacred his soldiers uselessly, but that his Conservative colleagues prevented him making a change.

The sole real encouragement to Lansbury and his colleagues came from abroad, and most of all from the American President, Woodrow Wilson. It is difficult, for those who did not live in it, to realise the atmosphere in which the President's speeches were received. To-day it seems impossible that they should have been objected to: they are moderate in phrasing, they are admirably written and in excellent English, their proposals are those of common sense and common humanity. In 1916 the President's chief request was that the belligerents, whose aims were phrased in vague rhetoric, should state in more detail what their terms were, so that it could be seen if they could possibly be reconciled; it is hard to believe that this could be regarded as an insult, but it was so received in Britain. Official reactions were kept in bounds by the need to be polite to the head of a great neutral nation on whom the Allies depended for supplies; the Northcliffe Press and Bottomley's *John Bull* were not so restrained. For by the end of 1916 the mood of 1914 had disappeared. There was a universal sourness. The papers were filled with abuse of Germans, of Wilson, of 'conchies', of 'slackers' in industry; the army was tired, sick and angry— parts were near to mutiny; 'brave little Belgium' was rarely said now without a sneer; strikes were reappearing even in essential war industries, and the South Wales miners had successfully defeated an attempt to put down a great walk-out by legal action. There was, potentially, a deep division between the speakers, too frequently women or men well over military age, who proclaimed the nation's determination to fight to the last man, and the workers at home and soldiers in the army who were both becoming steadily more disquieted by the never-ending suffering. But at no time during the war was any unity achieved between the two discontents. Men in uniform lived in a different world from civilians: they came for a brief space to what seemed to them a civilisation of which no one need complain— there were drinks offered by anxious relatives; there was *The Bing Boys* in London, or comparable shows in the provinces; there was a perpetual if feverish atmosphere of gaiety as long as leave lasted; and, above all, there were no shells, no lice, no blood-spattered trenches. They saw few reasons for strikes and discontent; they were prepared to believe *John Bull* (which dealt fiercely enough with meannesses over pensions and separation allowances, which they understood) when it said that strikes in South Wales were incited by German agents who wanted to stop the supply of shells for the guns. Wilson's speeches almost alone appealed equally at home and in the trenches.

In any conflict, be it a wrestle between schoolboys or a death-struggle between nations, he who first suggests peace negotiations runs a risk; he may be thought to be weakening. It is a matter of record that the Germans first took that chance. In December 1916 the Chancellor, Bethmann-Hollweg, who could look over his shoulders at politicians as merciless as Carson or Bonar Law, nevertheless risked making an open appeal for peace. He said, in the rhetorical phrases to be expected:

' During these long years the Emperor has been moved by a single thought: how peace can be restored so as to safeguard Germany after the struggle in which she has fought so victoriously. In a deep moral and religious sense of duty towards his nation and beyond it towards humanity, the Emperor considers the moment has come for official action towards peace. . . . At the fateful hour we have taken the fateful decision; it is drenched with blood of hundreds of thousands of our sons and brothers.'

Lloyd George's answer in the House of Commons was derisive; for neither British nor French politicians had any knowledge of what was happening in Russia. They added up Britain, France, Italy and Russia, and said that four was twice the size of the two that Germany and Austria made—Turkey and Bulgaria could be regarded as cancelled out by Serbia and Rumania—and thought they need only wait long enough for complete victory to be theirs. Wilson's ' peace note ' asking that each side state its peace terms was profoundly resented: when it reached London in January 1917 Northcliffe's *Evening News* placarded all the streets with the one word ' NO ! ' Lansbury and his colleagues printed a special edition which had as its placard simply ' YES ! '; for the first time, it had a showing equal to Northcliffe's, and, despite fumings, the Lloyd George

Government did agree to formulate terms. As a result, the President went one step farther: he delivered a speech in which he declared that the best thing that could be hoped for was ' peace without victory ', a peace by negotiation between the combatants, and not one dictated by either side. There was an explosion of anger and contempt; but Lansbury and the *Herald* declared that the statement was ' magnificent '—it was ' an evangel '—and cabled their ' heartfelt thanks ' to Wilson. They were still isolated; even the Labour Party did not share their enthusiasm. At its conference at the end of January 1917, when *Herald* policy was put forward (among others) by David Kirkwood, a shop-steward from the Clyde, and Fairchild, of the British Socialist Party, the Cabinet Minister Henderson got a vote of 1,850,000 to 300,000 against it. The Party ' is hopeless ', the paper reported.

In just a few days more than a month everything was changed. At the beginning of March (February in the Russian calendar) the news came through that what was in those days admittedly the most cruel and oppressive Government had ceased to exist. The Russian Tsardom, the terror of all Liberals and Socialists for a century or more, had slid down to disaster with scarcely a struggle. A Power that had hung like a black cloud in the horizon for as long as men could remember had disappeared, but nobody knew what had taken its place. The British Government was as ill-informed as anyone else: its Ambassador was Sir George Buchanan, an aristocrat who once told Albert Thomas (an important French statesmen and Socialist) that he was appalled at the thought of having a Socialist at his dinner-table, and an eminent delegation sent to Russia just beforehand, headed by Lord Milner, had reported that talk of revolution was baseless. Lansbury, in the *Herald*, welcomed the news, but at first believed a new Tsar would be selected: on March 23rd, fantastically daring, the paper hoped that ' a social-democratic republic ' might result from the revolution. For weeks conjecture was all that was possible: even in Petrograd the situation was obscure, and the British censor held up most of what little information came through. The British Government seemed to be horrified; the disappearance of the Tsar had upset all its belligerent calculations and, if it had not been for the initiative of an independent Member, the Commons might not even have remembered to congratulate the Duma officially upon the achievement of Russian freedom. It clung to its belief that the real leaders of the revolution were the warlike Liberals, the ' Cadets ' led by Professor Miliukov; even after that Professor had been dismissed for demanding that Russia annex Constantinople, it still failed to see that the real popular passion in Russia was for peace, and hoped that the revolution was really a revolt against ' German intrigue '.

It soon was alone in that hope. The new ' Council of Workers' and Soldiers' Deputies ' (' Soviet ' was a word only slowly assimilated) of Petrograd was each day more clearly the real source of power, and its influence was thrown wholly on the side of peace. The programme which the American President was scholarlily phrasing in fourteen points, it summarised in two: ' No annexations and no indemnities '. If the British Government could pretend not to hear, the *Herald* saw to it that the British workers heard. Of all the many moving Albert Hall meetings that Lansbury organised, none stayed warmer in his and everyone's memory than that of March 31st, 1918. It was called simply to welcome the Russian Revolution; its resolution merely demanded in general terms that all governments follow the Russian example in restoring freedom. But it was the first demonstration of any size, and it suddenly released the feelings which great masses of people were holding unexpressed—indeed, in many cases it first made them realise what they felt. From that day on there was a great change of heart and a great change of mind throughout Britain; what had been the unpopular propaganda of a small minority became, in a greater or less degree of fervour, the conviction of the greater portion of the thinking working class of the country, and of many outside the working class. ' How much it is, by far, the greatest and best thing that has ever happened in the history of the world,' said Fox about the fall of the Bastille: the same feeling filled the hearts of those who were celebrating the first days of the Russian Revolution. Not only had the worst thing that they knew disappeared, but the revolution that had killed it was opening unbelieved-in vistas. It was already clear that not only was freedom restored, but there was a possibility of the

Socialist changes which they had prayed for but never really expected to see; in the distance, and for a moment, they saw in a golden light the roofs and windows of Utopia. And in the present, and with a voice of authority, the new power was saying the one thing they needed to hear—a loud 'Stop!' to the slaughter around them.

Twelve thousand people packed the hall: all the seats were occupied, including those 'perpetually reserved' for stockholders and royalty. Five thousand or so were turned away. Men and women stood five deep even in the top gallery—a great circle far up in the roof, seatless, barely lit and, as it seemed, misty, and from which the speakers on the platform looked like midgets. Ordinary speakers could scarcely be heard—there were no microphones in those days. Three voices only rang plainly through to those vast heights—the chairman George Lansbury's, the transport-worker Robert Williams', and Clara Butt's, whose singing of *Give to us peace in our time, O Lord!* called all the audience to its feet to join with her—all those who could control their emotion and were not already in tears of relief and joy. At other times there was almost utter silence, of all the thousands straining to hear the weaker voices of Israel Zangwill, the author; Robert Smillie, the miners' leader; Henry Nevinson, the correspondent, or W. C. Anderson, the M.P.; it contrasted sharply with the full noise of all 12,000 singing the *Red Flag* as the speakers marched on to the platform.

Few of Lansbury's speeches have as yet been quoted in this book; for not many have been preserved, and those that have been convey hardly anything of the quality of his spoken words. But some portions of his speech on this evening should be reproduced.

'Now, we meet here, all kinds of people. All sorts and conditions of men and women are in this hall to-night. I believe that it is the most representative international meeting that had been held since the International Socialist Congress in this country. We have met here to celebrate one of the great historical events in the history of the world. I was going to say the greatest historical event, because those of us who have been in the Labour and Socialist movement have at times imagined that if there was one country in the world that would always be backward it was Russia. Yet here, in the midst of a tremendous war, a Russian revolution which thousands of men and women in the last fifty or sixty years have given their lives to make has been brought to a successful issue. (Applause.) It is a great and glorious thought that you gather up this work, that you gather up all the work of the men and women and the boys and girls of Russia who have given all they had to give for Russian liberty. This triumph has come, friends, because for the first time that I know of in history— at least, in modern history—soldiers, working-class soldiers, have refused to fire on the workers. (Loud and continued applause.) To me, comrades, that is the greatest lesson of all. On Bloody Sunday they had not learnt that lesson; they have learnt it now, and it is for us to learn it now—(great applause)—because we can understand that when the working-classes of all nations refuse to shoot down the working-classes of other countries, Governments won't be able to make wars any more. (Tremendous applause.) This war would end to-morrow if the troops on all sides march out into No Man's Land and refused to fight any longer. (Applause.)

' Mr. Lloyd George is head of a great Government. (Hisses.) Comrades, don't let us hoot anyone here. We disagree about lots of things, but we are all wanting to celebrate a giant proletarian revolt: we don't want to bother our heads about hooting anyone. After all, he is the head of our Government. I believe this—that if he and his colleagues would whole-heartedly back the programme sent out by the Revolutionary Labour Party of Russia, we could get an International that would be a bulwark for the future freedom of the whole of the human race. Now we English people have to clean our own door-step. I stood here just about three years ago: almost where Williams is sitting sat James Connolly. (Applause.) He and his murdered colleagues of a year ago were just too soon, that is all; and, friends, we British people have got to clear that Irish question up, because until we do it is not for us to celebrate other people's triumphs over reaction. Further, there are to-night hundreds of young men in gaol; there are to-night thousands of young men in India who are there in gaol. The people of India, the people of Ireland, the people of Ceylon, ask that we who claim to be the leaders in democracy in the world shall put our principles into practice at home. Now most of us here, every man and every woman who is gathered in this hall, have some sort of feeling and love and care for other men and women, and I think the one great outstanding thing to realise in regard to Russia and the working-class movement is just this, that if this great human race is to work out its salvation, it is by men and women like you and me doing it. You have to get rid of the idea that someone else can emancipate you, someone else can save you. We here in Britain—what is the thing that keeps us backward? It is our jealousies, our fears, and anxiety to find out where we disagree instead of where we agree. I want to see this Russian movement impelling you and me to catch their spirit, their enthusiasm, and be ready to suffer, and if needs be to die, for our faith. Men and women, the hardest thing is to live for our faith, and that is what you and I have got to do. Here and there in our country there are things that want clearing up. Some of them I just now mentioned. But do not go home without realising that in British prisons, for religious, for political offences, some of the best of the young men of this country are lying. Do not forget that in Russia they have thrown open the prisons. (Applause.) Do not forget that in Russia they have put down police spies.

' To the young men—if there are any here; to the young women—there are many here—I want to say this: you are celebrating to-night a tremendous thing. It is fine to cheer these other people, fine to feel you can sing about them, talk about them; a finer thing still is to emulate and follow their example. (Loud and prolonged applause.) It is men and women of goodwill, irrespective of race, who will redeem the world. You men and women gathered here in such magnificent numbers will go out with the words of the song you have sung ringing in your ears, and remember always the duty laid upon each of you, " Quit you like men, be strong ".'

The meeting had been organised by the ' Anglo-Russian Democratic Alliance ', which consisted of George Lansbury; Bert Harford, the *Herald's* business manager; Francis Meynell, a young man on the printer's staff; Harry Hease, an odd and rather piratical-looking sympathiser; and Robert Williams, its lone champion among trade union officials. To these were co-opted Robert Smillie, the miners' leader, and W. C. Anderson, an I.L.P. Member of Parliament; and Lansbury always afterwards regretted that this Alliance did not continue to direct the movement which was now started. He was ' jockeyed ' into dissolving it, he said; he thought that a small group of like-minded men, with himself as chairman, could have avoided the jealousies, the rivalries of organisations, and the vast confusions that followed. Typically, he could see no objection to this proposal: he knew his own disinterestedness, his perpetual willingness to listen to objections and take advice, his anxiety to give credit to others, and his capacity for hard work. He always preferred to work in a group (a clique, his enemies said), of which he always denied that he was the chief. For the formal processes of democracy, for committees, branch organisations, panels of candidates, business meetings and drafting resolutions he had great theoretical respect: and he never used them if he could avoid it.

Two months later the Alliance was responsible for the meeting of 1,200 delegates at the once-famous 'Leeds Conference'. The conference called for the setting up of 'Workers' and Soldiers' Councils' in England; though the majority of the delegates represented political rather than trade union organisations, the opinion which they spoke for was influential, and the Government had reason enough to be disquieted. Only one opposing voice was heard: Captain Tupper, of the Sailors' and Firemen's Union, damned the conference and all its proposals. Submarine warfare was at its height; his members were being drowned daily; and he told the conference in the crudest terms that nothing but war to the end against the Germans was a tolerable proposal. He was hooted, and told that his union was undemocratically run (as it was); but the bitter feeling that he voiced was more widely felt than the delegates knew. Ernest Bevin, of the Dockers' Union, a rising rival to Robert Williams, made a 'cleverly critical' speech; if the resolutions were passed, he demanded, would there be a guarantee that the Russians would vigorously re-start the war until the Germans 'do respond'? These were warnings for the future; perhaps a more immediate warning to the intelligent might have been the names of the delegates who moved the motions. Ramsay MacDonald 'hailed the Russian Revolution without any reservation': Philip Snowden, of the I.L.P., and Albert Inkpin, of the British Socialist Party, united in supporting a call for Soviets. No one who knew these various people could believe that they would for long co-operate in a revolutionary programme.

Not only was the Alliance rashly dissolved at this conference, but Lansbury himself was removed from the scene. He could not even attend the conference; he had to be hurried away to hospital for an operation for gallstones; all that followed occurred without his guidance. The *Herald* had spent much of its resources in organising the Leeds Conference; now it spent more in advertising 'the workers' programme' which was worked out by the Committees that it left behind. But though there was great excitement, there was no organisation behind these demands. No Workers' and Soldiers' Councils were founded, few soldiers even heard of the 'Workers' Charter' that was produced, and what action the workers at home took was directed by shop stewards on the Clyde and elsewhere, or by unofficial miners' committees in South Wales.

Internationally, it seemed for a while that there might be more success. Vigorous action came from two outside sources, Austrian and Russian. At the end of 1916 the Emperor Francis Joseph had died at a great age; his son Charles almost at once realised that the Western world, and with it his own empire, was racing to disaster. Openly, and secretly through a prince of the house of Bourbon, he attempted to make peace. He did not have the full approval of his northern ally; for though the unlimited submarine-sinkings campaign had in April brought the United States into the war, German officials nevertheless believed that Britain would be starved into submission before American troops could arrive. In May and June the Austrian Emperor made speeches calling for 'a victory of reason' which might almost have been Wilson's; though no comparably sane speeches came from the Allied side, the success of the private negotiations was such that the *Herald*, picking up rumours, in July hoped for 'peace in six weeks'. In the same issue it was recorded that the German Chancellor, Bethmann-Hollweg, had fallen and the Reichstag had accepted the Russian formula of 'no annexations'. Lloyd George answered cautiously, not vitriolically: in a fortnight's time a formal peace resolution was carried in the Reichstag by 214 to 116, and Philip Scheidemann, the German Socialist leader, said hopefully that if a parallel resolution was carried in the House of Commons 'peace negotiations can begin to-morrow'. But when it was moved in the House only twenty-one M.P.s voted for it: Asquith himself came to aid the man he most hated by endorsing Lloyd George's official doubts on whether Bethmann-Hollweg's successor had accepted the Reichstag resolution.   Something had happened to make it safe to continue the war; that something was nothing international, but a domestic victory of the kind in which Lloyd George was an expert.

The Russian demand for peace had not been addressed to Governments, nor through a prince; in accordance with the principles of the revolution, it had been an appeal from workers to workers.   It had come from the Petrograd Soviet—the ' Governments ' which succeeded each other no more controlled the revolution than seagulls control the waves over which they flit; even the Premier Kerensky, who seemed to have some permanence, only held his position by unfailing adroitness. There existed in Western Europe a thing called ' the Dutch-Scandinavian Committee ', a last relic of the Bureau of the Socialist International, which had been shattered in 1914; it had as secretary the Belgian Camille Huysmans, who carried on such desultory correspondence as was needed.   To this the Soviet addressed itself, and almost by violence drew it into the summoning of a conference of the International at Stockholm. The object of the conference, which Socialists of all nations should attend, was to investigate peace terms and, if possible, agree upon them; if this was done, the war might perhaps be ended forthwith. The proposal, which the Russian Government could not repudiate and did not wish to, seemed to the Western Governments not a hope, but a threat: the French sent two Right-wing Socialists to recall the Petrograd workers to sanity and the prosecution of the war; the Lloyd George Government sent (in June) Cabinet Minister Arthur Henderson, the Labour Party secretary, with authority to dismiss the Ambassador, Sir George Buchanan, and take his place if that would help in keeping the Russians in line.   On him they felt that they could rely, but they did not know their man.   Henderson was a silent, unimaginative man, loud-voiced, stiff, red-faced, with deep pouches under his eyes; an ironfounder by trade, a Nonconformist lay preacher from an early age; patiently hard-working, but rather rough and short-tempered in politics; a rigid teetotaller; with few individual characteristics beyond a trick of shooting his white cuffs at subordinates whom he rebuked.   He had worked steadily and silently in the Cabinet; he had acquiesced in the shooting of Jim

Connolly and other Irish Socialists after the Dublin rising of 1916;
surely he could deal satisfactorily with Russian Socialists.
Neither Lloyd George nor any of his colleagues realised that this
dull-looking man was an almost solid block of integrity; with
some of the less admirable qualities of the northern Nonconformist, he possessed his greatest asset, an inviolable and im-
perious conscience.   Henderson would always search out what
he thought to be right, and he would then do it; nothing else
would move him.   He might be influenced when his mind was
not clear; he had deferred to Lloyd George, and he was in the
future to defer too long to MacDonald.   But when he saw his
duty clear, he would do it; he might not even trouble to explain.
Moreover, though Lloyd George knew that he was loyal, he did
not suspect that his loyalty was not to the Cabinet, but to the
Labour movement which he represented in it.

What he thought during his six weeks in Russia his unmoving
face showed nobody; even his letters home merely said such
things as that ' the heat was exceptionally trying ', and that
' Moscow is not a bad city, though . . . it has a terribly mixed
population, including a good many Chinese '.   In fact, he had
decided it was necessary to hold the Stockholm Conference,
and for British Socialists to attend.   He would not agree to the
conference being ' mandatory ', as the Russians wanted; it
should be consultative only, and that would be enough.   If the
Allied parties failed to attend, and the Russians (who would
attend anyway) met only the Germans and Austrians, the stories
that the war was being carried on for French and British
imperialist aims would be universally credited in Russia; these
stories Henderson fully believed to be false.   If they did not
attend, it was not even certain that the Russian Government
would survive; certainly there would be no further co-operation
between Russia and the West; what would happen to the revolution, and to the hope of a just peace, no man could say.   He
told the Cabinet of his decision, bluntly perhaps, on his return.
Lloyd George was away, and for the first time he collided directly
with the blockheaded anger of Conservative upper-class
politicians.   They understood not a word of the arguments he
offered: for them he was a working-man who had become
difficult and was contradicting them on affairs which he could not

understand.   Politics made it necessary to have a Labour man in the Cabinet; but there were plenty of other working-men politicians—Barnes, Clynes, Roberts, Hodge, Wardle and such names—respectfully willing to take his place.   Why should they put up with him?   Only the fact that ' the Goat ', as Sir Henry Wilson called their premier, was away made them hesitate; he had been in favour of ' Stockholm ' once, might he not skip that way again?

But he was not going to.   He had been offended by the American President's speech on ' peace without victory ', and had replied by demanding a peace of punishment and restitution. No great successes had followed his assumption of the premiership a few months ago; instead, the Russians looked like quitting the struggle.   By an illogical but emotionally comprehensible reaction he turned against everything which they advocated, including the Stockholm Conference.   (It may be true that he even wished to offer peace to Germany on the basis of handing over to it slabs of Russian territory.)   Henderson, whose mental processes were slower, probably did not appreciate how completely Lloyd George had changed; when he was summoned to a special Cabinet on August 1st at four o'clock he attended in good faith, and was surprised to find the door locked.   After an hour, George Barnes, the Labour Minister of Pensions, a tall, good-natured, middle-aged engineer with a bald, egg-shaped head, came out of the door to say that he had taken his place by request in the Cabinet while his position was being discussed. Henderson's exact answer is not recorded, but in a few seconds he was inside the Cabinet room, in a formidable rage (' unusually resentful ', said Lloyd George afterwards); he felt that the working-class, as well as himself, had been insulted.   It is to be presumed (since the minutes are still not available) that the discussion which followed was inconclusive and disconnected. Henderson certainly considered at the end that he was still at liberty to recommend the Stockholm Conference to the Labour Party; Lloyd George had in mind an ingenious device which was to appear later; the Conservative Ministers, it may be, felt that the Labour man would on reflection accept his setback obediently.

The Labour Party conference met on August 10th; the Press,

173

tipped off from Downing Street, was sure that the ' pro-German ' proposal to go to Stockholm would be rejected. For Lloyd George's device was now ready. What exactly had occurred will probably never be known—certainly is not yet known— but it is clear that some authoritative person had gone to the Russian *Chargé d'Affaires*, M. Nabokoff (the Ambassador was dead) and persuaded him to send a cable to his Foreign Minister in Petrograd, a careless and temperamental Menshevik named Tereshchenko, asking for a return cable whose actual words were suggested. These were to the effect that the Stockholm Conference was ' a purely party concern, and in no way binding on the Russian Government '. The Petrograd Foreign Office was in chaos; the statement was, after all, technically true; and the cable called for was thoughtlessly sent. As soon as it was received a copy was hurried round to Henderson before the conference met, in the belief that it would give him the excuse, which he was presumed to be waiting for, to announce a change of mind. His fellow trade unionists valued him more correctly than Lloyd George; perhaps they did not love him (' Uncle Arthur ', whatever it may have been later, was originally a resentful, and not an affectionate nickname), but they respected him profoundly. The railwaymen, headed by J. H. Thomas, had changed their opinion merely because he had; the miners (600,000 votes) decided not to make up their minds until they had heard what Brother Henderson said. Brother Henderson (the prefix was in no way odd; it was as natural in a miners' lodge as in a Nonconformist chapel) spoke painstakingly and rather uninspiringly; some delegates, as he balanced one consideration against the other, were not sure until the end what it was he was recommending. He meticulously mentioned that a telegram had been received suggesting that the Russian Government had weakened in its opinion, but concluded by saying that the Stockholm Conference would be held anyway, that British Socialists must attend, and not leave it to the Germans, and that it would be an outrage to the Russian revolution, which they all had welcomed, if its effort for peace met with nothing but a rebuff. A few months ago a pious *Herald* resolution had been rejected by six to one; now this very practical proposal was passed by 1,846,000 votes to 550,000.

The Press was appalled, but its anger was nothing to that of Lloyd George, who worked in a world of political 'combinations' in which such things should not occur. Henderson had to resign from the Cabinet; on the 13th there followed the necessary debate in the Commons. It was Lloyd George's great parliamentary success; Henderson, advised by Shackleton, Asquith and the Speaker that ' there was a war on ', had decided not to expose his Prime Minister, who took every advantage of this. Henderson, he suggested, had lied to the Conference by suppressing ' Kerensky's change of policy ', he had lied to the Cabinet about his own intentions, he had overridden his colleagues. Like a bull vexed by gadflies, silenced by his own self-denial, Henderson could only repeat his assurance of his patriotic intentions, and flushedly demand that the Cabinet minutes which would exonerate him should be read. The Prime Minister smiled and refused.

But the House of Commons was not the Labour movement; Henderson's fellow-workers knew him better, and if they continued to back his new policy by more than three to one, it might still be successful. As soon as news of the debate had been telegraphed to Petrograd, both Kerensky and Tereshchenko re-affirmed in vehement terms their support of the Stockholm Conference, and a formal rebuke was sent to Nabokoff. But this, though enlightening, was late; a denial is not news, and few people read it. A quick propaganda campaign up and down the country—directed among others by Tupper of the Sailors and Firemen, Will Thorne of the General Workers, and Jimmy Sexton of the Dockers—endeavoured to make sure that the verdict of the Labour Party was reversed at the adjourned conference, called for August 21st. Its only effective opposition, for the moment, was Lansbury's *Herald*. If it was successful, and the resolution was annulled, then the whole agitation (from the point of view of the Government) would be happily ended; if not, it would be dangerous to defy what looked like a majority of the working people of the country; there might even be a possibility that the war would be stopped. The night before the conference was to meet it was still uncertain how far the ' Union Jack campaign ' had succeeded. As so often, the decision seemed to turn upon the miners' 600,000 votes; South Wales was for

Henderson, but other districts against; there was perhaps a 3 per cent adverse majority in the Miners' Federation. It was swayed largely by a reluctance to admit the I.L.P. pacifists, probably headed by Snowden and MacDonald, as part of the British delegation to Stockholm (constitutionally and by invitation the I.L.P. had a right to its own representatives); it knew too well what sort of speeches they would make in front of the Germans. A hurried meeting of I.L.P. delegates was held in the Fabian Society's basement in Tothill Street; if the Party would agree to waive its claim, perhaps the miners would change their mind, or would at least agree to vote not as a block, but region by region (and that would have done almost as well). One delegate remembers how Snowden, thin-lipped and sitting huddled up in the thick cigarette smoke, hour after hour prevented the proposal being made to the miners. 'I.L.P. representation is our right.' Never was Lansbury more missed than at that meeting; 'these people don't want peace, they want pacifism', complained G. D. H. Cole, who was pressing the motion. Ultimately it was agreed; and late in the evening Robert Smillie, the miners' leader, was telephoned. It was too late, the weary voice answered; the miners' delegates had decided to cast their vote, all in one block, against Stockholm.

The 'patriotic' delegates, some of them, had small Union Jacks stuffed in their waistcoats, to pull out and wave when the 'pro-Germans' were defeated. But despite the miners' vote, the decision was re-affirmed next day, though by a majority of only 3,000. 'Go on, wave 'em now!' shouted some of the majority, and there were some bad-tempered scenes. But they might well have waved them; 1,234,000 to 1,231,000 did not sound any more like a mass movement. The Government, at its ease, refused passports to the delegates for Stockholm; the Russians when they arrived met German delegates only. The Trades Union Congress, when it met on September 4th, was angry enough to pass (Tupper's union alone dissenting) by 2,849,000 to 91,000 a resolution protesting, and ordering its Committee to endeavour to call a conference itself, after trying first to co-ordinate Allied Socialists' war aims. Statements on war aims were drafted in the next few months; the *Herald*, the *Cambridge Magazine* and other papers printed them, but interest declined. It was too clear that the British and French Governments had destroyed in August any chance of reviving the International. Later next year the *Herald* published in book form an analysis and comparison of both Allied and enemy Socialists' peace terms, showing how close they had come together, and even outlining a treaty based upon them; it was hardly noticed. The Kerensky Government, having failed to secure peace, had been swept away by the Bolsheviks; the German workers' strike in reply to Trotsky's appeal at Brest-Litovsk had failed; Lloyd George and Clemenceau were unshakeably in power. Hope had gone, as the *Herald* said in an unusual mood of despair.

It is interesting, and perhaps not wholly useless, to speculate on what would have happened if these accidents had not occurred and the Stockholm Conference had been held. It is highly probable that after some tempestuous scenes the various delegates would have reached a considerable measure of agreement on peace terms. The analysis made by the *Herald* writer later shows how close the national parties were already; they probably would not have failed to realise (however uncomfortably) that they were now fighting about nearly nothing at all. There would have been brought into existence (the further one speculates, the less convincing become the probabilities; but so far they are still probabilities) a committee, bureau or other organ which, while it could not have issued orders, would have been able to make suggestions which it would be hard to ignore. The 'peace terms', as they would at once have been called, would have had an enormous influence on the organised workers of all the belligerent countries except the United States; they would have followed Wilson's speeches into the minds of the soldiers in the trenches. Their effect would have varied according to the country. In Russia it is unlikely that the success of the Stockholm Conference would have saved the Kerensky Government for very long; it fell because of its general ineptitude, as well as because of its failure to make peace. But the Bolshevik revolution, if it came, would have been less bloody—there would not have been, for example, years of armed invasion by foreign Powers—and this would have had its effect upon the later history of the revolution. Certainly, the Russian armies would have taken the ' peace terms ' as agreed facts; the Eastern front, already quiet, would have ceased to know any fighting at all. It is not unlikely that Austria-Hungary and Italy, already sick of the fighting, might have let their fronts relapse into a similar silence. What effect it would have had upon the better-disciplined armies, and nations, of Germany, Britain and France it is harder to say; but great week-long strikes in Germany followed Trotsky's appeal at Brest-Litovsk; mutinies as well as strikes were occurring on the Allied side. It is possible that the governments might have been forced to placate their peoples by taking some apparent steps towards peace negotiations; such steps would have been easier to take than retrace.

But these are merely speculations; the long night continued. All through the winter the steady slicing down of young soldiers continued; the roll of the ' intolerably nameless names ' grew longer and longer. There was almost nothing that the *Herald*, and Lansbury, could do; it was a winter of despair. Some propaganda successes were all that could be secured. One was so dramatic that it ended the most visible scandal of food rationing: it was a story published in the issue of November 24th, 1917, called ' How they Starve at the Ritz '. A contributor (Meynell), chosen for his appetite and aplomb, was sent to the Ritz with instructions to eat as grossly as he could; he showed considerable imagination in this—calling, for example, for a bowl of cream to pour into his tomato-soup, on the ground that it was not rich enough. The anger caused by his faithful account and the reproduction of the menu was enough to curb sharply the amount of public piggishness that went on afterwards. More important was the publication (already analysed) on May 11th, 1918, of the text of the secret treaties, edited and assembled by Seymour Cocks. But although this number reached a record sale (250,000 copies), the reaction was not what it once might have been; readers seemed cynically to have decided that there was nothing that they could do to end the nightmare, and that this was only one further evidence of how extensively their rulers would lie.

In the earlier months of 1918 it seemed momentarily as if there might be an end to the war, but not the one Lloyd George had anticipated. Soldiers in the trenches had begun to believe that the process of mashing up troops could never end in any important advance one way or the other, but the use of great reinforcements from the East by Ludendorff and Hindenburg appeared for some weeks to be contradicting this.   At great cost and with great slaughter the Allied troops were pushed back steadily, and real alarm spread in London and Paris.   Even Cole and Hutchinson (of the Engineers) wrote in the *Herald* (March 30th), ' There must be no strikes '; though other columns of the paper rejoiced that Glasgow engineers had prevented a comb-out of young men by Sir Auckland Geddes (' the Great Auk is extinct ').

The advance was at last stemmed; and the process reversed, mainly by the throwing of fresh American troops into the mincing-machine.

Victory came to the Allied troops in November 1918, not from the skill of generals so much as from the effects of the blockade. Privation, amounting to near starvation of non-combatants— that is, children and women—had broken the strength of the German nation.   The Allied soldiers as they advanced to the Rhine found the German families emaciated and ravenous; they shocked the patriots at home by sharing their rations with ' the Huns '.

Chapter Thirteen

PEACE was sudden; the soldiers in the trenches had not been alone in subconsciously believing that the mechanical massacre would never end; all men were unable for a while to collect themselves. The *Herald*, in the first peace-time issue, openly said that it could think of nothing but that the killing was at last over. In the next few days, however, as a man may do looking round after a long stupor, all England, including Lansbury and his colleagues, realised that many things had happened whose importance they had scarcely appreciated. Women had received the vote early in 1918 (not on fully satisfactory terms, it is true, but so little was there left of the ' Suffrage spirit ' that it was ten years before the women who had the vote troubled to correct them). Dublin had risen in revolt in 1916, and the Irish leaders were now armed Sinn Feiners—modern Fenians who had no use for English allies. Webb and Henderson, two right-wing Labour men, had produced and imposed on the Labour Party a Socialist programme, detailed and practical, called *Labour and the New Social Order*. Lansbury and his colleagues had had nothing to do with it, and it bore no trace of their syndicalist or ' Guild Socialist ' ideas—in fact, they seemed a little startled at any good thing coming out of such a quarter. Henderson had reorganised the Party, giving it a modern structure to go with a modern programme, and in particular setting up local Labour Parties with individual members. In the end these parties were to make the I.L.P. superfluous, and to put immense power into the hands of the trade union delegates (who could outvote them by hundreds of thousands, and whom they could not frighten, as the I.L.P. might have done, by a threat to walk out and take all the electoral machinery with them). But at the moment the improvement seemed obvious; Lansbury was as pleased as anyone, and in February 1918 had personally intervened at the Party conference to get the new constitution hurried through.

Organisation was anyhow what interested him least in the

Labour movement. He had already written and published what he thought were the most important things he had to say, and the book was now selling in larger numbers than his books had reached before or would again. It had the admirable title *Your Part in Poverty*; it was limpidly and earnestly written, and it probably turned more people away from selfish preoccupations into working for Socialism than anything else that he ever wrote. The book is short—126 small pages of large print—and was sold for a shilling. Its body was in four parts: one chapter contrasted the life of the working class with that of the rich; the second examined more closely what this meant in the case of women and children (always his first interest); the third inquired what sort of a life the business community got out of its preoccupation with money-making; the fourth tried to compel the Churches to compare their preaching with the actual conditions in industry. As an introduction and an epilogue he added what was in part a statement of faith, in part an appeal to others to join him in his work. He had in mind particularly young men and women of the middle class, who heard faintly the call of duty, came down to Toynbee Hall or elsewhere to help the poor, and before long went back to take a job in the Civil Service or elsewhere, regulating and improving a working-class which they had proved was unable to save itself. This, he felt, was profoundly un-Christian and arrogant.

'In the old-fashioned orthodox Christian religion [he wrote] great stress is laid on the necessity of "conviction of sin"; that is to say, on the necessity for men and women to convince themselves of their own wrong-doing. I think that in some ways this is an excellent doctrine, and I should like to see it expressed in regard to social and industrial matters. We must all clear our own minds of cant and be quite honest with ourselves as to the means whereby we secure our daily bread. . . . If we are convinced that the means whereby we live come to us in an honest and straightforward manner, and that taking usury and profit-making are true and right methods of living, there is not much more to be said. But if we decide for ourselves that profit-making and usury are evils which enable some of us to live at the expense of others, then our duty is quite plain: that is, to assist by every means in our power in destroying the system which gives to us so great a material advantage over our fellows.

N   181

' There is a school of people who say that we ought to go on making money because, unless we do, others will do it, and that if we beggar ourselves we do not improve the social position at all. This may be true to some extent, but, all the same, it is also true that if men and women fill up their time simply money-making, no matter what they may call themselves, or what opinions they may hold, they are exactly in the same position as people who support the present order. Therefore, those who are convinced the present methods of money-making are wrong are called upon to live in the simplest manner, and to devote every hour of leisure and every penny of money they can spare to assisting the workers in their task of organising the transformation of the present social order from competition to co-operation. I say this because so many people imagine that they have really done their duty when they have denounced the present order as iniquitous, while others think they have fulfilled their duty when they have distributed large sums of money, either in charity or for similar purposes.'

Lansbury applied these words to himself: he did live in great simplicity, and it was clear to those who knew him that he even felt guilty over the small comforts he allowed himself; while others were in such abject poverty what right had he to a study of his own? He never allowed his rich friends who poured out money for his various causes to feel they had bought a right to an easy conscience; he thanked them warmly for their generosity, but reminded them that they had no right to the money in the first place, and that they would never be at ease until they gave personal service to the cause as well as all the money they could spare.

This, however, was his Socialist gospel, part of his timeless mission. For the moment he was wholly delighted to see the Labour Party suddenly stand out vigorously for its principles. The moment the war ended it decided it could no longer tolerate Lloyd George's leadership; at a special conference, and after that rare thing, a moving political speech by Bernard Shaw, it overrode the protests of the remaining Labour Ministers and left the Coalition. It seemed to many, including Lansbury, that this was the first step to a victory which would come as soon as the air cleared. Even Conservative journalists forecast that in the Forces most votes at an election would be given to the Labour

Party; at home the rise in the cost of living, widespread profiteering, recurrent industrial unrest and the unending lists of dead and wounded were causes or signs of a similar discontent.

When the German collapse was accompanied by a general dethronement of enemy royalties and obvious disorder in Allied countries, Socialist hopes rose very high. ' Crowns and coronets three a penny! ' cried the *Herald* on November 10th. But their chief opponent was more artful a politician than any of the Labour men. The moment of relief and dizziness at the end of the war was chosen by Lloyd George for a sudden election. ' Vote for me, the man that won the war! '—a cartoon by the returned Dyson showed him bustling up to a falling Tommy with blood still streaming from his head. But the appeal, however vulgar, was successful. The poll was low—only a quarter of the uniformed Forces was able to vote—but most of those who voted, voted for their presumed saviour. The Parliament, which Keynes was to describe as one of hard-faced men who looked as if they had done well out of the war, consisted of 359 ' Coalition ' Conservatives, 127 ' Coalition ' Liberals (Lloyd George's own) and 15 ' Coalition ' Labour, against only 60 Labour men, 34 Asquithian Liberals, a few independents, and 73 Sinn Feiners who refused to come to Westminster at all. What made the disaster worse was that the Labour Party lost all its experienced leaders: Henderson, MacDonald and Snowden were out, and Lansbury failed to carry Bow by a few hundred votes. (Blair, C., 8190: Lansbury, Lab., 7248; Dalton, Lib., 988). The Parliamentary leadership fell to Adamson, a kindly miner obviously unfitted for it, and to Clynes, who had just left the Lloyd George Government with open and great reluctance.

The shock was violent: under its influence the *Herald* even called, unsuccessfully, for a general strike against the new Parliament, to force a fresh election upon a proper register. Though the call was not heard, it was not as absurd as it would have seemed a few years later. The union members, freed of their war-time restrictions, were furious at the tricks they felt had been played on them, and anxious to recover their losses in working conditions and in real wages—or, in some cases, vaguely to do ' what the Russians have done '. The soldiers were mutinous:

183

camps were in chaos, a whole ' tin town ' was burnt down, lorry-loads of armed men came to Whitehall to threaten the Ministries. One powerful deputation at least called on Lansbury. What he advised them is not recorded, but they listened absorbedly, thanked him, and said they must now go on to consult Mr. Bottomley.

But the moment passed. Men who could not distinguish between Lansbury and Bottomley could not run a revolution; in any case, the soldiers' chief grievance (the prior release of so-called ' key men ') was swept away by hasty demobilisation. The unions' power to strike was suddenly diminished by a temporary slump which brought the unemployment figures up to nearly half a million. The *Herald* had to content itself with minor successes, one of which was dramatic enough, and showed a gratifying affection for it among the London workers. It had booked and paid for the Albert Hall for one of its great meetings, to announce its decision to reappear as a daily. Hilton Carter, for the Council of the Hall, cancelled the letting arbi-trarily and returned the money. An appeal to the Government was in vain: ' It has no power whatever to intervene,' said Lloyd George. Then the Electrical Trades Union acted. It took out the fuses from the Hall, and explained to the power-station manager that if he re-connected the place it would be obliged to put all Kensington in darkness. The Hall tried to carry on with a glimmering sort of emergency light. But a great Victory Ball was in the offing, and the Licensed Vehicle Workers and other unions were arranging that no buses should stop at the Hall, no taxis take customers to or away from it, and no electric trains stop either at South Kensington or High Street. The Government which had ' no power whatever ' to intervene acted hastily (' could Mr. Lansbury possibly make it convenient to come round to the Board of Trade at once ? '), instructed Hilton Carter, and Mr. Lansbury had not one but two great meetings for his announcement.

For over a year Lansbury and his colleagues had been working to make the announcement possible. He did not intend, if he could avoid it, once again to be in charge of a perpetually bank-rupt paper, always on the point of closing down and with a mere 50,000 circulation. Characteristically, he drew help neither from the Trades Union Congress nor the Labour Party: he had gone direct to the unions and to personal supporters. He had fixed £400,000 in his mind as an adequate figure to start with; he did not get it, nor even half. Just over £100,000 was raised from the unions, and £40,000 from Co-operative Societies; an additional amount, not of great size, came from private subscriptions. Later, £10,000 was collected for special advertising, which used a rooster designed by Lovat Fraser; the miners presented £42,000, and the National Union of Railwaymen acted as ' paper banker '—a most valuable service. It bought the paper, held it, and collected the price from the *Herald* as and when it was used. Not only did this save capital, but it made more difficult a boycott which had already been started. Paper-makers were refusing to supply the *Herald* at all, and Robert Williams even had to go to Lord Burnham, of the Newspaper Proprietors' Association, and threaten to call a strike at the mills before the ban was relaxed. Even so, the paper had often to be bought in various parts of the country and under false names before anything like an adequate amount could be secured.

There were plenty of reasons for saying the project was still an unwise one. But Lansbury would always take a risk. The staff was there, some money was there, the new Government was doing irreparable harm almost daily and must be stopped. With the full support of his backers, Lansbury went forward. After a week's trial run, all the issues of which were kept private, the first number of the new *Daily Herald* appeared on Monday, March 31st, 1919.

Chapter Fourteen

THE first issue of the new *Daily Herald* was a journalistic blunder. The most prominent place on the front page and a ' streamer ' headline were given to a story saying that if the Poles occupied Danzig (as they threatened) ' there would be a Nationalist rising in West Prussia ' and ' a new war would be almost certain '. Nobody believed that Germany could fight a new war; but this ' scare ' tale was allowed to overshadow the real news story which should have been featured, and was written by the editor himself. It disclosed that peace terms had been received from the Russian Republic and were at that moment in front of the Allied Governments. There were to be in the future other instances of amateurishness in handling news. The *Daily Herald* often had ' scoops '—news which others could not get, or would not print, or (more often) were too prejudiced to realise was true—but it did not always get full value out of them. All the same, as a whole the paper was a brilliant production; even technically the (mostly) young men who ran it were before long the equals of their older Fleet Street rivals, while the list of contributors reads like a honours roll of the newer names in English literature. There was nothing like it in the London daily Press.

There was no doubt in anyone's mind who was chiefly responsible for its character, next to Lansbury himself. Gerald Gould had been appointed by him ' Associate ' (not ' Assistant ') Editor, and Lansbury always treated him as his equal and contemporary. ' You and me, Gerald,' he would say, and ' The young people don't know '—faintly vexing Gould, who felt himself to be of the same generation as Ewer, Mellor, Meynell and Ivor Brown. Gould had secured Lansbury's affection during the war; he had gone with him on a brief visit to the front (where he fooled him into drinking brandy in his coffee, saying that ' cognac ' was the name of a syrup that the French liked;

he only confessed the trick when he found G. L. was proposing
to order it daily), he had written regularly for the weekly *Herald*,
he had helped him throughout the long negotiations for raising
money for the daily. Himself, he was a minor poet, most of
whose verse is now forgotten; an essayist whose wit and charm
were not expected to survive; a literary critic whose clarity and
fairness of judgment made him a power, but only in his day.
Yet though he left, perhaps deliberately, very little by which he
would be remembered, he had a strong personal influence upon
the young writers of his day, and brought to the new paper
many whom Lansbury, with his working-class manner and background, could never have influenced. His individuality counted
for much: he was tall, athletic, gentle and amusing; not handsome, but with brilliant blue eyes and an unusual helping of
personal charm. Mainly, if not wholly, through his intervention the early pages of the *Daily Herald* were spotted with the
signatures of men and women who were, or were going to be,
famous writers. Siegfried Sassoon wrote the 'Literary Notes'.
Havelock Ellis reviewed books on sex. W. L. George, Israel
Zangwill, H. M. Tomlinson, H. W. Nevinson and Alec Waugh
were names signed recurrently; less frequently were those of
Rebecca West, Rose Macaulay, Philip Guedalla, Aldous Huxley
and Robert Graves. E. M. Forster contributed steadily;
W. J. Turner, the poet, dealt with music; Herbert Farjeon with
the drama; among other writers (a full list would be tiresome)
were Robert Nichols, Edward Garnett, W. H. Davies, Walter
de la Mare, Frank Swinnerton and Osbert Sitwell. 'Tom-
fool's'—Eleanor Farjeon's—light verse deserved and found
later publication in book form; one poem Lansbury liked so
much as to use it on his Christmas card:

THE CAROL SINGERS

They come in ones and twos and threes,
    Small ragged girls and boys,
Whose homes will show no Christmas-trees,
    Whose stockings hold no toys;
And shuffling on the step at night,
They—sing? Well, to be kind, not quite—
    They make a sort of noise.

Not in the hope of myrrh and gold
And frankincense they sing,
As they a hackneyed verse unfold
About a new-born King.
They rate their gabbled effort at
A penny, and it's scarce worth that
When they go carolling.

A try-on? Yes. But as for me
I never can refuse
The rough unpractised minstrelsy
That tells of heavenly news.
A child once in a stable lay—
How can I empty send away
These children from the Mews?

Perhaps more important than literary success was the collaboration that the new paper secured on political matters. Shaw wrote for it a series of articles on ' How to Repudiate the National Debt ', and in July produced a ' cod ' interview with the Kaiser which greatly annoyed the Conservative and Liberal Press. Vernon Bartlett sent ' Our Paris Letter '. M. Phillips Price, who, as *Manchester Guardian* correspondent, had produced almost the only (exception: Michael Farbman) informative stories from Russia, went to Berlin for the paper. But for the sub-editors who sat in the long, dirty room looking out on Tudor Street the most exciting messages which came through—apart from the short, jumbled Russian wireless intermittently provided by Marconi's—were those of H. N. Brailsford, who was sent out to travel through Germany—in the throes of an aborted revolution—Poland, where an ancient State was trying to revive in a man-made desert, and Hungary, where a romantic Socialist-Communist Government was in power. Much of what was printed was too hopeful: the reports of Freddy Kuh, Hiram Moderwell and other passionate American ' Reds ' were even less restrained than native enthusiasms, but, with all this, the picture of the world through *Daily Herald* columns is, after thirty years, seen to be truer than that of the *Daily Mail, Morning Post, Times* and other papers which almost monthly reported Lenin and Trotsky cutting each other's throats.

' The tone was more moderate; the policy was the same', was Lansbury's own appraisal (six years later in *The Miracle of Fleet Street*) of the new *Daily Herald* as compared with the old. But there were changes, even if they were not fundamental. He was forced, as has already been noted, to include ' tips ' in the sporting news; he tried once to omit the ' Honours List ' because of his deep contempt for the source of class snobbery, but the annoyance of his readers was so marked (justly, for he was suppressing news) that he never did so again. Syndicalism was no longer an operating philosophy, but the vague distrust of M.P.s into which it had degenerated presented no problem. The Labour Party in Parliament was so inept that it could be ignored without discomfort, or its performances relegated to a back page. It was not even loyal to its Party programme. When Lloyd George returned from Paris in July with a treaty which the Party officially condemned, all the Labour M.P.s but three stood up to sing ' He's a Jolly Good Fellow ', all but one stood up for ' God Save the King ' that followed. So incompetent was its leadership, even technically, that the thirty-four Asquithian Liberals were allowed to become the official Opposition in face of Labour's sixty; the preoccupation of the M.P.s, who were mostly ageing trade unionists, was in deploring and restraining the seditious behaviour of their own members. It was good journalism as well as common kindness to ignore them. What had been in part the real purpose of the old syndicalism was transmuted into a steady campaign for the reorganisation of trade unions. Nearly 1,800 separate unions still existed; most, though not all, belonged to the Trades Union Congress, whose sole central body was the ' Parliamentary Committee ', a group of elderly gentlemen who from time to time interviewed Lloyd George or other Ministers and accepted with unvarying simplicity the explanations that were offered. The paper vigorously supported every attempt to amalgamate the small unions (one of these amalgamations, constituting the Transport and General Workers' Union, headed by Ernest Bevin, ultimately destroyed the livelihood of its old supporter, Robert Williams, the Secretary of the Transport Workers' Federation); it also tried to modernise the organisation of the Congress. In December 1919 it recorded a great success; at the same special Congress at which Bevin officially appealed on behalf of the paper, it was decided to abolish the Parliamentary Committee and replace it by a General Council scientifically representing all sections and with (it was hoped) the power to act as leader of the movement.

Abroad the paper's chief enemy was British imperialism. Lansbury saw three countries in which his Government was, by violence, holding down the population: Ireland, Egypt, India. There was no question, in his mind or that of his colleagues, but that justice and the professions of the Allies demanded that British forces should be withdrawn from all three countries and the people allowed to decide their own future. The Egyptians and Indians who visited London found in Tudor Street their only unquestionable friend in the London Press. Other papers, even the *Manchester Guardian* or the *Daily News*, seemed to them to put British interests first and to expose outrages mainly because Britain would ultimately be benefited by the truth; only in the *Daily Herald* did they find their own people's interests regarded as of equal importance. News was censored and delayed; it was not for nearly six months that the facts of the massacre of Amritsar were known, for example. But what could be discovered, the *Daily Herald* printed. Lansbury was closely associated with Zaghlul Pasha, the only Egyptian politician of really statesman-like quality; the Indians with whom he worked were unnumbered—Srinivasa Sastri, Motilal Nehru, Lajpat Rai, Ramaswami Iyer and Shiva Rao were among those in whom he had most confidence. (Gandhi he met later.) Although it was, naturally, whispered that Egyptian and Indian money was 'poured' into the *Daily Herald*, it was not true; the nationalists received and did not give. That the link was less close with the Irish was no fault of the paper: it was due partly to the choice of the Sinn Feiners, who wanted no English friends; partly to the superior journalistic skill of the *Daily News*, whose exposure of the Black and Tans by Hugh Martin anticipated all Fleet Street.

Lansbury had visited Cologne and seen the misery of the German people. 'I saw babies whose bodies were transparent,' he wrote, with excusable exaggeration. The starvation of the German people—of non-combatants, necessarily, first—had been perhaps a legitimate weapon of war; but the war was now over, and there was no possibility of Germany resuming it. The blockade, whose hideous effects he had now seen, was being continued as an act of policy, to break the Germans' will and self-respect completely. Mr. Churchill put the policy clearly in a speech made shortly before the first number of the paper appeared:

' At the present moment we are bringing everything to a head in Germany; we are holding all our means of coercion in full operation or in immediate readiness for use. We are enforcing the blockade with rigour, we have strong armies ready to advance at the shortest notice. Germany is very near starvation. All the evidence I have received from officers sent by the War Office all over Germany shows, first of all, the great privations which the German people are suffering; and, secondly, the danger of a collapse of the entire structure of German social and national life under the pressure of hunger and malnutrition. Now is therefore the moment to settle.'

Lansbury had interviewed Woodrow Wilson and been impressed by his sincerity, though worried by his Olympian aloofness (the President received him magisterially, expounded his own views patiently and warmly, urged him to support them in public, and did not listen to what he answered); he had interviewed Lloyd George and, alone among his colleagues, still considered him a good man and potentially a popular leader, ' but fallen among thieves '. He was less prepared than they, therefore, for the terms of the Versailles Treaty when they became known in summary form in May 1919. (The full text was kept secret—the *Daily Herald* secured a copy a month later, but did not publish it because in fact the summary was a fair summary and the ban was bureaucratic pettiness.) It was not ' an open covenant openly arrived at '; it was a private bargain made secretly between four men—Wilson, George, Clemenceau and the Italian Orlando. Discussion of the terms was not allowed; the Germans were required to sign, or to be punished until they did. Simple evasions had been thought out to dispose of the promises in the President's Fourteen Points. The German Empire was not ' annexed '; it was merely seized and distributed among the Allies, with an obligation to report to a League of Nations which was to be created; consequently it was said to be

' mandated '. ' Indemnities ' were not exacted; they were re-
named ' reparations ', and not only was the poverty-stricken
country carefully pillaged, but tribute was fixed upon it for an
unknown amount into the unknown future. The details of the
Treaty cannot be summarised here; the subsequent treaties with
Turkey, Bulgaria and the broken pieces of Austria-Hungary
were of a similar kind. A Covenant was promulgated establishing a League of Nations, but ' ex-enemy ' nations were
excluded from it.

The despairing criticisms with which this document was
received in the paper were to be endorsed by time. Many
of its provisions were carefully thought out; much good might
have come from some portions. But its essential vices, of
injustice and greed, made retribution certain. In these months,
as certainly as ever man built for the future, the Allied politicians
constructed Nazism. They broke the promises in faith of which
the Germans had surrendered, they forced on the Republic a
false statement of exclusive guilt, they made its future life
economically impossible, and they ensured that a generation
should grow up distorted by underfeeding as well as political
oppression. Some, like General Smuts, knew what they had
done, but in the hope of a world-wide League of Nations
(torpedoed by the American Senate), decided that it was better
to sign than to refuse; Lansbury and the *Herald*, despite their
disappointment, had in the end nothing else to suggest. But a
drawn comment that they made was to last longer than any
printed word. When Clemenceau led the others down the steps
of the Hall of Mirrors in Versailles after the signature, he is said
to have stopped and said: ' Curious! I seem to hear a child
crying.' Dyson drew the picture on May 17th, 1919, ' straight '
with hardly any caricature. In the far corner, away from the
four great men, was the weeping child, a naked baby; round
its head, with uncanny prevision, Dyson had drawn a sort of
halo marked ' Class of 1940 '.

But if it was unsuccessful here, the *Daily Herald* team's
Russian policy, and the news which it printed, were more
effective. In 1919 there were several armed pretenders who
were trying to destroy the Soviet Republic, and in all cases but
one they depended directly upon Allied support. The one

exception was in the Baltic, where German armies under Von der Goltz for a while assisted Yudenitch, a general who nearly reached the gates of Petrograd. Elsewhere the support was Allied, and more and more purely British as the months went on. Winston Churchill, the Secretary of State for War, was the 'Whites'' only consistent supporter. The Americans withdrew early, the Japanese were only interested in the Far Eastern province, the French had other preoccupations. Only British money and soldiers could be called on, and for them there were five claimants. Two were foreign Powers with limited aims; the Poles were extending their authority over non-Polish lands up to the limits of 1772 (the year in which their political thinking seemed to have stopped), and a general named Petlura, who may have been a statesman or may have been a bandit (distinctions were hard to make in these ravaged lands), was constructing an independent Ukrainian State. These received but little support; either because they were ill-placed or because they needed it less. In the East a very serious threat to all Russia was the pseudo-Tsar, Admiral Kolchak, who had occupied all Siberia and was entering the great plain of European Russia. He had Allied advisers and military missions with him, and was so sure of victory that he had already demanded the cession to him of Constantinople and the Dardanelles. In the south was General Denikin, operating from the Crimea, Rostoff and Odessa (secured for him by an Allied bombardment). There was some speculation as to whether they would kill each other when they met, but none as to the regime they would instal; indeed, the physical experience of the peasants at their hands of what a Tsarist restoration would mean was one of the chief reasons for the Bolshevik victory. In the north, based on Archangel, was a government with more democratic and constitutional characteristics, but it depended openly upon British support. Denikin, in October 1919, was sent 'a final gift' of £15,000,000 worth of arms by Mr. Churchill; but British soldiers were sent to fight in the Murmansk and Archangel areas, and the British Navy sank two Soviet destroyers in the Baltic.

To stop the war on Russia, and to print the truth about the revolution, were Lansbury's chief preoccupations in 1919. In April his paper published the text of the terms which William

Bullitt and Lincoln Steffens, two American journalists, had brought from Lenin himself. Bolshevik policy had not by then stiffened into its later rigidity; how much the world has lost may be deduced from the peace offer, which included the abandonment of Soviet propaganda abroad, an amnesty for anti-Bolshevists within Russia, self-determination of all the border States, an all-party conference upon the future government of Russia, and a composition on foreign debts. Bullitt at least had been authorised by Lloyd George to make his journey, but once again the Premier had changed his mind and covered himself by disavowing his past. There was some story, he said, of a young man who was said to have come back from Russia; and so he dismissed it. The war went on. Moreover, it was to be intensified; the blockade which had reduced Germany to such misery could be used effectively here. Two months after the Government had officially denied (in August) that there was any blockade of Russia, the *Herald* published a secret document sent to Germany requiring that unfortunate country to co-operate in cutting Russia off from the world—no ships, no trade, no passports, no bank facilities, no post, no wireless communications were the instructions.

Perhaps the most irritating blow to Government prestige was struck on May 13th, when the *Herald* published a secret War Office circular to all commanding officers. It required them to find out three things—whether their troops would assist in breaking strikes, whether they would parade ' for draft to overseas, especially to Russia ', and whether there had been any growth of trade unionism among them. The state of mind that this revealed, and the plans that it suggested, created an uproar; Bonar Law at first announced that the prosecution of the paper was being considered, but after a few days' thought it was admitted that the news was accurate. Mr. Churchill accepted responsibility for the circular, and stated that, in view of the replies, troops would not be used for breaking strikes; but the war in Russia was to go on. However, British troops would in due course be brought home. The *Herald* replied in violent terms that this last was a lie; preparations were being made not to go, but to stay. Soon the rest of the Press joined in; the *Daily Express* in September published a series of revelations by Colonel Sherwood Kelly, V.C., who had just returned from Murmansk, which seemed to prove the accusation, and included a disastrous statement by the General in command, General Ironside.

In July the paper made a fresh discovery. (Later, Official Secrets Acts would have made it impossible to tell these truths.) In order to stop the soldiers finding out the purposes for which they might be used it had been decided to stop the circulation of the *Herald* under the scheme for sales to the Army agreed with the Newspaper Proprietors' Association for all papers. But as this could not be done publicly, it must be done secretly. The circular ordering it, brought out into the open, read rather wretchedly (issue of July 9th):

CONFIDENTIAL

Bundles containing copies of the *Daily Herald* newspaper are being received at railhead. If addressed to units under your command will you please ensure that *no copies are issued to the troops*, and give instructions for them to be collected and burnt at your Brigade Post Office under the supervision of an officer.

It is important that the collecting and burning of these papers involve as little publicity as possible.

It was about this burnt-offering that Osbert Sitwell wrote ' A Certain Statesman ', the only free-verse poem ever printed as the leader in a London daily. It began:

> ' The *Daily Herald*
> Is unkind.
> It has been horrid
> About my nice new war.
> I shall burn the *Daily Herald*. . . .'

At home the *Daily Herald* for a few years after the war held a position which no other paper was likely to have again. Because the trade union world had not organised its own leadership (the structure of the General Council was not approved until a year after the vote proposing it, and even then it only slowly acquired authority), and the Parliamentary Labour Party had no leadership to offer, it provided almost the only central source of coherent policy. (The I.L.P. was still isolated from most of the Labour movement.) It carried its responsibilities less lightly than before the war; perhaps because it had no *Daily Citizen* to scold after it. It never incited strikes (as it certainly used to); but it came directly to the help of any union on strike. (Wildcat strikes were rarely a problem; so much did the unions dislike and distrust the Lloyd George Government that they supported almost any strike.) It advocated, synthesised and pressed on the unions a policy of ' direct action ' which came very near to adoption, and in one case at least was to have a notable success. That the Government had been elected by a trick, and did not represent the people, seemed to it proved not only by the by-elections (which all showed a sharp fall in Coalition popularity), but by the local elections which in the autumn swept the Labour Party into power in scores of towns where it would never previously have had a chance. There was nothing morally wrong in using industrial force (Lansbury felt) against a Government so elected which was carrying on two illicit wars, as well as ignoring its own domestic promises.

' Direct action ', specifically at this time, meant strikes, either by all the unions in Congress, or the three great unions in the Triple Alliance (Miners' Federation, Transport Workers' Federation, National Union of Railwaymen), against using troops for strike-breaking and the continuation of conscription, for the release of political prisoners, and to stop the wars in Russia and Ireland. The first three objects were, partially and tardily, conceded; to the last two was added later, and more tentatively, direct action on behalf of the miners, though whether this was to be to enforce nationalisation or merely to hold up their wage standards was not always clear. Markets were starved, prices were going up, and for most of 1919 it paid the Government and owners to prevent a big coal strike. The Miners' Federation was induced to cancel a strike threat by the promise of a Royal Commission, half of whose members should be approved by it, and whose recommendations would be implemented by the Government. The *Daily Herald* had splendid ' copy ' in the cross-examinations by Robert Smillie of the Duke of Northumberland and other coal-owners about the social service they performed in return for the large incomes they drew from the coalfields. But the Labour movement had yet to learn that verbal successes and moral victories meant nothing against a Government like Lloyd George's: when the Commission reported in favour of nationalisation it coolly announced that the report would be put aside in favour of a complex scheme put up by a single coalowners' nominee called Duckham; when this scheme was rejected by everyone concerned, it blandly declared the industry had best revert to private ownership.

The *Daily Herald* (Lansbury's history for this period is the paper's history) gave direct help to the lightning and ill-advised police strike in August; it was more useful to the railwaymen next month in the national strike for which Lloyd George stated later the Government had been preparing for months. The Government intention was to break down the railwaymen's wages: prices had been soaring, and there was perhaps behind this brutish resolution a trace of economic thought. If wages, which were a large constituent of prices, were forced down, prices might fall and Britain be assured of large export markets. (In fact, when this operation was completed, Great Britain fell into a fifteen-year depression.) Lloyd George and his advisers, thinking in terms of the war still, made the attack on the railwaymen almost a military operation. Their advertisements called J. H. Thomas's members 'anarchists'; the public were even asked to regard them as they would the Germans. No negotiations, said Lloyd George, would be allowed until the men were back at work—thus making the quarrel a matter of Government prestige. All wages, the Government spokesmen were confident enough to add, would have to follow the railway pattern. The *Daily Herald* produced special editions in Manchester and Glasgow, costing £12,000 to £14,000 above its usual expenses (even though the circulation rose for the moment to the then sensational figure of 500,000, the money could ill be spared). The railwaymen needed the paper's help, for the attitude of all of the rest of the Press in the opening days was bitterly hostile. 'A strike against the community,' said the *Star*; 'Unfair, unreasonable,' cried its elder brother, the *Daily News*; 'Throttling the public,' said the moribund *Pall Mall Gazette*; 'Condemned,' said the *Daily Mail*; 'This junta of unknown and irresponsible men called the Executive Committee,' wrote *The Times*. Others besides the National Union of Railwaymen thought the *Daily Herald* was in part responsible, after a week, for a victory in which the Prime Minister not only agreed to negotiate where he had declared it impermissible, but conceded a large proportion of the union's demands.

The paper which Lansbury had organised had a far wider influence than anything that he had published before. *Daily Herald* readers were in hundreds of thousands—figures cannot be exact, for no one can say certainly through how many hands each copy of the paper passed. It was no uncommon thing for a man carrying a copy of the paper to be approached by a stranger doing the same, and spoken to as a friend. The readers had, towards the staff and especially towards the Editor, a feeling that was both proprietary and filial; they thought the paper was ' theirs ', but at the same time relied affectionately upon the good and wise man at its head. There was something of the same paternal relationship to be seen also in the paper's offices, above the Victoria House Printing Company's machine-rooms south of Fleet Street.

> *Dear George rang up to-night from Bow.*
> ' *The meeting filled my soul with light.*
> *There were twelve dockers in a row,*
> *Apostles of the coming fight.*
> *And if the hall was empty quite*
> *Apart from them, O brothers know*
> *From twelve, the middle of the night,*
> *The path is straight to morning glow.*'

That is part of a poem in a book which almost nobody bought, *Fleet Street in Starlight*, by Felix Boyne, published in 1923, when the story was nearing its end. ' Felix Boyne ' was the pen-name of W. P. Ryan, the night editor of the *Daily Herald*, who wrote this, with other *vers d'occasion*, in the silences before and about ' twelve, the middle of the night '. It may bring back to a few people—not many more than a hundred—a sharp memory of something that happened again and again during the four years which began in 1919.

It is an evening memory. The rhythmic thumping of the

great presses in Victoria House has ceased only a short while
ago; this is the silent period between one edition and another.
As much as there ever can be in a newspaper office there is peace.
The tall, bare, shiny windows seem polished black, for the
unshaded electric bulbs glare against them, and nothing outside is
visible. The three tape-machines (Reuter, Exchange, Central
News) clack intermittently only; the tape-boy is leaning against
them and picking his teeth. Sometimes a proof-reader comes in
with a prim Victorian protest: ' The correctors of the press take
exception to that phrase ' or, ' The Head Reader questions this
paragraph '. Intermittently a door swings open and a reporter
may perhaps be heard on the telephone, bawling curses and the
automatic blasphemies which are still regarded as professionally
necessary. The Chief Sub-editor is drowsing: he may be
' Sam ' Everard, the jovial ' Gadfly ' who survived from the pre-
war *Herald*, or Victor Canonbury, who had once been chief sub
on the *Chronicle* and the *Star* and had the most astonishing
anecdotes of old Fleet Street (and also rice-pudding in his gladstone bag), or Leslie Sheridan, his dark and handsome young
assistant, almost twisted with an ascetic anxiousness to do right.
The telephone bell rings; whoever it may be answers. ' Sub-
editors' room . . . yes . . . yes, G. L. . . . Oh, did you? . . .
The Poplar Branch of the Transport Workers? . . . Wait, I'll
take it down . . . yes . . . yes . . . yes . . . I'll see it does.
. . . No, there's nothing new. Practically nothing's come over
the machines for an hour now. . . . I will. . . . Thank you.
. . . Good night, G. L.' Then, with a sardonic grin, holding
some paper in his hand, he turns round. ' The old man's had a
meeting to-night.' ' Go on! What was it like? ' ' What are
all his meetings like? Inspiring. Probably fifty people there.'
' What's it worth? ' ' Oh. A stick at most. And Late
London only. Mucking up the paper with this bloody rubbish '
—the last phrase said with a fury almost masking the profound
serenity beneath it.

Night after night Lansbury used to ring up, paternally.
Everyone there would wish to know what he had done that day;
he must verify before he slept that everything there was all right.

Outside the *Daily Herald* only one thing of political importance had happened to him. As in so many other boroughs,

the November elections had wiped out the Tories in Poplar: Lansbury was to be the first Mayor of the new regime, without robes, mace or cocked hat.   In his advice to Labour Councils, published in December, he spoke almost exclusively of improved amenities and proper treatment of Council employees; his critics said already that he would have no care for the rate-payers.   But, despite the pleasure this victory gave him, his eyes were for the moment looking far away from Bow.   There were comrades of his in Europe who were trying to set up a Socialist State.   He was not sure that he could approve of their methods.   'I would not assist in establishing Socialism by brute force even if I had the chance,' he wrote in September.   But at least he would see what they were doing.   This ageing man (he felt tired, and in November he had said publicly he had 'only a few years more of active life') decided to smuggle himself into Soviet Russia.   If he succeeded, he would be the first British editor to get there.

Chapter Fifteen

IT seemed a well-chosen time to visit Russia. The British troops had, after all, been withdrawn from Murmansk and Archangel in the north, where the Government had promptly collapsed, most of its soldiers joining Trotsky's Red Army as soon as the British had sailed. Kolchak's forces in the east scarcely existed now: the area which the Bolsheviks controlled in Siberia was limited only by the distances their soldiers could march. Denikin in the south had been seriously defeated, and his destiny seemed similar (a general named Wrangel was to rally his followers for a while, but that could not be known). Von der Goltz's Germans in the west had returned home, where they were making trouble of their own, and a capitalist republic in the area where they had fought, Esthonia, had decided to defy the Allies and had opened negotiations for peace with Russia. The end of nearly six years of war and civil war seemed near, and the meetings between the Ests and Russians might open a crack in the blockade. The first step would be to Copenhagen, where Maxim Litvinoff for the Russians was carrying on with Jim O'Grady, the Labour M.P., and whoever else might be there, negotiations which were supposed to be about exchanging prisoners but which everyone knew were about peace—if, when, and to what extent Lloyd George would make up his mind to it. Moreover, Copenhagen was the place where Swedish and Finnish paper could be bought, and what more reasonable place could there be for an editor to go whose journal was already in difficulties for its raw material? Lansbury got his visa without trouble for Denmark; what he said to Litvinoff there he did not record, but he was not able to go, as he had hoped, in the baggage-train of the Russian diplomats after they had signed a treaty with the Ests. He crossed the Baltic to Finland at the end of January 1920, and there, so far as the *Daily Herald* knew, he vanished. There was no communication of any kind allowed with Russia;

some day, it was to be presumed, if his throat was not cut, he would reappear and tell what he had seen.

Days later, on February 8th, the tall mast which Marconi's had erected at Carnarvon received suddenly, in between Morse cracklings announcing weather conditions at sea, a private message, *en clair*, from. Moscow—the first time such a thing had happened. Godfrey Isaacs' staff somewhat sullenly sent it on to the *Daily Herald*. It was from George Lansbury. ' Arrived here to-day,' he began (' to-day ' was Sunday). ' The churches are all open, and people going in and out. . . .' Lansbury had momentarily forgotten he was a newspaper-man: he had sent a letter home as he would to his family, and on Sunday, naturally, he was interested in what the churches were doing. (His opening sentence earned for him a careful denunciation by revolutionary puritans: it showed, they said, that he was impregnated with bourgeois superstition and potentially a traitor to the class-conscious workers. Incidentally, his whole life, since he left the S.D.F., must be envisaged as accompanied by this thin but unceasing chorus.) In his later messages, as in the book which he published (*What I Saw in Russia*), he recovered himself, and sent reports (which were mysteriously held up in England, sometimes for four days) that covered adequately whole areas of the unknown land he was exploring. He saw Melnichansky, the secretary of the trade unions; Nogin, the head of the socialised textile industry; Djerzhinski, the chief of the political police; Lezhava, the chairman of the Co-ops; Lenin, Krassin, Kameneff, Zinovieff, Chicherin and others—all destined to die of overwork or to be killed by the Stalinists.

Lenin's Russia was not Stalin's: the present (1951) regime bears no more resemblance to what Lansbury saw than did the Empire of Bonaparte and Fouché to the France of the Convention, and far less than Cromwell's dictatorship did to the Commonwealth of 1649. Even the great Chief of later days was inconspicuous. (Stalin held the minor post of ' Commissar for Nationalities '. Lansbury, who was a keen observer, did not think him worth mentioning. Phillips Price, who had gone right through the revolution, mentions him once in his monumental *Reminiscences*, and his name is spelled wrong. Accounts which suggest he was playing a part of importance at the time of Lansbury's visit are written later, for propagandist purposes.)   Lenin himself worked harder and fed no better than his fellow-workers. How spare this regime was Lansbury recorded: the food was meagre even to him.

' Breakfast, three slices of black bread, a little butter substitute and cheese, two glasses of tea without milk. . . . 5.30 our main meal, two platefuls of vegetable soup, cusha—I think this is correct, it is a kind of rice or birdseed—bread and two glasses of tea . . . at bedtime cusha boiled in fat, bread, jam, tea.'

Banquets with many courses and seventeen toasts in vodka were far distant; while Lenin was alive they were unthinkable.   Lansbury recognised at once the habits, thoughts and morals of the men whom he met; they had been his own in the early days of the S.D.F.

His interpreter, in the nine weeks he spent in Petrograd and Moscow, was Alexander Berkman, the Russian-American anarchist, a convinced and open opponent of Bolshevism; the fact made no difference to his reception.   He interviewed at length Chertkoff, Tolstoy's executor, who opposed the regime on pacifist grounds, and old Kropotkin, who attacked it on patriotic grounds.   He tried to interview the Patriarch of the Russian Church, Tikhon, who refused on the ground that he was ' under domestic arrest '; Lansbury checked up on this statement, and decided it was hardly even nominally true.   He found, in fact, the most astonishing freedom of discussion, and even of action: nothing could be more different from the later regime of strictly controlled thought and speech.   Some phenomena, such as the experiments in drama, painting, decoration and poetry, meant nothing to him; some, such as the almost complete freedom of divorce, disquieted him.   But, viewed as a whole, what he saw exhilarated and inspired him.   What he wanted, all his life, above everything else was freedom for the average woman and man: here it had been found.   There was no *master-class*— that was the most important and irrevocable change.   However badly the Russian workers might manage their industries (and he saw several lamentable examples), they were now *their* industries.   When he addressed the Moscow Soviet he spoke to a body which was as democratic as an English town council.

Indeed, its proceedings reminded him closely of the L.C.C., and Kameneff of Cyril Cobb; the difference was that instead of debating if the Council could take charge of some minor productive activity, this Council was discussing the running of industries which were already in the people's hands.

He may have been dazzled, he was not blinded. He saw, what was indeed proclaimed, that politically there was a dictatorship. The Communists were a minority, but they accepted as comrades all who were on the workers' side against the Whites—the days of ideological persecution had not yet come. Moreover, it was a dictatorship *of*, and not yet *over*, the proletariat. Organs like the Moscow Soviet were still in fact responsible to their constituents; opposition existed within them; the leaders genuinely deferred to the opinions of their electors. In due course the Soviets were to become hollowed-out, and real decisions be taken elsewhere, within the Party; but for the moment there was a democracy, based on industry and military in its harshness, but nevertheless a true one. And with the disappearance of class privilege there had gone another division: the Republic was international in its mind and policy. There 'are no such things as strategic points', said Chicherin, the Foreign Commissar (who worked all night and slept all day). There was, and could be, no quarrel with the Finns, Letts, Poles or any other of Russia's neighbours. Invaded, the Red Army would defend Russia; but the days of Imperialism were over. For these border countries the Soviet programme was to get out and stay out. Anything else was a crime against the world's workers.

Lansbury inspected with particular suspicion the political police, soon to be known as the Cheka. Under Djerzhinski it was untypically efficient—'it would rejoice Sidney Webb,' he wirelessed sardonically. But he eventually accepted the Chekists' belief that they were really saving life: the Revolution had been accompanied by the most barbarous, disorganised and wanton massacres and murders, but steadily the police were containing, diminishing and preventing this violence. Political executions were rarer and rarer: more and more was attention being turned to ordinary crimes and unsocial behaviour, and more and more also was punishment giving way to re-training and rehabilitation. The police force, according to Lenin's theory in *The State and Revolution,* was an organ of coercion which would in due course disappear; give Russia peace and the end of Allied intervention, and that ideal would before long be achieved.

It was impressed on Lansbury everywhere that Allied action was mainly responsible for the faults which he saw around him. Relatively immense sums had been voted for education and the care of children; the Allied blockade and the devastation of a civil war which had almost reached Moscow made more than half the plans useless. Semashko, the Commissar of Public Health, had a programme which sounded like paradise to the Mayor of Poplar; but the blockade had successfully prevented the arrival of any medicines or stores. Operations were being carried out with ordinary knives and no anæsthetics; as soon as the snow melted, the masses of filth which encumbered the towns would start epidemics that could not be checked.

When Lansbury first entered Russian territory (he noted the time—4.50 on the afternoon of Thursday, February 5th, 1920) he was ' almost shouting for joy ' at the sight of the Red Flag over the local Commandant's office. But he soon realised that to admire was not enough: ' go thou and do likewise,' was the message. It was driven home by the man he most respected of all whom he met there.

' When I saw Lenin [he wrote] he had just recovered from a serious illness, and yet he was cheerful and apparently vigorous; not for one moment did conversation on his side flag, nor for an instant did he hesitate to answer the most direct, clear-cut questions in a straight-forward, honest manner. Cabinet Ministers in other countries would have talked of their troubles, of their difficulties, would have sur-rounded themselves with a group of officials to prevent the possibility of any mistake in their answering of questions: but Lenin takes the field alone, and this because he is not a diplomat—that is, he does not use language of a double meaning but wants you to understand what he means. He hates compromise. . . .

' I believe his strength comes because he is absolutely impersonal. He is the best hated and the best loved man in the world, but I believe he is absolutely indifferent both to love and hatred. I do not mean that he has no feeling, because I am confident that he loves little children, but in the pursuit of the cause of socialism he cannot be thwarted or turned one side or the other by personal considerations of any kind. He would go to the scaffold as calmly as to a meeting of his cabinet. He is not the " boss " of Russia, but he is the inspiring spirit of Russia. If there is such a thing embodied in humanity as the spirit of religion, then Lenin has got it to a larger extent than any other man I have met.'

Lansbury—not unexpectedly, perhaps—found it difficult to believe Lenin had no religion.

' Like the saints of old [he said of him] he has devoted his whole life to the destruction of capitalism, which he believes is the most awful cancer in the life of humanity. Those who would be his friends must be as pure hearted as he: he has no room for any of us who are half and half, and he wants us to be one thing or the other. He does not understand patriotic socialism. He does understand the pacifist attitude although he does not agree with it, but h e will have nothing to do with those socialists who cry out for the d efence of the father-land, because the fatherland to him is the world. He typifies in my judgment, a living expression of the saying of Tom Paine: " The world is my country, to do good is my religion, all mankind are my brethren ".'

On one thing both men agreed, and they were wrong. This was that shortly the Labour and Socialist movements of the whole world, bar a few useless leaders who had taken part in carrying on the recent war, would join the new International which the Bolsheviks were setting up. But would there be room in it for those like Lansbury who were opposed to violence and wanted to use constitutional methods? They discussed the question at length, and Lansbury believed that he had from Lenin a definite and considered ' yes '. Though such a permission is contrary to all later Communist theory, it was not impossible at the time. Bolshevik policy had not yet crystallised. In Lenin there was a strain of Peter Poundtext: though he was never so dim-sighted a commentator on Marx's words as his successors, he nevertheless had an inordinate reverence for the master's writings, and used to bandy texts with Kautsky and other pundits. And there was an important passage in which Authority had named Britain and Holland as the only two countries where violence might not be necessary.

The concession may not have seemed important to Lenin:

it did to Lansbury. His way was now clear. When he returned to London he spoke, on March 22nd, to a meeting in the Albert Hall so packed that it dwarfed all but one even of his earlier meetings. He quoted Lenin's message to him in these words:

'If you can bring about a peaceful revolution in England, no one will be better pleased than we in Russia. Keep in your trade union movement; keep in your Labour movement. Don't divide until you have to divide. Don't become disintegrated by premature strikes or premature upheavals. Keep together till you are homogeneous and do not be led into resorting to violence.'

He took the opportunity to repudiate the charges, already being sedulously spread, that the *Daily Herald* was subsidised by the Bolsheviks. The paper, he said, had received 'not a single penny from outside this country'.

From then on his personal policy (his colleagues had more hesitation) was to induce all British Socialist organisations—the Labour Party as well as the I.L.P. and the British Socialist Party, which had succeeded to the S.D.F.—to join the new International *en bloc* and make of it a tolerant, world-wide organisation which would achieve Socialism in his lifetime. The policy was impracticable: neither in London nor in Moscow could it have been accepted, and within a year he had seen this. But the effects of his Russian visit never wore off; co-operation between British workers and the Russian Government remained his consistent object, and he even extended a sentimental affection and protection to the small British Communist Party in later years.

He put his policy before the Labour Party conference at the end of June, in a speech which was received politely and no more. Its pacifism appealed neither to the revolutionaries nor to the patriots. The motion to leave the old International received only 516,000 votes against 1,010,000; the motion to join the new was rejected by 2,940,000 votes to 225,000.

Lansbury expected the defeat, and there were successes to console him. The policy of 'direct action' was steadily gaining support. The Poles had launched a great attack on Russia, supported by masses of Allied arms, and had even taken the Ukrainian capital of Kieff. The dockers in East London intervened in May: they stopped the loading of an arms-ship for Poland, the *Jolly George*, and the Dockers' Union conference, so far from repudiating them, extended and generalised the boycott: at the end of the month the railwaymen's union for a fortnight did the same. The Polish generals' supplies were partly cut off: perhaps because of this, their advancing columns soon began to falter. Their satellites had taken Odessa; they themselves had announced they would require the ' frontiers of 1772 ', which involved annexing an area of White Russia larger than Poland itself and absorbing incidentally the state of Lithuania. But their resources were strained and their troops tired; in June they began to retreat. Next month the strategy of Trotsky and the generalship of Tukhachevsky had their reward: Rovno was captured, and the Polish army broke into two. Now that the Poles were on the run, the ' hidden hand ' became no longer hidden: an Allied wire was sent to the Russians threatening intervention unless they granted an armistice to the defeated invaders. The Russians agreed, and negotiations were opened; but both sides were dilatory. The Poles' minds were still clouded with illusions of grandeur; the Russians were in no hurry to halt their victorious armies. In August their troops were nearing Warsaw. The British Government now took open steps towards war on Russia. The Navy was ordered to the Baltic; Lloyd George announced that ' pressure would be brought on everyone ' to come to Poland's aid; an ultimatum was sent to Kameneff, the Soviet envoy in London. On August 7th the blockade was re-established in its fullest vigour; Lloyd George and the French President, Millerand, met next day at Lympne with their two army chiefs, Sir Henry Wilson and Marshal Foch. Lenin rejected the ultimatum; Millerand and Lloyd George referred the question of warlike action to Marshal Foch.

The unions had voted in Congress, less than four weeks ago, in favour of direct action—a strike—to stop any war in Russia and Ireland. Perhaps they had not expected to have to honour their promise so soon: certainly, the Government had dismissed the resolution as wind. If it was wind, it was a wind that was rising; the waves were beating higher and higher; during the past four days of crisis, in branch meetings, party meetings,

lodges, ports, pits and factories men had been becoming angrier
and more anxious; they were determined to stop any war, and
this war more than all. The *Daily Herald's* columns had been a
crescendo of alarm, a tocsin; breaking Fleet Street custom, it
published on the 8th a Sunday edition with a streamer: ' NOT A
MAN, NOT A GUN, NOT A SOU '. The call was heard; the next
evening at the House of Commons a hastily convened meeting
of the Parliamentary Party, of the National Executive and of the
Trades Union Council decided on quite unprecedented action.
All the strength of the workers, it declared, would be used to
prevent a new war, including a general stoppage of work. All
union executives were required to hold themselves in readiness
to implement this decision, and a Council of Action was selected
from the meeting to carry it out. There was no doubt, from the
reports of the country, that the instruction would be obeyed if
the leaders were firm. Firm they would be; there was no
division between Left and Right; Henderson was as determined
as Robert Williams —indeed, curiously enough, he seemed to
the *Herald's* observers rather more steadfast.

Seldom can a government with so huge a majority in Parliament have received so jarring a blow. There was now no
question of proceeding with its Polish policy. Overnight
Lloyd George's confident bullying tone turned to a scolding,
shrill denial that any warlike thoughts had been in his mind.
Assistance to the Poles stopped dead; they rallied, indeed, but
with French aid alone. There was no British war on Russia;
a major part of Government policy had been altered, forcibly,
by the intervention of another power. That other power was
the organised working class of its own country; it was probable,
indeed inevitable, that the Government would take steps to break
it. Some of those steps were conscious; some, the most
effective, were the results of an economic disorder which it may
have caused, but certainly did not desire.

The *Daily Herald*, an antagonist perilously alone and very
dangerous, was now probably at the height of its power. Its
certified paid circulation, two months later, was found to be
329,869—in those days a very considerable figure, and its
influence was vastly greater than these figures suggested. (The
Daily Mail, ' a million sale ', could not have brought out a single

brickworks on strike, nor altered a by-election in one industrial town.) It had been partly responsible for striking the Government a reeling blow, and for months now had been printing revelations which officials least desired to see. The latest—the once-famous ' Golovin interview ', published a month before the crisis—had shown the Secretary for War privately making the most injudicious promises of help to White Russian generals. Some of the galaxy of literary men had withdrawn their support —one famous novelist explaining rather injuredly that he had never intended to support working men in activities against their employers—but Lansbury and his colleagues felt themselves on the whole strengthened by such desertions. The taking over of power by the workers was not going to be easy; it would demand patience, tenacity, clearheadedness and sacrifices. People who had called themselves ' Socialists ' out of vague benevolence and vaguer discontent were better away.

Ten days after its defeat, the Government made a direct attack on the *Herald* and its editor. The Admiralty issued what was claimed to be evidence that Lansbury was secretly in Russian pay. The method as well as the matter of the revelation excited suspicion. Even in 1920 for Lloyd George to accuse George Lansbury of monetary dishonesty had an element of the grotesque, but, in addition, the release of the charge was peculiar. The statement was sent to the rest of the Press, and not to the *Daily Herald*: had it not been for the courtesy of the *Manchester Guardian* and the *Daily Mail*, the journal would have appeared on the first day in all innocence without any answer. An attempt had also been made to persuade a news agency to issue the documents as its own discovery; only when it refused had the Government come into the open. The papers consisted of eight telegrams alleged to have passed between Litvinoff and Chicherin, some at the time of Lansbury's visit to Copenhagen and some in the summer. The earlier ones dealt with Lansbury's efforts to buy paper from the Russians, which seemed innocuous enough, but in the later there were references to a gift of money. The Admiralty admittedly had inserted the figure (' 6,000 francs '!) of the amount supposed to have passed, and as convincing detail it was added that payment was made in ' Chinese Bonds ', whatever those might be.

' Chinese Bonds, Chinese Bonds
With which Lansbury absconds;
Chinese Bonds, Chinese Bonds,
Smuggled by Peroxide Blondes;
Tightly packed by Spiers & Ponds;
Chinese Bonds, Chinese Bonds,
CHINESE BONDS! '

sang the *Daily Herald* poet disrespectfully. Lansbury immediately printed the complete list of all persons and organisations who had produced money for the paper. ' Not a bond, not a franc, not a rouble', ran the headline; and it was justified. Not even the most trifling subscriptions had come from overseas. The defence was unanswerable, for audited figures were there, and even if Lansbury had been the man to fake the accounts of a company, he would have been discovered. For the moment, the Government was silent.

Nevertheless, the paper was in considerable difficulties. By the calculations of 1918, 330,000 sales should have established it comfortably; but the calculations had been falsified. All papers now lived by their advertisement revenue, not their sales, and a stiff and effective advertising boycott had been applied to the *Herald*. It was so open that it was even discussed in the trade Press. Very few advertisers could be obtained at all: those that bought space expected and received much lower rates than its specialised and steady type of reader would have justified. In one or two cases possible advertisers were frank enough to point to items of news or articles which they would require to be altered or omitted if they patronised it. (One item was a criticism of the floating of a company, another an account of bad wages in the firm's trade.) Mostly, if they discussed the matter at all, they said that they saw no reason to aid a paper which was an enemy of private property. Moreover, costs to the paper were soaring. The 1920s were the years in which the multitudinous British Press was being killed; only the monsters were to survive. Partly this was of intention, for Northcliffe was well aware of the effect on smaller journals of the high wages he agreed to so easily. Exuberating wage and salary bills, however, were less alarming than the rocketing price of paper. Supplies were short—a great part of the pre-war sources in Russia was unavailable—and bidders with enormous purses were racing the price up; the *Daily Herald* was only one of many papers in grave difficulties.

It suffered more than others from a third difficulty. Unlike some of its rivals, it depended wholly upon the workers having pennies with which to buy it. And by now British economy was on the edge of the abyss. The ' hard-faced men ' were not hard-headed; they seemed to have imagined that the sellers' market at the end of the war would go on indefinitely. Prices of exports had been forced up (coal prices had been almost doubled), and, so far from using the short golden age to re-equip old factories, mills, furnaces and pits, the business community had gone out on a speculative ' jag ' in which, for example, Lancashire mills already obsolete were sold at 100 and 200 per cent above their previous value. By the autumn of 1920 the British employers were pricing themselves out of the export market and out of the home market too. Among the few advertisements which the *Herald* did secure were sinister full-pages from Selfridge's, announcing 10 per cent slashes in all prices in an endeavour to start sales up again. Goods were not moving; the paralysis was spreading back to the factories and mills; *Herald* readers were going on the dole. The fifteen years of mass unemployment and industrial stagnation were beginning. Now it looked as if the price would have to rise to twopence. What would happen to its circulation then?

At that moment a way out seemed to be opened. The issue of September 10th, 1920, carried on its front page the question: ' *Shall we accept £75,000 of Russian money?* ' An offer of that amount had, in fact, been received. It was a plain subscription from the Bolshevik Government—there were no conditions attached, nor any demand for a directorship; if accepted, the money would carry rather less than more obligation than that received already from the miners' and railwaymen's unions. The journal commented only that, as an internationalist, it saw in principle no objection, but was uncertain about the propriety of taking money from so devastated a country. It asked its readers' opinions; it also consulted the directors, debenture-holders and (privately) the staff.

The first category—the readers—seemed in favour; all the rest answered ' No '. The gift might be—indeed, probably was —innocuous; the manner of its arrival was too unfortunate. Francis Meynell, a director, had been in Copenhagen buying paper soon after Lansbury; some echo of his activities must have sounded in the Admiralty ' revelations '. He had agreed (strictly on his own authority) to bring back to London an amount of money amounting to £75,000, to be offered to the *Daily Herald* without conditions. Transference of a sum of that size, or indeed of any size, was in 1920 a matter of great difficulty. Any transactions with Russia were officially forbidden by the Lloyd George Government; the money was eventually brought across by Meynell not in ' Chinese Bonds ', but in jewels. To reconvert the jewels into currency he had secured the help of Edgar Lansbury, G. L.'s second son, who was in the timber trade in East London. There was nothing in this that was wrong, but there was plenty that was unwise. Disregarding the fact that no money had been received or even (till that day) been offered, the Government at once issued a statement claiming that all its accusations had been proved. Was not Meynell a director of the paper? Was not Edgar's name Lansbury? The argument was flimsy, but the clamour was enormous. The *Morning Post* was gross, *Punch* sneered, and other papers exhibited their individual characteristics. Meynell, having presented the offer, resigned his directorship, apologising to Lansbury for any embarrassment he had caused. He received a typically affectionate reply; but acceptance was now impossible. The money was refused, and the price of the paper was raised to twopence; everyone knew how dangerous that was.

The price-change was made on October 11th, 1920, one day after all the miners in Great Britain had come out on strike. The conjunction of dates was a warning. The strike was settled in a few days (the miners' colleagues in the Triple Alliance, the dockers and the railwaymen, came to their aid, though the machinery seemed to creak), but had it not been, the position would have been disastrous. The miners would have needed the paper more than ever, but its price would have been so raised that neither they nor their allies could have bought it. However, it was for the moment only a warning; to its own surprise and that of its rivals (Northcliffe called it ' the miracle of Fleet Street '), the *Daily Herald* at twice the price of any other paper still kept a 200,000 circulation.

The subsequent history of the *Daily Herald*, for the next two years was a part of the history of the British people as a whole. The marsh of economic depression into which the nation fell made it very difficult to defend the standard of living, which, for a while, the working class had secured. Nor was it prepared to defend it. The Labour Party in Parliament was still a tiny minority; the General Council of the Trades Union Congress still had no over-riding authority. Neither was there unity of will among the leaders. Great hopes had been pinned upon the Triple Alliance, of miners, railwaymen and dockers, but in April 1921, when a direct attack was made upon the miners' wages, their allies failed to come to their aid. The Alliance leaders, Thomas and Cramp for the railwaymen and Bevin and Robert Williams for the dockers, decided (with their executives' consent) on Friday the 16th that an incautious speech by Frank Hodges (the miners' secretary) gave them sufficient reason to refuse to strike on the miners' behalf. The *Daily Herald's* leader on this ' Black Friday ', written by Gould, began:

' Yesterday was the heaviest defeat that has befallen the Labour movement within the memory of man. It is no use trying to minimise it. It is no use pretending that it is other than it is. We on this paper have said throughout that if the organized workers would stand together they would win. They have not stood together, and they have reaped the reward.'

Lansbury frequently quoted that leader as the best that he had printed in his paper, and one by which he would wish it to be remembered. But words could not, for the moment, help; nor yet the £86,000 which the paper raised to help the miners in their struggle. They were defeated after many months, and the next year (1922) the richest union in Britain—the Amalgamated Engineering Union—was faced by a similar attack, whose outcome was the same. By then the paper itself was in deep water; it seemed likely to be swept away in the disasters which were overwhelming the whole Labour movement.

Moreover, its editor was entangled in an equally obstinate

conflict in local affairs. He had vacated, at the end of his term, the mayoralty of Poplar, but he remained the most influential member of the borough council, and was determined to use its power to resist the Government's policy of bringing down the standard of living of the workers. To all appearances, no local council could affect the issue; however, neither Sir Alfred Mond, the Minister of Health, nor any of his officials knew the law as well as George Lansbury and his colleagues, or had the least expectation of what they were about to do.

Chapter Sixteen

IN 1921 the number of unemployed was over a million. It was never going to fall below that figure in peace time—it was to rise much higher, indeed—but nobody then, not even the Government whose policy had caused it, thought this slump was to be permanent. The ex-servicemen who formed a very large proportion of the unemployed were angry that it had ever occurred; they had been promised a newer and happier world, ' homes fit for heroes ' and other slogans that they refused to forget, and many of them were in an ugly mood. In quite a short while they had exhausted their benefits under the Insurance Acts; some were given for a while an ' uncovenanted benefit ', insultingly called ' the dole ', some were forced to go to the Poor Law Guardians to receive ' relief ' on the old system. Perhaps, since they are now extinct, it should be explained that the Guardians were separately elected for their job, but their expenditure was met from local funds. None of them dared, it is true, behave as the Whitechapel Guardians once had done; half a dozen small authorities in London, however, did still refuse any relief outside the workhouse. Poplar, though, like most Labour boroughs, its administration was economical, took particularly generous care of the thousands who could not get work.

It was impossible, however, for councillors or Guardians like Lansbury and his colleagues to go on paying decent rates for long; Sir Alfred Mond, as successor to John Burns, could watch them with equanimity. For the poor were once again helping the poor: the enormous sums that had to be paid came largely from the pockets of men nearly as hard up as the helpless unemployed. Poplar's rates had been 11s. 5d. in the pound in 1917; in 1921 they were 22s. 10d. For by law the disaster which had fallen on East London was East London's responsibility. Apart from some trifling and inadequate payments made under an old Act, the wealthy West End boroughs were evading responsibility, as though the desolate and silent docks were the results of a failure of the Poplar Borough Council. The councils in working-class areas were rushing to bankruptcy (they were mostly Labour Councils, naturally), for the resources they should have used were locked up elsewhere. Lansbury quoted typical figures:

	Westminster	Poplar
Population	141,317	162,618
Rateable Value	£7,913,538	£947,109
Product of 1d. Rate	£31,719	£3,643

Poplar Council's position was worsened because it had been encouraged by Mond's predecessor, Dr. Macnamara, to spend between £30,000 and £40,000 on particular projects for which the Ministry had afterwards, by a trick (as it felt), refused to pay. But there seemed no way out for the Council: it would have to cut relief. A most agreeable thought for the Government; for if the Labour Councils were to be forced to take the initiative in forcing down the working class's standard of living, then the 'salutary effects of unemployment' would be felt on wage rates throughout the country without political inconvenience.

Lansbury was later called 'the uncrowned king of the East End'. But he was never that; the unexpected and infuriating way out found by the Poplar Council was due as much to four of his colleagues—his old friend John Scurr; Charlie Sumner, a short, jovial, old-style trade unionist; Charlie Key, a dapper schoolmaster who succeeded him as M.P. for Bow; and his son Edgar. A large part of the Council's bill consisted of 'precepts' —sums which, like all London boroughs, it was compelled to levy for the use of outside authorities, particularly the London County Council, whose demands had doubled themselves, and for Poplar were now over £270,000. It was decided on March 22nd, 1921—moved Sumner, seconded Key—merely to refuse to levy these precepts, and raise a rate only for the expenses of the Poplar Council itself.

Instantly there was an uproar. Certainly the action was illegal; but the Council pleaded in effect that it was compelled. It could neither turn the workless on to the streets to beg, nor screw money from its ratepayers which they had not got. The results of the economic disaster the Government had brought on

London must, at the very least, be dealt with by London as a whole. Let the L.C.C. (and the Metropolitan Asylums Board, which came in as a minor party concerned) levy its own rate if it chose, or seize the Poplar Council's property. The Councillors would not take actions which were probably impossible and certainly disgusting.

Some time was spent in litigation, which the Council sustained only for propaganda purposes. (Lansbury, as usual, was acute enough to discover a flaw in the writ of *mandamus*, which should have named the Councillors affected, and so to prevent the L.C.C. getting costs off Poplar.) Eventually it was summoned to the High Court on July 29th. It attended in procession, marching from Bow with the mace-bearer at the head; a band played it through Whitechapel and the City, and a banner preceded it, saying ' POPLAR BOROUGH COUNCIL marching to the HIGH COURT and possibly to PRISON '. Its behaviour ruffled the Court: ' What would happen if all borough councils did this?' asked one judge. ' Why, we should get the necessary reforms,' explained Lansbury benignly.

The issue was not in doubt, though the Council fought it through the summer. The Court ordered it to levy the precepts; it would not, and in the first days of September nearly all the Council (thirty members) was sent to prison ' for contempt '. Key was left outside to act as Deputy Mayor, a few Conservatives were not arrested, one Alderman repented and was excused. The rest, in law, must stay in prison till they ceased to be contemptuous, if ever they did.

Brixton Prison was none too pleased to have them: as soon as they arrived and the chief warder spoke to them in his usual tone he was answered: ' Where's your union card?' They refused to do any work; they demanded footballs, exercise, open cell doors, and newspapers to read. Daily the staff whom they had left outside insisted on seeing them ' on business '. The other prisoners, envious, sent a deputation to the Governor asking for the same privileges: the Governor sent for Lansbury to explain to it why they could not have them. But when he arrived, what Lansbury said was: ' These people should have the same privileges as us; after all, they've only broken the law, just as we have ', and the meeting broke up suddenly. But prison was all the same not a holiday: the privations and inconveniences were probably in part responsible for the deaths soon after of old Charlie Sumner and Edgar's wife Minnie (who was in a cell in Holloway). Lansbury himself had an experience of what prison discipline meant. He was taken ill one night, and rang the bell.

' A face came to the grating and asked me what the hell I was ringing about. I told him and he just went away and nothing happened. I rang again, the door opened and a man leaned across me and said he would smash my b——y head in if I did not stop it. Well, I then began to talk rather loudly and my friends each side of me heard something was wrong and they passed the word out of the window to the rest of the cells, and then, of course, pandemonium broke loose in rather less time than it takes me to write. The result was the chief warder, doctor, and deputy governor appeared, only to find me in a more or less state of collapse. Of course, they were all very sorry and in the end the warder who was guilty was punished.
' I am confident that if I had been in that prison alone without any friends, I should have been quite thoroughly set about that night and should, in the morning, have been charged with assaulting the warder.'

But if the Governor was uncomfortable at seeing them in Brixton, the Government was even more so. It had gained nothing by jailing them. On the contrary, Bethnal Green Council voted to do the same as they had; Stepney and Battersea were likely to do so, too. The ' moderate' Labour mayors, headed by Herbert Morrison, who deplored this, were up in Inverness clamouring to the Premier and Sir Alfred Mond that London Government was breaking down and action to placate Poplar must be taken at once. To appeals to levy the precept or to compromise, the Poplar men answered that they would not levy the precept and that they would negotiate only when they were all released and able to consult and debate freely. They ' sat tight', and Lansbury addressed crowds regularly through the gratings of his cell windows. ' Where's young E'gar? ' called the audience sometimes, and his son had to peer out above his father's head. In October the Councillors had their way: the High Court received an application from them for release in order to attend a conference to discuss the whole question.

The application apologised elegantly for any appearance of discourtesy to the Court (which was wholly irrelevant, as the Lord Chief Justice said), but it gave not the slightest indication of an intention to ' purge the contempt ' by carrying out its orders. The aged Lord Bray pointed this out rather querulously, but received no answer; counsel for the L.C.C., prodded towards asking formally for the Council's release, would not save the Court's face, and repeated merely that the L.C.C. would not object to whatever the Court did. In the end, ' with considerable difficulty ', as they said, the judges decided to release the Council. A conference was held forthwith: a bill was introduced equalising rate burdens; Poplar's rates fell six shillings and sixpence in the pound at once, and Westminster's and Kensington's went up a shilling.

J. H. Thomas, during the conflict, had called the Councillors ' wastrels '; Lansbury had replied to him that, while he only talked about it, the Poplar Councillors were acting on the official Party programme of ' Work or maintenance ', and the electorate would be grateful. He seemed to be right; the Guardians swept the board, carrying all seats but one; the Councillors were returned by increased majorities; ' Poplar men ' were even sought after by other boroughs as L.C.C. candidates; he himself carried Bow and Bromley in the 1922 Parliamentary election with a majority of nearly 7,000 (Lansbury, 15,402; Duveen, 8,626). From then on the seat was his whatever he did. He still patrolled the constituency at national and local elections, in a procession headed by a large stuffed black cat with a red neck-ribbon, and escorted by a flying corps of children chanting:

' Vote, vote, vote for Mister Lansbury
Poke old Someone in the eye '

(the ' Someone ' being the name of the Tory candidate). But this was only because electors must be treated with courtesy, and because he enjoyed it immensely; he could have won the seat henceforward without stepping out of his house at 39 Bow Road.

As soon as he entered the House he was elected to the Executive of the Parliamentary Party, and required to sit on the Opposition Front Bench, which he did, a little restive and embarrassed, as he always was when distinguished in any way, but delighted at the evidence of the respect in which he was held, despite his 'Poplarism'. He had need of consolation, for the *Daily Herald*, of which he was proudest, was now rushing to disaster.

It could no longer be kept alive as an independent paper. The workers could not pay twopence any more; circulation was falling, and all reserves had been eaten up. More capital must be raised, and it should obviously be raised from the Labour Party, or the Trades Union Congress, bodies which alone could provide the organisation to sell the paper. Since Stockholm, Lansbury and Henderson (the Party Secretary) had become friends; though they differed in policy, they respected each other's earnest honesty, and the changeover was thereby made easier. Lansbury had since 1918 told Henderson everything about the paper's finances; in May 1922 he proposed to hand the whole enterprise over. He was indignant later, when it was assumed even by his friends that he was passing across a liability and dodging a bankruptcy: nothing could have been more untrue. The debenture-holders had received their steady 5 per cent; Victoria House Printing Company was making good money; and as for the paper itself, he had received handsome offers privately for it, which he would not accept because the name of the *Daily Herald* was not for sale to a private capitalist. The offer was accepted after long deliberation; on September 11th a new editor, H. Hamilton Fyfe, a professional journalist converted to Socialism and approved by Lansbury himself, was installed as editor. Lansbury remained as General Manager (he had held both jobs for months, to save money) to keep the loyalty of the existing readers and as evidence to them that 'the cause' was not being betrayed.

But the ensuing months were unhappy. The changes in tone, in make-up and in policy introduced by Mr. Fyfe were not to the liking of the staff that Lansbury had trained. Discontent was particularly bitter in the journalists' chapel, and though Lansbury, with strict loyalty, refused to be brought in, in his heart he endorsed the criticisms. At Board meetings he found himself snubbed or treated with condescension; they acted, he said, 'as if any proposal coming from me was sure to be wrong'. Not all the distress that he felt was reasonable; in the change from an independent to an official organ the paper was bound to lose much of its verve and its reckless honesty. Criticism based upon nothing but a love of truth was no longer always possible; trade union and Socialist leaders must be admired; invective must be modified; compromises must be applauded. But Lansbury felt the new policy was going farther than he could bear; much that was printed seemed to him not so much wrong as silly and frivolous. Nor did the changes seem even commercially justified; in August 1923 there was a worse crisis than ever, and the Trades Union Congress very nearly closed the paper down. In February 1925, when he quietly resigned without even warning Henderson, it was, almost incredibly, a relief to leave the *Daily Herald* building.

Chapter Seventeen

DURING Lansbury's mute months on the *Daily Herald* there had been yet another conflict between Poplar and the Government. Twice the Local Government Board (now named the Ministry of Health) had tried to pull up the Poplar weed and found it was a thistle; it had had no more wisdom than to try a third time. Mond and his officials were naturally vexed at their dramatic defeat over the rates dispute; the loud condemnations of ' Poplarism ' in the Press and even in certain Labour circles may have suggested to them that an ' exposure ' of the Guardians such as Davy staged sixteen years before might be effective and popular. They sent down as investigator this time (March 1922) not one of the Ministry's authorised inspectors, but the clerk to the Bolton Guardians, Mr. H. I. Cooper. His inquiry was less sensational, for he only read documents, examined nobody, and saw none of the Committees nor the Board in action. His report was on the expected lines—it complained that the old principle of ' deterrence ' was not followed and a ' labour test ' like stonebreaking was not enforced, suggested that food should be cut down in the workhouse, and demanded that Laindon Farm Colony should be sold unless it could be used ' for test work for the unemployed '. It contained very little information that was not already published in Ministry reports, and ended with the grotesque remark that ' £100,000 a year ' could be saved. This, and some minor mis-statements of fact, enabled the Guardians to reply in a pamphlet *Guilty and Proud of It !*, which is among the more entertaining specimens of English political invective.

The Minister in June tried to bring the Guardians to heel by withholding an advance from the common Poor Fund to which they were entitled by custom: this he abandoned after two interviews in which Edgar Lansbury, their chairman, out-argued his own senior Civil Servants. He then issued an order to them requiring them to give relief at the rates which he, not they, approved. The District Auditor surcharged—that is, required

223

the Guardians and Councillors to refund personally—all expenditure on relief above the scale of the order and on wages above what he thought proper. Lansbury and his colleagues ignored both order and auditor: they neither reduced their relief nor cut the local officials' salaries. Nor did any penalty follow. In October 1922 the Conservative Party decided Lloyd George was no longer an asset, broke up the coalition, and turned him out of office, never to return. With him went Sir Alfred Mond, whose Tory successors had no wish to imitate him in thistle-cropping. They left the Poplar Council alone, and solved the question of the surcharges by never closing the audit—the books stayed open, and the account ran on for nearly three years.

In the 1922 election the Labour M.P.s had risen from 75 to 142. Henderson, whose merits were less obvious to electors than to trade unionists, lost his seat, as he had done in 1918, but every other Labour politician of eminence had been returned. Ramsay MacDonald, partly because he was experienced and competent, partly because a group of I.L.P. revolutionaries from the Clyde campaigned for him, had been made Parliamentary Leader. The Party had only a few months to get used to its enlarged size; at the end of 1923, Baldwin, the new Conservative Premier, held another election. The results were: Conservatives, 258 seats; Liberals (Asquith and Lloyd George in venomous partnership), 158; Labour 191. For almost the last time, the Liberal Party was able to influence British politics. According to what it decided, Baldwin or MacDonald would be Prime Minister. On December 18th Asquith announced that he would turn the Conservatives out and put the Socialists in.

There is no recapturing, to-day, the surprise and even alarm which this decision caused. Not many of the upper class were able to distinguish between Henderson's views and Lenin's; those few that could, accepted the I.L.P. view of MacDonald as an extreme ' red '. Up till the very meeting of Parliament in the New Year, Baldwin kept in office, refusing to accept the decision of the electorate. It was widely believed that the direct intervention of the King was responsible for this desperate and undignified holding-on; Lansbury, in a public speech, went so far as to remind him that the time for such interference had ended with the death of Charles I. Whatever solicitations he may have received, Asquith resisted them, and in January George V sent for Ramsay MacDonald. (One of the future Cabinet Ministers told Lansbury that for this supreme sacrifice the King put on a red tie.)

The member for Bow (Lansbury, 15,336; Albery, 6,941) could not be ignored: Henderson, for whom a seat was being arranged, asked him on January 15th if he would join the new Cabinet, and Lansbury, deciding (as he told his son-in-law Postgate) that the Party and Trades Union Congress were moved by wholly honest motives and not by ambition, answered that he would be honoured to do so. Three days later, however, there had been a change—it was asserted, and Lansbury was convinced to the end of his life, that the King had declined to have in his Cabinet a man who he thought had threatened to cut off his head. MacDonald offered Lansbury the post of Minister of Transport, outside the Cabinet; he replied he could not accept a post which gave him no share ' in the formation of general policy '. MacDonald showed formal regret, and said he expected to revise all his appointments in a few months, anyway.

The sole ' Left-winger ' in the new Cabinet was John Wheatley, the Minister of Health, who promptly cancelled Mond's order against Poplar. In June the High Court heard the Council's appeal against the District Auditor; it turned that official down, on the grounds that he was not entitled to substitute his opinion for the decisions of an elected body. This ended, at last, the long conflict between Whitehall and Poplar—though for some years still the District Auditor continued to send into the Councillors disregarded ' surcharges ' whose figures became more and more fantastic—in 1926 he asked Lansbury to pay out £43,000.

Lansbury's local anxieties might be over, but he shared all the general disillusionment over the rest of the Government's policy. The Party in January 1924 could have done one of three things. It could have refused office; that would have been pusillanimous, and the electors would have punished it. (' If they don't want office, they needn't have it '—Lansbury could remember 1912 and foresee that verdict.) It could take office knowing that every bill it produced, and every important administrative action, would have to be approved by a Liberal leader who had announced he would not allow anything which had the least taint of Socialism to pass. This had a definite attraction for MacDonald, who felt that in international affairs (he was going to be Foreign Secretary as well as Premier) an enormous advance could be made—a thing that must be to the advantage of the Party. Or, thirdly, it could bring forward a number of genuinely Socialist measures (as Lansbury would have wished), beginning with the nationalisation of the mines, and when they were rejected, go to the country—not expecting an immediate victory, but having offered a concrete programme to the workers and driven false friends and open enemies together into one camp. One election later the Party might reasonably hope to return with an independent majority and carry out a balanced Socialist programme.

The second was the policy adopted. The third was for a minute considered, but Snowden, the new Chancellor, recorded that it was rejected almost instantaneously. Snowden, MacDonald and Thomas were mainly responsible, as they were for many other decisions in the first and second Labour Governments. It was an odd triumvirate to have such power—each member thoroughly disliked the others, and none was of more than second-rate ability. Yet they were held together by an ultimate unwillingness to make any fundamental social change and a dislike of their colleagues who tried to push on them the text of the Labour Party's Socialist programme. As yet, however, they seemed merely affected by an understandable timidity; Henderson, Clynes, Webb and other Ministers who were unquestionably loyal to the Party supported them steadily.

There were undoubtedly successes in the international field. The French troops were got out of the Ruhr, which they had invaded and paralysed. A new ' reparations ' plan was worked out which appeared to be at least practicable. Russia was recognised, and trade negotiations were opened. But at home, apart from Wheatley's Housing Act, nothing whatever was accomplished, or even attempted. Moreover, in the autumn two monstrous follies were committed. First, a Communist paper, the *Workers' Weekly*, was prosecuted for a ' Don't shoot ' article, very like the Syndicalist leaflet of a decade ago to which all the older Socialists had rallied; then the prosecution was dropped in embarrassment; after a feeble defence in the Commons, Liberals and Tories united in condemning the withdrawal. On this muddled issue MacDonald decided to go to the country. The election campaign was in full swing, the Labour canvassers pointing confidently to the Government's international record, and in particular its restoration of friendship with Russia, when suddenly the *Daily Mail* published a letter (possibly forged—no one knows) signed by Zinovieff and instructing the British Communist Party on how to control the Labour Party and start an armed revolution.   This ' revelation ' might have been swept aside, but immediately—a second idiocy—there appeared an official note from MacDonald to the Russian Government, accepting the letter as genuine and reproaching the Soviet for allowing such intervention.

On what were the unfortunate Labour candidates to campaign now? What was the value of the Russian treaty? Even MacDonald's associates were horrified.   Thomas's verdict is smoothed by G. D. H. Cole into the ejaculation ' We're bunkered '; Snowden wrote to Jowett, ' It is the most incompetent leadership that ever brought a Government to ruin '. The Party membership after the election was reduced to 151; it was small consolation that the Liberals fell with an even heavier crash to 42.   Lansbury's own majority was lessened (15,740 to 9,806).

Chapter Eighteen

CLIQUES are generally condemned by historians; the word itself is an injurious one, only exceeded by ' cabal '. Yet it is doubtful whether a political democracy—certainly a Party system—could be operated at all without cliques. That they should not be very powerful, and that they should at all costs be short-lived, may be conceded at once. But in a party of any size men do not regard all their colleagues as equally attractive, even if they may agree with their theories; they work more easily with men whom they know and whose origins and ways of thought and talk are the same as their own—at any rate up to a time when they are separated by some prolonged and important disagreement on policy. Always, if they are at their ease, they will form a clique, often unintentionally, and sometimes without being aware of it. Parties which call themselves ' monolithic ' and pretend to have no cliques or divisions at all are Communist and Fascist parties; and they delude themselves. For the human divergencies which they repress merely express themselves in other ways—in delation, in intrigue and eventually in judicial murder.

A clique is not the same thing as a ' tendency ', a ' fraction ', or any other recognised and definable group which is based upon considered difference of opinion. Where such exists, either the party must split or the contending sections must make a bargain. This had been the condition of the Labour Party before 1914. The Liberal trade unionists and the Socialist ' I.L.P.-ers ' had come to a bargain whose terms were in effect discussed almost continuously in conferences and the Press, sometimes in very high words. At the beginning, the Socialists seemed to have the advantage; at the end, the trade unionists. Until the world war silenced them all, there were people on both sides who perpetually complained that the bargain was unfair and should be called off.

But there was no division in principle when Lansbury founded his own weekly in 1925. All the trade union leaders now called themselves Socialists, with perhaps two exceptions: the sectarian loyalty of the I.L.P. was also rapidly disintegrating. Yet the trade union group remained, and was, indeed, very powerful. It had become a clique. Its influence and character, in the quarter-century after 1914, can best be compared to that of one of the clubs which have played so interesting a role in the older Parties. As a club has its known bores and fools, which it nevertheless tolerates, so the group carried with it, on to the Labour Party executive and even to the Cabinet, good fellows whom it knew to be platitudinous and ineffective. A club will retain and even cherish old members whose probity is suspected, though there is not evidence enough to expel them, or young members who openly despise the rest as old fogies. So Havelock Wilson, of the Seamen, though he treated his fellows with the maximum of insult and non-co-operation, could have had their support as a fellow-trade unionist had he ever wanted it; J. H. Thomas, of the Railwaymen, was a most important member, though his integrity was suspected long before his fall and his ostentation was a standing embarrassment (for union leaders were very honest men, and simple in their lives); A. J. Cook, of the Miners, could denounce nearly all the older union leaders as traitors to the workers without ever becoming as much an outsider as Philip Snowden was all his life.

Entrance to the club was not to be secured just by working-class manners or habits. Frank Hodges, Cook's predecessor, retained no trace of his miner origin in voice, clothes or manner; but he left the circle only of his own choice. Nobody could be more obviously working-class than George Lansbury, but he was never one of ' them '. To be a union worthy—one of those who occupied or allocated seats on the General Council and Labour Party executive and must be placated by a percentage of Government posts in due course—a man must have begun his career as a stalwart in his union branch, must have proved himself by taking local office (paid or unpaid) and have proceeded to the district organisation, and so ultimately have earned a national position with his union. Then only could he project himself into political life with the clique's blessing: others, working-class or not, who attempted to arrive direct would never receive it.

The period when he was editor of *Lansbury's Labour Weekly* (first number, February 28th, 1925) was the only time that Lansbury had any direct access to the members of the ruling trade union clique or any decisive influence upon them. The record of the 1924 Labour Government had exhausted their patience with MacDonald, whose most established opponent he was. They were tempted by the thought of co-operation with the Russian trade unions, and he was one of the few who had succeeded in co-operating with Communists without quarrelling with them. Most important, he now had the ear of influential members of the General Council. Ben Turner, placid and bearded, and the only important leader the textile workers had produced, helped him to found the paper, and supported it regularly. A. J. Cook, the miner, though he regarded Lansbury as a back number, wrote for the paper and consulted with his group almost as much as with the Communists. But the closest liaison was with a group of three who during 1925 constituted a sort of triumvirate on the General Council—George Hicks, of the Bricklayers; A. A. Purcell, of the Furniture-Workers, and Alonzo Swales, of the Engineers. Hicks indeed sat on the editorial council, and was at one time in almost weekly contact. Co-operation, except for these three, was, however, still limited by the old prohibitions. G. D. H. Cole wrote many of the leaders for *Lansbury's* and largely shaped its industrial policy; but when he wrote an article advocating changes in union structure, he was rebuked in the next issue for interference by the assistant secretary of the Trades Union Congress, W. M. Citrine, with the zealous asperity of a steward banning a non-member from the Carlton Club.

Lansbury had some valuable aid to offer the union leaders. The *Weekly* was very effectively written: in addition to Cole, it had many of the most reliable contributors of the old *Daily Herald*. Ewer and Gould wrote intermittently; Meynell contributed most of a new and satirical series of ' Open Letters '; Postgate was Assistant Editor ; Margaret Cole was literary editor; a newcomer, Herbert Farjeon the dramatist, wrote a weekly diary of great wit, and the Parliamentary report by Ellen Wilkinson, illustrated by J. F. Horrabin, was the liveliest and most ruthless in the country. Originally, Lansbury had tried to call the paper the *Weekly Herald*, but was prevented by a veto from the *Daily Herald's* new controllers. He was greatly vexed—the personal title for the paper was no choice of his—and perhaps in unconscious revenge at first made the make-up an exact replica of the 1914 weekly *Herald*. It was nearly three months later that *Lansbury's* assumed its well-known format, with coloured cover and line illustrations. He had raised—privately, but from the same sources as before—some £5,000, and initially the venture was prosperous. The circulation was 172,000, probably more than double its nearest rival, and some seven times that of the sixpenny *New Statesman*, which was one of the few Socialist papers which announced its circulation. But in a very short time there was a warning: the Communist Party started the *Sunday Worker* as a rival. The journal (cordially welcomed by *Lansbury's*) had few claims to be a real newspaper, but it looked somewhat like one, had some hundreds of disciplined sellers and large funds in reserve. Its appearance neatly cut a third off *Lansbury's* circulation: the twenty-year slump was still on, and many workers could not afford two twopences a week.

The plans of the ' Reds ', as they were content to be called, in the General Council were far-reaching. Plausibly enough, they argued that the effects of the union defeats of 1921 were wearing off and the time had come to strike back. But instead of fighting individually on questions and at times decided by themselves, or even by their employers, the unions must act together, as an organised army with a general staff. Instead of making demands only for wages, which could easily be filched away again, they must concentrate on questions of hours, conditions and ownership which would mean a permanent benefit to the workers. Instead of limiting their views to one island, they must organise internationally. To reach these ends, the union leaders set themselves deliberately to do three things: first, to continue the process of amalgamating and ' streamlining ' the various unions; secondly, to acquire for the General Council the power to organise and direct the industrial operations of the unions as a whole, so that the whole power of the working-class could be thrown in to support any union whose entry into a conflict had been approved, and thirdly, to unite with the

Russian unions in reconstructing the international trade union movement.

The world's trade unions were split, internationally and in almost every free country except Great Britain, into two unequal parts. The larger part adhered to ' Amsterdam ', the International Federation of Trade Unions of pre-war days, led mostly by men who had supported their governments during the war and were reformers in principle; the smaller to ' Moscow ', the Red International of Labour Unions, consisting outside Russia mainly of skeleton organisations manned by a mixture of uncompromising revolutionaries and orthodox Communists (still usually the same individuals). The General Council persuaded the Amsterdammers to declare in principle that they would admit the Russians, and the Russians to join with it (in April) in an Anglo-Russian Trade Union Council; these were first steps which were to lead to a final union of both bodies. The effort was by no means foredoomed. There was still freedom of speech and even of action on the Moscow side; foreign workers could visit Russia freely, and were enthusiastically welcomed; the Western leaders had not yet decided that their critics were all Russian agents whose real object was to wreck the unions. Had the General Council, as it hoped, been able to act as a mediating and balancing force in a reunited international, it is possible that the deep, inflamed cut which divided the European trade unionists, to Hitler's ultimate benefit, might have been healed.

At home the programme had a more sensational result, but it was in fact less fully thought out. The double policy—of union reform and co-ordinated attack—might have had one of two results, if successful. It might have led to conflict, direct or veiled, with the Government, and so to a taking-over, on Syndicalist lines, of the chief industries by the reorganised unions. Hicks, Tillett and some other leaders had believed this possible and had written about it; but they had no clear idea of how in fact it would occur, and their faith in syndicalism as a workaday policy was almost extinct. They still spoke of ' the workers' revolution ', and even thought of it, but it was not a real thing to them. It was a threat, with which they hoped to scare their enemy; and an unbacked threat is more correctly described as a bluff. Alternatively, they might have been involved only in a struggle with various groups of employers, one after another; and by the use of the full powers of the workers in each dispute have forced their opponents to grant the required concessions, in hours, conditions and wages. This was, ultimately, though they did not realise it, an American policy; it would have forced (as did the A.F. of L. policy of high-priced labour) the employers to re-equip their industries and reorganise their companies, and was (whether they knew it or not) an unrevolutionary policy. It was a threat to the fuddy-duddies in coal, steel, engineering, cotton, wool and so forth, who hoped to protect themselves by cartellisation, tariff walls and low wages; but not to others. However, the distinction turned out to be of no importance; there were no Fords in the British business world, there were only Baldwins.

For the moment they were allowed to pursue their policy in peace. The Government was no less convinced than they were of the reality of the class struggle (in the 1920s the Marxist theories of the State were more crudely exemplified in practice than in any other period except the 1830s), and would have no hesitation in putting down their pretensions; but it was ignorant of what was going on. Its members never read Labour journals; victims of their own propaganda, they believed that the British working man was a Conservative at heart and despised the agitators who battened upon him. The conflict which they forced upon the General Council was hardly a conscious choice; they seem genuinely to have believed that the trade unions had been beaten for good in 1921 and that they had only to announce a decision with sufficient firmness for it to be accepted.

The financial policy of the Government made it certain that an unpleasant decision would have to be announced to the working-class; two actions in particular had made it inevitable. One was taken before the Labour Government, when Baldwin made a financial agreement with the United States. Abandoning the principle announced by Lord Balfour (that Britain would pay across to America as ' war debts ' what she received from the other allies, and no more) he had accepted unconditional obligations which later events were to show were unbearable. The other was taken after the Labour Government's fall; in May 1925 the pound sterling was put back on the gold standard, at a high level. Unless the cost of British products was sharply brought down, export trade would wither away.

Baldwin, who was to learn later to suppress untimely truths, in July announced bluntly that all working-class wages must come down; the attack, which was first made upon the miners, was, inferentially, no more than a prelude. The attack was, in form, the action of the coal-owners, perhaps the least reasonable of any group of British employers; it threatened a fall in wages, the ending of national negotiations, the destruction of the ' national minimum ', and an increase in hours. There could be no subsidy from the Government to soften the blow, added the Premier, with what seemed like gloating, but was in fact no more than indifference. Resistance must have seemed improbable. There were over a million and a quarter known unemployed, and many more (Lansbury, exaggerating, claimed the figure was a million) who no longer troubled to register. A quarter of a million, after all, had been turned off relief in the last ten months and were living as best they could; Lansbury had advised them to march on the British Empire Exhibition at Wembley and camp there.

The day after Baldwin's statement, July 30th, just before the miners were to be locked-out, a conference of trade union executives decided to forbid any movement of coal, and to authorise the General Council to call a strike upon any scale that might be necessary. The next day, which was naturally enough called ' Red Friday ', its chairman, Alonzo Swales, short, round and with the chubby face of an Anglican vicar, had the rare pleasure of telling a Conservative Premier that the whole life of the nation would stop if he pursued his policy, and of seeing his resistance collapse within a matter of hours. The Government was taken completely by surprise; it had made no preparations, and Baldwin announced that a subsidy would, after all, be paid to the mine-owners for nine months so that they could continue to pay the existing rates, and a Commission would be set up to advise what should be done with the industry. The trade union victory seemed to be absolute; certainly there had never been anything like it in English history.

One side rejoiced, rather unthinkingly; the other prepared for revenge. Until private memoirs have been published, it is not possible to say for certain what were the thoughts of the Government; but later events suggest that it had no intention of reorganising the coal industry, whatever the Commission reported (there had, after all, been more than enough inquiries already). The more bellicose members of the Cabinet, supposed by outsiders to be Sir W. Joynson Hicks, Mr. Winston Churchill and Lord Birkenhead, had taken the lead, and treated the nine-month interval as a period in which to organise such a defeat of the trade unions that their power should be broken for good. Coal stocks were to be piled up so that a miners' strike would be an empty threat. Communications would be safeguarded by an ' Organisation for the Maintenance of Supplies ', O.M.S., which would break any transport strike at once. A network of Commissioners was organised which would use emergency powers in the provinces and put an end to any interference with other services. The planning was military in conception; the initial steps were taken very shortly after Red Friday, and fairly openly. But the trade unionists took no comparable action. Not only were they humanly anxious to rest on their laurels and naïvely confident in their opponents' statesman-like qualities, but there was also a significant change in the constitution of the Council itself. After the September Congress, Swales was succeeded as Chairman by Arthur Pugh, a steel-worker, a man of great probity and no fool, but so far to the Right that he was one of the first two trade union leaders to shock their colleagues by taking a knighthood; in his belief, another conflict such as Red Friday must be avoided at almost any cost. The railwaymen were now represented, moreover, by the very versatile J. H. Thomas, one of the few leaders who still declared himself not a Socialist and who believed that, if any such conflict did occur, the Government ought to win.

The September Trades Union Congress, though it voted vociferously in favour of whatever the General Council put before it, could make very little progress towards the ' Reds' ' goals. A proposed ' Workers' Alliance ' of big unions had broken down; a suggestion to give the General Council powers to call the unions out on strike had to be referred back because union constitutions made it premature. All left-wing sentiments were cheered; the delegates even listened benignly to the Communist Party leader, Harry Pollitt. He was a boiler-maker, he had been educated in union lodges where the members still called each other ' worthy brother ', he spoke the language, and indeed was almost one of the club himself. Oddly enough, a month later, at Liverpool, the Labour Party Conference, consisting as to two-thirds of the same people, voted and spoke very differently. Lansbury, now on the executive, moved a resolution calling for Indian self-government. It was satisfactory in itself, but his position meant that he could organise no revolt from the floor. The Communist Party speakers took the lead there, and they antagonised nine-tenths of the delegates. ' The Party richly deserved its rout,' said *Lansbury's* bitterly afterwards, damning the Left for allowing itself to be represented by its least reputable and attractive element. The Conference was a prolonged personal triumph for MacDonald; when Bevin, for the Transport Workers, moved that no more minority governments should be allowed, even he was voted down by 2,587,000 to 512,000. It was to be the last time that heavy man would move without being sure the big battalions were behind him.

Lansbury's repeatedly and earnestly offered the General Council plans to organise the struggle that it foresaw. Trades Councils should be reorganised so as to net the country, in reply to the Commissioners. They should be strengthened by the adhesion of the local branches of all the main unions, and made into regional representatives of the General Council. Feeding arrangements should be fixed up with the Co-ops. Workers' Defence Corps (unarmed) should be set up. All the plans necessary to organise a 100 per cent general strike are still to be found in the files of the paper, but the editor and staff no longer knew if they were being read or acted upon. The speaking tube, so to speak, was obstructed; they did not know if their voices were heard, and no replies came through.

Lansbury was forced to turn his attention more to politics: here he was very little less of a thorn to MacDonald than he had been in 1911. ' I intend,' he said in November, ' on every possible occasion to obstruct, hold up, and in every way hinder the progress of business ' in Parliament. In March next year he moved to abolish the Navy by discharging 100,000 men, and took twenty Members into the lobby with him. When the Communist Party leaders were arrested for ' don't shoot ' propaganda to soldiers, he held one of his usual monster Albert Hall meetings, at which he made the audience stand up and repeat after him the same appeal. He was only prevented from printing similar articles in his paper by the printers taking his paragraphs out and leaving white spaces. At the end of the year he was fuming in the old way at the Party leadership; he felt, he said later, ' the time had come either to break away or give up '. Instead, he was to be forcibly more closely identified with it, for in February 1926 the Party voted that Executive members, and not MacDonald's ex-Ministers, should sit on the Opposition front bench. Lansbury was compelled once more to descend from his back bench perch and sit embarrassedly among the leaders. ' How do you like being on the front bench ? ' Baldwin asked him honeyedly next day. ' You looked like an old watch-dog brought into the drawing-room.'

He was handicapped in his influence in the Labour movement (and was to be for some time to come) by his continued patronage of the Communist Party. The literature of the time is filled with references to its 5,000 or 10,000 members; they bulked too large both in history and in the thoughts of men at the time. This was because they had the prestige of the Russian revolution, which they hardly deserved, and also because they were practising a new policy of ' nucleus work ' devised by Zinovieff that out-raged and startled trade unionists and Labour Party members. It required them to act as an organised conspiracy within the branches, not discussing, but pushing through pre-arranged programmes, using deception at need and treating their colleagues not as comrades, but as *chair à canon*. None of this induced Lansbury to withdraw his protection. He acted as treasurer of the committee to defend and maintain their arrested leaders; he advised them patiently when they called for his assistance at 39 Bow Road; he still advocated their admission to the Labour Party. Even their perpetual vituperation and their ascription of the vilest motives to those who disagreed with them (a habit he detested) he defended as being no worse than language which had passed unnoticed in the days of Hardie,

Burns and Hyndman. He refused, indeed (and this shows he had changed since 1911), to countenance a 'Left-Wing Movement' set up by the *Sunday Worker* to defy the new Conference decision barring them from Labour parties; he reminded his readers that if the vote had gone the other way they would have insisted on the Right obeying, and must give the loyalty they expected from others.

He had had enough of fabricated 'movements' where the Communists pulled the strings.

'Speaking for ourselves [his journal said editorially] we repeat that we will gladly meet and discuss with any sincere comrade whose mind is open for discussion. But we are *not* prepared to waste our time and tempers in meetings where a block of people are present who have come to a decision before, and whose sole object is to wirepull the meeting to a certain decision. If you are not prepared to argue, why send delegates at all? Why not send a gramophone record?'

The truth was, he had practically no respect for the Party he was aiding. 'That lot run a revolution?' he used to say. 'They couldn't run a whelk-stall.' But those who remonstrated with him did not realise their ineptitude made their claim on him more urgent. All his life he was helping lame dogs over stiles; the lamer, more useless and unloved the dog, the more obvious his need to help it.

The Coal Commission reported in March 1926; it was in favour of the nationalisation of coal royalties, of the amalgamation of coal companies into economic units, of lower wages and of longer hours. The Government and the coal-owners heard only the last two items; lock-out notices were posted in the pits on April 16th, for the 30th, the day the subsidy ran out. The Labour side was still unprepared, and, what was worse, dissension was appearing between the miners and the General Council. The miners were insisting on their slogan 'Not a minute on the day, not a penny off the pay'; the Council, knowing the poverty of some of its unions, wanted the right to make some concessions at need. It would agree to some fall in wages, but not to the big drop the Government demanded, and that should occur after, and not before, reorganisation. The Government, however, was adamant; it believed the Council was bluffing, and it wanted to call the bluff. On the night of May 2nd, when Pugh and his colleagues, ' begging and imploring —grovelling for peace ' (as Thomas said picturesquely), thought they had made some advance, the Cabinet impatiently broke off negotiations, on an almost nonsensical ground. (Some printers of whom the Council knew nothing had refused to print a *Daily Mail* leader.) The Conference of trade union executives then voted by 3,653,529 to 49,911 for a general strike, to aid the miners, to begin at midnight on May 3rd.

The nine days which followed have, in retrospect, something of the character of a long dream. Silence and solitariness settled on the island. Railways did not run (the ' O.M.S.' was almost useless) and newspapers had vanished (*The Times* on Wednesday was a piece of paper thirteen inches by seven); the quietude was made almost more marked by a thin, strange voice, the new ' wireless ', which piped fanciful stories of returns to work, provided by the Government. Long lines of old cars and lorries ran along the main roads, private, official or with yellow T.U.C. permits; when a courier arrived, the waiting Strike Committees would hear for a moment how things stood upon the route he had followed, and when he left, the darkness would fall again. The workers, whom the Cabinet thought were bluffing, had struck, after all; the General Council, wisely, had not called everyone out, but only the railwaymen, transport workers, printers, builders, steel and metal workers, gas and power workers, and chemical workers. These came out, and when Tuesday of next week the engineers and shipyard workers were called, they came out too. What men had hoped for and talked of for many years had happened; those who toiled had folded their arms and said to their exploiters: ' We will do no more '. The result was as if the bones of society had been exposed.

Neither Lansbury nor any of his colleagues had any share in the direction of this astonishing campaign. He went down to Bow, and produced, like any Trades Council secretary, a local bulletin upon a duplicator; his colleagues walked from the suburbs to *Lansbury's* office but did no work when they were there. The General Council wanted no assistance; once again this was an affair for club members only. But there was no harmony within the club. The Council was ready to settle for ' a ' minimum wage; the miners insisted on ' the ' minimum wage; that one word represented an unbridgeable division. Sir Herbert Samuel, of the Coal Commission, acting as a sort of mediator, produced a memorandum which required some concessions from the miners, but also some from the Government. The miners refused it, and pointed out that the Government had not agreed to it; the Council approved it and hoped, apparently, that a united acceptance of it would force the Government to implement it. But by that act the line had been broken; on Wednesday the 12th the General Council called off the strike in defeat. It made things worse for its followers (who, looking round them, saw the strike wholly victorious) by pretending the now meaningless Samuel memorandum was the terms of peace; there is extant a copy of a draft issue of *Lansbury's* acclaiming the end of the strike as a victory, and Ben Turner on the Council at least believed it was. But the fraud was soon clear from Baldwin's rejoicings on the wireless, and the greatest single effort of the British working class ended not only in defeat, but in disgust.

The disaster ended an epoch in trade union history. The immediate effects were that the Conservative Government passed a Trade Union Act forbidding general or half-general strikes, ordering the unions of Government employees out of the Congress, and altering the method of subscribing to the Labour Party (' contracting in ' replaced ' contracting out ') so as to injure its chances at the next election. Congress itself abandoned both union reform and the Anglo-Russian Alliance. But that was not all. The strike, as anyone could see, had been as effective as any general strike was likely to be; the Government had been shown to be inevitably the stronger. A century-old belief in the unions' economic power, and in direct action, had been disproved. Syndicalism had vanished. Political action through the slow and often exasperating parliamentary machine was now the only hope (since nobody really believed in armed revolt).

Among other things, this meant that there was no longer a reason for Lansbury's own journal; there were political journals enough already in existence, and though it continued to publish for over a year longer, it was fatally wounded in May. For the moment it seemed lively enough: it was able to break still yet another boycott by pressing out and selling Labour gramophone records. The existing companies forbade the recording of the *Red Flag*, the *International, England Arise* or any of the Socialist chants thousands of families knew: the small and frightened firm which agreed to make Lansbury's records stipulated that its name should never be disclosed and the records be delivered unlabelled (they were labelled in the office, and since one blackface is like another purchasers often found the *Red Flag* entitled *Talk by George Lansbury* and a speech by Cook called *Song of the Volga Boatmen*). It supported the miners in their hopeless fight, which lasted until mid-November. It raised funds, and held the traditional great Albert Hall meetings for them. It attacked both Neville Chamberlain's connection as contractor with the Government in which he was Minister of Health and his assiduity in enforcing cuts in relief. There was great suffering, especially by the children, and Lansbury ever afterwards had a personal dislike of the man he held responsible; he always believed that although most of the children that grew up in his later years were happier and stronger than in his youth, there could be seen in any school two 'bad crops' of stunted and diseased children, as obvious as faults in geological strata, and that they represented the years when Mond and Chamberlain were at the Ministry of Health. The pinched and white faces he saw in playgrounds and streets in South Wales and Lanark made him bitter; for all his kind heart, this was a thing he could not forgive, and he wished never to speak again to a Tory Minister. 'We should give up,' he wrote next year, ' all social intercourse with our avowed enemies either in or out of the House of Commons. This was the policy this paper advocated twelve months ago. Only one person agreed with it, the editor of this paper.' Collaborators had from him a harder condemnation than ever before: when Frank Hodges became Electricity Commissioner, he wrote: 'We all find our way to our appointed places', though not all his readers knew their bible well enough to realise how harsh a sentence that was. But, with all his vigour, it was clear that *Lansbury's* was in grave danger. No advertisements could be secured. Circulation fell as poverty and unemployment spread; there was wealth and waste enough in other circles, but twopence a week was too much for more and more workers. Contributors had to be asked to forgo their fees, expensive features were abandoned, the staff's salaries were cut, cheaper printers and poorer paper were found, and the offices moved into a derelict shop in Camden Town.

In the August of 1926 he had visited Russia again with his wife. They went for medical reasons, to take a cure at Essentuki in the Caucasus, on the Soviet's invitation. They were escorted by their daughter Violet (a passionate Communist working in Moscow), and only incidentally made political observations. Lansbury found his hopes of 1921 were being fulfilled. The country was still far behind the West, and was still a party dictatorship; but it was rapidly rising out of the devastation of war and famine. Increasing prosperity, happiness and comradeship seemed obvious everywhere; above all, there was no master class, and the common people everywhere owned the fields, factories and workshops. If there was incomplete political freedom, there was certainly no persecution. Trotsky—the ' Russian workers' Danton ', as he called him—came to see him, and talked freely and amicably, even though Stalin and Zinovieff had turned him out of office. He was refreshed and invigorated by what he saw; once again he put to himself seriously the question, ' Why am I not a Communist?' He found no new reasons, and returned the same answer as before; he was as much a pacifist as ever, and even more a democrat; but the self-examination was typical. Most men, once they have passed forty, have fixed minds and change their ideas with difficulty; Lansbury at the age of sixty-seven was still earnest in testing his beliefs, and would revise them if they seemed untrue. At this very time he made one exceptionally difficult change: he was convinced by the advocates of birth-control, and the columns of his paper altered accordingly. It cannot have been easy: he was the father of twelve children, he had a typically Victorian unwillingness to discuss sex, and the mechanics of contraception disgusted him. He was convinced, not by the economic arguments of the neo-Malthusians (which he distrusted), but by the argument that women should be allowed to control what happened to their own bodies. It was, once again, for him a matter of personal freedom.

His *Weekly* was now very close in policy to its nearest rival, the I.L.P.'s *New Leader* (successor to the *Labour Leader*), which was pressing a policy of ' Socialism in Our Time ' thought out by Brailsford, James Maxton—the Clyde M.P.—and a few others, and indistinguishable in practice from his own. During November and December 1926, moreover, he published in his paper a programme for the next Labour Government which was drafted in the Labour Party headquarters itself by four of its chief officers. (It was signed ' S.I.O.T.', a rebus; but except that one was the chief woman officer, Marion Phillips, the names are lost.) It was in effect a reduction to immediate Parliamentary terms of the I.L.P. programme; many workers in the country must have wondered if it was necessary to publish two weeklies whose policy had become so closely alike. *Lansbury's* was losing money steadily; the institution of a ' Ginger Club ' of its supporters had come too late to save it; Lansbury would not allow a big appeal for funds to the workers. In July 1927 it was peaceably amalgamated with the *New Leader*, under Maxton's editorship.

It was a severe blow to him. He was ill, for the Russian holiday had only temporarily eased his stomach trouble; he was very tired, and felt older than his sixty-eight years. With all his hopefulness—his last article was entitled ' Onward, ever Onward '—he could not but feel that the repetition of the *Herald's* story by *Lansbury's* marked him as a failure. Also, he was in financial difficulties: he now had no income except his M.P.'s salary. He could not, or would not, reduce the help he gave to others, and he could scarcely live more simply himself. As a patriarch, he felt equally responsible for all his relatives' distresses: ' I've never known the family have such a doing,' he said lugubriously to an unemployed son-in-law. If he had not had a fairly generous cheque from Messrs. Constable for writing his autobiography in 1928, he would probably have been seriously in debt.

He had, it is true, some successes in other spheres. Locally, he presided at the opening of the Poplar municipal electricity works, a power-station which was at its date the most economical and most effective unit of its size in Europe. The luncheon celebrating it was a curiosity among congratulatory ceremonies:

chilly and ill-cooked food was served by insolent or inept waiters in a pretentious hotel, to guests who heard Sir Hugo Hirst for the contractors elaborate the thesis that congratulation was really due to the Conservative majority in a previous Council which first suggested the station, and Mr. Lansbury for the Council return thanks to the labourers, skilled workers, foremen, working managers and designers who were its true builders. Nevertheless, its existence and performance shook the belief of those who had really believed the Poplar men to be a group of ' wastrels ' incapable of local government.

Nationally, he was more widely respected than before. He was elected Chairman of the Labour Party for 1928—it was almost as strange that he should take the post as that he should be chosen. He was able, from that momentary eminence, to insist officially on an independent Socialist policy.

' Any attempt [he said in his official address to the annual conference] to unite our forces with the decadent remains of Liberalism is foredoomed to failure. Our one and only goal is Socialism and all other parties in the State are violently opposed to it. Between them and us there can and will be no coalition or compromise.'

The conference solidly approved; whatever reserves they might have over I.L.P. and S.I.O.T. programmes, the Party members felt it unthinkable that they should again take office as in 1924, in circumstances which prevented them carrying out any Socialist programme, which excused any weak or evasive Ministers, and which enabled the Liberal leader to throw them, like lassooed horses, whenever he felt the circus had gone on long enough.

Yet that was exactly the practical joke the electorate was preparing for them. The 1929 election gave them 289 seats, the Conservatives 260, and Lloyd George's Liberals 58.

Chapter Nineteen

THE new Labour Government was in the same position as the old: a Liberal leader held the balance and had vetoed all Socialist plans. It looked very like the old, too; the same man was Premier, the same clique (MacDonald, Snowden and Thomas, inner ring; Henderson, Clynes and Webb, outer ring) dominated it and distributed offices. But there were some changes: MacDonald reluctantly left the Foreign Office to Henderson, instead of taking it himself, and for his Left-winger in the Cabinet he picked Lansbury instead of Wheatley. Lansbury had not expected a post. 'I feel sure they—that is, the Nabobs—' he wrote to Postgate, 'would rather not have me, and I hate being where I am not wanted. If they were really sensible they would send me to Russia', as Ambassador. The position given him was First Commissioner of Works. The Office of Works was almost the smallest department that could be made to carry Cabinet rank; he would have to preserve ancient monuments, care for the royal parks, look after the buildings of other departments, and that was practically all. As a compensation he was given the more important task of drawing up policies to relieve unemployment; with him were two Socialists outside the Cabinet, Tom Johnston and Oswald Mosley. But, with that odd schoolboy cunning which he took for political sagacity, MacDonald put in supreme charge of this Committee the new Lord Privy Seal, J. H. Thomas, the Right-wing railwaymen's leader, who would be almost certain to veto anything these three proposed.

Other appointments were unsensational. Snowden had to be Chancellor: Mr. Justice Sankey as Lord Chancellor gave wiser legal advice than was given in 1924. The Home Office under Clynes, the War Office under Tom Shaw, Agriculture and Fisheries under Buxton, the Scottish Office under Adamson and the Labour Ministry under Miss Bondfield were run, broadly speaking, by their senior Civil Servants. Wedgwood Benn, an ex-Liberal at the India Office, showed a great deal more energy than his older colleagues. Greenwood at Health and Trevelyan at Education were set to drafting a Housing and Education Bill respectively. Webb was transferred to the Lords as ' Lord Passfield ' (MacDonald, for all his backslidings, followed strictly the Socialist principle of ennobling only the son-less), but his tenure of the Dominions Office was not remarkable. A great deal was expected from William Graham's brains at the Board of Trade. Among the others perhaps one should mention Lord Thomson, at the Air Ministry, an exuberant soldier killed in the explosion of the *R101*, a terrifying disaster which ended, in Britain and perhaps for ever, man's attempts to fly by balloons.

Lansbury's wish was to work loyally for his chief: this was not 1911, and guerrilla warfare against MacDonald was the last thing he intended. That he was almost at once involved in a dispute with him was due to a curious obsession of that distracted man. Of all things, the argument was over clothes. It was fore-shadowed in the letter calling him to the Palace to take the oath: ' A black frock coat or a black tail coat will be worn, with silk hat ', wrote the Clerk. Lansbury greatly disliked all pomp, and particularly dressing-up; for this ceremony he reconciled himself to a Prince-Albert-like black frock coat, which became him very well, and wore a tall hat, to which he was not reconciled, considering it to the end something for children to throw snow-balls at. He looked a very dignified and respectable figure, but that was not enough for MacDonald; even though the *Evening News* photograph of Webb and Noel Buxton looking like Sancho Panza and Quixote had shown what Court dress did to the elderly and oddly shaped, he tried to compel Lansbury to wear knee-breeches. When the indignation with which this was received made him recoil, the Premier still tried to force his senior into full evening dress. This was to Lansbury the uni-form of a class which he did not respect and to which he did not belong: moreover, A. G. Gardiner, a Liberal journalist, had already written a sermon in the *Star* upon his top hat, contrasting it with the ' cant ' of Keir Hardie's cloth cap and saying that it proved ' Labour had ceased to be a rebel '. The comment was too true, in Lansbury's opinion; he begged to be excused from the further humiliation of a boiled shirt, but the more he resisted, the more MacDonald's snobbery was inflamed. Messages were sent that it was a personal request of the Premier: Cabinet dinners were arranged at which full dress was compulsory. Lansbury yielded so far as having the miserable garments made, but on each occasion he succeeded in finding an excuse for not wearing them. To the end the two men's relations were worsened by this grotesque dispute.

But the fault was not always MacDonald's. Lansbury was determined to be loyal, but he still had not learnt caution. When the Cabinet had decided to present a Coal Bill, he promptly spoke to a public meeting in Bow, saying that the mine-owners should be organised into a public utility corporation, ' a monopoly working under public supervision with limited profits'; next morning he got a handwritten letter from 10 Downing Street:

' My Dear George,
    ' I have had requests to say whether your pronouncement or mine on the coal situation is the official one. I made mine as the first move in pressure which I propose to apply to both sides. . . . Do pray remember every word you now say about policy is studied as the pronouncement of a Cabinet Minister. . . . Yours always J. R. M.'

His apologies appear to have been more ample; there is extant a further note from MacDonald saying: ' Be easy. No throwing to wolves. Only let us be careful.'

He found in the Office of Works a neat, small and rather Victorian department, settled in its ways, which looked on him with a reciprocated apprehension. Novelty was rare in the office; tradition was preferred, and even the files were very long lived. The first entry in the file which was presented to him when he raised the question of bathing in the Serpentine gave the ruling of Lord John Manners in 1866, and he might at that have been shown older ones. It was not, indeed, Lord John who had impressed his views most strongly on the Office, but a later and even less democratic peer, Lord Crawford. For Lord Crawford, and therefore for the Office, the parks were to be places of serenity and stillness, for the comfortable contemplation of persons of leisure. When they discovered that Lansbury proposed to pull down railings, to build shelters for children, to construct pools in which they could paddle and sail boats, and even to arrange for mixed bathing in the Serpentine in the heart of Hyde Park, the Civil Servants in the Office were scandalised. Their alarm was genuine; they saw the quiet green parks being turned into Hampstead Heaths.

In a very short time they had completely reversed their opinion. Only one official of importance remained hostile to the end; most were soon proclaiming Lansbury the best First Commissioner in living memory; the Permanent Secretary, Sir Lionel Earle, became a friend and companion. He had secured their confidence in the best way to impress Civil Servants, by competence in dealing with documents. They were astonished to find that a man who sometimes dropped his ' h's ' could nevertheless grasp the contents of a thick, wordy file with exemplary speed, that his decisions were prompt, clear and almost always right, that his tact in dealing with difficult deputations and dangerous questions was much greater than his predecessors'. They gave him that last seal of Civil Service approval; they said that when he departed in the House of Commons from the briefs they prepared the result was always happy. He was criticised, it is true, for over-kindness; he would believe that petitioners and correspondents were honest and truthful until he found out the opposite. But when he discovered trickery, they found that he could be alarming. A deputation of Jewish barbers once asked him to support Sunday opening in the East End; Lansbury received them so favourably that after a while one of them, as a ' try-on ', claimed that he had promised to ask Lord Swaythling to give a party at his West End house for some purpose of theirs. The Private Secretary did not remember afterwards exactly what Lansbury said; he only remembered his expression, and that the barbers left the room with such terrified speed that they actually trod upon one another.

His officials were impressed by his reverence for the past; no previous First Commissioner had delighted more in preserving ' ancient monuments ' or been more willing to visit them. They did not perhaps realise that he treated them according to a plan—the ' sweet reasonableness ' on which he prided himself. He always listened with the most patient attention to explanations of why nothing could be done on the lines he had suggested,

and then would say something to the effect of: ' Well, brother '
(his favourite address to everyone), ' you've given a very fine
explanation of what *can't* be done.   Now I want you just to sit
down and work out what *can* be done.'   Often enough the result-
ant plan was very much what he wanted all along, and the official
defended it with an author's pride.

Moreover, his reforms led to no disasters.   When the railings
inside the parks were pulled down, or replaced by low-slung
chains, the Londoners did not stamp over the flower-beds,
tearing up the rhododendrons.   The spectacle of children
paddling in pools and sailing boats seemed not to be revolting,
but almost agreeable.   The opening of the Serpentine to mixed
bathing did not lead to riots, or to mass indecencies, even though
the First Commissioner, supported by his Permanent Secretary,
had resisted a demand that men should be forced to wear ' a slip,
and on top of that a costume reaching from neck to knees '.
(To one correspondent who objected that the introduction of
female bathers had ended a male privilege of bathing as God made
them in the early morning, he had answered, ' I should myself
not object to men and women bathing in a state of nature if what
are described as morality and public opinion would allow me to
give permission '.)

The reforms in the parks made Lansbury immensely, dis-
proportionately popular.   The Press was full of his praises.
When the Treasury declined to find money for his proposals, he
was almost at once able to raise all that he needed by voluntary
subscription.   Space for space, cartoon for cartoon, the First
Commissioner in the summer of 1930 occupied almost as much
room in the Press as the Foreign Secretary or the Chancellor.
There were, of course, exceptions to the chorus of praise.   The
legs and arms of the young women and men who sunned themselves that summer on the banks of the Serpentine, the squeaks of
the children paddling in Regent's Park, seemed to have roused
some strange rages.   The more responsible the newspaper
considered itself, the more irresponsible its adjectives.   The
Morning Post, with not even a faint regard for facts, said ' The
" Lido " is a prey to hooligans and thieves '.   *The Times* called
Lansbury the Caliban of the Parks; it told him his plans were
' grotesque and horrible '; starting dignifiedly by referring to

'ill-considered innovations' it suddenly lost its temper and charged him with 'clownish fussiness' and with turning Hyde Park into 'Coney Island'.

These anatagonists he ignored; but he could not wholly ignore what he called the 'unco guid'. When he decided that a licence to sell wine, beer and spirits (at meal times only) could be applied for by the restaurant in the Tilt Yard at Hampton Court, the London Free Church Federation in a long denunciatory letter signed by the Reverend Bagnall demanded the reversal of his decision. Ill-manneredly, it had sent the letter to the Press before delivering it to him; he asked for the same publicity for his answer, but did not get it until a second sharper letter had been sent by his secretary. 'I should regard it as an impertinence', he wrote to the angry Nonconformists, 'on my part to attempt to impose total abstinence on other persons on the ground that I am an abstainer', and told them that people should be allowed 'to consume beer and spirits in healthful and happy circumstances', and in places to which they would bring their families.

More dangerous was an attack from a body calling itself the 'London Public Morality Council', which covered itself with the authority of the Bishop of London. Its thesis was that the reforms had led to an orgy of obscene misbehaviour in the Parks. The reports of the parks purity police (as their unofficial investigators were called) were sometimes—how shall one put it?—in such physical detail that their authenticity was unlikely; it was unfortunate also, in dealing with an experienced campaigner, that so many of the 'spontaneous letters of protest' were phrased in identical language. Lansbury was convinced after a short while that he was the victim of an organised campaign to which his Bishop had given his name. He reacted with unusual sternness: he toured the parks himself with the police and one of the amateur narks, and told the Press afterwards that the allegations were false. They were the product, he said, of 'depraved minds' which had nothing better to do than look for nastiness. He did not forget to add that whatever wrongdoing there was was in fact due to miserable housing conditions, the result of years of Conservative misrule. If young people—and old, too—had rooms of their own, or even a little privacy occasionally, there would be no problem.

A Tory or a noble First Commissioner probably could never have stood up to such attacks; in religion, temperance, probity and decency Lansbury could dominate his opponents; only from such as him were these unhappy and perverted people forced to accept defeat. He became a sort of symbol of personal freedom to Londoners; when, for example, he commented that London restaurants, like Parisian, ought to serve dinners out on the pavement, a number of proprietors forthwith set out their tables, and photographers followed him round until they snapped him obligingly lunching out of doors in Charlotte Street.

His innovations in the parks led to a complication that troubled no other Minister. George V was not only King but also 'Ranger' of the central parks, and so had a right to be consulted about the details of any changes that were made in them; he was, too, a faithful reader of *The Times*. It was not long before Lansbury was called to an interview to which neither party can have looked forward with comfort. To him, George V was a short-tempered, narrow-minded, out-of-date Tory, with a tendency to interfere in matters in which the Crown had had no business for 200 years. To the King he was probably a boisterous plebeian, whose intention was to wreck the whole structure of the society he loved and who had been personally offensive about him in public. There was enough truth in both pictures to make both men uncomfortable. The King's views and tolerance, originally at least, had not been much wider than those of a back-bencher in the House of Lords; Lansbury certainly intended to overturn society and, though he had not in fact threatened to cut off his head, it had not been respectful to say publicly, 'George Five should keep his fingers out of the pie'. Yet it was not really surprising when they got on extremely well together. They had three qualities in common, which they respected in each other: a simple and strong piety, a genuine kindheartedness, and an unusually compelling sense of duty. The King's flaws of temper and tolerance were not likely to be shown in his relations with his First Commissioner, and he was probably surprised by Lansbury's natural courtesy and patience. Lansbury, on his side, was hardly likely to lecture the monarch upon Socialism—indeed, the only general subject which he seems ever to have discussed with him was the welfare of children, on which he was sure of the King's sympathies. He had, indeed, to use his domestic tact from time to time. There is an anecdote, probably but not certainly true, of the time when the King tried to make him replace a sound if orthodox design by Alfred Hardiman for a statue to Lord Haig by a deplorable object proffered by Lady Haig. The interview had lasted uneasily for a time when Lansbury said, not in feigned sympathy: ' If you will excuse my saying it, Sir, you are looking tired, and far from well.' Some while later, the official whose duty it was to remind the King when he over-ran his engagements discovered the two old gentlemen sitting with their heads close together discussing the faults of doctors (' like two charwomen ', it was said disrespectfully); the King was saying with appropriate gestures ' . . . but they called it a minor operation, Mr. Lansbury; and they opened me from *here* to *here* '. All he remembered to add, as he closed the audience, was, ' Well, I am sure you will do what you can about the statue, Mr. Lansbury '.

But however popular his policy at the Office of Works might be, Lansbury knew how small its importance was. What mattered was the Unemployment Committee; and here he met continual frustration. His two immediate colleagues were all that could be wished, personally. Tom Johnston was a tried Scots Socialist; but his position was insecure, for he was merely Parliamentary Secretary to the Scottish Office, and for weeks could not find out from the Premier if he was a full member of the Unemployment Committee or not. More assistance, at first, came from the Chancellor of the Duchy of Lancaster, Oswald Mosley, rich and ambitious son of a Tory baronet, with white teeth, metallic charm and a Douglas Fairbanks smile, married to the well-to-do, half Jewish Lady Cynthia Curzon. Lansbury worked closer for a while with him than anyone else in the Ministry. But if Lansbury had not himself had access to the Cabinet, none of the Committee's plans might have been considered; for its titular chief, J. H. Thomas, the Lord Privy Seal, would neither discuss their plans nor disclose his. At the very beginning he had disagreed with Lansbury; the economic position would improve, not worsen, he said; his sub-committees, of eight knighted Civil Servants, and of as many bankers and employers, had proved it to him. Big schemes would be unnecessary; in any case, he had his own plans, and he visited the Dominions on a tour which was little more than a holiday. True, in a few months the rapidly rising unemployment figures sent him into a panic—for he had no policy or plans; he was not clever, he was merely artful. But he did not then turn to his colleagues; he looked elsewhere to find the assurance he needed. There was only one man in the Cabinet who seemed completely confident, the Chancellor of the Exchequer, and he soon effaced himself behind him.

The Party thought Philip Snowden was a rigid Socialist. Had he not denounced MacDonald for his miserable 1924 record? 'I never trusted J. R.,' he had written to Jowett, 'but he has added to the attributes I knew an incapacity I never thought him capable of, and his colossal conceit prevents him being in the remotest measure conscious of what he has done.' But it did not realise that this was just ' anti-MacDonaldism '; Snowden's proclaimed Socialism was merely a form of words. All industries (he believed) should be nationally owned and controlled, but how this could be done he had never thought out; the phrase ' State ownership ' was enough. Now that he was in a position where nationalisations were forbidden, even if he had had a practical scheme for them, his mind became politically a void. There were still the sharp nose, the arrogant manner, the tight mouth and vindictive tongue, the obstinacy and the angry blue eyes. He was still a sharp-cutting instrument, but the driving direction behind it had vanished. And to his other qualities was added in the autumn a great increase in vanity; for at an international conference at The Hague he beat down and outwitted the French delegates, securing 87 per cent of the German reparations discussed there. This fairy gold (for it was never to be received) and the deafening applause in the Press went to his head. He believed himself to be a great statesman; he had never listened much to others, and now he did not listen at all.

But Nature abhors a vacuum, even in politicians' heads; and Snowden's lost Socialism was replaced by a primitive Liberalism. It may have been a natural reversion to what had been ' advanced ' thought when he was a child, or it may have been (as Lansbury thought) an indoctrination by Sir Warren Fisher and his colleagues at the Treasury; in any case, two things became sacred to him—Free Trade and the Gold Standard (neither of which had anything to do with Socialism). The Budget must at all costs be balanced; the gigantic waste of the ' dole ' must somehow be ended.

There was nobody in the Cabinet to resist his domination. Willie Graham, at the Board of Trade, knew better, but could not stand up to him. Margaret Bondfield, Minister of Labour, became almost at once his echo (or that of her senior Civil Servants), forgetting that it was resentment at that Ministry's behaviour which had largely brought the Party to office. Arthur Henderson was wholly preoccupied with Foreign affairs, and, as usual, loyally followed MacDonald. Trevelyan was entangled in a desperate attempt to get through a new Education Act; it was destroyed eventually by the Lords, who had reverted to their wrecking policy of Asquith's day, but until then he had no ears for other questions. The rest were either amiable trade unionists ' along for the ride ' or, like Buxton at Agriculture or Webb at the Dominions Office, refused to help when Lansbury appealed to them. Indeed, the chief effective opposition to Snowden came from MacDonald himself: the Premier was at least not malleable, like his colleagues, any more than a cushion is. But the resistance he offered was the resistance a pillow offers to a sword. With his verbosity and indecision, he could hold up and prevent the Chancellor's more destructive actions; he could not enforce an alternative policy.

Snowden was thus able almost to make Lansbury his butt in Cabinet meetings. But his charges of throwing about public money were unjustified; the proposals Lansbury put up (for Thomas soon could offer nothing but lamentations) were by no means impracticable, and they had substantial support behind them. Ernest Bevin backed, and perhaps inspired, the scheme for retirement pensions; Frank Wise of the I.L.P. that for Import Boards. The first scheme was for retirement pensions for workers at sixty; it would have cost, according to their calculations, £21,000,000 to £22,000,000; there would have been a saving of £10,000,000 on the Unemployment Fund and poor relief. It would have meant a fall of approximately 300,000 in the unemployment figures; together with the raising of the school age to fifteen (which would have withheld 400,000 juveniles and was later sabotaged by the Lords) it would have wiped out two-thirds of the unemployment figures and made solvent the Fund which was perpetually borrowing vast sums from the Treasury. But when it came before the Cabinet in December 1929, Snowden refused even to consider raising the money. Lansbury circulated extracts from speeches, pamphlets and the election manifesto showing that the Government was pledged to the scheme; only Henderson seemed even worried by the inconsistency.

He attached particular importance to a scheme for blocks of self-contained settlements in Western Australia; they would be financed by a British corporation using mostly, but not wholly, Government money, and over a period of time not making a loss. The settlements (which he reckoned would absorb 10,000 men, including a large number of miners—the worst hit by unemployment) would rapidly become self-supporting, and the Premier of Western Australia (Mitchell) cabled Lansbury his enthusiastic support. But the Dominions Office objected that some part of the proposed land was said to be salt (it was an idle rumour; the land has now been cultivated for years) and that the present price of wheat was low. W. Lunn, Webb's assistant, complained that Western Australia, with its 400,000 population, did not offer to pay for part of the scheme. MacDonald said that Mitchell had made a disloyal speech; and under such fatuous comments the project was buried.

His proposals for the reclamation and cultivation of derelict land (of which there was plenty in Britain in 1929) arose directly from his experience of Laindon and Hollesley Bay; he was provoked at the dull departmental negative that he received. ' I cannot accept this as the last word,' he replied, with a flash of his old impatience; and indeed others found Buxton too wooden. He was replaced late in 1930 by the more imaginative Christopher Addison; he, too, met the unchanging refusal of Snowden to help. Snowden, who liked to be called ' the Iron Chancellor ', by now enjoyed his negations and never, even in after years, realised that he was asking for a miracle. He was demanding that unemployment (1,630,000 in June 1929; 1,912,000 in June 1930) should be ended without any expenditure that was not ' remunerative '—remunerative expenditure being mostly what would have been financed by the banks anyway. So all that happened was a grant, extracted from him in the first days, of £135,000,000 for public works by local authorities, coupled with a condition by which the authority concerned had to employ a proportion of men transferred from the most depressed areas instead of its own. The condition was ' mad ', Lansbury wrote vainly to Thomas in October 1929; and indeed it soon had to be abandoned, for it was merely spreading unemployed around the country. There were excellent Reports on the cotton, iron and steel, and shipping industries, but they were not acted upon; there was a Coal Bill which might have set up a sort of corporation under public control, but the alert Lords wrecked all of it but the provisions which encouraged cartels. Even when Lansbury, as First Commissioner, drafted a scheme for developing the Montagu House site and rehousing and centralising four Ministries, for efficiency's sake, Snowden prevented its adoption, saying it should be regarded as a scheme for relieving unemployment and filed away with the rest.

As early as July 1929 Lansbury had sent to Thomas and his colleagues letters laying out plans which would, in a smaller way, have had something like the effect that Roosevelt's ' New Deal ' later had in America. Only slowly did he realise that none of them would be tried. In the spring of 1930 he decided, in consultation with Mosley and Johnston, to assemble the most obviously useful of them into one document and force it on his colleagues' attention. Mosley, the least occupied and the best writer, was the draftsman; he sent the text to Thomas, as was the correct procedure; Thomas refused to show it to the Cabinet. This at least would not do; Lansbury used his position as Cabinet Minister to put it on the table himself. The memorandum proposed a liberal use of credit to revive home purchasing power, to be enforced by public control of banking. Imports would be controlled by direct limitation and by bulk purchases from the Dominions, which were crying out for these. Social services were to be improved, and the promise of retirement pensions fulfilled. Existing schemes for the taking and re-cultivating of derelict land were to be approved, with great demonstration farms run by the State. The ' rationalisation ' of industry—the current cant term for the re-equipment and reorganisation of

British industry which everyone saw was years overdue—was to be taken under control, and so directed that it did not throw more men out of work, but led to a rapid increase of production, both for home and foreign markets.

This was a programme which was in general practical, and indeed urgently needed, but it provoked Snowden to a storm of fury worse than he had yet treated the Cabinet to. His mind was now scarcely even Liberal; he reflected the views of Conservative financiers, and almost every sentence of this seemed to him provocative, revolutionary nonsense. The Memorandum was rejected; Mosley resigned and made a very telling attack in the House of Commons.

Lansbury did not resign; he thought of it, but the recollection of 1912 held him back. He wrote an earnest appeal to MacDonald asking that he and Snowden should come to a Party meeting and ask the M.P.s to ' open their hearts to you '. In return they should open their own minds to the M.P.s and say what they really meant to do. He got no satisfaction; nor could he have done. If MacDonald had opened his mind to them, the M.P.s would have found nothing; what they would have found in Snowden's head would have appalled them.

The summer of 1930 passed with unemployment figures rising steadily, and Lansbury, more and more fatigued, protesting against Cabinet inaction. There was a Panel of Ministers, an Economic Advisory Council, and a Joint Committee with the Liberals; all worked separately, and their advice never coincided; nothing was done. Clynes broke an old tradition of asylum by finally refusing to admit Trotsky. The *Daily Herald* was taken over, with Lansbury's blessing, by Odhams Press, and shot up to a million sale. Meanwhile the Parliamentary machine, never very efficient, slowed down almost to a standstill. Asquith had allowed the first Labour Government a short run, and then pulled it down with a crash; Lloyd George was letting it stay in the ring longer, but hobbling it all the time. In eloquent speeches he denounced the Government for its timidity and depicted the glorious vigour with which the Liberals would have dealt with unemployment; but he refused to give the Cabinet the one assistance which would have allowed it to put through any programme at all—the regular voting of the Closure. The rare permitted Bills moved slowly through an unending treacly sea of debate; month after month hope had to be abandoned even of measures on which the Government was unanimous. Lansbury's frustration was by no means wholly the fault of his colleagues.

But as the Labour Party conference, dated for October, came nearer, it was made clear to him what his real value was to his colleagues. He was a screen; his duty was to defend them against attacks from the Left, and in the name of Cabinet solidarity he could not refuse. The ' dangerous ' topics that he was assigned were India, Communist affiliation and unemployment policy. Two of these were assignments he could accept cheerfully. He had had a bellyful of Communist tactics; he answered their demand for affiliation with the round statement that they were in favour of violence, and the decisiveness of his words had a great part in putting an end to their recurrent applications. On India he was equally at ease. The Conservative ' strong ' policy had resulted in widespread civil disobedience and a breakdown of constitutional government. But Ministers had seen the regnant Viceroy, Lord Irwin, and been impressed by his sincerity; he had worked in complete harmony with Benn, the Secretary for India, and a better regime was almost in sight. An obstacle was the hostile report of a Commission of Inquiry headed by Sir John Simon and unfortunately containing a Labour Member, Major C. R. Attlee, but the Government had decided to over-ride it and call as soon as it could what the Indian Congress had long demanded, a Round Table Conference. Lansbury was helping Benn directly and continuously; there was every reason (if the Conservatives did not come back to office) to hope for an enormous and irretrievable advance towards Indian self-government within a year. Was not the freeing of four hundred millions more important, perhaps, even than the continued unemployment of two millions? Gandhi could be coaxed into direct negotiations with the Viceroy if there was a thumping vote telling the Government to go forward on its path; Lansbury was glad to secure it.

But unemployment policy? Here it was sharp practice to command him to defend it; and artfulness was met by artfulness. Lansbury's defence of the Cabinet was a defence in form; but this was the last time his colleagues treated him as a mug. He explained painstakingly why the text of the Mosley memorandum could not be published; it was because he had brought it himself to the Cabinet, and so made it a Cabinet paper, and Cabinet papers were not published. Everyone could understand, as he went along, that he fully agreed with its proposals. To give a semblance of criticism, he wondered whether Mosley had not under-estimated in his figures the effects of what had been done; he should have added in certain indirect employment. However, it should be remembered that only Socialist measures could cure unemployment; under capitalism it was bound to continue. As for Mosley's concrete proposals, did he appeal to the conference to lay them aside and trust the Government? He did not; he appealed to Mosley to re-phrase them so that they would no longer be a secret Cabinet paper, and put them up for consideration again. The Minister on the platform, in fact, was deliberately throwing the cards across the hall into the lap of the critic, sitting Byronically among the rank and file with folded arms. But they were not picked up: Mosley was not the sincere and ardent Socialist he seemed, but was already embryonically the Fascist leader. The triumph he wanted was personal; even so, he polled 1,046,000 votes against 1,251,000, and was also elected to the new executive, while Thomas was defeated.

Many of his comrades reproached Lansbury for even this Pyrrhic defence of the Government; he may have reproached himself. But he had good reasons still for supporting the Government; outside of this one problem it had done remarkably well. The advance in India has just been described; in Egypt Henderson had startled the world by bluntly dismissing a noble proconsul, Lord Lloyd, who attempted to carry on the old domineering policy. Irak had been freed and a treaty signed. British imperialism, which Lansbury so much detested, was being stopped in the areas where it was doing most harm. The Conservative quarrel with Russia had been ended; a Soviet ambassador sat in London, and a trade treaty was on the way. Henderson was the first Foreign Secretary to take charge of the Foreign Office and force it to change its habits; he had even compelled its ruffled chiefs to buy and study the Labour Party pamphlets and Conference reports. He had had a great share in persuading the French to evacuate the Rhineland; he had strengthened the power of the League of Nations, and was preparing the ratification of the ' optional clause ' on arbitration. If MacDonald's Treaty of naval limitation had only covered America, Britain and Japan, it was, even so, a big advance; and France and Italy, the two recalcitrant Powers, were being coaxed along by Henderson.

By what narrow margins do men miss happiness! The heart is cold, to think how near the British came in the summer of 1930 to securing the peace that everyone desired. The Labour Ministers were hesitant sometimes, weak often, and a few were unfit for their task; but they did reach out for what was nearly in their grasp, and they seem models of courage and forethought compared with the wretched men who succeeded them. Gandhi did meet Irwin next year; if the Government had remained in office, India might have become a partner and an ally fifteen years earlier. The League of Nations, still undamaged, might have been so strengthened that war would have been made impossible. The Soviet Union, not yet a Stalinist dictatorship, might have become closely and pacifically linked with the West, and its later history have been very different. Nor, though nothing that a British Government could do would have arrested the American economic collapse, need the effects have been so disastrous in this island if 5 per cent of the votes at the Party Conference had swung across and the Mosley plan had been adopted. But none of this was to be; a storm was approaching from America which was to blow the Government away and replace it by men who had electoral cunning but little else. Russia was to be alienated. India was to suffer many years more of foreign rule and to be hostile in the hour of Britain's greatest need. The economic crisis was to be met by building tariff walls behind which British industries ossified in a pool of unemployment millions wide. The League of Nations was to be destroyed, and Britain and the world to slide stupidly into the second worst disaster of recorded history.

Chapter Twenty

WHEN George Lansbury died he believed he had left safely behind him for his biographer all the papers necessary for a true history of the second Labour Government and his share in it. How some of these documents were abstracted will be found recorded in the *Foreword* to this book ; here it is only necessary to describe what remains. There are many letters to him, and some from him; there are his drafts of memoranda, notes, minutes, extracts and odd papers; there were conversations with the writer of this book; and there is a narrative of the whole course of events, written by him, but never published. Some things are missing. The names of the Cabinet Ministers who turned against MacDonald in August 1931 are not recorded, but only their numbers. There is nothing to establish or contradict the widespread belief that it was the King who, stepping away from the traditional neutrality of the Crown, was responsible for MacDonald's astonishing final action. But there remains enough to make clear the general course of events, and also to show that on one important point the official story was an apparently intentional untruth.

In 1931 the Socialists were seeing the predictions which they had made for fifty years fulfilled, but that was small consolation to them. Socialists had always contended, even if they were not Marxists, that the innate contradictions of capitalism caused it at intervals—usually of about ten years—to grind to a convulsive stop. The working population, because of the profit system, would not be able to buy what it created; factories, mines and mills would be slowly paralysed; starving, unemployed men would drift about the streets, and raw materials and food would be thrown away, because there was no ' purchasing power ' or (as the more delicate writers called it) ' through a lack of effective demand '. This had seemed to be confirmed by history since the Victorian days when Marx first formulated the theory (Hyndman had even written a book on *The Commercial Crisis of the*

Nineteenth Century in which the spasms seemed to recur almost by clockwork), but since 1910 it had been derided. Normal developments had been deranged between 1914 and 1918 by war, and the check of 1921 had been explained away or slurred over. In America, in particular, a school of economists had arisen which claimed that there would never be a slump again. Mortuary investigators will find, if they go to the trouble, that this theory was based on the spread of instalment selling ('hire purchase'), and amounted to little more than the belief that no article need henceforward be paid for. The Socialists had said that the American boom could only postpone, and maybe make worse, the inevitable crash; they were being proved to be right. They also said that the predatory economic arrangements of the Versailles Treaty—the dreams of limitless German reparations and the slicing up of Eastern Europe into states which could not live on their own resources—would worsen it and wreck the prosperity of the world unless they were drastically changed. In this, too, they were proved to be right.

The Labour Party was not altogether what a few years later would be called 'Keynesian', but J. M. Keynes' theories were far more powerful inside it than elsewhere. Not only Lansbury, but the whole General Council of the Trades Union Congress, were convinced that the only immediately practical method of dealing with the crisis was to increase Government spending on useful projects. For the moment they were prepared to suppress (in deference to Liberal votes) their belief that the disease could be cured only by taking the main industries and the whole of the financial system under public control; they would have been content with what Roosevelt's advisers a year or two later called 'pump-priming', and with the compulsory re-equipment and reorganisation of the British industries which had fallen into ruin under their existing proprietors. Unfortunately, there was among them a small group which no longer had any Socialist beliefs and shared to the full the orthodoxy of the Treasury. (Among the beliefs which then ranked as orthodox was one that there was a limited amount of real money available for investment anyway, and that any attempt by the Government to restart paralysed shipyards and factories must result in an equal withdrawal of funds elsewhere.) The small group happened to occupy the key positions in the Government; its leaders were MacDonald, Snowden and Thomas. What Thomas's policy was is not very clear, nor does it matter much (he was probably a Tory Tariff Reformer by now); but the other two before long were following a course of action unsuspected by, and indeed hostile to, their colleagues, whom they had both begun to despise and dislike. Snowden, whose ignorance of the trade unions was colossal, seems to have intended to let the crisis mature until it was desperate and then to produce a ruthless special budget, cutting down the social services and turning the unemployed back to the workhouses. The Cabinet, the M.P.s, and even the national Party Conference at need, would be so panic-stricken by then that they would submit gratefully to their saviour, the Iron Chancellor, and he would be quit for ever of the witless ' Left ' which was frustrating him. What was in Mac-Donald's mind must, as usual, remain uncertain. From hints that Mrs. Hamilton has noted in her life of Henderson, it seems that he may have been contemplating his desertion some months before it occurred. The apparently meaningless phrase ' a Council of State' was used by him more than once; he was absenting himself from the circles of his old friends, and moving with a naive pleasure in ' high society '. If that is true, his inactivity was not mere muddleheadedness; he was preparing for a crash which would enable him to get rid of his now unwanted colleagues and link up with his social equals.

The two men most powerful in British political life, and the symbols to foreign observers of British financial strength and policy, are the Prime Minister and the Chancellor of the Exchequer; these two now were not trying to ease a crisis; perhaps they were intentionally worsening it. They had, no doubt, only the unemployment problem in view; they did not suspect that the difficulties would be suddenly greatly worsened by a financial crisis. They did not even know that the Bank of England (without apparently telling the Foreign Office) had been lending large sums to insolvent Central European banks, or that bankers and financial houses had been lending anything up to £400,000,000 to equally embarrassed borrowers—money which their depositors would recall and they might not be able to pay. They may have presumed they had several months to play in, and that the bankruptcy of the Unemployment Insurance Fund was their most immediate problem.

Lansbury made three, if not more, attempts to bring the Cabinet round to at least some action on unemployment. Late in November 1930 he re-phrased the main items of his previous programmes, putting the Western Australian project in the forefront; it had the same reception as before. In January 1931 he took advantage of a looming coal crisis to propose the constitution of a Public Corporation, such as the Conservatives could be told they had already set up for electricity. He reminded the Government that all sections of the movement, themselves included, were pledged to this by the 1926 pamphlet *Coal and Commonsense*, which he forced under their noses and made them re-read. This may have secured him some momentary attention, but no more. In February he sent a letter or memorandum in answer to the Premier's general request for suggestions on unemployment finance. The mass of the workless were unemployed, he said, either because of the special results of 'rationalisation'—the amalgamations of competing firms, the closing of obsolete units, and the introduction of labour-saving machinery—or because of the usual sickness of capitalism, which lived by unemployment. They must not be penalised: the funds needed for unemployment relief must come from the top end of the income scales. An emergency tax, graded from 2 to 10 per cent, should be raised on all incomes that amounted to more than £500 per year (after taxes had been paid); if the Treasury officials objected, let them draft a compulsory loan at low interest. This money should not be used for keeping men idle; it should be used for useful work. The whole official policy of cutting expenditure and throwing more men out of work was senseless: in times of bad trade Governmental and municipal expenditure should be increased.

If his plan was ever considered, it was not adopted; and he was already dispirited: 'I know', he wrote, 'I am a solitary person who, having seized on an idea, refuses to give it up.' Nothing, indeed, which he sponsored was to be carried out, with the odd exception of a Bill for safeguarding the ancient monuments of Britain, made necessary by a proposal to quarry away the foundations of the Roman Wall. It was introduced into the House of

Lords, passed down to the House of Commons, where Opposition members, on personal appeals from Lansbury (he thanked them for ' your compassion for one of the ancient monuments '), pushed it through Committee, and received the royal assent on June 11th, 1931—the sole work of Lansbury's hand that is on the Statute Book.

He was lucky; there was an almost Canadian log-jam of held-up Bills in Parliament. There were Bills for the repeal of the Trade Union Act of 1927, for electoral reform and the abolition of university seats and plural voting, for consumers' councils and for agricultural marketing. The Education Bill was being picked to pieces; the Town and Country Planning Bill and the Mining Welfare Bill were stopped dead. It was not even worth drafting a Bill on the Report on cotton reorganisation, nor on that on the iron and steel trade, which proposed a public corporation. On the last item some of the Ministers were rather scandalised to hear at the beginning of May from Snowden that the Governor of the Bank of England, a bearded and eccentric autocrat named Montagu Norman, disapproved of any such plan, and that if the Government continued to consider it he would stop the reorganisation of the steel trade that the banks were sponsoring through their Securities Management Trust. The Premier promised to secure an explanation of this arrogant ultimatum: oddly enough, he was never able to ask Mr. Norman about it. None of the Cabinet, moreover, except Snowden and MacDonald was allowed to meet any of the financiers concerned.

Lansbury had made one effort to break the jam, which must have surprised him almost as much as its object. He listened to his old enemy Lloyd George's speeches in the Commons, passionate, apparently sincere, opening wide vistas of reform, and eloquent as only Lloyd George could make them. Then on February 13th, 1931, he wrote to him: ' I have thought of writing to you many times during the past few years. Why won't you join the Labour Party? ' He went on to point out that all the existing proposals of the party were ' expedients ' which Lloyd George ' as an outsider ' had approved. ' Your help would be invaluable, *as one of us.*' It was true Lloyd George could not bring all his half-hundred Liberal M.P.s, but he could bring most of them, and the best of them. Lansbury did not add in so many words that if Lloyd George joined up with the Labour Party he would have to be given at least the vice-premiership and three or four Cabinet posts for his friends. Lloyd George still had most of his old power and energy; imported into the Cabinet, he would have blown away the vacillations of the wuffling MacDonald. He would have had a harder job with Snowden, but he would probably have dominated him in the end. Certainly, once the Liberals were in one group with the Socialists, the legislative traffic block would have been broken and the held-up Bills have sailed through—as far as the House of Lords, at least. Lloyd George answered him at some length, in a hand-written letter, on February 16th. He did not agree, but at least he had given the appeal serious consideration. He assured Lansbury of his whole-hearted desire to co-operate, but ' as to the best method of ensuring co-operation I should like to speak freely. " Coming over " is not the best way to help. It would antagonise millions of Liberals with hereditary party loyalties. . . . I am sure I can render more effective assistance where I am.' As for other possibilities: ' Personally I have had enough of office. Seventeen years is just as much as anyone can put up with.' He ended with a shrewd remark: ' Your colleagues are too easily scared by obstacles and interests. Unless you can inoculate them with some of your faith and courage your party and ours will be landed in an overwhelming catastrophe.'

It would not be true to say that Lansbury was wholly unhappy during the first half of 1931. There was much cause of anxiety, but some things were going well. He liked his work at the Office. Afterwards, when the Labour Cabinet was charged with having ' run away ', he said indignantly to his son: ' Run away? what did I run away from? £2,000 a year and a job I enjoyed enormously.' Wedgwood Benn at the end of March reported a warming success: the Indian Congress had agreed to take part in the forthcoming Round Table conference. Peace and freedom were in sight for a sub-continent whose population was ten times that of Britain. At Geneva there had been two further great advances: Henderson had signed the ' optional clause ' binding Britain to arbitration on all questions, and that was starting a rush of other States to do the same; a World Disarmament Conference (a thing Lansbury longed for above everything) had been called. Henderson, because of his great success as Foreign Secretary, had been asked to become President of it, and had agreed.

If only home affairs had been as hopeful! Snowden, it was true, had produced a Budget which was curiously colourless, the Unemployment Insurance Fund had been allowed to borrow again from the Treasury, and the Liberals had been placated by an ' Anomalies Act ' which made it more difficult for some thousands of the unemployed to draw their relief. But the unemployment which had been started by the gigantic American collapse was spreading across the world in great consecutive waves, as it were from a huge underwater explosion. By July the figures in Britain of unemployed had passed 2,750,000; at the end of that month Snowden detonated the bomb which he had, perhaps half-consciously, laid. Earlier in the year, to placate the Liberals (Lloyd George was ill and Sir Herbert Samuel and Sir Donald Maclean took his place), he had, with an air of indifference, appointed a Royal Commission to investigate the financial position. There were only two Labour representatives on it; the majority were resolute opponents of the Labour Party, and the chairman was Sir George May of the Prudential. Now it delivered a report which was more alarming than even the Chancellor had hoped. It declared that the British Government was in effect bankrupt; by £120,000,000 a year it could not meet its obligations. It demanded savings of £96,000,000 pounds forthwith, of which over £80,000,000 should come out of the social services. £66,000,000 should be taken from the unployed, by a cut of some 20 per cent in benefits. The Cabinet was not warned before this furious document was published, and it did not realise its gravity. It was just separating for the recess, so it left a Committee of MacDonald, Snowden, Thomas, Henderson and Willie Graham of the Board of Trade to consider what should be done.

What passed in that committee is not known, but some of the proposals that were made are. The Budget was loaded with the heavy payments exacted by the Americans under Baldwin's agreement for the war debt: each year since 1923 two payments had been made, one of over £19,000,000 and one of nearly £14,000,000. The fall in prices had added nearly a third to them in real value, and many outside the Labour Party thought they were preposterous in size and morally unjustifiable. Could they not be suspended? No, replied Snowden (according to his own account); that would be a confession of bankruptcy as well as common dishonesty. Could not the £50,000,000 for the Sinking Fund be held back? Certainly not; that was a device for faking the books—besides, he had in mind a great conversion operation which would in due course save a lot of money, and which would be defeated by it. Should not heavy taxes be put on the upper classes, who were benefiting enormously by the heavy fall in prices? That might be attractive in principle, no doubt, but would the Conservatives and Liberals agree to something like £100,000,000 a year being taken off their chief supporters? Thomas hinted at a tariff, but Snowden's reaction was so violent that he apologised at once.

While these discussions were going on something had occurred which neither MacDonald nor Snowden foresaw (nor probably their advisers, whoever they may have been). To the economic crisis there was added a financial crisis. The *Credit Anstalt* was the name of a bank which practically controlled the life of Austria; it was in grave difficulties, partly owing to the frantic recall by Americans of moneys that they had invested in Europe. In the hope, among other things, of saving it, the German Chancellor had negotiated a Customs Union with Austria, but the French had successfully forbidden this, and the terms that they offered for restoring Austrian finances amounted to an economic protectorate. British and Germans banks tried to shore up the *Credit Anstalt*; they failed, and its doors were closed. This was grave enough, but on top of that the great Darmstadt and Dresden Banks in Germany crashed, and the whole weight of what was now a European financial collapse fell on London. Now the great foolishness of the British financiers was exposed; they were not indeed bankrupt, but they had been borrowing on short terms and lending on long, and they could not meet their obligations except by drawing on the Bank of England. And the Bank of England's gold was vanishing day by day. At a time like this, a British Royal Commission, endorsed by the Premier and the Chancellor, had declared that Britain was insolvent. The crisis could not have been more alarming.

Snowden and MacDonald intended only to scare their colleagues; but they seem to have scared themselves and all around them. Certainly, when the Cabinet was recalled precipitately on August 19th, both problems—the run on the Bank and the unemployment crisis—were presented in a fine confusion. It met daily, sometimes several times a day, until the 24th. Only gradually did a division of opinion become clear, and it was marked, to outside observers, by the increasing number of the Cabinet Ministers who came back with the First Commissioner of Works after each meeting to talk with him in his big room in Storey's Gate overlooking St. James' Park. After the first meeting there were only three; before the last there were ten out of twenty-one. The names are not recorded: one of his earliest allies, to his surprise, was Clynes; next was Graham; but the great shift in opinion occurred, as ever, when Henderson changed his mind.

The course of events was recorded by Lansbury: none of the other published accounts contradict him. At the beginning the Ministers seem to have examined the crisis coolly and tried to solve it in accordance with their principles and the party programme. The run on the Bank, they were assured, could be stopped if the Budget were balanced. Very well, then, let the higher incomes pay for it. High salaries should be cut, economies could be made in administration and (reluctantly) in projected public works; taxes must be increased. The May cuts in unemployment pay were put aside as indecent. (If relief had gone up ' 30 per cent ' because of the fall in prices, so had contributions, argued Lansbury.)

MacDonald, having seen them, reported that neither Neville Chamberlain for the Conservatives nor Herbert Samuel for the Liberals would even contemplate anything like £100,000,000 from taxation. The money must come, they considered, from the unemployed. Moreover, the May estimate of £120,000,000 deficit was too small; it was more like £180,000,000. Under pressure, he agreed to see the Trade Union Congress, but reported that they had a pre-crisis mentality and could not understand that both unemployment benefit and wages must be decreased. He and Snowden next went to see the Bank of England (members of the Cabinet were already grumbling because they were not allowed to see the financiers face to face, but they grumbled in vain) and brought back what was nearly an ultimatum. The run on the Bank could be stopped only if very considerable cuts were made in unemployment insurance; the danger was very close. The majority of the Cabinet (how large a majority is unknown) wanted to accede: a 20 per cent cut in unemployment pay was intolerable, but might not 10 per cent do? There was a wrangle; some of the Ministers seem to have suggested that the pound might be devalued to meet the financial crisis ('abandoning the gold standard' was the phrase then used), and Snowden, in one of his most emphatic phrases, told them that he would rather wreck the Labour movement than agree to what would mean cutting the workers' wages in half. His colleagues rejected the 10 per cent cut, but were shaken enough to allow MacDonald to inquire of the Opposition leaders, as a mere hypothesis, whether they would agree to such a cut and whether that would meet the crisis. They were told at the same time that the King was returning to London.

The same afternoon—the 22nd—they heard that the Opposition leaders had said that the matter of the 10 per cent cut should be put to the financial authorities responsible for raising the loan in New York without which the Bank of England could not carry on. They were still not allowed to meet these financial authorities: MacDonald, with an anxious air, asked if he might ask the Deputy Governor (Norman was away) of the Bank—for information only, of course, and stressing that the Cabinet had not agreed to any such plan—whether the 10 per cent cut would be satisfactory. Yes, he might. The Bank, it turned out, had to consult the Federal Reserve Bank of America. And Mr. Harrison of that Bank must make confidential inquiries in New York.

By now some members of the Cabinet, including apparently Henderson, were becoming angry; it seemed to them as if the policy of the Government of Great Britain was to depend upon the word of a New York banker. Next day, Sunday the 23rd, they had evidence that this was exactly the case. They were called to hear the latest position, and for a fleeting moment saw the Deputy Governor of the Bank; they were sent away because Mr. Harrison had not telephoned, called back again when he had spoken. The message he had sent to the Premier was smooth, but quite clear. The credits needed would be granted only if the Government's policy had the sincere approval and support of both the City and the Bank of England. All present must have known what that meant; there was clearly a tense scene. In the end, eleven were for accepting Mr. Harrison's ultimatum, ten against; but the ten were prepared to resign, and that would mean that the Labour Government was at an end. (It was afterwards denied that the Ministers ever hung as it were on the end of a line, awaiting a New York decision; but Lansbury's notes make it clear it was just that that happened.) MacDonald received, in the usual form, all the Ministers' resignations, and said that he would notify the King; the Opposition leaders must be told about the Harrison messages, and there would be a last meeting of the Cabinet next day at noon.

The Ministers assembled on Monday in the usual way, not one —not even Snowden—suspecting what they were going to hear. MacDonald told them that they had indeed lost office, but he had not. The King had agreed to invite certain individuals, of whom he would be the chief, to carry on the Government. The others would include Baldwin, the Conservative leader, and Samuel, the Liberal leader. There would be a small Cabinet—only about a dozen—and it should last only as long as 'the emergency' did. Deprecatingly, and for a moment it seemed almost ashamed, he assured his colleagues that there would be no 'coupons', or pacts, or such inter-party arrangements at the next general election when it came; his new colleagues had pledged themselves to that. Nor would there be any party legislation, and non-controversial Bills, like the London Transport Bill, promoted by the valued new-comer to the Cabinet, Herbert Morrison, would be carried through. When he had finished, the Cabinet broke up. Three Ministers, like good boys, were asked to stay behind—Snowden, Thomas and Sankey, the Lord Chancellor.

As he left the meeting, Lansbury looked white enough and haggard, but the face of his most powerful ally was ghastly. An onlooker said that Henderson seemed shrivelled and bowed, and his usually ruddy face was yellow. Disloyalty was a thing he could not understand. He had given his most unswerving support to the handsome, eloquent leader who had helped him build up the movement; he had never allowed himself to be influenced by the fact that he had not in his heart liked Mac-Donald and had more than once received discourtesy from him. Now that man had deserted the people in its greatest misery. He could not understand, though he would try to forgive; he looked like a man who had been given a mortal wound.

Chapter Twenty-one

THE Trades Union Congress, the Labour Party and the Labour M.P.s, through their various executive committees, met on the Wednesday, two days later. MacDonald was still in name their leader, and he may have hoped—perhaps he had even promised his new colleagues—that he would bring his party with him. Thirty-six hours, from Monday afternoon to Wednesday morning, dispelled the hope. The decision of the meeting was in doubt, if at all, for a few seconds only. The new Government was to be ' vigorously opposed ', and the Labour Party of 261 M.P.s (of whom only about fifteen deserted) was to constitute itself ' the official Parliamentary opposition '. The trade union delegates spoke rather harshly to the Ministers who had agreed to MacDonald's plans up to the very end when they did not accept—or were not offered—posts in what was already calling itself ' the National Government '. An echo of their adjectives sounded through to the *Manchester Guardian*, but no recriminations were allowed in the open. The Party had difficulties enough without personal dissensions: MacDonald would make excellent play with the weakness of some of his colleagues as soon as Parliament met.

He did indeed, and for some weeks to come there were bitter wrangles, in which the ex-Ministers vainly demanded publication of the Cabinet minutes. It was a trivial squabble in such a crisis, but MacDonald excelled in it; his vigour seemed to have returned, and he pursued his ex-colleagues with the fury of a leader scorned. It was only because he had at last ejected them from office, he cried in a phrase that made the Press headlines, that Parliament could meet with ' the pound still worth twenty shillings '. Henderson, now Leader of the Opposition, made some attempt to bring back MacDonald to his old mind, saying:

' He and I have occupied the most important offices—shall I say? —of the Labour movement in this country. It has had only two secretaries in thirty-one years. The Prime Minister was secretary

273

for the first eleven years, and at his request I became his successor, a position which I have held just upon twenty years. We have been in two governments. . . . I want to say this, whether the withdrawal of our colleagues be long or short, whether it is temporary or permanent, it is a direct loss to the Labour movement.'

There was no response: his leader of a few days ago sat and watched him from the other side of the House, five yards away, with a steady expression of contempt. He had waited twenty years (he seemed to be thinking) to be quit of the man. Curiously enough, he was obviously discomposed when Lansbury spoke for the party a day or two later, on September 14th. The new Government was putting through an ' Economy Bill ' which made various savings, but whose chief object, as the Press happily said, was ' to turn unemployed off the dole '. Lansbury spoke vehemently: he quoted Tennyson:

> ' Tho' niggard throats of money-lords may bawl,
>> What England was, shall her true sons forget?
> We are not money-lenders all,
>> But some love England and her honour yet.
> And these in our Thermopylae shall stand,
> And hold against the world the honour of this land.'

' These bankers have said to us, " Your social services are attracting the notice of the unemployed masses in the United States, who marching with banners demand unemployment benefit as in this country ". The bankers and the capitalists have said, " Wages must come down, social services must be stopped, and Great Britain is the country that we must attack." This has been going on all through these two years. We have been discussing in committees one after the other what to do in order to meet this situation, and we are told that we ran away. We are told that we gave up. The people who ran away are those who sit over there [pointing to MacDonald]. They have capitulated to the moneylenders, and what have they capitulated to do? The right hon. Gentleman [Neville Chamberlain] is now to be put in charge of the whole of this business of crushing and beating down the unemployed. I know the right hon. Gentleman's administration. I know what his cruel orders can do. Before the ink is dry on his appointment, already the London County Council are plundering the poor old dames' pensions and reducing the relief of these old people by a shilling a week. I suppose that is equality of sacrifice.'

The Economy Bill was passed, but the disaster could not be checked by such means; Snowden and MacDonald had created panic only too well. In a few days nothing seemed to be left of the prestige for which they had sacrificed so much. The pound broke, after all: on September 20th the gold standard was abandoned and all the countries which had used London as their bank and sterling as their wealth found they had lost 20 per cent overnight. There had even been a worse shock to British power: the Admiralty just before had announced that the cuts had caused such insubordination in the Navy that the autumn exercises could not be held. The unemployment figures were passing 3,000,000.

It may seem odd that at this moment of failure the new Government chose to hold a general election. Very precise pledges had been given against this. But promises were no longer a sufficient obstacle—Europe was entering the Decade of the Lie; it was to see a German Chancellor whose proclaimed principle was that the grosser the untruth the greater was its political value, and to hear a British Premier state that he had not told the electors the truth because if he had they would not have voted for him. There were considerations now that outweighed any matter of a broken promise. The probable political results of the panic were clear to any professional. The slump that started in 1930 was a world-wide phenomenon, and wherever there were democratic institutions it produced the same result. The ruling party, whatever it might be, was violently thrown out. The swing might be to right or left; it was almost a matter of chance. In the United States it was the Republican Party that was shattered; in Spain it was the King who fled; in Germany it was the Nazis who came into power; in Poland 'the Colonels'. If the National Government had stayed in power only a few months it would have been punished in the same way. The men at its head were electioneers, and they knew that speed was needed; elections must be held within a very few weeks, while the Labour Ministers could still be blamed for everything. A general election was hurried through, therefore, in October, even though the pound was no longer worth twenty shillings. 'Coupons' (that is, letters giving coalition approval) were issued to 600 men. The coalition, of all parties except Labour, could not agree upon a programme (it differed particularly upon Free

275

Trade), and asked for ' a doctor's mandate ' to do whatever it thought best. Such a plea could succeed only with a hysterical patient, but the electorate was easily made hysterical. Mac-Donald brandished on his platforms a German million-mark note, saying that the pound would become as worthless as that if Labour was returned; Snowden or Runciman the Liberal—the honour is disputed—thought of the even more effective allegation that Labour had arranged to steal the deposits in the Post Office savings bank. The campaign was brilliantly successful. The Labour Party was not merely defeated, it was almost annihilated. From 289 seats (in 1929) it fell to 46. There were five ' I.L.P.-ers ', but otherwise nearly every M.P. was a supporter of the coalition (471 of them were Tories; the Liberals split in three, ' Simonites ', ' Samuelites ', and the Lloyd George family, each hating the other). Only one Cabinet Minister survived—George Lansbury. Only two minor Ministers survived—C. R. Attlee, who had been Postmaster-General, and the new recruit, Sir Stafford Cripps, who had been Solicitor-General. Lansbury, perforce, became first deputy leader and then (since Henderson did not return) full leader.

The Nabobs had vanished, never to return. For almost twenty years now a group of men had shared among themselves, and allotted to others, positions of power in the Labour movement and later in the government. The names of influence recurred regularly, and part of the art of politics (as in the days of Whig Dukes) consisted in allotting to each its niche. Arthur Henderson, William Adamson, J. R. Clynes, J. H. Thomas, Philip Snowden, Tom Shaw, J. R. MacDonald, Sidney Webb, Margaret Bondfield, F. O. Roberts, Ben Turner—these and others had all their prescriptive claims, and the modern Taper or Tadpole would know precisely what they must receive. Now they were swept away for ever: Henderson alone made a ghostly reappearance for a few months after 1933, ill and interested only in Geneva politics. It was as though a huge tide had smashed through a breakwater, sweeping it away and carrying the timber far out into the sea, leaving standing only one tall, stout and solitary stanchion.

The shore was perhaps not quite as empty as it seemed. Trade union leaders are not swept away by an election, and in time they might occupy the vacant places of the Nabobs; the two most influential of them, Citrine and Bevin, were no friends to Lansbury. But this no one noticed for the moment; the Trades Union Congress, shaken by the defeat, was as angry with MacDonald and 'right-wing policy' as Lansbury could be; moreover, while Henderson lived and supported him, not one of them would move against him.

Probably there could have been no better leader for the Party in 1931 than George Lansbury. 'Could I ask for anything more,' said Ponsonby in accepting the leadership in the Lords, 'than to be quit of those people and to have Lansbury as my chief?' The Party did not want another Olympian autocrat, or a Parliamentarian who could slur over difficulties by wordy formulas; it was reeling from the double shock of treachery and defeat. It wanted someone who could restore its confidence in human decency and its belief in its future; perhaps (in psychological cant) it wanted a father. Certainly, the disillusion had been horrible: one eminent woman worker for the movement spent a fortnight in bed from shock when she learned of MacDonald's defection; for months many provincial parties could not bring themselves to take down their large framed pictures, with the flowing quiff and elegant moustaches. In Lansbury they found not only someone whom they loved and who loved them with no touch of patronage, but also a man who would repeat, in his full, hoarse voice, disregarding sniggers in the House of Commons and elsewhere, the truths about justice, kindness and equality that they wanted to hear again. His technique as leader of the tiny Opposition was unorthodox, but it was brilliantly successful; he turned it into a propaganda meeting such as he had known from 1890 onwards. His followers were mostly middle-aged, upright trade unionists, more loyal than eloquent; they made simple, straightforward speeches on general principles, challenged every motion that they could, and often marched through the division lobbies singing the *Red Flag*. Sometimes Jack Jones, the ribald old docker who sat for Silvertown, would lead them, 'in his rather spoiled voice', as Lansbury said, in singing 'It's the poor that helps the poor', which especially vexed the Conservative sense of propriety.

It was incessant, wearying work for his forty-six, to attend at all debates, to raise all the necessary questions, to pounce on every error and every usurpation of the Government; it was galling to see the easy way in which the majority could idle in and out as it chose. Their hearts had sometimes to be raised by a fight: in May 1932 Lansbury took on their most bellicose opponent, and one who had been most cavalier in his treatment of the House. Mr. Winston Churchill, who had not been included in the National Government, sauntered in at half-past ten on the night of the 26th and interrupted the discussion on the Finance Bill by a speech, in a rather dominant tone, on the beer duties. The Leader of the Opposition rose to comment on the injustice to private members who had sat ' hour after hour on the off-chance of getting an opportunity to speak '. ' I will tell the right hon. Gentleman,' he went on, ' what ought to have been told him long ago, and it is that he usurps a position in this House, as if he had a right to walk in, make his speech, walk out, and leave the whole place as if God Almighty had spoken.' The two statesmen became heated, and Lansbury told Mr. Churchill ' to hold his tongue '; the Chair, on the whole, supported him, and his opponent had to be contented with complaining later of the ' perfect cataract of semi-coherent insults from the so-called leader of the so-called opposition '.

He made all the use he could of the small resources he had. Help that he had hoped for was refused him. He begged Maxton, as the leader of the five ' I.L.P.-ers ', to sit next him on the front bench; but that party had decided that the time had come to break away from the tainted Labour Party. It declared itself a separate party and seized, after a childish scuffle, a small room in the House allotted to the Labour Party. But it reaped no reward for its righteousness: to the class-conscious workers to whom it appealed it seemed to be merely deserting a ship that it thought to be sinking. For a while personal loyalties kept it alive as a Clydeside group, and after that it was nothing.

His two chief aides were C. R. Attlee and Sir Stafford Cripps, and both men, it is fairly certain, would admit they owed more to his training than to any other man. Training, indeed, was his chief work; he had to sit almost perpetually upon the front bench, shepherding his flock and tapping his glasses against his knee: he had not merely to find speakers to deal with every subject that came up and to brief them, but even to supervise their delivery. ' Speak up. Put your chin up, X., put your *chin* up,' he would say in his too-penetrating whisper that sometimes reached to the Press gallery. From his two principal supporters he received all the help that he could have hoped: they held up his hands as against Amalek ' the one on the one side and the other on the other, and his hands were steady until the going down of the sun '. In Attlee he found a very clear brain, an immense capacity for work, an invaluable assiduity in absorbing and classifying the vast amount of material that descended upon any leader of the Opposition, and an unassuming willingness, as his deputy, to carry out all the work that was laid upon him. But no more than anyone else did Lansbury foresee a great future for this rather diffident committee-man; his successor, as party leader and in due course Premier, he expected to be Cripps, and one of his most delicate tasks was to bridge the gap between this extreme ' Leftist ' and Henderson on the Right, who was still the official voice of the party and the unions. The gap was wide: when Lansbury incautiously told Henderson that he hoped Cripps would succeed him, the answer was: ' If that happened, I would feel that all I have worked for had gone for nothing '. There existed, when Henderson's life was written, ' a long and intimate ' correspondence between him and Lansbury; but it seems to have been wantonly destroyed; however, there still remains part of the correspondence between Lansbury and Cripps.

' I saw Uncle Arthur yesterday [he wrote to him in an undated letter, probably at the end of 1931]. I do not think he is very well, though he says he is. I found him a bit upset with the sort of forward policy we aim at. He talked of miners and others demanding something to go on with, and not being content to wait for Socialism; this seemed like our old friend Gradualism with a vengeance. I reminded him that at Scarborough [the Labour Party conference there had adopted a programme Lansbury might well have written himself] all our speakers deliberately and after due consideration declared we could not deliver the goods re Social services etc. within the capitalist system. I also said that what mattered was that the programme we fight on shall be a Socialist one, full blooded and unmistakeable; but he seemed to doubt, even if he had a majority, the wisdom of punching our policy right home. I tried hard to make him see that if we had a majority we could not be turned out, and told him I am certain the bankers and financiers will endeavour to sabotage us and whether we like it or not we should be forced to deal with the Banking system. . . .

'But my final thought is that A. H. is terribly worried about the party, that he feels Labour is in the wilderness for a long period unless we can trim our sails so as to catch the wind of disgust which will blow Mac and his friends out and that he is not anxious for us to be too definite about Socialist measures as our first objectives. Put them in our programme but be sure when we come to power we keep on the line of least resistance. He is not dishonest or to be blamed for this attitude; like me he has spent his whole life doing small things while advocating his " changes ". You must make him see the movement he has done so much to foster will perish if once again it gets lost in the morass of opportunism.'

Stafford Cripps was to be, for the next six or seven years, one of his closest political comrades. But Cripps did not have with him the independent and occasionally defiant relations that his old colleagues on the *Daily Herald*, say, had had. He was as much a disciple as a colleague. He was thirty years younger than Lansbury, and he looked to him, as he honestly said, for ' inspiration '. ' Every day I am grateful to you for your friendship and your guidance. God bless you ', ended one of his letters in January 1932. He was young politically, as well as in years; only a few weeks earlier he had written to congratulate MacDonald on his ' courage ' in breaking up the Labour Government, and now he was denouncing him in the more vehement phrases of class-conscious Socialism. He had quite recently been inducted into the Party by Herbert Morrison, and was already censuring his mentor for weakness. Even physically he was different from the Cripps of the 1940s; his face was plumper, his hair more copious, and horn-rimmed glasses accentuated an impression of rotundity far different from his later austerity. His speeches were vehement, and gave a misleading impression of passion. Passionate, politically, he never was; his moving periods were the eloquence of a very able lawyer; he was sincere and deeply earnest, but in himself he was, if anything, ' cold '—in a friend's phrase. Lansbury, with his instant apprehension of personal qualities, saw in him a potentially great servant of the people, and set himself, with the natural authority of an older man, to train him.   He admired the power and clarity of his mind, but he saw in him a proud tendency to follow out his own reasoning and not listen to the arguments of others (to facts he would always listen); ' Stafford,' he would say, ' you have not heard a word that I have been saying. Listen,' and at once the younger man would stop, and with a conscious humility (for he was as profoundly a Christian as Lansbury), attend carefully to what he had ignored.   For some time, indeed, he seemed almost to swing towards him as a magnet to the Pole; for example, once, when Lansbury (using an habitual phrase of despondency which was little more than what would have been an oath in others) said that he ' felt like joining the Communists ' if something was not done, Cripps was so shaken that he replied that if Lansbury ' went wrong ', then ' I would lose faith in everybody '.

There was a great weight of work which fell upon Lansbury's shoulders.   His team was smaller in numbers than MacDonald's in 1910, it was weaker individually, some did not support him as he had expected, and the tasks were more difficult.   More than 500 M.P.s were against the Party, and when they mocked it (as they often did) as ' unable to function as an opposition', there was some truth in what they said.   The thirties were the period of the growth of Fascism; political opposition was bloodily extinguished in Berlin, Moscow, Tokyo and Madrid, and the National Government in Britain seemed sometimes like a grey shadow of what was in power on the Continent.   It was due, in part, to Lansbury and his colleagues that the House of Commons never became a Reichstag.   But the ceaseless work of questioning, of exposing inhumanity, cowardice or injustice, was very hard.   The documents on India alone which Lansbury left for his biographer are a pile 24 inches high, largely of closely-typed matter; the *Hansard* columns of his speeches and those of his colleagues are more than can conveniently be counted. The labour was not wasted. The Government of India Act for example of 1935 was much better than it might otherwise have been, even though it ultimately failed to satisfy the Indian Congress.   Much work had to be done behind the scenes, for forty-six M.P.s could never affect a vote in the House; before long Lansbury was using his position as Parliamentary leader more for extra-Parliamentary activity. Newspapers now were almost obliged to print his letters; one, an appeal to the Church in *The Times* of October 11, 1932, produced fifteen personal letters the next morning from beneficed clergymen, saying that he had convinced them it was their Christian duty to use their pulpits to aid the unemployed. He was less successful in July of that year in appealing to the Archbishop of Canterbury, the Chief Rabbi and the President of the Free Church Council to mediate in the quarrel that had broken out between De Valera, the Irish President, and J. H. Thomas, the Dominions Secretary; but at least the Archbishop (once Cosmo Lang, the Socialist bishop of Stepney) covered his formal refusal with a private letter implicitly admitting an obligation to intervene in politics. (His excuse was the particular one that De Valera was ' incapable of reasoning '.)

As a broadcaster, though he spoke too long, Lansbury was developing a technique almost as good as King George's—the most ' fatherly ' broadcaster of the thirties. ' My sister writes to me that she nearly cried over your broadcast,' wrote Lord Ponsonby to him in October next year (1933). ' I wish I had your faith and hope.' On civil liberties Lansbury soon had an immense *dossier* of cases (for the new Government was vigorous at least in putting down any disagreement with its policies). ' It was quite easy to see Hannington in the room,' read the deposition of a police officer who seized the organisers of the unemployed. ' His room is on the top floor. It has three windows to the best of my recollection. I remember the first letter produced here; I found it personally. . . . I know Devine. He did not ask me to sign a record of the documents I removed. Had he done so I should not have signed one.' And so on for pages; it has a dreadful likeness to the papers of Sidmouth's Home Office of 110 years before. Lansbury, with his historical knowledge, was profoundly alarmed. When Tom Mann was arrested for his share in the unemployed agitation, he did all he could to help him, and visited him after his release, deeply discontented with himself because he was not in prison too. He told the friend who helped him up the hill (he was seventy-three and tired) that if he had had Tom's courage he would have been where Tom was, instead of being a sentimental windbag.

(Not all his Parliamentary activity was opposition. He welcomed the Statute of Westminster, giving independence and equality in 1931 to the Dominions, as ' a piece of Socialist legislation '; the Communist *Daily Worker*, which had by now despaired of him, rebuked him for ' sanctimonious impudence '.)

He was not, initially, worried by difficulties with his own party; in fact, the only disagreement that he had with headquarters in 1931 and 1932 was one in which it was more ' to the Left ' than he. The National Government was fulfilling its promise of throwing masses of the workless off the dole, by imposing what was called a Means Test. This, reverting to a practice of the Whitechapel Guardians forty years before, involved calling upon the relatives of an unemployed man to declare their income, and disallowing a claim for relief if it appeared that they could have contributed more. The inquisition, as much as the meanness, revolted a generation which had almost forgotten the days of Bumble. Lansbury, knowing the realities of Poor Law administration, said publicly that he was in favour of a *personal* Means Test—he would not give public money to a man who himself had adequate resources—but the anger which the Government had roused was such that the Party voted against any Means Test at all, and he had to submit. He did so in a typical way; his secretary wrote to inquirers repeating his views, and merely adding that he would follow the party policy, since he had been outvoted; in the House he said that the Labour Government, when it returned, would find a way of preventing fraud without tormenting the poor.

To the overwork was added a private burden. He had been unable to save money even on his £2,000 salary as First Commissioner; now that he had only an M.P.'s £600, poverty was coming near again. The Labour Party, since he was Leader, met some of his expenses and a part of his gigantic postal bill, but it was not enough. He could not diminish his personal expenditure except by cutting down his generosities or charging for his meetings, and neither of these would he do. Soon he was slipping seriously into debt.

It was not such difficulties which were straining him, however.

It was a sense of his own unworthiness; his religion, which had served him so well in other crises, was now doing him no service in filling him with doubts when he most needed enthusiasm, both for himself and to give to others.

'The fact is [he wrote to Stafford Cripps in July 1932] life becomes more and more difficult for me. Everything gets so mixed; persons, causes, tumble into each other and form such a hotch-potch of ideas that truth or what seems like truth gets just smothered. Sometimes my daily tasks come and go quite easily; at other times my whole being gets overwrought and I am not certain of my own action because sometimes you, sometimes others, see the right course differently to myself. One day the party seems all important, the next day quite unimportant because its interests seem to conflict with truth.

'Then I find myself smothering my own mind and thoughts because others think a certain way better than mine; but over-riding everything is the simple fact that, full of guile of sorts as I am, my wickedness is not of the kind that can stand up to the guile of men like L. G., Simon or J. R. M. I hear words which mean certain things to the ordinary man and something else to the men who use them. . . .

'But my chief thought is of the multitudes outside who *trust* us, those thousands who pin their faith to our assurance that given power big things will be attempted. I think of myself; " even if I live to see us in power, will it be possible for me to keep my faith?" *The thought of leadership does not enter; it is as one of the 350 in the House.* And when the others come under review what a mixture of personal ambitions and ignorance confronts us! and this appals me.

'You know me well enough now to know what a mixture of self-consciousness and some self-sufficiency I am and how much I like appreciation. This latter is not sought after; yet it is true, I would rather give pleasure than pain, even to those I dislike. It is a very human failing which in varying degrees is in us all.

'Somehow, in ways it is impossible to describe, I get bewildered by the fact that though we cannot live without bread is true, it is equally, if not more, true we *cannot* live by it alone. I have striven hard to make myself and others see that we must each lose our lives in the life of the community and while fighting for bread and rights for ourselves, we must never forget the *common* weal. But the last has been buried in words and as a result our movement is full of men, and women, who measure success by what it brings to them. This is not a fault of mine. It is perhaps the only decent thing that has remained firm and fixed since my earliest enthusiasm—I could not ever measure success of a movement by any personal measure. I like success but, it is true, personal success such as mine is has come without the asking (that is, if anything any of us attain to should be counted as success in a personal sense).

' I believe the world, and our people especially, need a purely religious message, not theological. In fact the world needs this more than anything else. Is the House a place where such a message can be given? You remember Savonarola turned Romola back to Florence when she was fleeing from her husband and told her to give her witness in the place she had been given to fill. It is this thought, and others, that at present bids me hold on. Yet there come days when the jealousies (*my own*, as well as other people's), and want of faith both in our actions and our courage and discretion, worry me to distraction. I laugh and keep as stout a heart to the hills of difficulty as is possible, but often my heart fails and my soul seems to cry out within me whether I am spending my old age in the way that is best. At the start I felt God had given me a task to do. It may be he has; my doubt is whether I am good enough to do it or whether the way is right. You must not imagine there is self righteousness in what I say now, but it is true my mind does not allow me to see more than a very few who see the impersonal side of life as I know I do; yet if we cannot within the framework of our party get together a body of men and women, especially young ones, who will see the cause of Socialism as a religion to be served as St. Francis, Savonarola, and Tolstoy served their faiths, all our work is hopeless. You know the saying: " God is waiting for the people who are good enough to enter and enjoy the Promised Land." The daily question which hits me in the face is: Are we teaching and living our lives in the way best calculated to produce such people?

' It is me and my own faults, shortcomings and misgivings which perplex and baffle me and make me so tiresome in thought and action. DON'T answer.

Always. G. LANSBURY.

' P.S.—I was a prig to object to meeting Salter or anyone else; if you are able to change again, ask your wife to change over and let me come when he is there. I ought not to be so self-righteous about anyone, even on economic matters.'

While he reproached himself, his own most severe critic, for weakness, pride, muddle-headedness and love of popularity, he could not fail to see that others were worse than he. He had gone north to Lossiemouth in Scotland to appeal to MacDonald against the Home Secretary, Gilmour's, action against Tom Mann.

'I must *tell* you about J. R. M. when we meet [he wrote to Cripps on his return (December 31, 1932)]. He is a terrible mixture of vanity, cowardice, and utter lack of principle. He is like a rudderless vessel, just drifts. Does not attempt to see an argument, just repeats "Gilmour". . . . He will see Gilmour, as he, Mac, was obviously impressed by the fact that most of the press and lots of Noncons. are not with him. But I came away terribly distressed that a man with his mentality should have led us all for so many years. He never could have believed in civil liberty or Socialism. His whole mind is one web of tortuous conservatism; he has no solid rock of conviction anywhere except perhaps a lingering kind of Protestant faith as expounded by John Knox.'

He soon had a more pathetic evidence of his old chief's degeneration. As the M.P.s walked in ceremonial passage to the Lords to receive a royal message, the Prime Minister and the Leader of the Opposition together at their head, MacDonald suddenly said to him under the noise: 'George, do you feel your age now?' Lansbury made some indifferent answer, and MacDonald went on in a perplexed tone: 'I do. I do not always know what I meant to do. Often in the House I am speaking and I have no idea how the sentence I am saying should finish.'

Foreign policy was what troubled him most. On the surface he was in full agreement with his party, but there was an anxiety at the back of his mind which he did not want to bring to its front. All were agreed that the League of Nations must be supported with immovable resolution, and that if this were done war would be impossible. A member of the League—Japan—in 1932, attacked another member—China—and before long had overrun Manchuria; Lansbury, with Bromley of the Trades Union Congress and Lathan of the Labour Party Executive, signed a reproach to Simon, the Foreign Secretary, for rebuffing an American hint at common action against Japan, and a demand that he should initiate an economic boycott through the League against the aggressor. The Government refused; it was walking already on the path towards the Second World War, and this was only the first of many suggestions to be treated with derision. But Lansbury momentarily wondered what would have happened if it had agreed, and if economic ' sanctions ' (the cant word) had failed. Would ' military sanctions ' (the cant phrase for war) have followed? And could the Labour movement, a second time in a generation, support a ' war to end war '? Fortunately, the dilemma was postponed, and he did not, any more than anyone else in England, realise how much nearer it was brought by the Nazi seizure of power in Germany. That disaster seemed to him and his colleagues not much more than a local catastrophe for the German Socialists, ruining the greatest Labour movement in the world and turning tens of thousands of the best Germans into refugees. It certainly was making impossible the task of the World Disarmament Conference, to which Henderson was devoting his failing energies; though serious, this was a limited damage, and seemed comparable, for the moment, to the failure of the World Economic Conference of 1933, which had been the focus of so many hopes and which was frustrated by the United States' sudden devaluation of the dollar.

His anxieties were not lessened by the behaviour of his assistant, Lord Ponsonby, the leader in the House of Lords, who wrote to him that this was an appropriate time to demand that Britain disarm totally 'an an example '. He evaded this proposal (his aristocratic supporter noted that he liked popular applause, and wrote later to his biographer asking him to stress this failing), but he was ill-at-ease, for he had often enough proposed something like that before. But now he was leader of the Labour Party, and had realised not only that his followers would not agree with it, but that he himself did not really approve. He was not, he decided, and told his intimates, in favour of ' unilateral disarmament '; he wished British armament lowered to the very Plimsoll line of safety (which he probably would have drawn low) but he was not (despite occasional rash rhetoric) in favour of Britain going naked in an armed world.

If they had known of this decision, his opponents within the Labour Party might have been mollified. For an opposition was forming at the beginning of 1933. The trade union leaders, reasonably enough, did not want another autocrat to take the place of Ramsay MacDonald, least of all a sentimental pacifist. Any eccentricities of Mr. Lansbury should be checked early. The Nabobs had been blown away; that was a good thing, and it meant that the room was swept and garnished for themselves to enter in. They were, after all, more genuinely representative of the working class than the intellectuals like Snowden and MacDonald (the name of Thomas was slurred over in these discussions), and had recently proved it. While Henderson extended his protection to the Victorian survival who led the party, no direct attack was possible, or even necessary, but the principle of control of all political policy by the National Joint Council of the Labour Party and the Trades Union Congress (in which they had a majority) might as well be affirmed. Ernest Bevin, in March, when an Albert Hall meeting was called by a small body called the Socialist League, wrote to Lansbury, condemning him for agreeing to speak at it without the permission of the Council, in such terms that he was answered: ' Your note has made me utterly miserable. I despair of making a suggestion or taking any action without being completely misunderstood.' Lansbury patiently went over the details of the arrangements for the meeting and his right to speak for the Labour movement.

' Whenever I feel it is impossible to state the Party's own view I shall of course resign, not merely from leadership but from membership; but I do maintain my right to put the Party's case . . . wherever an opportunity occurs, and I do not think I am called upon to ask permission from anybody to do this—and certainly have no intention of doing so.'

The dockers' leader was silenced for the moment, but he was to return. It was unfortunate that the two most powerful leaders of the trade union ' club ' were men temperamentally hostile to Lansbury, and irritated by what they considered his emotional and old-fashioned thinking. Ernest Bevin had spent his life and energies in building up the giant Transport Workers' Union that had displaced Robert Williams' Federation; he was not by origin a docker, but he had assimilated his habits of mind and language to those of dockland. He had courage, independence,

George and Bessie Lansbury, about 1925

George Lansbury, after resigning the leadership

obstinacy and directness, as well as a quite unusual keenness of mind. But he also had a roughness of phrase, a shortness of temper and an overbearingness of manner, which he seemed at times actually to cultivate, as being genuinely proletarian. He had something of Burns' vanity; in a moment of humorous self-knowledge he had referred to himself as a *prima donna*. The next most important trade union leader, the Secretary, Walter Citrine (afterwards Lord Citrine), was as different as Shaw's chauffeur, Henry Straker, was from a builder's labourer: indeed, the two were in some ways epitomes of two types of British worker. Citrine, who had come to his post from the Electrical Trades Union, was clerkly and almost finicky. Stiff-collared, blue-suited, thin and tall, he was even physically a contrast to the stout, short and lowering Bevin. His mind was as clean, clear and precise as himself; his office was run to exact schedules; his speeches, if sometimes too long, were models of passionless and convincing argument. Divergencies and rebellions he rebuked, never with a labourer's oath, but with an instant reference to the resolutions which they contravened. He was, probably, rather less fitted to collaborate with George Lansbury than his blunter colleague.

A far heavier burden than overwork and suspicious colleagues was to fall upon Lansbury. Late in March 1933 his wife, Bessie Lansbury, died. What this loss meant to him was, he said, inexpressible; and there is no sense in attempting to express it here. Politically as well as personally he had relied upon her during a half-century of unquestioned affection and fidelity; neither of them ever spoke willingly about the link between them, but it was his own conviction that the character of Bessie Lansbury was greatly responsible for the character of George Lansbury. Certainly, her disappearance knocked as it were a centre out of his life, leaving only the outside interests. He had always come back to 39 Bow Road from his meetings up and down the country, from his late sittings in the Commons, from his tiresome sessions with the Executive, or from his evening work at the Editor's desk. Now there was no home, and no wife to whom he could come back.

There still exists a cinema news-reel, taken five weeks after her death, and showing George Lansbury leading, and then speaking to, the May Day marchers to Hyde Park. The figure is unchanged; the body tall, strong, upright, if a little heavy; the step is unusually firm for a man of seventy-four. The head has the Roman grandeur which had replaced the simple geniality of 1912—a big, Wellingtonian nose, sparse white hair blown in the wind, firm jaw; the voice is deep and full, though husky. But the eyes, as the face turns to the camera, are haggard and in deep hollows; there are deep sympathy and profound tiredness in both them and the set of the shoulders. He looks round upon the crowd as if he were solely responsible for their future and their belief, and as if the responsibility were more than his exhaustion could bear.

From his desolate house he went out, even more frequently than before, to meetings up and down the country, where he would find at least some inspiration to his work and an assurance of an affection which was still his, even if it was a thin substitute for what he had lost. He went farther afield, stayed away longer, spoke more frequently than ever before. He was overworking, even to the most casual eye; but there was nobody to prevent him, or to order him to rest. Where could he rest?

The inevitable result came on December 9th, 1933. He opened a bazaar at the Gainsborough Town Hall, and walked briskly away to prepare his speech for a Socialist meeting that was to follow. In the dark he did not see a step on the balcony above the main hall; he was thrown forward and fell several yards. When he tried to move, he found his thigh was broken. His answer to the comrades who rushed to help him was typical; in a strong voice he said: ' This is only an incident. Carry on with the meeting ', and so firm was his authority that they retired and did as they were told.

He was in great pain. The bone was set locally, but in such a way that it had to be re-broken when he reached London by ambulance. There he was cared for skilfully and with loving kindness in the trade union hospital, the Manor House. But his condition was grave and gave his doctors anxiety for many days. He himself believed that he was dying.

Chapter Twenty-two

'In the very earliest, darkest hours of my illness, I was not afraid of what would befall me; I had no dread of God as my Father and my Judge.' Lansbury wrote this in *My England*, a book which he composed in hospital as his considered political programme for his country, and which abounds in passages that could hardly be written in 1951 by a Labour leader. He spent only a few weeks in the near shadow of death, but many in the fear of being crippled; he was in hospital, all told, from December 1933 to July 1934, often in pain. Much of the time he spent in meditation; 'during the long nights around Christmas and Easter,' he recorded, ' often feelings of sheer exultation and sometimes of despair would flood my mind.' ' I tried,' he writes in the same passage ' on several occasions to make pressmen understand that my illness and nearness to death had made some things clearer to me.' He did not at the time succeed; maybe he had chosen the wrong audience. But in the next year or two it became clear that he had changed, perhaps not as much as he believed, but certainly changed. Immediately, the alteration showed itself in a greater confidence; the diffidence which had intermittently plagued him almost disappeared. He seemed satisfied that he had a duty to do, and assured that he was able to do it. He knew that he was unworthy, indeed, and admitted it frequently. He objected to any praise that seemed excessive, and still refused money when he could. Raymond Postgate, for example, arranged with Odhams for a £1,000 payment for a series of important and exclusive articles—a generous but not fantastic sum—but when the cheque arrived he refused to accept it, though his bank account badly needed it. It was only the mortified disappointment on his son-in-law's face that made him relent, and there is little doubt at that that most of the money was given away. But he ceased at least to regret so seriously his occasional lapses from extreme simplicity of living. It may sound absurd, but in fact it was a significant change when he admitted that he liked cold lobster, and would order it even if it was a trifle dearer than other things on the menu. When he travelled, he stipulated for comfortable accommodation, without feeling the need to apologise. Nothing that he did could by the wildest exaggeration be called indulgence, but there disappeared the morbid thought that he ought to live as uncomfortably and poorly as his least fortunate constituents.

Even before he resumed his leadership, his colleagues noted his decisiveness. He did not, even while he was still ill, leave Parliamentary affairs wholly to Attlee and Cripps: in May 1934 he was writing to Cripps telling him to ' dot Simon in the eye ' and outlining the argument to be used. In February of that year, with almost excessive assurance, he was cajoling the Bishop of Lichfield into accepting his nominee (a ' Catholic Crusader ') for an important parish vacancy. He carried on a steady guerrilla warfare with Sir John Reith, the Director-General of the British Broadcasting Corporation, to secure a fairer proportion of Labour speakers on the wireless. He got little satisfaction, but he was at least indefatigable, and once or twice almost discountenanced that autocratic man.

Some of his new confidence was no doubt due to the enormous number of letters that were sent him. He had never, except after his wife died, received such a flood of affectionate correspondence. Some were from his political enemies—there was even an ungainly note from Neville Chamberlain—but most were from supporters, women and men whose only object was to tell him that they admired and loved him, and needed him; it would indeed have been a cold man who was unaffected by them. But the main cause of the change was within himself; it was a deepening of his religious belief. In his long, anxious nights he arrived slowly at an assurance that he was himself both a part and an instrument of a power that he could not and did not need to define, though he called it God; his wife, whose absence he felt every day, was equally a part of that power, and a part to which he would soon be reunited. It is hard for one who does not share it to explain, or even describe this calming certainty. He expressed it in conventional phrases about love— he had no other language—but those who listened to him speak, or merely watched the way that he behaved, did sometimes fleetingly understand that Socialism was for him, and perhaps should be for them, nothing but a practical working out of the order, ' Love one another '. Love was not only the will of God, it was also the will of man (if there was any difference, for God expressed Himself, and existed, in and through men of goodwill), and might be as practical a method of testing Acts of Parliaments, by-laws and foreign policy as ' the greatest good of the greatest number ', ' the interest of the workers ', ' the defence of the nation ' or any other of the conventional criterions. (For those who pondered upon the question, it must have been clear which way his decision would now go if there ever was a conflict between his pacifism and his Socialism.)

His altered emphasis—for it was that rather than a new method of thought—meant gradually an alteration in his relationship with his colleagues and followers. After his illness he had many more clerical friends than before. His earlier distaste for parsons (never very logical) seemed to vanish. The change was not, of course, wholly on his side: Temple, Gore and others had changed the Church too, and it was by no means certain now that the vicars in the towns that Lansbury visited would be the Tory bigots of 1900. A good many priests were now Socialists or near-Socialists; it was said, and may have been true, that in the thirties George Lansbury's voice was more influential in the Church than the average bishop's. But against this must be set the fact that he was less easily understood by his lay colleagues. Many of his fellow Left-wing Socialists were Marxists, or at least agnostics. They found they had to translate what he said into their own language; sometimes it would not translate at all. He did not secure, mainly for this reason, the same unquestioning loyalty from the Labour Party headquarters' staff that he had had from the Office of Works. He seemed to them good-hearted, but a preacher more than a practical politician. Henderson had had all their respect, but only some of their affection; Lansbury had some of their respect and all their affection. He did not even play any important part in the revival of Socialist militancy within the Labour movement. This revival was largely connected with the movement for the ' United Front ' (between Labour Party, I.L.P. and Communist Party) in which his aide Cripps took an excited interest. He could not constitutionally support this, as he was leader of the Labour Party, and anyway he had the strongest doubts of the Communist Party's usefulness. But these were not the only reasons; it was more important that he spoke a different language from the Socialist Leaguers, G. D. H. Cole and his neo-Fabians, the surviving ' I.L.P.-ers ', Victor Gollancz's ' Left Book Club ' members and the Communists. To them he was only a benevolent old fighter whose approval was an encouragement, but who could give no practical advice.

Nevertheless, his most important activity in 1934 was political. While he was still leader of the Party, and his influence was at its highest, he composed and published his book, *My England*, in which he gave both a picture—intermittently—of England as he hoped to see it, and—consecutively—of the legislative means by which his modern Utopia would be reached. Interspersed were general statements of principle and reflections like that already quoted. It was disorderly in appearance (though a close analysis shows it is far more cunningly arranged than appears) and deliberately conversational in style; but that did not make it any the less effective. It would indeed be possible, if anyone cared to spend the time, to reconstruct from it and from the abandoned Bills of the 1929 Government a good half of the home legislation of the third Labour Government. Lansbury appeared, when he died, to have failed; but on the Government which took power five years afterwards there were not many precursors whose influence was greater than his.

There is no room for an analysis of the book, and most of what he proposed has already been described, especially his plans for innocent enjoyment. One or two points surprised some of his readers. His programme for the next Labour Government included a reform of Parliamentary procedure (with more normal hours of meeting), an educational Bill, a big rebuilding and rehousing effort, land reclamation and the restoration of agriculture, bank nationalisation, Import and Export Boards, and other expected proposals; but it seemed to some people odd that, with 2,000,000 men out of work, he should say that the problem under a Socialist Government would be more likely to be a shortage of labour than unemployment. ' Leftist ' critics were pained because he said that the shibboleth ' Reform or Revolution? ' was no longer helpful, that a Socialist Government would introduce non-Socialist and palliative measures as well as Socialist Bills, and that the people could not be expected to starve while the foundations of a Socialist State were patiently laid. He repeated, defiantly, his often-rejected plans for the emigration of whole balanced communities to the empty places of Australia and Canada. He discomposed some of his pacifist friends by saying that force would be needed, and would be employed to put down the hooligan 'British Fascist' gangs which were being organised; he added that the Mosley movement was connived at and encouraged by the Government (which incidentally he suspected of being in a secret alliance with Japan as well). One other principle that he announced brought him into conflict with a man who now might well have been an ally, Herbert Morrison. He did not think his own experience with the staff of the Office of Works was typical. On the contrary, the events of 1930 and 1931 had convinced him that the future Government could have no confidence in the higher Civil Servants. Not only did they not understand Socialist policy, they would probably actively sabotage it. Socialist measures, he said, must be carried out by Socialists: the existing Treasury experts could not be 'tolerated' in their offices. Outside experts, Royal Commissioners, referees and so forth should no longer be drawn from upper-class men like the May Committee-men. Nothing could have more displeased Herbert Morrison, fresh from his sensational capture of the London County Council, and with his mind set upon reorganisations and reforms through the willing service of public officials. Lansbury's dictum, which he had contested before, seemed to him to open wide doors for the introduction of an American 'spoils system'. The fat jobs would be allotted and re-allotted, as the parties went in and out; Socialist administration would be impossible, progress would stop, and corruption would flourish. He knew of one corner in London at least where the danger of Labour jobbery was not at all imaginary.

The difference of opinion was less profound than it seemed. Lansbury detested patronage and corruption as much as Morrison, and knew more about them. Morrison could hardly have believed that immovable enemies like Sir Warren Fisher could carry out a Socialist financial policy. There was, indeed, a real difficulty; but time and the terrible lessons of a war were to remove it. When the third Labour Government came to power there was no phalanx left of upper Civil Servants who believed that Socialist proposals were either disasters which they ought to prevent or fantasies which in fact could never be carried out.

In 1934 and 1935 the politicians could see clear signs of a change in public opinion. It might be said that in 1931 the Labour movement had been knocked senseless, and that three years later it was beginning to stir and, like a boxer, rising to its feet. But the metaphor would be only partly illuminating. The change was mostly in the unpolitical mass of the population —the people whom the statisticians called ' the floating vote '. They had recovered from the hysteria of 1931; the electoral pendulum was swinging back. Unemployment was still enormous; the National Government had fulfilled none of their expectations; in itself it was beginning to fall apart. Since Free Trade had been abandoned, most of the Liberals had left it; those who remained (as ' National Liberals ') were already almost indistinguishable from Conservatives. The ' National Labour ' element was even more of a wreck; Snowden was sitting in unemployed solitude in the Lords; MacDonald's mind was growing cloudier, and he abandoned the premiership to Stanley Baldwin; Thomas, the sole survivor, was already isolated by suspicions which became certainties when a Budget scandal broke some months later. Moreover, the results of a privately-organised ' Peace Ballot ' had been announced. Eleven million electors had declared for peace and full support of the League of Nations. A vote of that size could turn an election; at the moment the Labour Party was accepted as the more sincere supporter of the League, and the Conservative Head Office was worried.

As Lansbury worked and spoke, the Labour movement seemed to strengthen under his hand. He fought the ' Sedition Bill ' in October 1934. He broadcast on India in February 1935, explaining why the Government proposals could not satisfy Indians. He negotiated, once again, with Lloyd George in 1934, to find that all that the Liberal leader wanted was an election compact, which he could not have. So far as home affairs were concerned, everything pointed to a possible Labour victory in a short while. Parliament was four years old, and an election must be held soon; the country was disappointed and nervous; half of Baldwin's five hundred seats were vulnerable; there was a possibility that the newly confident Labour Party would gain a majority, and in that case George Lansbury would be Prime Minister.

There were others, besides Lansbury himself, to whom that thought brought anxiety. In home affairs no one more than he could have expressed adequately the desires of both trade unionists and Socialists. But there was a looming danger in foreign affairs, in which it seemed he could not speak for them. No one in Britain, it is true, knew what was really in the mind of the ' National ' Government; the problem was discussed in the belief that it would support the League of Nations, and much of the debate consequently to-day seems off the point. Mussolini knew better; he was not, like Hitler, a criminal fanatic, he was a pin-table crook, a spiv, a ' wide boy ', and, as such people do, he knew intuitively when and where the police were slack, inattentive or corrupted. His intention to attack Abyssinia, a member of the League, was already formed. He had met the British and French spokesmen at Stresa and listened carefully to what they had to say, but more carefully to what they did not say. They would not, he decided, keep their promises to the League; he could recognise (who better?) a welsher, and in the summer of 1935 he moved his troops to the attack.

But in Britain his calculations were not understood. The question which the Labour Party thought it had to answer was: ' When the support which the Government will give through the League to the Abyssinians brings us near to "military sanctions " (that is, war) shall we support this war, with all that that implies? ' Its leader was beginning to answer *No*, its members *Yes*. For many years it had been enough to say that the united use of ' economic sanctions ' (meaning boycotts, trade and financial blockades and such) would prevent war, but that seemed no longer true. (Sardonically, even this was a mistake, as was shown by the instant success of the Nyon threat in 1937. The actual use of force was not needed against Italy; an economic blockade by all the forty-two nations which were ready for it, and the closing of the Suez Canal would probably have stopped Mussolini in 1935.) War was war, even if limited in scope and carried on by order of an international authority. An answer would probably have to be given at the Labour Party conference in October.

But before it met there had to be a prelude. The question of war and peace was not the only one that had to be settled; for certain leaders there was also the question of the effective control of the Labour Party. The Trade Union group, which has been compared to a club, had determined to reaffirm its authority. The Labour Party was frequently called a trade union vassal by its opponents; the charge was never nearer to truth than in 1935. The Trades Union Congress was usually held a bare month before the Party Conference, and it discussed political questions. The same delegates (in most cases) would reappear at the Party Conference and put through the resolutions they had already debated, using their overwhelming ' card vote '. To the delegates of Labour Parties, who provided the only new faces, the less civil trade union leaders would say that they were infected with middle-class fantasies; the only people who knew the facts of industrial life were they themselves, the true workers. There was no effective reply (a local party which had over a thousand votes was a monster; the Railwaymen alone had 208,000), but of verbal replies there were plenty. The trade unionists were told that they had no right to use their card votes on proposals on which their members had not voted; that they traded behind the scenes in seats on the executive (which was true; there were no real contests for the trade union seats—only for the local societies' seats); that their members paid, per head, about a tenth of what the local parties' members paid; and that it was the individual members who did all the work in the constituencies of which the new Nabobs expected to take the reward. The union leaders were unmoved; for they were motivated by a queer last survival of Syndicalism, not a class-consciousness but a caste-consciousness, which made them rather pleased to contemplate an arrangement by which they neither fought elections nor took office, but annually or in General Council issued instructions to those who did.

There was nothing like a unanimous desire among them to

remove Lansbury: they had joined with their colleagues at the Southport Conference in refusing peremptorily his offer to resign the leadership lest his pacifism became an obstacle. But they did not feel so keenly as the politicians that his loss would end the chances of a victory at the polls. He was only one of many others in the Party who might have to be brought into line; he would, no doubt, be a loss; but, then, his successor might be more amenable. Henderson had resigned the previous year, was ill and in fact dying; no opposition could come from him.

There was one thing which weakened Lansbury's position, if he wished to resist an attack; for the first time in his life, he was a solitary man. 'In the midst of a very busy life,' he had written to the Crippses in December, 'I am often very, very lonely, except for the persistent faith that that which we think of as God is all around us, and my darling is not really dead.' To the loss of his wife had been added another; Edgar, his second son— the one with whom he discussed politics regularly, and who was his obvious successor—died of cancer in the summer of 1935. Nor had he—as he had had on the *Daily Herald* or *Lansbury's Weekly*—a group of people with whom he worked regularly and who modified his policy as he changed theirs. Even the son-in-law with whom he had worked for years no longer agreed with him. He had disciples, such as Cripps, in plenty; but they looked to him for guidance and decisions; they could not help him now.

He tried to avoid being sent to the Trades Unions Congress at Margate in August as fraternal delegate, suggesting Attlee to take his place. But the executive objected; there had been rumours of disunity, and his absence might be considered intentional. He attended in time to hear Walter Citrine, now full Secretary of the Congress and a knight, urging the delegates to vote a resolution pledging themselves to ' military sanctions ', and not ' to let George Lansbury down ' by voting against it. This he thought was intolerable; the Congress leaders knew what his views were, and his name should not have been used; when he had to make his delegate's speech he would have to say he would not have supported the resolution. Sir Walter, hearing this, was alarmed; he discussed the problem with his colleagues, and brought back the reply that as Lansbury's only right to speak rose from his being the Labour Party's fraternal delegate, he must only deliver the Party's message. There seems to have been something either in the bureaucratic ingenuity of this message, or in the pedagogic manner of its delivery, that vexed Lansbury; in the account which he wrote, but apparently decided not to publish, the tenseness of his feeling about Sir Walter is obvious. Yet the provocation had an unexpected effect on him. He was alone at the Congress; he spent forty-eight hours in self-examination; he went for a long walk by night upon the cliffs by himself, hoping to find a solution. Finally he seems to have been swayed both by a decision not to be influenced by any personal resentment and by a recollection of his disastrous mistake of 1912. 'Never resign'; he once again consulted his colleagues, and with three exceptions they told him that his resignation would be a disaster to the Party. Everyone knew, they added, that if war came he could not be their leader; but that might be far away, and he had a duty to the Party whose revival was to a high degree his own work. He was persuaded; to an immensely enthusiastic audience he made a speech which denounced war but did not repudiate Sir Walter; he was hideously uncomfortable when delegates asked him afterwards if he had changed his opinions. He attended a meeting of the executives of both the economic and political wings of the movement; he told both them and the Labour candidates emphatically what his real views were, and how deeply he felt them in his conscience. He was assured again that his position was understood, and that his work as leader was indispensable. One of those present was revolted by his reference to his conscience, and classed him (it seemed later) as a canting nuisance; but this he did not realise.

The Party conference was to meet at Brighton in the first week of October. There were two groups pulling at Lansbury, both afraid that he might not resign. The one was personified by the leader in the House of Lords, Ponsonby, who wrote to him on September 17th, 'I cannot wait any longer!' and sent to the Press a letter resigning his position, on the ground that no honest pacifist could consistently 'hold a position as leader' in the Party. If this failed to force his hand, the other group— the trade unionists—would probably succeed. They were headed by a powerful triumvirate, Ernest Bevin of the Transport Workers, Charles Dukes of the General Workers, and John Marchbank of the National Union of Railwaymen. Before the Conference met, Lansbury made a fresh effort to abdicate quietly; the executive again told him that this would be inexcusable, and that he was essential for the forthcoming election.

If he had not been haunted by his 1912 mistake he would probably have insisted; certainly, by the time the Party Conference met on the last day of September he had determined that he must go. The Italian troops were now actually invading Abyssinia; at any moment the British Government would have to support the League with ' military sanctions '. The resolution calling on the Government to use ' all necessary measures ' through the League to stop the Italians was moved for the executive by Mr. Hugh Dalton on Tuesday, October 1st. Though his voice was even louder than usual, there was nothing bullying in his argument: it was a clear and fair statement of the case for using force through the League to stop a war before it could spread, buttressed by some telling quotations from Mr. Lansbury (who had taken care to say that in these sentences he was expressing official party policy) and Sir Stafford Cripps (who had not). The debate at first seemed rather to go against the pacifists; Lord Ponsonby was clever, but no more, Miss Cox and Dr. Salter sentimental; Sir Stafford Cripps made a speech which they did not care for, for it claimed that armed force was quite suitable if used by a workers' government but not otherwise. On the other side Major Attlee, Sir Charles Trevelyan, Lees-Smith and others had the easier task of proving that inactivity would only lead to further war, and that to fail to support the League Covenant made nonsense of all the Labour Party's programmes of the last sixteen years. Marchbank and Dukes, with some heat, resented the ease with which intellectuals like Cripps advised the unions to organise strikes and boycotts instead. The speeches were not great oratory, but they were thoughtful and were carefully followed. A great political party was seriously endeavouring to make up its mind upon a profoundly important question; democracy could for a morning be seen at its best.

When Lansbury rose in the afternoon he had a tumultuous

reception, such as he had never had before; the whole conference, with the exception of two glowering trade union groups, rose and sang ' For he's a jolly good fellow '.   But his opening words spread disappointment.   ' I agree with my friends,' he said, ' who think it quite intolerable that you should have a man speaking as Leader who disagrees fundamentally on an issue of this kind.'   As the Leader was elected by the M.P.s, he had called a meeting of them for the following Tuesday, where the matter would be put in order; but if anyone wished to move that the Conference sent a recommendation to the M.P.s that he should go, ' I should not consider that as hostile but perfectly natural '. The Conference bellowed ' No, no ', but though he was obviously moved he went on:

' I have gone into mining areas, I have gone into my own district when people have been starving or semi-starving; I have stood in the midst of dockers who have been on the verge of starvation (before there was any " dole " or Poor Law Assistance, excepting the workhouse), and I have said to them: " No, you must not rise, you must have no violence, you must trust to the winning of this through public opinion."   I have never at any time said to the workers of this country: " You must take up either arms, or sticks, or stones, in order to force your way to the end that you seek to attain."   And when I am challenged on all these issues, I say to myself this: I have no right to preach pacifism to starving people in this country and preach something else in relation to people elsewhere. . . . I have said the same thing on the continent when I have had the privilege of speaking abroad.   I have said it in Russia when my Russian comrades allowed me to see a review of their air force, and when they took me on one of their warships.   I have never under any circumstances said that I believed you could obtain Socialism by force.

' And why have I said that?   I have said it, first, because One whose life I revere and who, I believe, is the greatest Figure in history, has put it on record: " Those who take the sword shall perish by the sword ". . . .

' It may be that I shall not meet you on this platform any more. (Cries of " No ".)   There are things that come into life that make changes inevitable.   It may very well be that in the carrying out of your policy I shall be in your way.   When I was sick and on my back ideas came into my head, and one was that the only thing worth while for old men to do is to at least say the thing they believe, and to at

least try to warn the young of the dangers of force and compulsion
. . . it is said that people like me are irresponsible. I am no more
irresponsible a leader than the greatest Trade Union leader in the
country. I live my life, as they do, amongst ordinary people. I see
them when I am at home every day; I meet them and know all there
is to know about them; and they do about me. . . . If mine was the
only voice in this Conference, I would say in the name of the faith I
hold, the belief I have that God intended us to live peaceably and
quietly with one another, that if some people do not allow us to do so,
I am ready to stand as the early Christians did, and say, " This is our
faith, this is where we stand, and, if necessary, this is where we will
die." '

He had rarely spoken as movingly: his voice was at its full
strength, and some of the delegates may have been shaken.
It was not possible that he could change the result of the vote;
but one man at least was determined that the pacifists should not
only be beaten, but so beaten that it should be made impossible
for their leader to stay. Moreover, this talk of conscience disgusted him. Ernest Bevin's speech that followed was described
even by the *News Chronicle* correspondents (David Keir and Ian
Mackay, who shared his views) as of ' a virulence distasteful to
many of the delegates. . . . In one vitriolic passage he even went
so far as to say, "It is placing the executive in an absolutely wrong
position to take your conscience round from body to body asking
to be told what to do with it " '. The sneer roused angry protests,
but he shouted the objectors down: ' There is one quotation
from the Scriptures which George Lansbury has quoted to-day
which I think he ought to apply to himself—" Do unto others ".
I am a democrat,' he continued angrily, ' and I feel we have been
betrayed.' Lansbury, he said, had taken part in drafting and had
approved the Party's pamphlet called *Socialism and Peace*,
advocating sanctions. He had told the executives at Margate
that he had seen Sir Samuel Hoare and pledged the Party to
sanctions. Sir Stafford Cripps, too, was stabbing the Party in
the back. ' People have been on this platform to-day talking
about the destruction of capitalism. The middle classes are not
doing too badly as a whole under capitalism and Fascism.
Lawyers and members of other professions have not done too
badly. The thing that is being wiped out is the Trade Union

Movement.' Anyhow, it was not politicians who had formed the Labour Party—it was the trade unionists, and Keir Hardie had had nothing to do with it.

Bevin's speech was not an argument, but a calculated bad temper—one says ' calculated ' because the jovial jests with which he commented on his success afterwards seem to rule out a deep anger. But it served its purpose. The Conference became a wrangle. Lansbury listened with surprise and mounting anger, and as soon as Bevin stopped went straight to the microphone. When he tried to speak it was at once switched off; white with anger, he said to the responsible person that unless it were turned on he would shout loud enough for all to hear. He told Bevin that, as he knew, he was helpless in hospital when *Socialism and Peace* was drafted and had never agreed to it; when he had reported his interview with Sir Samuel Hoare he had also explicitly stated his own views on sanctions.

He also reproached Bevin on a point that is now obscure. His real anger, however, was against the sneer of trailing his conscience around. His expectation was that some member of the great majority on the executive which had repeatedly refused to accept his resignation over sanctions would step forward and say so. But none of them did; they sat stonily looking in front of themselves. Only Morrison, as he left the platform, unexpectedly leant forward and shook his hand, saying something to the effect of ' Stand by your beliefs, George '. It was a kindness at a moment of personal disillusion; Lansbury never forgot it.

Next day the executive resolution was carried by 2,168,000 to 102,000. On Tuesday George Lansbury met the M.P.s and resigned. By thirty-eight votes to seven—five abstaining—they refused to accept his resignation; but this time he insisted, Major Attlee, his deputy, taking his place. He returned home to Bow Road, in a state of great distress, almost unable to speak to the Press. Politically, he felt that the country might be at war any moment; personally he felt he had been meanly deserted by the colleagues who had so roundly told him a few days before that he could not be allowed to resign.

Within a fortnight the Government had drawn its own, unexpected conclusions from the Conference drama. An immediate general election was announced. Baldwin's programme was one of support for the League, more armaments to back 'collective security', and renewed efforts for Abyssinia. Now that they had lost their only popular leader, it was enough to wreck the Labour men's hopes of a victory. Their numbers rose, as they were bound to do, but only to 154 (Lansbury polling 19,064 to 5,707); the Conservatives and their appendages numbered well over 400. The 'National Government' was re-established; under its reign Abyssinia was abandoned to Italy and the League was broken up.

Chapter Twenty-three

IN the four years of life that remained to him Lansbury was a physically as well as a mentally changed man. He could only walk with a stick, slowly, and as a result he became heavier and plumper. He wore glasses all the time now, and his face was an old man's. But in other ways he was healthier. He suffered less from the stomach troubles which had tormented him all his life, less, too, from the heart palpitations which used to scare him suddenly. Both these were probably due in part to worry, and now that some of his responsibilities were removed they diminished too, though they never disappeared. One worry, indeed, returned, but it was not an important one for him. He was a poor man again, but he could not live as one. He had his salary as M.P. and a small income from his son's revived timber firm; anything more had to be earned by writing, for he still would not charge a fee for speaking, though it would usually have been willingly paid. Later it was pointed out to him that, as an ex-Cabinet Minister in need, he was probably entitled to a pension, but he forbade any application to be made. More than a quarter of a century ago he had criticised a Conservative ex-Minister (apparently Lord George Hamilton) for applying for such a pension, and this, he considered, made it indecent for him to think of using the Act himself. If he had had only his own personal needs to think of, he could have subsisted on his income, but the public assumed that the Right Honourable George Lansbury, M.P., P.C., J.P., ex-leader of His Majesty's Opposition, and an ex-Cabinet Minister, must be a man of substance. Appeals for help in money, which he would not refuse, came steadily in; his postal bill was enormous (frequently even the 'stamped addressed envelope for reply' was omitted). Lady de la Warr and her friends had once supplied the funds for the Bow Labour Party; now she was dead the Party equally looked to its member to keep it going. He had therefore to write articles profusely for *Reynolds'*, *John Bull*, the *Star* and whatever other paper would take them. Necessarily, before long he became repetitive; he was not a natural writer and, besides, he had by now only one theme.

He had told Raymond Postgate, who tried after his resignation to re-enlist him in the cause of Socialist militancy, that he was now seventy-seven and had no longer the energy to do 'everything at once'. He was going to concentrate on one thing, and that one thing would be stopping the Second World War which he saw coming. The decision was not absolute or immediate. For a long time he carried on with some of his old Socialist activities. He was Mayor of Poplar again in 1936. He resumed energetically his warfare with Sir John Reith of the B.B.C. In 1937, when the Government quarrelled with the Indian Congress, he became almost his old self in the House of Commons. He questioned the Ministers concerned, cabled the Viceroy that he ought to meet the Congress leaders personally, and on June 14th raised on the adjournment of the House the whole question of the breakdown of provincial self-government. His pressure had a good deal to do with the resumption of negotiations and the restoration of autonomy, partial though it was.

He was a most pertinacious helper of the refugees who were now pouring out of Hitler's Germany. The British Government, not welcoming these human evidences of the results of its foreign policy, had suspended the right of asylum. Only those wretched people who could prove themselves 'special cases' were to be admitted; Lansbury's files were full of ingenious arguments from him to Sir John Anderson proving almost every case 'special'. In 1937 he joined the Board of a new Socialist monthly called *Fact*, under the general editorship of Raymond Postgate. Each number consisted of a Socialist book, garnished with reviews or special articles, and revised and polished by members of the Board. Lansbury wrote one number (*Why Pacifists Should be Socialists*) himself, and took some part in editing others. His colleagues included Stephen Spender, Joseph Needham, Storm Jameson, Margaret Cole, Francis Meynell, Rudolph Messel, H. G. Wells and others; but he was rather aloof from them already. In fact, at one of the rare full Board meetings he said to Margaret Cole, in his unfortunately resonant whisper: ' I don't think Ray's going to get much out of *this* lot.'

The motionless silence of his colleagues, at the final scene in the Brighton Congress, made his parting from the official Labour movement easier. It would have cost them nothing to defend his honesty then; they had failed to, and he no longer had respect or affection for them; it was not a pain but a relief to be separated from them. Charles Dukes' General and Municipal Workers, which he had represented at Labour Party Conferences for nearly thirty years, wrote to tell him he could no longer be a delegate if he spoke against the official policy; for ' we should never then have control of the Districts, if we allowed this to proceed '. He told them in answer that they were unwise to suppress minorities, and came as delegate of the Bow local party instead; he was saddened, but at least it made it easier for him to speak his mind about the Labour Party. It was now, he thought, a machine only. ' I think my work for the Party, as a Party, is finished,' he wrote to Cripps. ' I see life ever so much broader than in the days gone by. . . . The Party nearly chokes me; I want to shout out *against* them.'

This last period of concentration upon pacifism, is mostly responsible for Lansbury's reputation as a man whose heart was stronger than his head. Even friends (except those who agreed with him totally) noticed the growth of characteristics unlike the clear-headed ' G. L.' with whom they had worked for so many years. The most marked, and the most surprising in him, were an unwillingness to see facts which obstructed his hopes, a disinclination to follow out arguments that pointed in a direction he disliked, and a habit of repeating general statements (such as that war was supremely evil) as if they were contributions to the discussion, and not platitudes. They were still by no means typical of him, or to be found in everything that he said or wrote; but they were observable tendencies, and they were growing. At first he maintained his opposition to one-sided disarmament, and over the Spanish war he had doubts which distressed his stricter colleagues. Arguing with Postgate after the Franco revolt, he stressed the contributory faults of the Republican Government, especially the violence of its supporters. ' But, allowing that these mistakes were partly responsible, what would

you have done, G. L., if you had been a Spanish worker in July
1936? Suppose you found that a secret military plot had in fact
exploded in all the main cities, to kill the Republican and Socialist
leaders and install Fascist dictators, where would you have
been?' The answer, with a deprecating half-smile, was:
' I suppose I should have been with my own people.' But these
qualifications soon disappeared; in 1937 he told the Labour
Party Conference that Britain should disarm as an example to
others; by then, too, he had decided that the Abyssinians
had been wrong to resist the Italians.

His last sympathies with the Russians, also, vanished at this
time. Like all his friends, he watched with growing perplexity
the horrifying series of the so-called ' Trotsky ' trials, and for
him, as for everyone else, there came a time when the grotesque
crimes charged against, and admitted by, all but one of the
leaders of the revolution could no longer be believed. For him,
the deciding date was that of the appearance in the dock of
Sokolnikoff, once Ambassador in London. He knew him
personally and well: ' Those things,' he said, referring to the
charges against him, ' are not true; I know the man and they
can't be.' But his only deduction was the confused one that
' violence never settles anything '. If this had been true—it is
not; the centuries-long existence of Moslem civilisations founded
on force would alone disprove it—it still provided no programme
for the future, nor even an explanation of why what had been the
hope of the world was declining into a police-state. He was no
longer interested in such questions.

This hardening, this closing of his ears, had more than one
cause. Undoubtedly the chief was his passionate wish to avoid
war; he was not the first man whom great anxiety and anguished
desire induced to mistake hopes for facts. He *must* succeed;
the obstacles could not be allowed to be too great. Those that
might be too serious he merely did not see, with an unconscious
blindness. Perhaps, too, the advancing age which he gave as
the reason for his concentration on pacifism meant a narrowing of
mind as well as of objective; it may be so, but in other ways
there was no sign of a failing in mental power. More important,
probably, was the lesser stature of his new collaborators. Previously he had always been ' first among equals '; now, with the

possible exception of Lord Ponsonby, there was no one who could be compared with him for experience, character and political importance. It is dangerous for any man of determination, established position and great energy to have no counsellors, but only admirers. His clerical colleagues could provide enthusiasm, sincerity and the eloquent re-statement of general principles; but of these things there was plenty. Of his political colleagues, probably the most independent was Dr. Arthur Salter, the Member for Bermondsey, a more decisive man than his paler confrères. He was honestly religious, indefatigable in his work, a fine organiser, and an incorruptible public servant; and the results of a lifetime of devotion could be seen all over his poverty-stricken borough. But he was so gauche as to be almost boorish at times, so intolerant that he seemed to ascribe any difference of opinion to moral turpitude, a Prohibitionist where Lansbury was a teetotaller, and one who had not for years even heard a political statement unless he agreed with it before it was spoken. Yet this man was now Lansbury's most helpful adviser.

Lansbury considered himself, and often was, more practical than his friends. He knew it was not sufficient to ask only for a ' change of heart ': years of Socialist training had shown him that most of the causes of war were economic. The growing threats to peace, from Germany, Italy, Japan and Franco Spain, were in origin largely due to the economic effects of the 1919 treaties and to the usual destructive effects of private capitalism. Men were standing around out of work in millions in the richer countries; in the poorer countries, such as the Balkans, they were surrounded by natural wealth which they could not get the capital to exploit. Yet in the great centres there were accumulations of capital that could not be used. A pointless paralysis held all countries except Russia; instead of trying to end it, statesmen were using tariffs and exchange-juggling to make the movement of wealth even more difficult. An international conference of the Heads of States could meet and take direct steps (as Roosevelt was doing inside the U.S.A.) to provide funds for investment in backward areas, to stabilise currencies, to lower tariffs, and so set going again the wheels of industry all over the world. The sacrifices would be almost nil; the reward would be such a prosperity that no nation would be driven by despair into war-like preparations.

The plan was by no means visionary in itself; two years afterwards the Belgian Liberal ex-Premier, M. Van Zeeland, at the request of the British and French Governments, produced a detailed plan based on similar principles which was recognised almost universally as completely practicable. Lansbury immediately adopted it, and included it in his propaganda.

But to remove the cause is not necessarily, as Lansbury seemed not to realise, to cure the disease. Any surgeon knows that an operation may successfully remove the origins of an illness, and that the patient may still die; long-neglected illness may have set up secondary complications which can no longer be treated. No doubt the original causes of the threatening war were the general effects of uncontrolled private capitalism and the special effects of the Versailles Treaties, but by now they had had results which no economic reforms could undo. On one side there was a fixed will towards war; on the other a timorous unwillingness to take any determined action, in any direction, to prevent it. Lansbury's appeals for his economic peace conference met evasions and resistances which he could never out-manœuvre.

He began his propaganda by a motion in the House of Commons on February 5th, 1936, instructing the Government to endeavour to call, through the League of Nations, the conference that he desired; it was lost by 228 votes to 137, though both Lloyd George and Lees-Smith (for the Labour Party) supported him. However, he had already decided that orthodox methods would be ineffective; he had made a decision which some people thought was sublime and some people thought was silly. Since what was said in the House or the Press was not heard, he would use his unique position and his new leisure to take his proposal to the rulers of the world himself. He would visit both the people and the heads of States, and present to them directly his simple but practical proposal. It may have been a folly—it certainly looks in retrospect like a one-man endeavour to push back the wheel of history. But if so, it was at least a noble folly.

The plan had been simmering in his mind ever since August 1935, when *The Times* had printed a long letter from him calling

311

for a Truce of God. It was made more practical in conference with several Christian friends, including notably Canon Raven, the Rev. ' Dick ' Sheppard, the Rev. Henry Carter, Mr. Corder Catchpole and Mr. Percy Bartlett, mostly belonging to a pacifist organisation called the Fellowship of Reconciliation. Originally the intention had been that several people should undertake ' embassies of reconciliation '; but before long it was clear that only Lansbury's visits were being effective, and only a couple of others were, in fact, undertaken.

His first visit, before the scheme was organised, was to the United States, in April and May 1936, with his secretary and daughter Daisy and his fellow-M.P., Dr. Salter. He did not see the President, Franklin Roosevelt, until the end of May; the preceding weeks were occupied by a highly successful series of meetings. He visited twenty-six cities in six weeks, the ' Emergency Committee ' driving him with no regard for his age. Within twenty-four hours of being picked off the liner in a swaying boat he had addressed two mass meetings and broadcast under roasting Klieg-lights. He was seeing for the first time what well-organised American publicity could do. The Mayor of Philadelphia rang the famous ' Liberty Bell ' for him. At one meeting a flock of carrier-pigeons descended upon him, each bearing on its leg a message in favour of peace. At another there appeared an even more attractive flock, of young women who announced that they were demanding pensions in advance from Congress, as the probable mothers of the soldiers who would be killed in the next war. He was greatly enlivened by these stunts and by the enthusiasm of his audiences; if he was very tired, it was in part his own fault. The experienced American lecturers who accompanied him delivered in each city exactly the same speech. There was no strain; everything was learnt by heart. The phrase on which the voice should quaver; the moment when emotion should prevent one proceeding; the occasion to draw back and flash the eye with indignation—the fixing of all these is a device without which American lecturing as an institution could not exist. But Lansbury would not have it; for each meeting he composed a new speech, and delivered it with a renewed expenditure of energy and emotion.

What passed when he met the President he did not tell, for

he had given a promise of secrecy, and was reduced to such platitudes as that Roosevelt was a friend of Britain but his first allegiance was to America. The President received him cordially, but he clearly did not agree to call the desired conference at once, although he seems to have given a half-promise to do so if Lansbury could line up enough acceptances elsewhere.

Soon after his return, in August 1936, he crossed to Paris to see Léon Blum, the Socialist Premier put in office by the ' Popular Front'; again he received warm encouragement, but Blum's position was too shaky for him to take the necessary initiative. Next month he went to Brussels to confer with Van Zeeland, the Belgian Liberal leader; from there he went on to Scandinavia. He had a long discussion with the Danish Premier, Thorvald Stauning, a square man with an enormous white beard, the last survivor of the great generation of European Socialists like Bebel, Jaurès, Iglesias or Engels. In Oslo he saw the Prime Minister Nygaardsvold; in Stockholm the Premier, Per Albin Hanssen. All these, and their Foreign Secretaries, were Socialists and near-pacifists; they cordially agreed with his proposals, but considered there was no chance for a tiny Power successfully to call such a conference. Still, he was refreshed by their encouragement; he was troubled, it is true, by the attitude of ' some out-and-out Christian pacifists' at Sodertalje, outside Stockholm, who believed literally the words of the Gospel, and were not interested in economic change nor in ' applying our principles to modern life'. But he was changing; he had decided, when he published a book next year, that such selfish people were ' the driving force of our movement'.

There was an obvious criticism of his journeys; he was preaching only to the converted. What danger to peace was Denmark? or the United States? When he spoke in the House the Members interrupted him, kindlily or impatiently, with: ' Go and tell that to Hitler!' The reproach was justified, and his response was direct; he went and told it to Hitler. Through the help of the Foreign Office he secured a long interview with the Führer in Berlin on April 19th, 1937.

Exactly what passed at that interview is not known. Hitler bound Lansbury to secrecy, holding out to him as bait the promise of a general amnesty of Nazi victims, provided there was no publicity (which would, he said, prevent it, since he must never appear to yield to foreign pressure). Lansbury went to see Lord Halifax some time after his return, and gave him an account of the interview; but he made no notes, and Lord Halifax has forgotten what he said. (He urged Lansbury to go on to see the Premier, Neville Chamberlain; but old recollections were too strong, and Lansbury could not bring himself to, though he probably did so after Munich.) But the main lines of the interview can fairly easily be reconstructed. Hitler received him with great courtesy, settled him comfortably where his injured leg could be at ease, and discussed whatever Lansbury advanced in a friendly manner, and with none of the tirades which were habitual. Only on two subjects—the Jews and the Russians—did he become excited and let be seen the lunatic that there was behind the politician. For this interview he was mostly as determined a peace-lover as Lansbury himself. He even discussed political prisoners for a quarter of an hour and made the promise already mentioned. All his offers of disarmament, he told Lansbury, had been perfectly genuine; it was not his fault they had never been accepted. He would have been glad to call Lansbury's conference himself, but he could not take the lead. Nobody trusted him, owing to Soviet propaganda, and his initiative would spoil any chances it might have. He ran over the names of those Powers who should attend, and with a marked effort of self-restraint said that even the Bolsheviks should not be excluded. He even agreed to issue a joint statement that Germany would attend a conference ' for economic co-operation ' if ' President Roosevelt or the head of another great country would call it '. Lansbury privately noted the interview as ' a triumph '.

Hitler, when he chose, was a man of great charm, and he seems to have enchanted Lansbury. ' He *will not* go to war,' Lansbury wrote to Clifford Allen, who had also been to see him, ' unless pushed into it by others '; he wrote of him publicly as ' one of the greatest men of our time '. Privately he described Hitler as a distressed and lonely man; he believed quite honestly that if he had been able to speak German and could have stayed with the Führer a short while at Berchtesgaden he could have calmed him and perhaps converted him to ' Christianity in its purest sense '. He was so convinced by his assertions that he wished only to free Germans, that when Hitler occupied Prague in 1939 he sent him a personal telegram reproaching him for breaking his promise.

After this it was unsensational when he had a warm reception from Mussolini in July. The Italian dictator had once been a Socialist, and was glad enough to talk economics sensibly; moreover, there was nothing he wanted less than a major war. For a moment it seemed even to the hard-boiled that something might result from all these journeys: ' No one took his mission very seriously until they met Mr. Lansbury ', telegraphed the *Observer's* correspondent in Rome, and the American, British, German and Italian journalists interviewed him when he left Mussolini as a matter of routine, but ' as Mr. Lansbury spoke it was as if a spell had been thrown over the assembly '.

His December journey, after that, seemed almost too easy a task. He called on President Benesh of Czechoslovakia, Marshal Smigly-Rydz, the Prime Minister of Poland, Dr. Schuschnigg, the dictator of Austria, and their Foreign Secretaries. All of them were enthusiastic. By now he had so far crystallised his proposals as to suggest a £1,000,000,000 international development fund, to be levied as a proportion—say 20 per cent—of existing war-like expenditure. It was received with almost pathetic enthusiasm by these smaller States: the heads of them begged him to go forward, and Dr. Schuschnigg even freed some political prisoners.

On his return he put whatever pressure he did upon the British or American Governments—there are no records, but he certainly took some action—and wrote a book about his journeys, called *My Quest for Peace*, which, rejecting criticisms, he made more uncompromising than ever.

' I have just got my mind settled about the book [he wrote on January 16th, 1938, to Postgate who prepared it for the press as usual]. It cannot be exciting and will from some points of view be quite dull. This is due to the nature of the book, and its continued repetition, but most of all, because the actual foundation of my thought is based more on religion than ever before. I know you cannot understand how it is possible to hold my kind of faith. The fact is, it has hold of me quite firmly. I am absolutely convinced there is no

315

hope in the world for any decent future, unless we can banish Hate and substitute Love which will enable us to forgive as we hope to be forgiven. I know you so well, that you are not unforgiving but on the contrary very understanding and full of true tolerance, so let us do our best with the book; it will not please many of my best friends. But it is my book and I *must* try and say what is in my mind. All good wishes and sympathy in having to read so much you will not agree with. . . . Don't trouble to reply; we two do understand each other.'

In August he was travelling again. In Bucharest he saw King Carol and his ' patriarch-premier ', Myron Christea; in Belgrade he saw the Prime Minister, Stoyadinovitch, and returned early in September to see the Regent, Prince Paul. In Budapest he saw the dictator, Admiral Horthy; King Boris of Bulgaria saw him in London at the Ritz. In every case he was warmly encouraged: Horthy, who began by inflicting nationalist propaganda on him, ended by asking him to draft a letter for him—Horthy—to send to President Roosevelt asking him officially to call the conference. His hopes were still high—if Roosevelt would not, probably King Leopold of Belgium would call the conference— but events were near which altered the prospect completely and put an end to his journeys. For September 1938 was the month of the Munich crisis.

In March 1938 Hitler had taken his first warlike action: he had invaded and conquered Austria. But there had been no bloodshed, Austria was a German State, and Hitler had promised that this was his last territorial demand in Europe. However, in August he mobilised his armies for the invasion of Czechoslovakia, demanding the cession of the border districts occupied by Germans (the ' Sudetenland '). Czechoslovakia was allied by treaty to France and to Russia (though not to Britain); such a cession would have made it militarily helpless before Germany. War seemed near, but Chamberlain, the British Premier, flew to Berchtesgaden to meet Hitler, and, in concert with Premier Daladier of France, recommended Czechoslovakia to hand over all districts with more than 50 per cent Germans. But now even that would not do; Hitler increased his territorial demands, and Czechoslovakia, France and Britain mobilised. At this crisis Mussolini persuaded Hitler to agree to a last meeting, at

Munich. This time Chamberlain and Daladier agreed to Hitler's enlarged demands (with but trifling changes) and enforced them on Czechoslovakia. Hitler announced that this was his last territorial demand in Europe, and signed a joint declaration with Chamberlain promising not to go to war. Chamberlain on his return said this was 'peace in our time'.

As everyone knows, Hitler invaded and conquered the rest of Czechoslovakia in March 1939, and in September 1939 invaded Poland, so starting the Second World War.

At the time of Munich, Lansbury was an ardent supporter of Chamberlain, having no more doubts than that unfortunate man himself. He cabled to Hitler begging him to hold his hand, and to Benesh suggesting that true courage was to yield. He received a flood of correspondence supporting him, many from people who seemed to imagine he still had some direct political power. Telegrams arrived proposing various actions—one that he should arrange for 'a flood of visitors' to Germany and Czechoslovakia preaching peace; another that he should get the ex-Kaiser Wilhelm to broadcast to Germany from Doorn about the unprofitability of war; a third that he should recruit an unarmed army from the Peace Pledge Union and the Oxford Group to patrol the mountain borders of Czechoslovakia night and day for twenty miles on each side of the frontier. He adopted none of these nonsensical suggestions; indeed, he did very little, because there was very little he could do. But what he could do he did, and he was resolute in his support of Chamberlain.

No doubt he was proved wrong by later events. Still, there has been a great deal of cant written since then about Munich; in particular, it is not true that any important part of the population opposed Chamberlain's action at Munich. Major Attlee, for the Opposition, wished him 'God-speed' before he took his aeroplane, and there were very few who did not echo it. Probably there would have been many more if they had known what they did later, and what Chamberlain should have known then. But in the actual week of Munich, apart from refugees, there were only two sizeable groups who were in favour of defying Hitler. One was the Communists and their fellow-travellers, politicians of no integrity who a year later were cheering the Nazi-Soviet pact; the other consisted mostly of optimists who had convinced themselves that Hitler was bluffing and ' the Nazis would not fight '. Lansbury at that moment was no wiser, but he was no more foolish, than most of his countrymen.

Chapter Twenty-four

AFTER Hitler had seized the rest of Czechoslovakia in March 1939 even Chamberlain was disillusioned; there was little indeed that Lansbury could do. What he did looks like the action of a despairing man; he can hardly have hoped for a result. He wrote to the Pope (who had declined to see him in Rome in 1937) thanking him for a recent speech and asking him to call a peace conference of the Powers for Easter Day on the Mount of Olives. He telegraphed to both Mussolini and Hitler in April reminding them that the promises they had made him the year before bound them morally to respond to an appeal in favour of peace that President Roosevelt had just made. A speech by the King of the Belgians seemed to him to be a flicker of light; for a moment he thought his peace journeys might be resumed. He visited Brussels in July 1939; he talked both to Pierlot, the Premier, and to his royal master. He found that Leopold was contemplating a joint appeal by all the small Powers to the large Powers for an economic and political peace conference before the storm burst. He adopted the idea enthusiastically. What Powers should participate? Was King Carol of Rumania, whose support was assured, too seedy a potentate to be asked to sign? Leopold seemed very anxious to bring in Dr. Salazar, the Portuguese dictator. Moreover, nobody had enlisted Finland. So the Reverend Henry Carter should go next month to Helsingfors; Lansbury would arrange to visit Lisbon. Carter reached Finland and saw Ekkro, the Foreign Minister, through the intervention of the President of a Temperance Society; the Finn arranged for the delegates of the four Scandinavian Powers to consult before the winter meeting of the League of Nations Assembly and approve Leopold's proposal. Lansbury's visit to Salazar was delayed; perhaps because in Lisbon, as in Vatican City, he was, after all, a heretic.

Meanwhile, he spoke to meetings steadily up and down the country. Most were organised by the Peace Pledge Union, of which he was President—a body made up of young men and women who pledged themselves to take no part in any war. He enrolled a considerable number; how many is not known, nor is it known how many honoured their pledge when war came. Similar pledges were being taken in America, Scandinavia and other western countries, but none in Fascist countries. Neither Lansbury nor his colleagues would agree that this fact was a valid objection to their activities. Even so, he was becoming discouraged, and beginning to doubt if his crusade would be successful. ' I am very hopeful that the miracle will happen,' he wrote after seeing Leopold; the phrase is not really that of a confident man.

On September 3rd, 1939, with all the rest of England, he learned that there would be no miracle. It was obviously his duty to speak in the Commons on behalf of the pacifists; he did so in words of adequate dignity:

' The cause that I and a handful of friends represent is this morning apparently going down to ruin. But I think we ought to take heart and courage from the fact that after two thousand years of war and strife, at least even those who enter upon this colossal struggle have to admit that force has not settled and cannot settle anything. I hope that out of this terrible calamity will arise a spirit that will compel people to give up reliance on force. . . .'

The House listened to him respectfully, as it did in ensuing months when he rose to speak (and whenever he rose he ' caught the Speaker's eye ' automatically). The Members called the R.A.F. raids which dropped nothing but leaflets over Germany ' Lansbury's War ', and they even treated gently a proposal which he got twenty M.P.s to sign in November, after the fall of Poland, proposing that Hitler's suggestion of a peace conference be accepted.

But all his activities now were the activities of a man who was waiting. It would be an exaggeration to say of him, as could have been said of Keir Hardie in the First World War, that he died of a broken heart. He was an older man, and the natural term of his life was nearer. He knew he had done all that a man could do to stop the catastrophe; he had foreseen it, and if his efforts had been insufficient, he could not blame himself either for blindness or for inactivity. Perhaps God had a reason for his failure, perhaps even (as he thought sometimes) the great catastrophe was in itself to be a challenge or an opportunity. But that would be for younger men to meet; he, meanwhile, was a soldier who was awaiting the order to ' dismiss '. He was naturally dejected and disappointed, it is true; war, he knew, was an incomparably horrible thing (though he can hardly have foreseen how dreadful it was, in fact, to be). Moreover, his energy was running out; since he had been rushed down to an underground air-raid shelter in the City after a false alarm in the winter of 1939, his stomach and heart troubles seem to have returned; he was intermittently sick and easily exhausted. Yet he was certainly not depressed all the time, nor even usually an unhappy man; joy in life kept reviving in him and, as always, he was a support and comfort to others. He could still joke: when the Editor of the *Fortnightly Review* called on him to discuss the philosophy of Christian pacifism, he surprised him by opening the front door of 39 Bow Road in person, and saying gravely: ' I am sorry. The second footman is out '. In March 1940, when he was eighty-one, he wrote for the magazine *Lilliput* a charming piece called ' It's Lovely to be Old '; but those who read it carefully could notice that nearly all the pleasures he listed were those of memory.

As a man who is waiting may do, he spent a good deal of time in tidying up. He began to arrange his papers, talked to his biographer about his *Life*, and tried, so far as he could, to put those who would survive him on the right way. He spoke in the Commons against the danger which he saw—the working up, as in 1918, of a spirit of hatred against all Germans. Here he had, unexpectedly, the support of Lloyd George. But his great anxiety was provided by his friends of the Peace Pledge Union. These young men, impressed by the importance of the pledge they had taken, naturally tried to call attention to their views as flamboyantly as they could. They resolved publicly to stand for their principles, to take up an inflexible position, to emphasise their attitude, to maintain their standpoint, and so forth. Their phrases remind the traveller of that remarkable collection in the Thorwaldsen Museum of Sculpture in Copenhagen, where the visitor looks down long avenues of smooth, white, slightly oversized statues of heroes, all perpetually paralysed in noble poses. One of the attitudes which the P.P.U. members wished to assume was to stand outside the Labour Exchanges where men were called up for enrolment, calling their attention to how easy it was to register as conscientious objectors. Their organiser also proposed to hold a series of monster meetings denouncing the war and demanding peace negotiations.

Lansbury, however, could compare 1939 with 1914, as they could not, and could see that these things were uncalled for. There was no jingoism now. No brass bands escorted the men who joined up; there was no lurid propaganda about ' Hun atrocities ', nor any excited young women singing *We don't want to lose you, But we think you ought to go*. The soldiers did not need to be told that war was evil; they knew it very well, and marched away as a melancholy duty. Conscientious objectors were now not merely tolerated: they were treated liberally. Public agitation was not only unnecessary; it would endanger that tolerant and sober mood; and Lansbury was determined to prevent his young friends making fools of themselves. The means he used did not always show a great respect for their intelligence; Mr. Roy Walker, their organiser, has recorded his frustration:

' We younger men deeply respected George Lansbury, but were sometimes annoyed at the shrewd and unscrupulous way he used his age. In National Council, if anybody wanted to do other than George wanted on any important issue he would promptly wax tragic: " You young fellers don't want to take any notice of an old chap like me. I've had my say long ago. I'm a back number. You young people don't want to be bothered with me. You do what you like and just let me slip out quietly." Two minutes of this in a quavering voice would reduce the toughest rebel to shamefaced acquiescence. Whereupon George would brighten up magically and the meeting would continue smoothly, with no sign of failing powers—or of renunciation of power.'

But he did not treat them with artfulness only. He was too ill to attend their annual conference in 1940, but he sent them a reasoned letter on their tactics:

' We did our best to prevent the catastrophe. Now it is upon us, it is our bounden duty to do everything in our power to understand the motives of the vast majority who cannot accep our point of view, and let them know we respect and honour them for their courage, self-sacrifice and earnest endeavour on behalf of what they consider right. Because I think this way, I desire to appeal most earnestly to all members of the P.P.U. to give up picketing the Employment Exchanges when men are registering for Service. Such picketing cannot win or convert those worth having and men who are C.O.'s can easily discover how to make their position clear without aid from us. The main argument against this picketing is this: we are not playing fair with Government or Parliament. We possess rights and privileges such as no other nation allows pacifists in war time. I beg you all to keep this in mind and do nothing to prejudice these privileges. It is never a good thing to exact the full " pound of flesh " when arguing or asserting one's rights.

' As for Peace by Negotiation and stopping the war, we are allowed freedom to advocate this in and out of Parliament, and this we should do with reason and discretion. There are times when " Silence is golden ". Even so, we can at all times meet in our Groups and cheer and inspire one another to hold on to the faith, and when possible tell our neighbours and friends why we cannot take part in war. We need use neither slogans nor words which hurt the feelings of people who are quite as sincere as we think ourselves to be.'

He did not wholly trust his colleagues, writing in a covering note that ' if read ' the message must ' be read in full '; but he may have been unjust. The letter was read, and, on the whole and with some heavings, acted upon.

The winter of 1939–40 was a hard one, and he felt very tired. He was worried, more than he would have been normally, by financial difficulties. (He left almost nothing when he died.) Within a month of his death a letter from Barrow Cadbury, a model of delicacy and kindness, almost forcibly relieved him of an anxiety he hated even to mention; but until the promise of the £400 annuity which it contained arrived he had been distressed— for his dependants, not for himself. He was more troubled by his continued weakness; the coming of spring did not revive him as he expected. He went down to Farnham to stay with Graham Pole, an old friend from the days of Lady de la Warr and the early *Herald*. There he was cosseted; he was even persuaded, after serious thought, to take an occasional glass of wine, which eased his stomach. But the relief was only temporary; he consulted with the doctors at the Manor House Hospital, Golders Green, and in April went into that hospital ' for observation '.

He may not have known, but the doctors had known for some while, that the disease which had killed Edgar was attacking him. It might have been operable in a younger man, but at eighty-one an operation would have been fatal. There was nothing to be done but to make him as comfortable as might be and hope for the unexplained and sudden recovery which does sometimes come in cancer cases. No such recovery came.

Perhaps he suspected the truth. He rallied his energies to give a last message, as solemnly as he could, to the British working class, which he had served. He wrote it laboriously with his hand in bed, and handed it to the *Tribune* on April 18th. The editor, Postgate, published it on the 25th, and brought the issue to his bedside. In the article he had said:

' If—and it is a big if—anything is left on which to start a new world of life based on true co-operation, the war will have left the organisation used for slaughter available, at least in some men's minds, for the work of construction.

' But, comrades, I desire to express my unshakeable belief born of experience. It is this: *our call to the workers must be an unselfish one.* We must ourselves understand that neither personal, class, sectional or any other such interest shall be the driving call which bids us unite. We must be honest and declare that a class-less society is only possible when our minds are free of class hatred and prejudice.

' As you know, I try to preserve my faith in the Christian religion. This faith is stronger, more sustaining than anything else ever can be. I hold fast to the truth that this world is big enough for all: that we are all brethren, children of one Father. It is not His fault that we misuse His world, because the fault is in ourselves. I beg all my readers to join, not in creating a new British world, but a new world wherein will be practised the true way of life: " Each for all and all for each ".'

But in the week since he had written this his mind had passed over a dividing barrier. He thanked the editor with his unvarying kindness, but did not look at the paper. His face, and even his head, seemed smaller: his blue eyes were still, and he appeared to be looking at something a great distance away. During the next few days he spoke very little, and meditated for long periods: he was very weak, and slept a great deal.

On May 7th his relatives were summoned urgently. To one daughter he said when she came: ' Did the doctors send for you? ' She made some conventional answer, intended to relieve his anxiety. He again asked her, separating the words in the tone of impatient patience so typical of him: ' But did the doctors send for you? '

' Yes.'

' Thank God. Then it will not be long.'

A little while later he fell asleep; and some time in that sleep he died.

Until May 14th his body lay at 39 Bow Road—lay in state, it might almost be said, covered in flowers and visited by a continual stream of mourners. On that day it was moved to St. Mary's, his parish church, islanded in Bow Road, where the Rector conducted a brief service, ending with an old Benediction that he had liked:

' O Lord, support us all the day long of this troublous life, until the shades lengthen, and the evening comes, and the busy world is hushed, the fever of life is over, and our work is done. Then, Lord, in Thy mercy grant us safe lodging, a holy rest, and peace at the last, through Jesus Christ our Lord.'

The church was packed, not only with the workers of Bow, his friends and his relatives, but with men of distinction of many nations: Mr. Maisky, the Ambassador of the Soviet Union; Mr. Quo Tai-chi, the Ambassador of the Chinese Republic, and others. Some, not all, followed the body to Ilford Crematorium, where the Reverend C. G. Langton was to commit it to the fire. The morning was cold, but clear; the sunlight was steady, but light-coloured and weak; a gusty wind blew Mr. Langton's white surplice about him and carried away some of his words. There had been, till now, little ceremonial for those of his followers who were Socialists, but not Christians. But at the moment when the coffin (so small to the eyes of those who remembered him in the days of his health) began to move upon the rollers to the furnace, someone quietly began to sing *The Red Flag*. It was taken up by all the audience, and his body went upon its last journey to the sound of the tune that had been of all others most familiar to him.

Nine days later a memorial service was held in the still-undamaged Westminster Abbey. Such a service is among the most solemn and most beautiful rites of the Church to which he had belonged; yet in its perfection it was less moving than the rather ragged singing outside the furnace doors—until, perhaps, the unseen choir sang the poem which he had loved best and which most clearly symbolised his work and his life:

> *Bring me my bow of burning gold;*
> *Bring me my arrows of desire;*
> *Bring me my spear: O clouds unfold!*
> *Bring me my chariot of fire.*
>
> *I will not cease from mental fight,*
> *Nor shall my sword sleep in my hand*
> *Till we have built Jerusalem*
> *In England's green and pleasant land.*

Then the congregation filed out into sunlight. The sky was blue, with small white clouds and with a blurred grey-red on the horizon beyond the river; the air was still; Parliament Square, for a Westminster noon, was quiet. Before long, the air-raid sirens would be heard howling. Before his ashes and his wife's were scattered, as he asked, in the English Channel, half his borough of Poplar was to be laid in ruins, and of his own house in Bow Road nothing would be left but a doorway and a door.

INDEX

Doreen
(d. young)

(t